LATIN FOR READING

LATIN FOR READING

A Beginner's Textbook with Exercises

REVISED EDITION

Glenn M. Knudsvig, Gerda M. Seligson, and Ruth S. Craig

Ann Arbor   **The University of Michigan Press**

Preface

Extensive tryouts with over two thousand students of all ability levels, mostly college but some high school students, provided feedback on virtually every detail of the instructional materials that became the first edition of *Latin for Reading*. Another thousand students and more than thirty instructors at a number of schools and colleges have now used that first edition. The feedback from these students and instructors, plus our own continued growth in the fields of language analysis and description have enabled us to develop this revised edition that we, and many others, know is a success-oriented course for Latin students. The validation process for the two editions has indeed been long, but the outstanding results in terms of student learning have made the whole process worthwhile.

Great care has been taken to make the course effective for a heterogeneous classroom population. We assume that this course is the first formal study of a foreign language for some students. Furthermore, we know that this is the first time that most students, with or without a foreign language background, have studied the systematic nature of language. We know that ability levels and levels of preparation vary greatly. Nevertheless, instructors have found that through the careful use of the information and procedures of this course, even the weakest students will be able to acquire at least the central concepts and skills related to Latin, and to language learning in general. Students better prepared for the study of Latin will indeed excel and become ready for a more thorough study of Roman authors.

The textbook attempts to combine the useful principles and descriptions found in textbooks representing the so-called traditional approach (exemplified by Wheelock's college-level textbook) with the insights from linguistic research of the past several decades, as well as from a reexamination of the best grammars of a century ago.

As the name of the book indicates, the purpose of this course is to enable students to learn to read—rather than to write—Latin. Everything follows from this purpose. The explanations, the rules, the procedures, and the exercises all reinforce the fact that the first task of readers is to recognize and respond to the Latin stimulus on the printed page. The reader must be able to process the morphological, syntactic, and semantic information carried by each word or set of words. A separate task is that of expressing the sum of the information in an English translation; this course formally addresses this area too.

Thus, the course seeks to introduce students to the systematic nature of language in the following areas:

> morphology: words and their parts;
> syntax: sentences and their parts, as well as their completeness requirements;
> semantics: meaning-related features of words and groups of words.

The interrelationship of all of these is most apparent in one of the major themes of the book, that of learning to use the various sorts of information about words and groups of words as a basis for forming expectations of other words or groups of words. The ability to form and hold expectations is a universal human characteristic. When a door opens, one expects somebody to enter, be it a person, an animal, a ghost, or, metaphorically, a gust of wind.

It is this ability that enables us also to understand each other's speech and to read. A text-book designed to teach a person how to read a foreign language must take advantage of this ability and build upon it.

If a learner has an adequate active understanding of the devices of his or her own language, a textbook for a new language must equip this learner with a knowledge of the foreign language devices, i.e., in Latin of its morphology and its syntax. To this must be added a study of the main points of overall difference, e.g., in Latin, absence of the article, different role of word order, and different rules for abbreviated sentences (now called gapping). If a learner has a less than adequate understanding of the devices of his or her own language, the textbook must also acquaint the learner with the basic building blocks of language, i.e., the sentence kernels, the modifiers, and the connectors. Furthermore, the textbook must make the learner aware of the systems of syntactic equivalents because the basic syntactic functions are often filled by equivalents, e.g., the subject of a verb may be a noun, an adjective, a pronoun, an infinitive, or a dependent clause.

We have tried to respond to these necessities by sustained emphasis on the points mentioned. We have also tried to do something similar for semantic expectations, but our convictions are much firmer for syntax since there has been more research in this area.

It is our hope that continued research in Latin syntax, and particularly in semantics, will provide enough information to further advance this approach to learning Latin. In the last few years, we have begun to develop new course materials, in cooperation with Professor Roger Hornsby of the University of Iowa, for Cicero and Vergil based on the concepts contained in *Latin for Reading*. The results have been most satisfactory. The profession is in great need of new materials for these first-author courses that our students encounter.

We are deeply indebted to Waldo E. Sweet, who was the first to describe Latin in terms of modern linguistic science and who assembled many of the Basic Sentences and Readings. Next we are indebted to many generations of teaching assistants at the University of Michigan who taught from the various drafts of the textbook as it was developed. Among them special thanks are due to Deborah Pennell Ross, who has taught and talked with us for many wonderful years; she has been an exceedingly valuable resource person. Thanks are due also to Martha Welborn Baldwin, who was our typist, editor, and conscience for the preliminary edition. We are extremely grateful to the many reviewers and instructors elsewhere, especially those at the University of Iowa, Lawrence University (Wisconsin), Sherman College (Texas) and in secondary schools in Illinois, Michigan, and Virginia, who provided us with confirmations, observations, and suggestions based upon their experience with the preliminary edition of *Latin for Reading*. We feel grateful to the many students from whose progress and problems we learned so much.

Last, not least, we thank our families and each other for the patience and the faith that enabled us to come to this point.

Features

Lesson Text

Each lesson begins with an overview and Basic Sentences. The presentation of material follows this outline:

Morphology
Discussion of Syntax and Semantics
Guidelines for Metaphrasing and Translation

This breakdown trains students to attend separately to form, function, and semantic categories as sources of information for getting to meaning. It establishes the habits necessary for dealing with advanced reading. The treatment of metaphrase and translation as a separate topic emphasizes the fact that expressing the English equivalent of what one sees in Latin is a separate skill and does not follow automatically from a mastery of morphology, syntax, and semantics.

Exercises

Exercises interspersed throughout each lesson serve to

accustom learners, independent of their instructor, to observe and acquire each of the subskills necessary for mastering a new construction or topic,
maintain previously learned material,
isolate items that learners traditionally consider tricky, and
provide student performance data to instructors for use in determining class activities and assignments.

Summary Tasks

Summary tasks at the end of each lesson provide suggestions for further drill and review. Most of these can serve as models for tasks in other lessons as well, in order to maintain and integrate all skills.

Latin Corpus

The major part of the Latin material consists of genuine or slightly adapted Latin; only the Narrative Readings have been composed to fit the needs of each lesson.

Basic Sentences in each lesson contain the new constructions. The sentences are described in the lesson text.
Readings in each lesson include single sentences and connected passages of various lengths. They are divided into Required and Optional Readings. The Readings, as well as the Basic Sentences, provide a focus for discussions of history and culture.

Narrative Readings provide additional practice in learning to read connected passages. They are present through lesson 17. Themes for these stories are taken from mythology and fables.

Selections from *The Menaechmi Twins* by Plautus are available beginning in lesson 22. They are adapted to lesson level where necessary.

Selections from *Eutropius* are included in order to provide a Latin text for various practice tasks at early stages or for translation work later.

Vocabularies

The following types of vocabularies occur in each lesson:

Lesson Vocabulary, which is to be memorized, contains the words occurring in the Basic Sentences, a limited number of high-frequency words from Readings, and, where appropriate, words from lists associated with the new constructions of the lesson.

Vocabulary for Readings and Narratives. Words that occur three times are marked by an asterisk at the third appearance and are not provided in Readings Vocabulary after that. They are, however, listed in Review Lessons Vocabulary and in the General Vocabulary at the back of the textbook.

Vocabulary for the selections from Plautus and Eutropius is provided. Vocabulary for the Optional Readings in later lessons must be looked up in a dictionary.

Word Studies

Word studies in this textbook include exercises on English derivatives and exercises on Latin stems.

Stem List

A list of many frequently occurring Latin stems is provided to aid in systematic vocabulary acquisition. Lists of words to be entered onto the stem list occur in the lessons.

Basic Sentences

A list of all of the Basic Sentences, without translations, is provided for use as a quick reference and for drill and review purposes.

Appendix

The appendix contains a summary of morphology of Latin nouns, adjectives, pronouns, numerals, and verbs.

General Vocabulary

This is a complete listing of all required vocabulary. The number of the lesson where the word first occurs is provided.

Abbreviations

The abbreviations as used especially in the vocabularies and charts are listed together for easy reference.

Glossary

The glossary provides the general meanings of some of the technical terms used in the course.

An Introduction to the Pronunciation of Latin

Here are some general guidelines to follow in pronouncing Latin somewhat as it was pronounced in ancient times. With these in mind you will be accurate in spelling what you hear and in reading/pronouncing what has been written.

• There are no "silent letters" in the Latin writing system. For example, in the Latin words *cane* and *regere* the final *e*'s are pronounced as part of the final syllable of each word, i.e., of -*ne* and -*re*.

• Vowels are either short or long. A long vowel is marked in this and many other books with a macron or "long mark" over the vowel, e.g., *ā, ē*. A short and long vowel differ in *quantity* (a long vowel should be sounded approximately twice as long as a short vowel) and *quality*.

Vowel Chart

long		Latin		short
ā	about as in f*a*ther	→ *fāta*	← about as in *a*gain	a
ē	about as in th*ey*	→ *cēdet*	← about as in p*e*t	e
ī	about as in mach*i*ne	→ *fīnit*	← about as in s*i*t	i
ō	about as in c*o*ne	→ *cōnor*	← about as in *o*rbit	o*
ū	about as in r*u*de	→ *lūdus*	← about as in f*u*ll	u
	(cf. n*oo*n)			

There are three common vowel combinations, or diphthongs, that have sounds different from those of the separate vowels:

ae about as in *ai*sle, e.g., *ae*quus
au about as in th*ou,* e.g., *au*get
oe about as in *oi*l, e.g., p*oe*na

Other diphthongs are *ei, eu,* and *ui.*

• Each letter (with a few exceptions) always represents the same sound.

• A Latin consonant has much the same sound as the same consonant in English. But note the following:

   c is pronounced as a hard sound, that is, like the *k* in "kite" and "like," *not* like the *c* in "city"

   g is pronounced as a hard sound, that is, like the *g* in "go" or "log," *not* like the *g* in "gem"

   j has a sound similar to the *y* in "you"; it is actually both a vowel and a consonant, much like the *y* in English. Some books use the letter *i* instead of the *j* when it is used as a vowel; other books use the letter *i* instead of the *j* everywhere. We have elected to print *i* where the letter is a vowel and *j* where it is a consonant.

---

*The short *o* is least like the English sound.

s has the sound of *s* in "son," never the sound of *s* in "ease"

the letter *v* has the sound of English *w*

ch is pronounced as a *c,* not as the *ch* in "church"

doubled consonants in Latin stand for a doubled sound. (In English they indicate the length of the preceding vowel, e.g., "*later*" vs. "*latter*.")

Word Accent

• The last syllable of a multisyllabic word is *never* accented in Latin.

• In a two-syllable word the accent is always on the first syllable.

• In a word of three or more syllables, the syllable just before the last one receives the accent if possible. This is possible when the syllable is "long," that is, if it meets *one* of these three criteria:

the syllable contains a long vowel, i.e., is marked by a macron, *or*

the syllable contains a diphthong, *or*

the syllable ends in a consonant.

For practical purposes, if the short vowel just before the last vowel of the word is followed immediately by two or more consonants (with a few exceptions), the syllable is usually "long," and receives the accent.

Your instructor will provide additional information about pronunciation, the alphabet, and syllabication.

Contents

Lesson 1 1
Introduction to the Latin Sentence 2
Introduction to Latin Nouns and Verbs 3
Syntax: The Complete Sentence 8
Metaphrasing: A Technique for Learning to Read Latin 10

Lesson 2 15
Part of Speech: Coordinating Conjunction 15
The Gap 17

Lesson 3 21
The Complementary Infinitive 21
Questions 23

Lesson 4 28
Part of Speech: Adverb 28
Part of Speech: Preposition 28
Syntax: Adverbial Modification 29

Lesson 5 35
Part of Speech: Adjective 35
Gender 37
Syntax: Adjectival Modification 38

Review Lesson 1 48

Lesson 6 53
The Passive Kernel: A New Kernel Type 53
Another Adverbial Modifier: Noun in the Ablative without a Preposition 56

Lesson 7 63
Number and Number Agreement 63
Part of Speech: Pronoun 66

Lesson 8 72
Number and Number Agreement Continued 72
Cardinal Numbers 75

Lesson 9 80
Principal Parts of Latin Verbs 80
The Present Perfective Tense 84

Review Lesson 2 91

Lesson 10 97
The Linking Kernel 97
The Factitive Kernel 99
Part of Speech: Pronoun 100

Lesson 11 105
Dependent Clauses 105
Dependent Clauses as Adverbial Modifiers 107

Lesson 12 115
Adverbial Accusatives with Prepositions 115
Adverbial Accusatives without Prepositions 116

Lesson 13 123
Relative Pronouns 123
Relative Clauses as Adjectival Modifiers 124
Relative Clauses as Noun Equivalents 128

Review Lesson 3 134

Lesson 14 141
The Participle: A Non-Finite Verb Form 141
Participial Clause as Adjectival Modifier 144

Lesson 15 151
The Ablative Absolute: Participial Clause as Adverbial Modifier 151

Review Lesson 4 158

Lesson 1

Introduction to the Latin Sentence
Introduction to Latin Nouns and Verbs
Syntax: The Complete Sentence
Metaphrasing: A Technique for Learning to Read Latin

From the first lesson to the last, the *sentence* is the focus of *Latin for Reading*. The goal of lesson 1 is to enable the beginner to understand how Basic Sentences 1.1–1.6 mean what they mean and to read and translate other sentences of the same kind.

Basic Sentences

1.1. Manus manum lavat.—Petronius
Manum manus lavat.
Manum lavat manus.
Lavat manus manum.
Lavat manum manus.
Manus lavat manum.

A hand washes a hand = One hand
washes the other.

1.2. Impedit īra animum.—Cato
Īra animum impedit.
Animum impedit īra.
Impedit animum īra.
Īra impedit animum.
Animum īra impedit.

Anger obstructs the mind.

1.3. Spem successus alit.—Motto
etc.

Success nourishes hope.

1.4. Fugit hōra.—Motto
Hōra fugit.

Time flies.

1.5. Occāsiō facit fūrem.—Medieval
etc.

Opportunity makes a thief.

1.6. Vincit vēritās.—Motto
Vēritās vincit.

Truth prevails.

Introduction to the Latin Sentence

In order to begin to understand how the Basic Sentences mean what they mean and to read other sentences of the same kind, it is necessary to know that *sentences* are put together from *words* and that words, as indicated in dictionaries, are *nouns* or *verbs* or some other *part of speech*. Parts of speech were described and named by the ancient Greeks because of their interest in describing language. The Greeks thought about the structure of language as they thought about other fields such as mathematics, astronomy, logic, etc. They distinguished groups of words according to several criteria, among them meaning: e.g., *nouns* (words for names of persons, places, things, ideas, etc.), *verbs* (words for actions or states of being), *adjectives* (words describing nouns), etc. The Romans took over the Greek terminology, and with some adaptations this terminology is still used today. Lesson 1 introduces Latin sentences consisting only of *nouns* and *verbs*.

■ Exercise 1

From the English translations of the Basic Sentences, copy five words that are nouns and five words that are verbs.

Nouns	*Verbs*
1.	1.
2.	2.
3.	3.
4.	4.
5.	5.

In order to find out what part of speech a Latin word may be, it is helpful to look at its ending. Latin word endings carry a great deal of information. Each of the words in the Latin Basic Sentences is a verb or a noun. The ending *-t* indicates a verb.

■ Exercise 2

Copy all verbs from the Latin Basic Sentences.

1.

2.

3.

4.

5.

6.

Nouns in these Basic Sentences appear with a variety of endings. However, these endings fall into two groups: those that end in *-m* and those that do not end in *-m*.

■ Exercise 3

Copy the Latin nouns that end in *-m*. Next copy those nouns that do not end in *-m*.

Nouns that end in -m	*Nouns that do not end in* -m
1.	1.
2.	2.
3.	3.
4.	4.
	5.
	6.

The nouns *function* in these sentences as *subjects* or as *direct objects*. In English, function is indicated by the *word order*. The noun before the verb functions as *subject*, the noun after the verb as *direct object*.

■ Exercise 4

From the English translations of the Basic Sentences copy five nouns that function as subject and three nouns that function as direct object.

Subject	*Direct Object*
1.	1.
2.	2.
3.	3.
4.	
5.	

In Latin, word order does *not* indicate function. Instead, word *endings* indicate function. Nouns in these Basic Sentences that do not end in *-m* function as subjects, those that end in *-m* function as direct objects.

In contrast to English that uses word order to indicate function, Latin uses an older system, a trace of which is preserved in English pronouns. For example, the English pronouns *him* and *she* each retain their same function whether they occur in a sentence using regular English word order, "she likes him," or in the unusual order "him she likes." *She* is the subject and *him* is the direct object in both word orders. *Him* is never subject, *he* is never direct object. The contrast between such pronoun forms as *he* and *him* or *they* and *them* is the closest thing in English to the Latin system of word endings.

In the Latin language it is not only pronouns, but also nouns and adjectives, that have different endings indicating different functions in the sentence. These different forms are called *cases*.

Introduction to Latin Nouns and Verbs

The Paradigm of the Latin Noun

The Latin noun has five *cases*. Only two occur in the Basic Sentences for lessons 1 through 3. The names of these two cases are *nominative* and *accusative*. The remaining three cases are called ablative, dative, and genitive.[1] Lesson 4 will introduce the ablative case, lessons 16 and 17 the dative and the genitive cases. However, the genitive will appear throughout the course as part of the dictionary listing of nouns.

Latin nouns, like English nouns, also have different forms for singular and plural number, e.g., in English, "opportunity/opportunities" and "success/successes." Latin nouns therefore have ten forms. The ten forms together are called the *paradigm* of the noun. Here is the paradigm for *hōra* (time, hour), a noun in Basic Sentence 1.4 (S1.4).[2]

Singular	
Nominative	**hōra**
Accusative	**hōram**
Ablative	hōrā
Dative	hōrae
Genitive	hōrae
Plural	
Nominative	hōrae
Accusative	hōrās
Ablative	hōrīs
Dative	hōrīs
Genitive	hōrārum

Note that some of the cases look like other cases. These ambiguous forms require the careful attention of the reader.

There are a number of nouns that have the same set of endings as *hōra*, e.g., *īra* (anger) in S1.2 and *pecūnia* (money) in S2.3.

■ Exercise 5
On the model of *hōra,* write the paradigm of *īra* and of *pecūnia*. Write the names of the cases.

Case Name
Singular

nominative	īra	pecūnia
_____	_____	_____
_____	_____	_____
_____	_____	_____
_____	_____	_____

Plural

_____	_____	_____
_____	_____	_____
_____	_____	_____
_____	_____	_____
_____	_____	_____

---

1. Another case, the vocative, is quite different in use from these five cases and will occur only late in the course.
2. S, as in S1.4, indicates a reference to a Basic Sentence.

In addition to the set of endings used above, there are four other sets of endings for nouns. Each noun has one of these sets. All nouns that have the same set are said to belong to the same *declension*. For example, *hōra*, *īra*, and *pecūnia* all belong to the declension that is called the First Declension. Here are the nominative and accusative of nouns from each of the five declensions. The differences among sets of endings don't always appear in these two cases. (See p. 6 of this lesson or the Appendix for the complete paradigm of a noun from each declension.) All of these nouns appear in lessons 1 and 2.

			Declension		
Case	First	Second	Third	Fourth	Fifth
Singular					
Nominative	hōra	animus	fūr	manus	rēs
Accusative	hōram	animum	fūrem	manum	rem
Singular					
Nominative	īra	populus	occāsiō	successus	spēs
Accusative	īram	populum	occāsiōnem	successum	spem
Singular					
Nominative	fēmina	vir	vēritās	senātus	diēs
Accusative	fēminam	virum	vēritātem	senātum	diem

■ **Exercise 6**

Examine the paradigms above and copy those endings that seem to be recurrent or predictable in each declension.

			Declension		
Case	First	Second	Third	Fourth	Fifth
Singular					
Nominative	_____	_____	X	_____	_____
Accusative	_____	_____	_____	_____	_____

Technical Terms Used to Describe Parts of Words

Manus and *manum* in S1.1 are forms of the same noun. It is clear that they are somewhat similar and somewhat different. Part of each of these two words is the same, {manu}, and part, {s}, {m}, is different. Each of these parts contributes to the meaning. The technical term for parts of a word that carry meaning is *morpheme*. The study of morphemes is *morphology*. Consider the following English words in terms of morphology.

English Noun
truth has one morpheme, {truth}.
truths has two morphemes, {truth} and {s}.
truth's has two morphemes, {truth} and {'s}.

English Verb
learn has one morpheme, {learn}.
learns has two morphemes, {learn} and {s}.
learned has two morphemes, {learn} and {ed}.

In the noun *truths*, {truth} is called the *stem morpheme* and {s} is called the *inflectional morpheme*. In the verb *learns*, {learn} is the stem morpheme and {s} is the inflectional morpheme.

Morphology of the Latin Noun

Inasmuch as the Latin word *manus* contrasts with the Latin word *manum* in S1.1, it appears that each of these words has two morphemes, i.e.,

the stem morpheme {manu} and the inflectional morpheme {s} in *manus*,
the stem morpheme {manu} and the inflectional morpheme {m} in *manum*.

The accusative singular of all but a few nouns to be presented later ends in the inflectional morpheme {m}. Some of the nominatives have the inflectional morpheme {s}.

All cases singular and plural of one noun from each declension are provided below as an overview of noun morphology. See the summary of morphology in the Appendix for more paradigms.

Noun Paradigm

	Declension				
	First	Second	Third	Fourth	Fifth
Singular					
Nominative	**hōra**	**animus**	**fūr**	**manus**	**rēs**
Accusative	**hōram**	**animum**	**fūrem**	**manum**	**rem**
Ablative	hōrā	animō	fūre	manū	rē
Dative	hōrae	animō	fūrī	manuī	reī
Genitive	**hōrae**	**animī**	**fūris**	**manūs**	**reī**
Plural					
Nominative	hōrae	animī	fūrēs	manūs	rēs
Accusative	hōrās	animōs	fūrēs	manūs	rēs
Ablative	hōrīs	animīs	fūribus	manibus	rēbus
Dative	hōrīs	animīs	fūribus	manibus	rēbus
Genitive	hōrārum	animōrum	fūrum	manuum	rērum

Morphology of the Latin Verb

Latin verbs have many different inflectional morphemes. In lessons 1 through 5 the morpheme {t} is the only inflectional morpheme that indicates a Latin verb. The {t} indicates that the subject of the verb is *third person* and *singular*.

In English, only the third person singular of the verb has an inflectional morpheme, i.e., {s} as in *indicate, indicates*. Latin, however, has separate morphemes for first, second, and third persons in both singular and plural. Here is an overview of a Latin verb.

Verb Morphology

	Singular	Plural
First person	alō (I feed)	alimus (we feed)
Second person	alis (you feed)	alitis (you [all] feed)
Third person	**alit** (he, she, it, or [noun] feeds)	alunt (they or [nouns] feed)

All verbs in the sentences in lessons 1 through 6 are in the third person singular. Later lessons will introduce the other persons and the plural number of the verb.

■ Exercise 7

Identify the part of speech and the form of each word in these Basic Sentences. For verbs, give person and number, e.g., *alit:* verb; third person, singular. For nouns, give case and number, e.g., *fūrem:* noun; accusative singular.

S1.1. Manus manum lavat.
S1.3. Spem successus alit.
S1.5. Occāsiō facit fūrem.

1. manus   _____

2. manum   _____

3. lavat   _____

4. spem   _____

5. successus   _____

6. alit   _____

7. occāsiō   _____

8. facit   _____

9. fūrem   _____

■ Exercise 8

On the basis of their morphology alone, identify these words by checking the appropriate column. The words occur in sentences from the Readings section of this lesson.

Līs lītem generat.
Brevitās dēlectat.
Vēritātem diēs aperit.

| | Noun | | |
	Nom. Sing.	Acc. Sing.	Verb
1. līs	_____	_____	_____
2. lītem	_____	_____	_____
3. generat	_____	_____	_____
4. brevitās	_____	_____	_____
5. dēlectat	_____	_____	_____
6. vēritātem	_____	_____	_____
7. diēs	_____	_____	_____
8. aperit	_____	_____	_____

Syntax[1]: The Complete Sentence

In order to read a language it is not enough to know the morphology of the language or the meaning of its words. If this were so, all that one would need would be a summary of morphology and a dictionary. To be a successful reader, one must have a feeling for *sentence,* that is, for whether or not a string of words forms a complete sentence. Few people would maintain that the following are complete sentences in English: "dog and," "dog chases," "chases." It is this feeling for completeness that enables one to read one word or phrase and at the same time set up *expectations* about what is to come in the sentence. Only in one's own language, however, is this feeling instinctive. It does not work automatically in a foreign language where rules for completeness of a sentence may be different or where a sentence may be put together differently. Therefore, learning to read a foreign language most of all means acquiring a conscious knowledge of how words form a complete sentence in that language. Only with this knowledge can readers set up and hold correct expectations while reading.

Kernel of the Sentence

The one requirement for a complete sentence is that there be a minimum framework or skeleton. This framework is called the *kernel.* As one reads one must expect kernels because every sentence has one or more kernels. Most sentences also have one or more words that are not part of the kernel. These are either modifiers or connectors (to be studied in later lessons). Look at these examples in English.

> *Dogs chase cats.* Each word is part of the kernel.
> Most *dogs* happily *chase* frightened *cats.* Three words, *most, happily,* and *frightened,* are modifiers.
> *Dogs chase cats* happily and confidently. Two words, *happily* and *confidently,* are modifiers and one word, *and,* is a connector.

Each Basic Sentence in this lesson has only one kernel. There are no modifiers or connectors. Each word or item in the kernel has one of the following functions:

    subject
    verb
    direct object

This course describes seven types of kernels. Two types occur in this lesson.

1. A *transitive active* kernel has items filling these three functions:
   a. verb
   b. subject
   c. direct object
2. An *intransitive active* kernel has items filling these two functions:
   a. verb
   b. subject

---

1. Syntax is from Greek *syntaxis* (putting together); words are put together into sentences.

In English, the items that are part of a kernel usually occur in the following order: subject, plus verb, plus direct object (if present). In Latin, the items that are part of the kernel may occur in any order, because the nominative indicates the subject and the accusative indicates the direct object.

■ Exercise 9

Name the kernel type of these English sentences that are translations of the Basic Sentences from this lesson.

1. One hand washes the other hand. _____

2. Anger obstructs the mind. _____

3. Success nourishes hope. _____

4. Time flies. _____

5. Opportunity makes a thief. _____

6. Truth prevails. _____

The items in the kernel of a Latin sentence, as well as the kernel type, will be entered on a chart such as that in exercise 10.

■ Exercise 10

Copy each kernel item and name its function. Name the kernel type. Sentence 1 has been given as an example.

1. Spem successus alit.
2. Vincit vēritās.
3. Manus manum lavat.
4. Impedit īra animum.
5. Fugit hōra.

	Item: Function	Item: Function	Item: Function	Kernel Type
1.	spem: direct object	successus: subject	alit: verb	trans. act.
2.				
3.				
4.				
5.				

The word *noun* names a part of speech only and does not correspond to a specific function within the sentence. On the other hand, the word *verb* is the name of both a part of speech and a function within the kernel. This double use of the word *verb* is unfortunate, but corresponds to current practice.

Each of the two nouns in transitive active kernels, one in the nominative and one in the accusative, has the same syntactic function in the kernel wherever it occurs in the kernel. Look again at the Basic Sentences. The first one of each set is the original sentence, but the others are equally correct.

■ Exercise 11

Write Basic Sentence 1.4 (*Occāsiō facit fūrem*) in five different word orders.

1.

2.

3.

4.

5.

Question: These five sentences retain the same meaning even though the word order is changed. Why?

■ Exercise 12

From the Readings (R) section (p. 13), copy each kernel item and name its function. All nouns in these sentences are either nominative case or accusative case (marked by the inflectional morpheme {m}). Sentence R1.4 is given as an example.

	Item: Function	Item: Function	Item: Function	Kernel Type
R1.4.	līs: subject	lītem: direct object	generat: verb	trans. act.
R1.1.				
R1.2.				
R1.3.				
R1.5.				
R1.6.				
R1.7.				

Metaphrasing: A Technique for Learning to Read Latin

Reading is a linear activity, i.e., the reader processes one word or group of words after another in the sequence in which they appear. This is so in Latin, as well as in English. But, because the sequence in which Latin words appear is rarely the same as in the equivalent clause or sentence in English, a person learning to read or translate Latin must develop a special technique.

Without such a technique the reader would have to look through the whole Latin sentence, first for the subject, then for the verb, and then for the direct object. This, of course, would destroy the linear nature of reading.

Thus, in order to help students learn to respond to the Latin in a linear fashion, this course introduces *metaphrasing*. This is a technique that relates the Latin system of morphology and syntax to English word order patterns. It provides a "slow-motion" simulation of the manner in which a proficient reader might process information from Latin and express it in English while proceeding through a sentence item by item. It is a most useful technique for beginners, but, if carried to extremes, may become cumbersome later.

Every metaphrase begins with a basic framework for English kernels:

"(subject) (verb)ₛ ± (direct object) ."

This is to be read as "blank" "blanks" "plus or minus" "blank." The symbol ± (plus or minus) allows for a transitive or an intransitive kernel. It is retained in the metaphrase until one is certain that there is or is not a direct object.

Example: Upon seeing the word *spem* in S1.3 (*Spem successus alit*), it is not enough to process only vocabulary information, i.e., that the word means *hope*. It is just as important to process the morphological and syntactic information and relate it to the English system and word order patterns. Thus *spem,* a noun in the accusative case, is to a reader of Latin what the word *hope* in the pattern "_____ _____s hope" ("blank blanks hope") is to a reader of English. The *form* of the word *spem* in Latin conveys the same syntactic information about its function as the *position* of the word *hope* conveys in English. In both languages the word has raised the expectation of a subject and a verb.

Likewise, the *form* of the word *successus* tells the reader that *successus* is to Latin what "success _____s ± _____" is to English. Both raise the expectation at least of a verb, and possibly of a direct object.

Metaphrasing does not yield a polished translation; it yields what is called a metaphrase or a structural translation. Additional skills are needed in order to produce polished literary translations.

The metaphrasing guidelines to be learned in this course cover some of the most common problems of learning to read Latin. They will be introduced as needed. The first two metaphrase guidelines are as follows.[1]

A subject precedes a verb.
A direct object, if present, follows the verb.

Note on the Latin noun: There are no articles in classical Latin; therefore, *fūr* means "thief" or "a thief" or "the thief."

Note on the Latin verb: Latin does not distinguish, as English does, between the simple, the progressive, and the emphatic forms of the verb. Therefore *alit* means "feeds" or "is feeding" or "does feed," according to the context.

A *cumulative* metaphrase (i.e., adding one word at a time) of *Spem successus alit* is as follows.

Item	Syntactic Information	Metaphrase
spem	direct object	_____ _____s hope.
spem *successus*	subject	Success _____s hope.
spem successus *alit*	verb	Success nourishes hope.

Here are examples of the metaphrase of Latin words in *isolation* (i.e., words not listed here as part of a sentence).

Item	Syntactic Information	Metaphrase
Cognōscit	verb	_____ recognizes _____ .
Fūr	subject	Thief _____s ± _____ .
Successum	direct object	_____ _____s success.
Īram	direct object	_____ _____s anger.
Spēs	subject	Hope _____s ± _____ .

---

1. There are, of course, exceptions but they are for reasons of emphasis, style, etc.

Summary

Metaphrasing shows how a Latin word with a certain morphology relates to English word order. It also shows how the information obtained from one word *raises expectations* of other words with specific functions. For example:

1. The presence of a direct object raises the expectation of a verb and of a subject.
2. The presence of a verb raises the expectation of a subject, and possibly a direct object.
3. The presence of a subject raises the expectation of a verb, and possibly a direct object.

Although metaphrasing is a specific technique used while learning to read Latin, the notion of *expectations* is central to the reading process at all levels of reading in all languages.

■ Exercise 13

Using the chart, write a *cumulative* metaphrase of the sentence *Animum vēritās alit*. The first word is given as an example.

Item	Part of Speech and Identification	Syntactic Information	Cumulative Metaphrase
1. Animum	noun: acc. sing.	direct object	_____ _____s mind.
2.			
3.			

■ Exercise 14

Complete this metaphrase chart for these words in *isolation*. Metaphrase each in the structural context of a complete kernel.

Item	Part of Speech and Identification	Syntactic Information	Metaphrase
animus			
hōram			
spēs			
lavat			
occāsiōnem			
vēritātem			
impedit			

Lesson Vocabulary

The standard practice for listing a *noun* in Latin dictionaries is to give the nominative and one other case, because the nominative does not always show the *stem morpheme. This is especially true of third declension nouns.* This book follows the practice of those Latin dictionaries that give the nominative and *genitive* cases.

The standard practice for listing a *verb* in Latin dictionaries is to give the principal parts of the verb; the first principal part is the first person singular, the "I ____" form. The second principal part is called the infinitive. This will be studied in lesson 3. The third and fourth principal parts will be introduced in lesson 9. Lessons 1 through 8 will list only the first two principal parts.

The English word(s) given with a Latin word in the Lesson Vocabulary represent the word's basic meaning, and are not always the same as those used in the translation of the Basic Sentences. The main reason for the difference is that the translations of the Basic Sentences are often literary, specialized, or idiomatic. The English words given with the Latin words in the Readings Vocabulary often represent the specialized meaning required in a particular sentence.

Nouns

animus, animī: spirit, mind
fūr, fūris: thief
hōra, hōrae: hour
īra, īrae: anger
manus, manūs: hand
occāsiō, occāsiōnis: opportunity
rēs, reī: thing, affair, circumstance
spēs, speī: hope, expectation
successus, successūs: success
vēritās, vēritātis: truth

Verbs

alō, alere: feed, nourish
faciō, facere: make, do
fugiō, fugere: flee
impediō, impedīre: hinder
lavō, lavāre: wash
vincō, vincere: conquer, prevail

Readings

1.1. Brevitās dēlectat.—Medieval
1.2. Vēritātem diēs aperit.—Seneca
1.3. Diēs dolōrem minuit.—Anon.
1.4. Līs lītem generat.—Anon.
1.5. Philosophum nōn facit barba.—Plutarch (translation)
1.6. Amor gignit amōrem.—Anon.
1.7. Necessitās nōn habet lēgem.—Anon.

Vocabulary

1.1. brevitās, brevitātis: briefness
  dēlectō, dēlectāre: delight, cause joy
1.2. diēs, diēī: day, time
  aperiō, aperīre: open, reveal
1.3. diēs, diēī: day, time
  dolor, dolōris: pain, grief
  minuō, minuere: diminish, lessen
1.4. līs, lītis: quarrel, argument
  generō, generāre: beget

1.5. philosophus, philosophī: philosopher
  nōn: not (this is an adverb)
  barba, barbae: beard
1.6. amor, amōris: love
  gignō, gignere: beget, create, give birth to
1.7. necessitās, necessitātis: necessity
  nōn: not (this is an adverb)
  habeō, habēre: have
  lēx, lēgis: law

Word Study: English Derivatives

The study of English words derived from Latin is helpful in learning both stem morphemes and meanings of Latin words. Likewise, a knowledge of Latin stem morphemes enlarges one's English vocabulary.

Find in the Basic Sentences or in the body of the lesson for the first column or in the Readings section for the second column a Latin word with which each of the following English words is connected by derivation. Write the Latin word in the form in which it appears. In addition it may be useful to give the dictionary listing. Underline the common elements in each pair of related words. Be prepared to explain the relationship in meaning. Use an English dictionary if necessary.

From Lesson	Latin	From Readings	Latin
1. animated	animum (animus, -ī)	1. amorous	
2. fugitive		2. aperture	
3. hour		3. brevity	
4. impede		4. delectable	
5. lavatory		5. diary	
6. manual		6. diminish	
7. occasion		7. legal	
8. verity		8. necessity	

Summary Tasks

____ 1. Name the part of speech of each word in the Basic Sentences and/or Readings.
____ 2. Name the syntactic function of each noun in the Basic Sentences and/or Readings.
____ 3. Write the accusative of each noun from the Lesson Vocabulary.
____ 4. Name at least one expectation that is raised by the first word in each Reading.

Lesson 2

Part of Speech: Coordinating Conjunction
The Gap

Lesson 1 introduced kernels and functional items within kernels. This lesson introduces *connection* through *coordinating conjunctions* or commas. It also introduces sentences with *gaps*, i.e., sentences in which words that are expected are not present.

Basic Sentences

2.1. Fūrem fūr cognōscit et lupum lupus.—Anon.
    A thief knows a thief (when he sees one) and a wolf a wolf.
2.2. Diem nox premit, diēs noctem.—Seneca
    Night follows day, day follows night.
2.3. Pecūnia nōn satiat avāritiam sed irrītat.—Medieval
    Money does not satisfy greed but inflames it.
2.4. Vītam regit fortūna, nōn sapientia.—Cicero
    Chance rules life, wisdom does not rule it.
2.5. Senātus populusque Rōmānus
    The Senate and the people of Rome (Note: Abbreviated *S.P.Q,R.*, this is the name of the sovereign Roman state. It is a phrase, not a sentence.)

Part of Speech: Coordinating Conjunction[1]

In lesson 1 all sentences consisted of one kernel, and all parts of the kernel consisted of one item, i.e., one subject, one verb, or one direct object. Through the use of *connection* any number of items having the same function can appear in both Latin and English sentences. E.g., in the sentence "I like math, physics, and geography," the items "math," "physics," and "geography" are all direct objects connected by either a comma or "and." Commas and words like *and*, a *coordinating conjunction*, function as connectors.

    In contrast to nouns and verbs, conjunctions have only one form. Words that have only one form are sometimes called *indeclinables*.

    Connection is expressed in this lesson by the coordinating conjunctions *et, -que* (and) and *sed* (but). Additional coordinating conjunctions will occur in other lessons. Connection is also expressed by the use of the comma. The comma in S2.2 (*Diem nox premit, diēs noctem*) indicates *and*, that is, parallelism. A comma followed by *nōn*, as in S2.4 (*Vītam regit fortūna, nōn sapientia*), indicates *but not*, that is, contrast. Of course, just as in English, not all commas indicate connection.

---

    1. *Conjunction* is from Latin *conjūnctiō* (a joining together).

15

Syntax: Connection

English coordinating conjunctions usually appear between the two items connected.

> sooner or later
> in and out
> slowly but surely
> "Give me liberty or give me death."
> men and women
> "to be or not to be"
> " 'Twas brillig and the slithy toves did gyre and gimble in the wabe."

Coordinating conjunctions in Latin do not always appear in the same place as they would in English. For example, *-que* (and) regularly appears attached to the second item. In S2.5 (*Senātus populusque Rōmānus*), the *-que* attached to *populus* connects *senātus* and *populus*.

Coordinating conjunctions indicate that two "sames" are connected to each other.

> a subject to a subject,
> a direct object to a direct object,
> a kernel to a kernel, etc.

A connector never connects a subject to a verb, or a whole kernel to a direct object, although it may look like it. For example, in S2.1 (*Fūrem fūr cognōscit et lupum lupus*), the *et* does not connect the verb *cognōscit* and the direct object *lupum;* instead it connects two kernels.

■ Exercise 1
Underline each of the sames that are connected, and name them by function within the kernel or as kernels.

Example: <u>He ran</u> and <u>the dog followed</u>.   <u>two kernels</u>

1. I hear the saxophone and the trombone.   _____

2. The man writes and paints.   _____

3. He lost the money yesterday and she found it today.   _____

4. Once upon a time there were knights and ladies.   _____

5. My sister skates and her husband swims.   _____

The Gap

Man's ability to read is truly mysterious. The Roman writer Quintilian in the first century A.D. said that a person could not read out loud correctly unless he understood what he was reading. In a well-appointed Roman household there was always a slave called the *lector* (reader), whose job it was to read out loud correctly texts that he had studied before or that he could read *ex tempore* (at the moment without preparation), because he was proficient at reading.

What this means, *inter alia*,[1] is that the *lector* had a sense of *completeness of expression*. Everybody has this sense, and it is a major reason for our ability to read. The fact of completeness of expression is, however, obscured or interfered with by another fact of language: often not all words that are expected are present, because in language identical items can be deleted or *gapped* (∅) according to rules specific to the particular language. The symbol ∅ is to be read as *zero*.

One-kernel simple sentences usually occur in isolated sayings, proverbs, slogans, and sometimes at the beginning of books, chapters, and paragraphs. Because all expected items of the sentences are present, one-kernel sentences are easy to analyze and to understand. Sentences of two or more kernels and sentences in connected passages are more difficult.

S2.1 has a complete kernel: *Fūrem fūr cognōscit*. The *et* indicates that there is a second "same." This "same" is *lupum lupus,* which is an incomplete kernel inasmuch as it shows no verb. According to the gapping rules for verbs in Latin, *an identical verb may be gapped in the first or second of two kernels.*

> *Fūrem fūr cognōscit et lupum lupus* ⟨∅ = *cognōscit*⟩ is possible.
> *Fūrem fūr* ⟨∅ = *cognōscit*⟩ *et lupum lupus cognōscit* is possible.

The rule is different for English.

> A thief recognizes a thief, and a wolf ⟨∅ = recognizes⟩ a wolf. (possible)
> A thief ⟨∅ = recognizes⟩ a thief, and a wolf recognizes a wolf. (not grammatically possible for most speakers of English)

The verb is not the only kernel item that can be gapped in Latin. *An identical subject in Latin may be gapped in any kernel of a two- (or more) kernel sentence.* The rule is different for English where an identical subject of the kernel cannot be gapped in the first kernel. For example, "Likes baseball but Matt prefers soccer" is not grammatical; "Matt likes baseball but prefers soccer" is grammatical.

An identical direct object of two or more kernels in Latin can be gapped in any of the kernels. On the other hand, an identical direct object of two or more kernels in English can be gapped in the first kernel only. For example, "Anna likes but Lisa dislikes rhubarb" is grammatical; "Anna likes rhubarb but Lisa dislikes" is not grammatical. Notice that the second kernel of the latter sentence could be completed by adding the pronoun *it*.

Note: A two-kernel sentence also is called a two-*clause* sentence.

---

1. *Inter alia* is a Latin phrase meaning "among other things."

■ Exercise 2

Copy and label all kernel items from Basic Sentences 2.2, 2.3, and 2.4. Include all ∅ items (example: ∅ = *cognōscit*). Cl. Conn. means clause connector, i.e., the connector that joins two clauses.

	Cl. Conn.	Item: Function	Item: Function	Item: Function	Kernel Type
S2.2.					
S2.2.					
S2.3.					
S2.3.					
S2.4.					
S2.4.					

■ Exercise 3

Complete the following chart for Basic Sentences 2.2, 2.3, 2.4, and 2.5 of this lesson. Include ∅ items. S2.1 is given as an example.

	Connector	First Same	Second Same
S2.1.	et	Fūrem fūr cognōscit	lupum lupus ∅ = cognōscit
S2.2.		Diem nox premit	
S2.3.		Pecūnia nōn satiat avāritiam	
S2.4.		Vītam regit fortūna	
S2.5.		Senātus	populus

■ Exercise 4

Rewrite the following Latin sentences supplying all gapped items. Follow the example.

Fūrem fūr cognōscit et lupum lupus. = Fūrem fūr cognōscit et lupum lupus ⟨∅ = cognōscit⟩.

1. Diem nox, diēs noctem premit.

2. Pecūnia nōn satiat avāritiam sed irrītat.

3. Vītam fortūna, nōn regit vītam sapientia.

■ Exercise 5

Metaphrase each item in the structural context of a complete kernel.

1. hominem

2. fēmina virum

3. avāritiam cognōscit

4. vēritātem vir

5. premit

Lesson Vocabulary

Nouns
avāritia, avāritiae: greed, avarice
diēs, diēī: day; time
fēmina, fēminae: woman
fortūna, fortūnae: chance, luck
homō, hominis: human being, man
lupus, lupī: wolf
nox, noctis: night
pecūnia, pecūniae: money
populus, populī: the people, a nation;
   populus Rōmānus: Roman people
sapientia, sapientiae: wisdom
senātus, senātūs: senate
vir, virī: man
vīta, vītae: life

Indeclinables
nōn: not

Coordinating Conjunctions
et: and
-que: and
sed: but

Verbs
cognōscō, cognōscere: recognize, learn,
   get to know
irrītō, irrītāre: stir up, incite
premō, premere: press, pursue
regō, regere: rule, direct
satiō, satiāre: fill, satisfy

Readings

2.1. Rem, nōn spem, quaerit amīcus.—Carmen de Figuris
2.2. Homō locum ōrnat, nōn hominem locus.—Medieval
2.3. Medicus cūrat, nātūra sānat.—Motto
2.4. Jam frāter frātrem, jam fallit fīlia mātrem,
     jamque pater nātum, jam fallit amīcus amīcum.—Medieval
2.5. Vulpēs vult fraudem, lupus agnum, fēmina laudem.—Werner
2.6. Lupus pilum mūtat, nōn mentem.—Anon.

Vocabulary

2.1. quaerō, quaerere: look for, seek
   amīcus, amīcī: friend
2.2. locus, locī: place, position
   ōrnō, ōrnāre: decorate, adorn
2.3. medicus, medicī: physician, doctor
   cūrō, cūrāre: treat, take care of
   nātūra, nātūrae: nature
   sānō, sānāre: cure, heal
2.4. jam: now (this is an adverb, not a noun
     in the accusative)
   frāter, frātris: brother
   fallō, fallere: deceive
   fīlia, fīliae: daughter
   māter, mātris: mother
   pater, patris: father
   nātus, nātī: son
   amīcus, amīcī: friend

2.5. vulpēs, vulpis: fox
   vult (from volō, velle): want, wish (an
     irregular verb)
   fraus, fraudis: trick, deceit
   agnus, agnī: lamb
   laus, laudis: praise
2.6. pilus, pilī: hair, skin, hide
   mūtō, mūtāre: change
   mēns, mentis: mind

Word Study: English Derivatives

Follow the directions given in lesson 1. Note the spelling changes in some words between the vowels in Latin and the vowels in English. If the Latin word is a noun in the nominative, write both the nominative and the genitive case forms, since the nominative does not always show the stem.

Some derivatives in this and other lessons appear with a prefix although the Latin word as it appears in the lesson has no prefix. In some instances a prefix different from that in the vocabulary is used.

From Lesson	Latin	From Readings	Latin
1. avarice		1. amicable	
2. furtive		2. filial	
3. irritable		3. fraternity	
4. nocturnal		4. fraudulent	
5. population		5. inquire	
6. regent		6. laudable	
7. satiated		7. maternal	
8. vital		8. mutation	

Summary Tasks

_____ 1. Rewrite Readings 2.1, 2.2, 2.4, 2.5, and 2.6 supplying all gapped items.

_____ 2. Write a cumulative metaphrase for Basic Sentence 2.2.

_____ 3. Write the noun stem and then write the accusative of each third declension noun from the Readings Vocabulary.

_____ 4. Copy any four English coordinating conjunctions and the "sames" they connect from the sentences in the first paragraph on page 2 (lesson 1).

_____ 5. Copy into your notebook, on a page labeled Coordinating Conjunctions, all coordinating conjunctions introduced so far. Add to this list throughout the course.

_____ 6. How many clauses in the Readings are complete, i.e., have no gaps?

_____ 7. What expectation is raised by a connector?

Lesson 3

The Complementary Infinitive
Questions

The first part of this lesson introduces the *complementary infinitive,* one of four major uses of the Latin infinitive. The second part introduces sentences that are questions rather than statements.

Basic Sentences

3.1. Fūrem fūr cognōscere potest. (S2.1 adapted)
    A thief is able to recognize a thief.
3.2. Quis fūrem cognōscere potest? (S2.1 adapted)
    Who can/is able to recognize a thief?
3.3. Quem occāsiō facit? (S1.5 adapted)
    Whom does opportunity produce?

The Complementary Infinitive

So far the item functioning as verb of the kernel has been a single word verb. From now on there also will be verb items consisting of two verb forms, one with a person ending (so far the morpheme {t}), and the other an *infinitive,*[1] which has no ending for person.

Morphology

The morpheme {re} at the end of the second principal part of a verb signals the verb form called the infinitive. Verbs fall into groups called *conjugations*. There are four main conjugations. The vowel before the {re} indicates the conjugation to which a verb belongs. The infinitive endings are:

    First conjugation: **āre** as in amō, am**āre** (to love)
    Second conjugation: **ēre** as in videō, vid**ēre** (to see)
    Third conjugation: **ere** as in regō, reg**ere** (to rule)
    Fourth conjugation: **īre** as in audiō, aud**īre** (to hear)

Some verbs are irregular and do not follow these patterns, e.g., *volō, velle* (wish, want); *possum, posse* (can, be able).

---

    1. A verb with a personal ending is called a *finite verb*. See Syntax, lesson 14.

Syntax

Certain English verbs occur regularly with an infinitive. The English verb *can/is able* is one such verb that patterns regularly with an infinitive. That is, it raises the *expectation* of the infinitive of another verb. For example, "the thief is able" raises the expectation of a "to _____" verb form, e.g., "to recognize." This use of the infinitive is called *complementary infinitive* (from *complement,* to fill out, to complete). Later lessons will introduce other uses of the infinitive.

Other English verbs pattern occasionally with an infinitive. The English verb *want* is an example of such a verb. Compare "the people want to rule" ("want" plus infinitive) with "the people want power" ("want" plus noun).

In Latin, too, certain verbs pattern with an infinitive either regularly or occasionally. Some verbs that pattern regularly with a complementary infinitive are:

potest: can/is able (from possum, posse)
audet: dares (from audeō, audēre)
solet: is accustomed (from soleō, solēre)

Some verbs that pattern occasionally with complementary infinitives are:

cupit: desires (from cupiō, cupere)
dēbet: ought, must (from dēbeō, dēbēre) (dēbeō + direct object = owe)
vult: wants (from volō, velle)

Fūr occāsiōnem *vult.* (The thief *wants* the opportunity.)
Fūr avāritiam *satiāre vult.* (The thief *wants to satisfy* his[1] greed.)
Fūr pecūniam *dēbet.* (The thief *owes* money.)
Fūr *fugere dēbet.* (The thief ought to flee.)

The complementary infinitive is considered as part of the verb of the kernel. For example, in S3.1, *potest* provides the *person* and *number* while the infinitive *cognōscere* provides information as to *kernel type.* Observe the kernel chart for S3.1. *Fūrem fūr cognōscere potest.*

Item: Function	Item: Function	Item: Function	Kernel Type
fūrem: direct object	fūr: subject	cognōscere potest: verb	trans. act.

■ Exercise 1

Rewrite each verb in the sentences below as complementary infinitive with one of the six new verbs: *potest, audet, dēbet, solet, cupit, vult.* Study the example.

Manus manum lavat: Manus manum lavāre dēbet.

1. Impedit īra animum

2. Spem successus alit

3. Vēritās vincit

___

1. Often words such as *his, her,* and *our* are not expressed in the Latin sentence, but can be understood from the context.

■ Exercise 2

Copy the kernels of the new sentences you produced in exercise 1 and give a metaphrase of each sentence.

Item: Function	Item: Function	Item: Function	Kernel Type
1.			
2.			
3.			

Metaphrase

1.

2.

3.

■ Exercise 3

Metaphrase the following items in the structural context of a complete kernel. Look at the example.

dēbet: _____ ought to _____ ± _____

1. pecūniam

2. īra potest

3. lavat

4. vult fugere

5. regit sapientia

6. audet

7. pecūnia

8. avāritiam irrītāre solet

Questions

The Basic Sentences in lessons 1 and 2, as well as S3.1, are statements. There are, of course, other modes of speech, namely questions and commands. This section introduces Latin questions such as in Basic Sentences 3.2 and 3.3. There is no difference between questions and statements in terms of kernel types and syntax.

One way in which a question can be distinguished from a statement is by the presence of an *interrogative pronoun*. These are *wh-* words in English (who, what, etc.) and the equivalent *qu-* words in Latin (see Morphology of the interrogative pronouns in this lesson). Such question words seek a specific word or words as answers. Look at this example.

Quis fūrem cognōscere potest? Fūr. (*Who* is able to recognize a thief? [Another] thief.)

In this example the question word is *quis?* (who?).

A second type of question is the *yes/no* question. In English this differs from a statement by the inversion of subject-verb word order, and the presence of an auxiliary verb such as *do* or *is*. In Latin this question is signaled by *-ne* added to the first word in the question. Compare these sentences.

> Statement: Fugit hōra. (Time flies. *or* Time is flying.)
> Question: Fugitne hōra? (Does time fly? *or* Is time flying?)

Morphology: Interrogative Pronouns

	Animate	Nonanimate
Nominative	quis? (who?)	quid?[1] (what?)
Accusative	quem? (whom?)	quid? (what?)

Syntax

Pronouns stand for nouns and have the same syntax as nouns. Examples of Latin questions are given here with corresponding statements. Notice that the phrase *quid agit* (what does _____ do?) is used in this course to ask for the verb ± object.

> Statement: Vir fēminam videt.
> Questions: Quis fēminam videt? Vir.
>   Quem vir videt? Fēminam.
>   Quid agit vir? Videt fēminam.
>
> Statement: Vincit vēritās.
> Questions: Quid vincit? Vēritās.
>   Quid agit vēritās? Vincit.
>   Vincitne vēritās? Vincit.

Note: The answer to a yes/no question in Latin is usually a repetition of the sentence or at least the verb, with or without the negator *nōn*.

■ Exercise 4

Based on the example given, compose questions to ask for each underlined item.

> The wolf wants the lamb.
> a   b
>   c

a. Who wants the lamb? The wolf.

b. Whom does the wolf want? The lamb.

c. What does the wolf do?⎫
c. What is the wolf doing?⎭ The wolf wants the lamb.

---

1. The accusative is identical to the nominative. Lesson 5 will explain this morphology.

1. <u>Success</u> feeds <u>hope</u>.
     a   b
                c

   a.

   b.

   c.

2. <u>A thief</u> is able to recognize <u>a thief</u>.
     a   b
                    c

   a.

   b.

   c.

■ Exercise 5

Answer in Latin the following questions on Basic Sentences (S) and Readings (R). S1.3 is given as an example.

      Quid alit spem? Successus.

S1.4. Fugitne hōra?

S1.5. Quem facit occāsiō?

      Quid agit occāsiō?

R1.1. Quid agit brevitās?

R1.5. Quem nōn facit barba?

R1.7. Quid necessitās nōn habet?

S2.4. Quid vītam nōn regit?

      Regitne vītam fortūna?

R2.2. Quis locum ōrnat?

R2.3. Quid agit medicus?

S3.1. Quem fūr cognōscere potest?

Semantics: Animate versus Nonanimate

Both Latin and English discriminate between nouns with the *semantic feature animate* or *nonanimate*. This is most clearly seen in the interrogative pronoun of both languages. A *who?* question calls for an answer such as "thief," "friend," "wolf," or "lamb," each of which has the feature *animate*.

      A *what?* question calls for an answer such as "hope," "success," "clothing," or "truth," each of which has the feature *nonanimate*.

The feature animate/nonanimate will be the most important semantic feature to be considered in reading and interpretation. For example, the figure of speech *personification* means that the feature animate is added to a word that does not have it naturally. The noun *highway* does not have the feature animate naturally, but it is personified in the sentence "the highway is humming with traffic today" because "humming" is associated with animate nouns. This process may occur for *fortūna* and *sapientia* in S2.4 since the verb *regit* (rules) commonly appears with animate nouns, such as *populus* or *vir*, as subject.

■ Exercise 6

Rewrite the following statements as questions, replacing the first noun by the interrogative pronoun. Be careful to observe the semantic difference between nouns with the semantic feature *animate* and those with the semantic feature *nonanimate*. Observe the example.

Philosophum nōn facit barba.   Quem nōn facit barba? Philosophum.
Barba philosophum nōn facit.   Quid philosophum nōn facit? Barba.

1. Manus manum lavat.

2. Spem successus alit.

3. Vēritās vincit.

4. Fūrem fūr cognōscit.

5. Fēmina virum audit.

■ Exercise 7

Write the kernels of the following sentences on the kernel chart. In the last column indicate whether it is a statement or question.

1. Quem lupus cognōscit?
2. Quis pecūniam vult?
3. Quid lupus vult?
4. Quid fugit?
5. Quid spem alit?

Item: Function	Item: Function	Item: Function	Kernel Type	Name
1.				
2.				
3.				
4.				
5.				

Lesson Vocabulary

Pronoun

quis, quid (interrogative pronoun): who, what

Indeclinable

-ne: signals a yes/no question

Verbs

agō, agere: do, act, drive, lead
amō, amāre: love, like
audeō, audēre: dare
audiō, audīre: hear, listen to
cupiō, cupere: desire, wish
dēbeō, dēbēre: owe; ought (with inf.)
possum, posse (irreg. verb): be able, can
soleō, solēre: be accustomed
videō, vidēre: see
volō, velle (irreg. verb): wish, want, be willing

Word Study: English Derivatives

Follow the directions given in lesson 1. Note the spelling changes in some words between the vowels in Latin and the vowels in English. If the Latin word is a noun in the nominative, write both the nominative and the genitive case forms, since the nominative does not always show the stem.

Some derivatives in this and other lessons appear with a prefix although the Latin word as it appears in the lesson has no prefix. In some instances a prefix different from that in the vocabulary is used.

From Lesson   **Latin**

1. agent

2. amatory

3. audacious

4. cupidity

5. debt

6. inaudible

7. possibility

8. volition

Summary Tasks

____ 1. List the Latin verbs that always or sometimes pattern with a complementary infinitive.
____ 2. Expand each of the verbs listed in summary task 1 with an infinitive and metaphrase the new verb set.
____ 3. What determines the kernel type if a complementary infinitive is present?
____ 4. Copy into your notebook, on separate pages for each conjugation and for irregular verbs, all verbs in the Lesson Vocabulary of lessons 1, 2, and 3. Add to the list from each new lesson.

Lesson 4

Part of Speech: Adverb

Part of Speech: Preposition

Syntax: Adverbial Modification

The Latin sentences in the previous lessons introduced the kernel of the sentence and connectors. This lesson introduces *modifiers*. The modifiers are *adverbs* and *prepositional phrases*.

Basic Sentences

4.1. Fortiter, fidēliter, fēlīciter.—Motto
   Courageously, loyally, successfully. (A motto meaning Live/serve courageously, loyally, happily.)
4.2. Vēritās numquam perit.—Seneca
   Truth never perishes.
4.3. Prūdēns cum cūrā vīvit, stultus sine cūrā.—Werner
   A prudent person lives carefully, a fool lives carelessly.
4.4. Gladiātor in harēnā capit cōnsilium.—Seneca (adapted)
   A gladiator forms his plan in the arena.

Part of Speech: Adverb[1]

Most words ending in the morpheme {ter} are adverbs, and some words ending in the morpheme {ē} are adverbs. Examples are *fortiter* (courageously), *fidēliter* (loyally), and *fēlīciter* (successfully) in S4.1 and *rēctē* in R4.3. There are also many adverbs, such as *numquam* (never) in S4.2 and *semper* (always) in R4.3, that cannot be recognized by their forms. Adverbs are indeclinables.

Part of Speech: Preposition[2]

Prepositions are words such as *cum* (with) and *sine* (without) in S4.3 and *in* (in, on) in S4.4. They are indeclinables. A preposition patterns with a noun in the accusative or ablative case to form a *prepositional phrase*.

---

1. *Adverb* is from Latin *ad verbum* (near a verb).
2. *Preposition* is from Latin *praepositiō* (a placing before), a word placed before a noun.

Noun Morphology: The Ablative Case

All of the *prepositions* in this lesson pattern with *nouns* in the *ablative case*. This is the first of several uses of the ablative case. The ablative singular *always* ends in a vowel. This ablative vowel is long unless it is an *-e,* which is a short vowel in the third declension (e) but a long vowel in the fifth declension (ē). Look at the declension chart.

	First	Second	Third	Fourth	Fifth
Singular					
Nominative	hōra	animus	fūr	manus	rēs
Accusative	hōram	animum	fūrem	manum	rem
Ablative	**hōrā**	**animō**	**fūre**	**manū**	**rē**

■ Exercise 1

Identify each word by part of speech and, if a noun or pronoun, by case and number.

1. vītam

2. rēctē

3. numquam

4. cum

5. populum

6. quem

7. sine

8. animō

9. occāsiō

10. fortiter

Syntax: Adverbial Modification

The words in the sentences in the previous lessons have all been kernel items or connectors. Items that do not have a kernel function or are not connectors are *modifiers*. They modify any item of the kernel or another modifier. The item that is modified is called the *head of construction. A modifier raises the expectation of a head.* Modifiers are of two kinds.

1. adverbial modifiers: the head of construction is a verb, adjective, or adverb, but not a noun
2. adjectival modifiers: the head of construction is a noun

The modifiers of the Basic Sentences of this lesson are all *adverbial modifiers.* They are of two types.

1. words that belong to the part of speech *adverb,* e.g., *fortiter, numquam*
2. *prepositional phrases* consisting of a preposition and a noun in the ablative case

In S4.3 (*Prūdēns cum cūrā vīvit, stultus sine cūrā*), there are two kernels.

Prūdēns vīvit (A prudent person lives . . . ,)
Stultus ∅ = vīvit (A fool lives . . .)

Cum cūrā is a prepositional phrase and so is *sine cūrā*. *Cum cūrā* modifies the head *vīvit* (not *prūdēns*), in the first kernel; *sine cūrā* modifies the head *∅ = vīvit*, not *stultus*, in the second kernel. These prepositional phrases describe *how* the person lives, i.e., in what manner he lives, *not* what or which person lives. Prepositional phrases seldom modify a noun in Latin prose, but frequently do so in English, e.g., "the man in the moon," "a hamburger with everything," "the man from Mars."

It is easier to understand the relationship between the verb and the adverbial modifier when the modifier is an adverb, as in *Gladiātor fortiter vīvit*. *Vīvit*, not *gladiātor*, is the head; *fortiter* describes "in what manner?" or "how?" the subject lives.

■ Exercise 2
Copy the kernels of Basic Sentences 4.2, 4.3, and 4.4 onto the kernel chart. Remember that Cl. Conn. means clause connector.

	Cl. Conn.	Item: Function	Item: Function	Item: Function	Kernel Type	Name
4.2.						
4.3.						
4.3.						
4.4.						

■ Exercise 3
Copy all modifiers of Basic Sentences 4.1 through 4.4 onto the modifier chart and complete the chart.

	Item	Description*	Syntactic Information†	Head of Construction
4.1.	fortiter	adverb	adverbial modifier	not expressed in motto
4.1.				
4.1.				
4.2.				
4.3.				
4.3.				
4.4.				

*adverb or prepositional phrase
†adverbial modifier

Semantics: Manner, Place, Frequency, Accompaniment

In the sentence *Prūdēns cum cūrā vīvit* the prepositional phrase *cum cūrā* answers the question "in what manner?" However, in the sentence *Prūdēns cum amīcō ambulat* the prepositional phrase *cum amīcō* answers the question "with whom?" This is so because the noun *amīcus* (friend) has the semantic feature *animate*, whereas the noun *cūra* has the semantic feature *nonanimate*. Therefore, *cum cūrā* indicates the semantic category *manner* and *cum amīcō* indicates the semantic category *accompaniment*.

In S4.4 *harēna* (arena) has the semantic feature *place* as does *culmen* (pinnacle, top) in R4.4. *In + place* indicates the semantic category *place where; ab/dē/ex + place* indicates the semantic category *place from where*.

In S4.2 the adverb *numquam* has the semantic feature *frequency*.

Both Latin and English reflect semantic categories in their questions.

Semantic Category	Latin Question Word(s)	English Question Word(s)
Manner	quō modō?*	In what manner?
Place where	quō (in) locō?* Ubi?	In what place? Where?
Place from where	quō ā/dē/ē† locō?* Unde?	From what place? Where from?
Frequency	quotiēns?	How often?
Accompaniment	quōcum? (= cum + quō?)‡	With whom?

*Consider these as phrases; later lessons will explain their structure.

†*Ab* is *ā* and *ex* is *ē* before a word beginning with a consonant.

‡The ablative singular of the interrogative pronoun *quis*.

■ Exercise 4

Underline any item that is a *semantically* possible answer to the question provided.

1. Quō modō populus vīvit?   in harēnā, cum sapientiā, cum fūre, numquam

2. Quotiēns impedit īra animum?   fortiter, in pecūniā, semper, sine cūrā

3. Quōcum fūr venit?   cum amīcō, numquam, cum cūrā, ā/ab harēnā

4. Ubi lupus est?   fidēliter, in harēnā, sine fortūnā, semper

Metaphrasing: Adverbial Modifiers

It is safest to metaphrase prepositional phrases after the kernel. Adverbs may be metaphrased before the verb or after the kernel. Adverbial modifiers may be moved elsewhere in a translation.

■ Exercise 5

Metaphrase each of the following. Remember that every metaphrase must show a complete kernel. Look at the example.

sine cūrā: _____ _____s ± _____ without care

1. cum sapientiā

2. gladiātōrem dē locō

3. quis cum īrā premit

4. sine fortūnā

5. numquam potest

6. in senātū

■ Exercise 6

The column on the left contains predictable endings for the nominative, accusative, and ablative singular of Latin nouns. Identify by case all declension possibilities for each ending. The case ending *-em* is given as an example.

Case Ending	First	Second	Third	Fourth	Fifth
-em			acc.		acc.
-ā					
-us					
-a					
-um					
-e					
-ō			*		
-ē					

*not a predictable ending on third declension nouns

Lesson Vocabulary

Nouns
amīcus, amīcī: friend
cōnsilium,¹ cōnsiliī: plan, advice
cūra, cūrae: care, concern
gladiātor, gladiātōris: gladiator
harēna, harēnae: sand, arena
locus, locī: place, position
modus, modī: manner, way
prūdēns, prūdentis: sensible person
stultus, stultī: fool

Indeclinables
Adverbs
fēlīciter: successfully, luckily
fidēliter: faithfully
fortiter: bravely
numquam: never
rēctē: rightly, correctly
semper: always

Prepositions
ā/ab (+ abl.): from, away from
cum (+ abl.): with

dē (+ abl.): from, down from; concerning
ē/ex (+ abl.): from, out of
in (+ abl.): in, on
sine (+ abl.): without

Question Words
quō modō?: in what manner?
quō (in) locō?: in what place? where?
quō ā/dē/ē locō?: from what place?
    where from?
quotiēns?: how often?
quōcum?: with whom?
ubi?: where?
unde?: where from?

Verbs
ambulō, ambulāre: walk
capiō, capere: take, seize, get
pereō, perīre: perish, die, pass away
sum,² esse: be, exist
veniō, venīre: come
vīvō, vīvere: live, be alive

Notes
1. The nominative morpheme {um} of the second declension will be introduced in the next lesson.
2. The third person singular of this verb is *est*.

Readings

Required

4.1. Latet anguis in herbā.—Vergil
4.2. Nēmō sine crīmine vīvit.—Dionysius Cato
4.3. Nēmō semper rēctē vīvit.—(adapted)
4.4. Ruit ā culmine Trōja.—Vergil (adapted)
4.5. Stultus cum stultō fēlīciter vīvere potest.—(adapted)

Vocabulary

4.1. lateō, latēre: hide, be hidden
   anguis, anguis: snake
   herba, herbae: grass, herb
4.2. nēmō, nēminis: no one
   crīmen, crīminis: crime, wrongdoing
4.3. nēmō, nēminis: no one
4.4. ruō, ruere: rush, fall, be ruined
   culmen, culminis: summit, peak
   Trōja, Trōjae: Troy

Optional

4.6. Palma nōn sine pulvere cēdit.—Motto
4.7. Suāviter in modō, fortiter in rē.—Motto

Vocabulary

4.6. palma, palmae: palm of victory
   pulvis, pulveris: dust, work
   cēdō, cēdere: yield, submit
4.7. suāviter: gently, sweetly

Latin Questions

Answer in Latin these questions on Basic Sentences and Readings.

S4.2. Quotiēns vēritās perit?

S4.3. Quis sine cūrā vīvit?

S4.4. Quō in locō gladiātor capit cōnsilium?

R4.2. Quō modō nēmō vīvit?

R4.5. Quōcum stultus fēlīciter vīvit?

Word Study: English Derivatives

Follow the directions given in lesson 1. Note the spelling changes in some words between the vowels in Latin and the vowels in English. If the Latin word is a noun in the nominative, write both the nominative and the genitive case forms, since the nominative does not always show the stem.

Some derivatives in this and other lessons appear with a prefix although the Latin word as it appears in the lesson has no prefix. In some instances a prefix different from that in the vocabulary is used.

From Lesson	Latin	From Readings	Latin
1. capable		1. correct	
2. capture		2. criminal	
3. felicity		3. culmination	
4. fidelity		4. herbarium	
5. fortitude		5. latent	
6. imprudently		6. pulverize	
7. stultify		7. ruin	
8. vivid		8. suave	

Summary Tasks

_____ 1. Complete a kernel chart for Readings 4.1 through 4.5.

_____ 2. Complete a modifier chart for Readings 4.1 through 4.5. For an example of a modifier chart, see exercise 3.

_____ 3. Write the ablative singular for each noun from the Lesson Vocabulary.

_____ 4. Ask one Latin question for each Reading.

_____ 5. Copy into your notebook, on a page labeled Prepositions + Ablative, all the prepositions in this lesson. Add to this list throughout the course.

_____ 6. Copy into your notebook, on a page labeled Adverbs, all adverbs in this lesson. Add to this list throughout the course.

Lesson 5

Part of Speech: Adjective
Gender
Syntax: Adjectival Modification

The last lesson introduced two parts of speech, prepositions and adverbs. This lesson introduces one new part of speech, the *adjective*. This lesson also introduces a new type of modification, namely, *adjectival modification*.

Basic Sentences

5.1. Ā fonte pūrō pūra dēfluit aqua.—Anon.
   From a pure spring flows pure water.
5.2. Fīnis corōnat opus.—Binder
   The end crowns the work.
5.3. In omnī rē vincit imitātiōnem vēritās.—Cicero
   In every situation truth conquers imitation.
5.4. Vānēscit absēns et intrat novus amor.—Ovid
   An absent love fades away and a new one enters.
5.5. Fortem Fortūna adjuvat.—Terence (adapted)
   Fortune helps the brave person.

Part of Speech: Adjective[1]

Morphology

Adjectives look like nouns and have nearly the same morphemes for case and number. One group of adjectives looks like nouns of the first and second declensions. The other group looks like nouns of the third declension except in the ablative singular.

The endings of Latin adjectives indicate three grammatical categories: case, number, and *gender*. There are three genders called masculine, feminine, and neuter (to be explained further in the section on gender). Some of the forms of adjectives are ambiguous with regard to these categories.

The beginning part of this lesson introduces the group of adjectives that look like nouns of the first and second declensions. These adjectives are then used in explanations of the syntax and metaphrasing of adjectives in general. The last part of the lesson introduces the group of adjectives that look like nouns of the third declension and adds information about the syntax of adjectives.

---

1. *Adjective* is from Latin *adjectīvum* (added).

Morphology: First and Second Declension Adjectives

Novus, -a, -um (new, strange) represents the group of adjectives called *first* and *second declension adjectives*. These adjectives have a dictionary entry that shows all three genders in the nominative singular, e.g., *novus, -a, -um* for nov*us*, nov*a*, nov*um*. Look at the paradigm chart of *novus, -a, -um*.

	Masculine	Feminine	Neuter
Singular			
Nominative	**novus**	**nova**	**novum**
Accusative	**novum**	**novam**	**novum**
Ablative	**novō**	**novā**	**novō**
Dative	novō	novae	novō
Genitive	novī	novae	novī
Plural			
Nominative	novī	novae	nova
Accusative	novōs	novās	nova
Ablative	novīs	novīs	novīs
Dative	novīs	novīs	novīs
Genitive	novōrum	novārum	novōrum

Other adjectives with this paradigm include:

> bonus, bona, bonum (good)
> magnus, magna, magnum (large, great)
> malus, mala, malum (bad, evil)
> parvus, parva, parvum (small)
> pulcher, pulchra, pulchrum (beautiful)
> pūrus, pūra, pūrum (pure)
> quantus, quanta, quantum? (how great a? what size?)

Note the following comparisons with the morphology of nouns of the first and second declensions.

> The first column is on the model of the second declension masculine noun *lupus, lupī*.
> The second column is on the model of the first declension noun *fēmina, fēminae*.
> The third column is on the model of the second declension neuter noun *vīnum, vīnī*, introduced in this lesson.
> The adjective *pulcher, pulchra, pulchrum* has the masculine nominative *pulcher* on the model of second declension nouns such as *aper, aprī* and *ager, agrī* whose stem does not appear in the nominative.

■ Exercise 1
Identify the following adjectives by case (nom., acc., or abl.), number (sing.), and gender(s) (m., f., or n.).

1. novum

2. novum

3. novum

4. bona

5. bonā

6. pulcher

7. pulchra

8. pūrō

9. pūrō

10. pulchram

■ Exercise 2

Write the paradigm (nom., acc., and abl. sing.) of the following nouns and adjectives.

	aper, aprī	pulcher (masc. only)	vīta, vītae	parva (fem. only)	quantum (neut. only)
Nominative					
Accusative					
Ablative					

Gender

Every noun belongs to one of three gender classes: masculine, feminine, or neuter. The full dictionary entry for a noun consists of its nominative, its genitive, *and its gender*, e.g., *fōns, fontis,* m.; *rēs, reī,* f.; *opus, operis,* n. Neuter means literally that a noun is neither masculine nor feminine, because the Latin adjective *neuter, neutra, neutrum* means "neither of two."

The gender of a noun must be memorized, but there are some helpful generalizations on gender. For example, most nouns in the first and fifth declensions are feminine, most nouns of the second declension are masculine or neuter, and most nouns of the fourth declension are masculine.

Gender is sometimes predictable from meaning. For example, nouns denoting males and females or their cultural roles are masculine or feminine, respectively. Most abstract nouns are feminine. But the gender of many nouns cannot be predicted from meaning. For example, a Latin word for water, *aqua,* is feminine, a word for fire, *ignis,* is masculine, and a word for air, *āēr,* is neuter.

Morphology of Neuter Nouns

The *paradigm of neuter nouns* differs from other paradigms inasmuch as the *nominative* and the *accusative* are *always alike.* This ambiguity is usually resolved within the sentence.

Neuter nouns of the second declension end in *-um* in the nominative.

Neuter nouns of the third declension have many different appearances in the nominative singular and, therefore, in the accusative singular also. In S5.2 *opus* is the unlikely looking direct object. See, e.g., *opus* and *culmen* in the paradigms that follow.

Paradigm for Nouns in the Neuter Gender

	Second		Third	
Singular				
Nominative	**vīnum**	**cōnsilium**	**opus**	**culmen**
Accusative	**vīnum**	**cōnsilium**	**opus**	**culmen**
Ablative	**vīnō**	**cōnsiliō**	**opere**	**culmine**
Dative	vīnō	cōnsiliō	operī	culminī
Genitive	vīnī	cōnsiliī*	operis	culminis
Plural				
Nominative	vīna	cōnsilia	opera	culmina
Accusative	vīna	cōnsilia	opera	culmina
Ablative	vīnīs	cōnsiliīs	operibus	culminibus
Dative	vīnīs	cōnsiliīs	operibus	culminibus
Genitive	vīnōrum	cōnsiliōrum	operum	culminum

*The genitive singular of second declension nouns ending in *-ius* and *-ium*
was regularly spelled with a single *-ī*, e.g., *cōnsilī*, until after the beginning of the reign of Augustus (31 B.C.).

Other neuter nouns of the second and third declensions include:

perīculum, perīculī (danger), second declension
vitium, vitiī (fault, vice), second declension
corpus, corporis (body), third declension

■ Exercise 3
Using the dictionary listings provided, identify the following nouns by case and number.

corpus, corporis, n.
dēceptiō, dēceptiōnis, f.
pāstor, pāstōris, m.
venēnum, venēnī, n.

1. pāstōrem _____

2. corpus _____

3. corpus _____

4. corpore _____

5. dēceptiō _____

6. dēceptiōne _____

7. venēnum _____

8. venēnum _____

Syntax: Adjectival Modification

Adjectival modifiers modify nouns; they do not modify verbs. An adjective is one kind of
adjectival modifier; later lessons will introduce other kinds of adjectival modifiers. The noun
that is modified is called the *noun-head*.

In Latin the adjective as modifier has the same case, number,[1] and gender as its noun-head. This is called *agreement. Caution:* declension is *not* an issue in adjective-noun agreement: an adjective can modify a noun of any declension. In S5.1 (*Ā fonte pūrō pūra dēfluit aqua*), the adjective *pūrō* is in agreement with its head, the noun *fonte;* both have the same form identification, i.e., ablative, singular, masculine, although they are not in the same declension. The adjective *pūra* is in agreement with its head, the noun *aqua;* both are nominative, singular, feminine. Look at the example.

Ā fonte pūrō pūra dēfluit aqua.

Because of agreement, the Latin adjective can precede, follow, or be separated from its noun-head. *Pūrō* follows *fonte,* and *pūra* is separated·from *aqua.* This is very different from English where in the most common word order an adjective precedes its noun-head. Later lessons will introduce additional information about word order in English and Latin.

Below are examples of the nominative singular masculine of the adjective *bonus, -a, -um* modifying a noun with masculine gender from each declension.

First	Second	Third	Fourth	Fifth
nauta bonus (good sailor)	animus bonus (good mind)	gladiātor bonus (good gladiator)	successus bonus (good success)	diēs bonus (good day)

Here are examples of the accusative singular feminine of the adjective *bonus, -a, -um* modifying nouns with feminine gender from each declension.

First	Second	Third	Fourth	Fifth
aquam bonam (good water)	(No nouns with feminine gender in this book)	mentem bonam (good mind)	manum bonam (good hand)	rem bonam (good situation)

In prepositional phrases Latin often separates the adjective from its noun-head in the order adjective—preposition—noun-head. If an adjective were added to modify *cūrā* in S4.3 (*Prūdēns cum cūrā vīvit*), the word order would commonly be *Prūdēns* magnā cum cūrā vīvit. S5.1 could be rewritten as *Pūrō ā fonte pūra dēfluit aqua.* This is the pattern in the well-known academic phrases *magnā cum laude* and *summā cum laude.*

Separation of adjective from noun-head is very common everywhere in Latin, especially in poetry where a noun and adjective often begin and end a whole line of verse.

■ Exercise 4

Underline the nouns that could be noun-heads for the adjectives given. The nouns in each set agree in number (singular) and gender with the adjective. Select those that agree also in case. Identify the form of the pairs by case, number, and gender.

1. pūram: nocte, manum, vīta, spem _____

2. bona: aqua, rē, vēritātem, occāsiō _____

3. novum: perīculum, culmine, vīnō, corpus _____

4. novum: locō, lupum, hominem, amīcus _____

_____

1. See lessons 7 and 8 for plural number.

Metaphrasing: The Adjective as Adjectival Modifier

According to the principle that a modifier raises the syntactic expectation of a head, an adjective raises the expectation of a noun-head. It has the basic metaphrase (adjective) (noun-head) . That is, there should be a blank for the expected noun-head if it has not already occurred. In the sentence *Pūra dēfluit aqua,* the words *pūra dēfluit* must be metaphrased "Pure ____ flows." The noun-head filling this blank must be nominative in case and singular in number, and in gender it must be feminine.

■ Exercise 5

Metaphrase the following items. Remember that every metaphrase must show a complete kernel. Look at the examples.

ā pūrō: ____ ____s ± ____ from a pure ____ .
pūram: ____ ____s pure ____ .

1. pulchra

2. sine parvō

3. malō in cōnsiliō

4. pūrus

5. pulcher

6. ex bonō

7. novam

8. novā cum cūrā

9. pulchrum

10. pulchrum

■ Exercise 6

Using the charts, write a cumulative metaphrase of the sentences given. Examples are given in the first chart.

Ā fonte pūrō pūra dēfluit aqua.

Item	Part of Speech and Form	Syntactic Information*	Cumulative Metaphrase
ā fonte	prep. + noun in abl.	adverbial modifier	____ ____s ± ____ from a spring.
pūrō	adj.: abl.	adjectival modifier	____ ____s ± ____ from a pure spring.
pūra			
dēfluit			
aqua			

Fīnis bonus magnum opus corōnat.

Item	Part of Speech and Form	Syntactic Information*	Cumulative Metaphrase
fīnis			
bonus			
magnum			
opus			
corōnat			

    *adverbial or adjectival modifier

Morphology: Third Declension Adjectives

Omnis, omne (every) and *absēns* (absent) represent the two main subgroups within the group of adjectives called *third declension adjectives*. They are so called because their inflectional endings correspond closely to those of third declension nouns. The major difference is that the ablative singular ends in *-ī* while the ablative singular of most third declension nouns ends in *-e*. Look at the paradigm chart for *omnis, omne*.

	Masculine	Feminine	Neuter
Singular			
Nominative	**omnis**	**omnis**	**omne**
Accusative	**omnem**	**omnem**	**omne**
Ablative	**omnī**	**omnī**	**omnī**
Dative	omnī	omnī	omnī
Genitive	omnis	omnis	omnis
Plural			
Nominative	omnēs	omnēs	omnia
Accusative	omnēs	omnēs	omnia
Ablative	omnibus	omnibus	omnibus
Dative	omnibus	omnibus	omnibus
Genitive	omnium	omnium	omnium

Other adjectives with this paradigm include:

    fortis, forte (*or* fortis, -e) (brave)
    facilis, facile (*or* facilis, -e) (easy)
    quālis, quāle? (*or* quālis, -e?) (what kind of?)

    A paradigm for the nominative, accusative, and ablative for *absēns* (*absentis*) is given here. The appendix has the complete paradigm.

	Masculine	Feminine	Neuter
Singular			
Nominative	**absēns**	**absēns**	**absēns**
Accusative	**absentem**	**absentem**	**absēns**
Ablative	**absentī**	**absentī**	**absentī**

Omnis and other third declension adjectives like it have the same form in the nominative for masculine and feminine. *Absēns* and the smaller number of third declension adjectives like it have the same form for the nominative in all three genders. The accusative of all third declension adjectives has the same form for masculine and feminine; the ablative (as well as the dative and genitive) has the same form for all genders.

Here are the dictionary entries for these sample adjectives.

omnis, omne (also found as *omnis, -e*) represents *omnis* (masculine), *omnis* (feminine), and *omne* (neuter).
absēns (*absentis*) represents *absēns* as nominative in all three genders. The form *absentis*, often given in parentheses, is the genitive case and shows the stem *absent-*.

A few third declension adjectives have a different form in the nominative for each gender. See the paradigm of *acer, acris, acre* in the appendix.

There are no adjectives whose paradigms correspond to those of fourth or fifth declension nouns.

■ Exercise 7
Identify the following adjectives by case (nom., acc., or abl.), number (sing.), and gender (m., f., or n.).

1. facilis

2. facilis

3. facile

4. facile

5. fortem

6. fortem

7. absēns

8. absēns

9. absēns

10. absēns

■ Exercise 8
Identify by part of speech, case, number, and gender each word listed below the sentences. The arrows indicate adjective-noun constructions.

1. In omnī rē vincit imitātiōnem vēritās.

omnī

rē

2. Gladiātor in omnī harēnā cōnsilium capit novum.

omnī

harēnā

cōnsilium

novum

3. Omnis spem alit bonam successus.

omnis

spem

bonam

successus

■ Exercise 9

Identify each adjective and underline any noun with which it agrees, as directed. Refer to the Lesson Vocabulary as needed.

Each of these adjectives agrees in *number* and *gender* with the nouns listed in that line. With which noun(s) does each adjective agree also in *case?* Underline those nouns. (Use nominative, accusative, and ablative cases only.)

Adjective	Identification	Nouns
omnem (omnis, -e)	_____	fontem, lupus, populum
fortī (fortis, -e)	_____	populum, fūre, fēmina
nova (novus, -a, -um)	_____	cūra, mēns, manū

Each of these adjectives agrees in *case* and *number* with the nouns. With which noun(s) does each adjective agree also in *gender?* Underline those nouns.

Adjective	Identification	Nouns
bonam (bonus, -a, -um)	_____	vīnum, aquam, mentem
novus (novus, -a, -um)	_____	fōns, aqua, opus
omne (omnis, -e)	_____	perīculum, opus, mēns

Metaphrasing: Adjectives without Noun-heads

All adjectives, whether first and second declension or third declension, raise the expectation of a noun-head. There are, however, two common situations in which the expectation of a noun-head is not overtly fulfilled, i.e., in which the noun does not appear. One example is provided in S5.4: *Vānēscit absēns et novus intrat amor* (An absent love fades away and a new one appears). Here an *identical noun-head,* i.e., *amor* (love) is *gapped* in the first of two connected constructions in a manner not possible in English, where it can be gapped only in the second of two constructions. The noun-head *amor* could also appear with *absēns* in the first construction and be gapped in the second.

S5.5 exemplifies another possibility common in Latin and other languages, namely that an adjective can appear without any noun-head at all. *An adjective without a noun-head is the syntactic equivalent of a noun.* The adjective in S5.5 is not a modifier but functions by itself as a kernel item (here the direct object) and is metaphrased "brave person." An adjective so used is commonly called a *substantive*.

In metaphrasing such adjectives it is safe to add "person" (or "man") if the adjective is masculine, "woman" if it is feminine, and "thing" if the adjective is neuter in gender.

A few adjectives occur so often without a noun-head that they are treated as nouns. For example *stultus, stultī*, m., as in S4.3, means "fool" but *stultus, stulta, stultum* is an adjective meaning "foolish." Another example is *amīcus, amīcī*, m. (friend) and *amīcus, amīca, amīcum* (friendly).

■ Exercise 10
Write a metaphrase of each sentence.

1. Gladiātor fortis cōnsilium capit.

2. Fortis cōnsilium capit.

3. Gladiātor fortis cōnsilium capit, ignārus fugit. (ignārus, -a, -um [cowardly])

4. Fūr fortem videt.

5. Gladiātor ducem fortem sed fūr malum audit. (dux, ducis, m. [leader])

6. Vir omnem fūrem capit.

7. Habet fīnem omne opus.

8. Omnis vitium habet.

■ Exercise 11
Copy all modifiers from the Basic Sentences of this lesson onto this modifier chart. Include both adverbial and adjectival modifiers.

		Syntactic Information		
Item	Description*	Adverbial Modifier	Adjectival Modifier	Head
5.1.				
5.1.				
5.1.				
5.3.				
5.3.				
5.4.				
5.4.				

*adjective, adverb, or prepositional phrase

Lesson Vocabulary

Nouns

amor, amōris, m.: love
aqua, aquae, f.: water
corpus, corporis, n.: body
culmen, culminis, n.: peak, summit
fīnis, fīnis, m.: end, goal; boundary
fōns, fontis, m.: spring, fountain
imitātiō, imitātiōnis, f.: imitation
mēns, mentis, f.: mind, judgment
opus, operis, n.: a work, accomplishment
perīculum, perīculī, n.: danger
vīnum, vīnī, n.: wine
vitium, vitiī, n.: fault, vice

Adjectives

absēns (absentis): absent
amīcus, amīca, amīcum: friendly
bonus, bona, bonum: good
facilis, facile: easy
fortis, forte: brave
magnus, magna, magnum: large, great
malus, mala, malum: bad, evil

novus, nova, novum: new; strange
omnis, omne: every, (pl.) all
parvus, parva, parvum: small
pulcher, pulchra, pulchrum: beautiful
pūrus, pūra, pūrum: pure
quālis, quāle?: what kind of?
quantus, quanta, quantum?: how great a?
    what size?
stultus, stulta, stultum: foolish, stupid

Question Words

quālis, quāle?: what kind of?
quantus, quanta, quantum?: how great a?
    what size?

Verbs

adjuvō, adjuvāre: aid, help
corōnō, corōnāre: crown
dēfluō, dēfluere: flow down
habeō, habēre: have
intrō, intrāre: enter
vānēscō, vānēscere: vanish

Readings

Required

5.1. Tempus fugit.—Anon.
5.2. Habet suum venēnum blanda ōrātiō.—Publilius Syrus
5.3. Mēns sāna in corpore sānō.—Juvenal
5.4. Vīnum bonum laetificat cor hūmānum.—Medieval
5.5. Commūne perīculum concordiam parit.—Anon.
5.6. Nōbilitat stultum vestis honesta virum.—Anon.

Vocabulary

5.1. tempus, temporis, n.: time
5.2. suus, sua, suum: his, her, its own
    venēnum, venēnī, n.: poison
    blandus, blanda, blandum: pleasant
    ōrātiō, ōrātiōnis, f.: speech
5.3. sānus, sāna, sānum: healthy
5.4. laetificō, laetificāre: make glad
    cor, cordis, n.: heart
    hūmānus, hūmāna, hūmānum: human

5.5. commūnis, commūne: common
    concordia, concordiae, f.: harmony,
        concord
    pariō, parere: bring forth
5.6. nōbilitō, nōbilitāre: ennoble
    vestis, vestis, f.: clothing
    honestus, honesta, honestum:
        respectable

Optional

5.7. In vīnō, in īrā, in puerō semper est vēritās.—Anon.
5.8. Ruit altō ā culmine Trōja.—Vergil *Aeneid*
5.9. Nōn semper aurem facilem habet fēlīcitās.—Publilius Syrus
5.10. Sub pulchrā speciē latitat dēceptiō saepe.—Medieval
5.11. Fraus sublīmī rēgnat in aulā.—Seneca
5.12. In pulchrā veste sapiēns nōn vīvit honestē.—Anon.

Vocabulary

5.7. puer, puerī, m.: boy
5.8. ruō, ruere: fall down, collapse
    altus, alta, altum: high
    Trōja, Trōjae, f.: Troy
5.9. auris, auris, f.: ear
    fēlīcitās, fēlīcitātis, f.: success,
      prosperity
5.10. sub (prep. + abl.): under
    speciēs, speciēī, f.: appearance
    latitō, latitāre: hide, lurk
    dēceptiō, dēceptiōnis, f.: deception
    saepe (adv.): often

5.11. fraus, fraudis, f.: deception, fraud
    sublīmis, sublīme: lofty, high
    rēgnō, rēgnāre: reign, rule
    aula, aulae, f.: palace
5.12. vestis, vestis, f.: clothing
    honestē (adv.): honestly

Latin Questions

Answer in Latin these questions on Basic Sentences and Readings.

S5.1. Quō ā locō pūra dēfluit aqua?

    Quālī ā fonte pūra aqua dēfluit?

S5.2. Quid fīnis corōnat?

S5.4. Quālis amor vānēscit?

R5.4. Quāle vīnum laetificat cor hūmānum?

R5.5. Quid agit commūne perīculum?

Word Study: English Derivatives

Follow the directions given in lesson 1. Note the spelling changes in some words between the vowels in Latin and the vowels in English. If the Latin word is a noun in the nominative, write both the nominative and the genitive case forms, since the nominative does not always show the stem.

    Some derivatives in this and other lessons appear with a prefix although the Latin word as it appears in the lesson has no prefix. In some instances a prefix different from that in the vocabulary is used.

From Lesson	Latin		From Readings	Latin
1. aqueduct			1. community	
2. coronation			2. concord	
3. facilitate			3. cordial	
4. final			4. humane	
5. fluent			5. nobility	
6. fortify			6. oration	
7. novelty			7. parent	
8. operate			8. vestment	

Summary Tasks

___ 1. Name one syntactic expectation raised by each of these words: *numquam, facile, et, novam, cum.*

___ 2. Expand the first noun in each Basic Sentence of lessons 1 and 2 with the appropriate form of *omnis, omne* and *novus, nova, novum.* Use the vocabulary list in Review Lesson 1 for information on the gender of nouns.

___ 3. Write a cumulative metaphrase for Reading 5.6.

___ 4. Copy the kernels of the Basic Sentences of this lesson.

___ 5. Copy each adjective-noun construction from Readings 5.1 through 5.6.

___ 6. Write the nominative, accusative, and ablative singular of each of the pairs copied in task 5.

___ 7. Write the nominative, accusative, and ablative singular of each of the neuter nouns in the Lesson Vocabulary.

Review Lesson 1

Lesson Vocabulary

Nouns[1]

First Declension
aqua, aquae, f.: water
avāritia, avāritiae, f.: greed, avarice
cūra, cūrae, f.: care, concern
fēmina, fēminae, f.: woman
fortūna, fortūnae, f.: chance, luck
harēna, harēnae, f.: sand, arena
hōra, hōrae, f.: hour
īra, īrae, f.: anger
pecūnia, pecūniae, f.: money
sapientia, sapientiae, f.: wisdom
vīta, vītae, f.: life

Second Declension
amīcus, amīcī, m.: friend
animus, animī, m.: mind
cōnsilium, cōnsiliī, n.: plan, advice
locus, locī, m.: place, position
lupus, lupī, m.: wolf
modus, modī, m.: manner, way
perīculum, perīculī, n.: danger
populus, populī, m.: the people, a nation;
    populus Rōmānus: Roman people
stultus, stultī, m.: fool
vīnum, vīnī, n.: wine
vir, virī, m.: man
vitium, vitiī, n.: fault, vice

Third Declension
amor, amōris, m.: love
corpus, corporis, n.: body
culmen, culminis, n.: peak, summit
fīnis, fīnis, m.: end, goal; boundary
fōns, fontis, m.: spring, fountain
fūr, fūris, m.: thief

gladiātor, gladiātōris, m.: gladiator
homō, hominis, m. & f.: human being, man
imitātiō, imitātiōnis, f.: imitation
mēns, mentis, f.: mind, judgment
nox, noctis, f.: night
occāsiō, occāsiōnis, f.: opportunity
opus, operis, n.: a work, accomplishment
prūdēns, prūdentis, m.: sensible person
vēritās, vēritātis, f.: truth

Fourth Declension
manus, manūs, f.: hand
senatus, senatūs, m.: senate
successus, successūs, m.: success

Fifth Declension
diēs, diēī, m. & f.: day; time
rēs, reī, f.: thing
spēs, speī, f.: hope, expectation

Pronoun
quis, quid? (interrogative): who, what?

Adjectives
First and Second Declension
amīcus, amīca, amīcum: friendly
bonus, bona, bonum: good
magnus, magna, magnum: large, great
malus, mala, malum: bad, evil
novus, nova, novum: new; strange
parvus, parva, parvum: small
pulcher, pulchra, pulchrum: beautiful
pūrus, pūra, pūrum: pure
quantus, quanta, quantum?: how great a?
    what size?
stultus, stulta, stultum: foolish, stupid

---

1. Note that the gender for all nouns is now given.

48

Third Declension

absēns (absentis): absent
facilis, facile: easy
fortis, forte: brave
omnis, omne: every, (pl.) all
quālis, quāle?: what kind of?

Indeclinables

Adverbs

fēlīciter: successfully, luckily
fidēliter: faithfully
fortiter: bravely
nōn: not
numquam: never
rēctē: rightly, correctly
semper: always

Prepositions

ā/ab (+ abl.): from, away from
cum (+ abl.): with
dē (+ abl.): from, down from; concerning
ē/ex (+ abl.): from, out of
in (+ abl.): in, on
sine (+ abl.): without

Coordinating Conjunctions

et: and
-que: and
sed: but

Question Words

-ne: asks for a yes/no answer
quālis, quāle?: what kind of?
quantus, quanta, quantum?: how great?
    how great a? what size?
quō ā/dē/ē locō?: from what place?
    where from?
quō (in) locō?: in what place? where?
quō modō?: in what manner? how?
quōcum?: with whom?

quōtiēns?: how often?
ubi?: where?
unde?: where from?

Verbs

adjuvō, adjuvāre: aid, help
agō, agere: do, act, drive, lead
alō, alere: feed, nourish
ambulō, ambulāre: walk
amō, amāre: love, like
audeō, audēre: dare
audiō, audīre: hear, listen to
capiō, capere: take, seize, get
cognōscō, cognōscere: recognize, learn,
    get to know
corōnō, corōnāre: crown
cupiō, cupere: desire, wish
dēbeō, dēbēre: owe; ought (with inf.)
dēfluō, dēfluere: flow down
faciō, facere: make, do
fugiō, fugere: flee
habeō, habēre: have
impediō, impedīre: hinder
intrō, intrāre: enter
irrītō, irrītāre: stir up, incite
lavō, lavāre: wash
pereō, perīre: perish, die, pass away
possum, posse: be able, can (irreg. verb)
premō, premere: press, pursue
regō, regere: rule
satiō, satiāre: fill, satisfy
soleō, solēre: be accustomed
sum, esse: be, exist (irreg. verb)
vānēscō, vānēscere: vanish
veniō, venīre: come
videō, vidēre: see
vincō, vincere: conquer, prevail
vīvō, vīvere: live, be alive
volō, velle: wish, want, be willing (irreg. verb)

Although all vocabulary is important, special care should be directed to learning *indeclinables;* they are few in number but frequent in use. Also, they are easily confused with words belonging to other parts of speech.

Morphology Review

This section in each Review Lesson will contain a summary of the new morphology presented in the last group of lessons and an exercise in form identification.

New Morphology: Lessons 1 through 5

noun: nominative, accusative, ablative, genitive, singular
adjective: nominative, accusative, ablative, singular
pronoun, interrogative: nominative, accusative, singular
verb: third person singular, infinitive

Form Identification

Using the dictionary entries provided, identify the following forms and indicate the entry from which each is taken.

   a. amor, amōris, m.: love
   b. amō, amāre: love, like
   c. amīcus, amīca, amīcum: friendly
   d. amīcitia, amīcitiae, f.: friendship

1. amīcum _____

2. amīcitiam _____

3. amōre _____

4. amāre _____

5. amor _____

6. amō _____

7. amīcam _____

8. amat _____

9. amōrem _____

10. amīcō _____

Narrative Reading

A Wolf in Sheep's Clothing (or Deceit May Backfire)

This passage is a fable told by Aesop, a famous storyteller in ancient Greece. With the help of the notes and vocabulary, read, metaphrase, and translate the following story.

Lupus Pilum Mūtat

Lupus malus agnum vult sed pāstor bonus gregem magnā cum cūrā custōdit. Lupus autem capit cōnsilium et ovis[1] pilum sibi[2] impōnit. Fraudem pāstor nōn cognōscit, et lupus lānigerō cum grege pernoctat. Jam pāstor ēsuriēns agnum capere vult. Ex ovīlī[3] agnum celeriter rapit—sed pāstor nescius lupum, nōn agnum, in manū tenet. Itaque lupum prō agnō pāstor occīdit.

Fraus pāstōrem fallit, sed lupum occīdit.

Notes

1. ovis: genitive singular (sheep's); ovis pilum (sheepskin)
2. sibi: upon himself
3. ovīlī: ablative singular of ovīle, ovīlis

Vocabulary

agnus, agnī: lamb
autem (sentence connector): however
celeriter (adv.): quickly
custōdiō, custōdīre: guard
ēsuriēns (ēsurientis): hungry
fallō, fallere: trick
fraus, fraudis, f.: deceit
grex, gregis, m.: flock
impōnō, impōnere: put upon, place upon
itaque (sentence connector): and so
jam: now
lāniger, lānigera, lānigerum: wooly

nescius, nescia, nescium: unaware, not
   knowing
occīdō, occīdere: kill
ovīle, ovīlis, n.: sheepfold
ovis, ovis, f.: sheep
pāstor, pāstōris, m.: shepherd
pernoctō, pernoctāre: spend the night
pilus, pilī, m.: fleece
prō (prep. + abl.): instead of, for
rapiō, rapere: grab, snatch, seize
teneō, tenēre: hold

Derivatives from Narrative Reading

Supply from the Narrative Reading the Latin word from which these English words are derived.

	Latin			*Latin*
1. accelerate			6. malice	
2. custody			7. pastor	
3. defraud			8. rapacious	
4. gregarious			9. recognition	
5. homicide			10. tenacious	

■ Exercise: English to Latin Sentences

Following the structure of the Basic Sentences or Readings given, write a Latin translation of the English sentences. Keep the order of words as it is in the model. (It may be necessary to expand with *nōn*.) Vocabulary assistance is provided below.

1. Manus manum lavat. (S1.1)

   a. The woman is washing a dress.

   b. The man wants praise.

   c. The woman helps (her) friend.

2. Fortem Fortūna adjuvat. (S5.5)

   a. A wise person likes a wise person.

   b. The king pursues the evil person.

3. Vēritās numquam perit. (S4.2)

    a. Wisdom does not always prevail.

    b. Praise often vanishes.

    c. The king reigns bravely.

4. Nōbilitat stultum vestis honesta virum. (R5.6)

    a. The new wine delights the beautiful woman.

    b. The wise friend produces a great work.

Vocabulary

This list provides a Latin equivalent of each English word. Words that have been memorized are listed without their full dictionary entry. It is a good review to add the remainder of the dictionary entry for such words. For words that have not been memorized, a dictionary entry is provided.

Nouns
dress: vestis, vestis, f.
friend: amīcus
king: rēx, rēgis, m.
man: vir
praise: laus, laudis, f.
wine: vīnum
wisdom: sapientia
woman: fēmina
work: opus

Adjectives
beautiful: pulcher
evil: malus
great: magnus
new: novus
wise: sapiēns (sapientis)

Indeclinables
always: semper (adv.)
bravely: fortiter (adv.)
not: nōn (adv.)
often: saepe (adv.)

Verbs
delight: dēlectō, dēlectāre
help: adjuvō
like: amō
prevail: vincō
produce: faciō
pursue: premō
reign: rēgnō, rēgnāre
vanish: vānēscō
want: volō
wash: lavō

Lesson 6

The Passive Kernel: A New Kernel Type
Another Adverbial Modifier: Noun in the Ablative
without a Preposition

All verbs in previous kernels have been *active* in *voice*. This lesson introduces a new kernel type that has a verb in the *passive* voice. In addition, this lesson introduces another type of adverbial modifier, a noun in the ablative without a preposition.

Basic Sentences

6.1. Occāsiō aegrē offertur, facile āmittitur.—Publilius Syrus
    Opportunity is offered rarely and lost easily.
6.2. Ā cane nōn[1] magnō saepe tenētur aper.—Ovid
    A wild boar is often held by a small dog.
6.3. Multitūdō nōn ratiōne dūcitur sed impetū.—Horace
    A crowd is led not by reason but by impulse.

Note
1. *Nōn* here negates the adjective *magnō*, not the verb *tenētur*.

The Passive Kernel: A New Kernel Type

Morphology: The Verb in the Passive Voice

Verb forms such as *amat, tenet, āmittit, capit,* and *audit* all end with the morpheme {t}, which indicates third person, singular, *active voice*. The verb forms *amātur, tenētur, āmittitur, capitur,* and *audītur* all end with the morpheme {tur}, which indicates third person, singular, *passive voice*.

The English equivalent for a passive verb is "is _____-ed" or "is being _____-ed." Thus, the translation of *capitur* is "is seized" or "is being seized."

The morpheme {tur} is attached to the stem morpheme, e.g., {amā} and {tenē}, that appears also in the second principal part of a verb, the infinitive, e.g., *amā*re, *tenē*re. The exception is the third conjugation where the vowel *i*, as in *āmittitur*, replaces the vowel *e* of the infinitive *āmittere*.

Examples of verbs from each conjugation are presented in their active and passive forms on the following chart.

| | | Third Person Singular ||
Conjugation	Infinitive	Active	Passive
First	amāre	amat	amātur
Second	tenēre	tenet	tenētur
Third	āmittere	āmittit	āmittitur
Third -iō	capere	capit	capitur
Fourth	audīre	audit	audītur

From now on include active or passive voice as part of the form identification of verbs.

The final vowel of the stem, when long, appears as a short vowel in the active voice form because of a linguistic law that operates throughout the Latin language. According to this law

> a long vowel becomes short before: another vowel
>> a final *m*
>> a final *r*
>> a final *t*
>> any *nt*

Infinitives have a predictable passive form marked by a final *ī*. Note that the passive infinitive of the third conjugation does not include the *-er* of the active voice.

Active Voice	*Passive Voice*
amāre (to love)	amārī (to be loved)
tenēre (to hold)	tenērī (to be held)
āmittere (to lose)	āmittī (to be lost)
capere (to take)	capī (to be taken)
audīre (to hear)	audīrī (to be heard)

Syntax: The Passive Kernel

So far there have been two kernel types.

> A *transitive active* kernel has items filling the three functions of
>> verb
>> subject
>> direct object
> An *intransitive active* kernel has words filling the two functions of
>> verb
>> subject

There is now a third kernel type, the *passive* kernel. It has items filling the two functions of

> verb
>
> subject

Note that the intransitive active kernel and the passive kernel each has only a subject and a verb. The difference between the two types is that the verb in the passive kernel is in the passive voice and the verb in the intransitive active kernel is in the active voice.

■ Exercise 1

Enter S6.2 and S6.3 into the following kernel chart. The example given is S6.1 (*Occāsiō aegrē offertur, facile āmittitur*). The adverbial modifier section of this lesson describes the modifiers in these sentences.

	Cl. Conn.	Item: Function	Item: Function	Item: Function	Kernel Type	Name
S6.1.		occāsiō: subj.	offertur: verb	—	passive	statement
S6.1.		∅ = occāsiō: subj.	āmittitur: verb	—	passive	statement
S6.2.						
S6.3.						
S6.3.						

Metaphrasing

The passive kernel is metaphrased as "_(subject)_ is/is being _____-ed."

Caution: Many speakers of English confuse the term *passive* with other terms describing verbs, especially the term *past*. For example, "the thief is being recognized" and "the thief is recognized," both in the passive voice, are *not the same* as "the thief recognized" or "has recognized" or "had recognized," all of which express *past times* and are in the *active voice*.

■ Exercise 2

Metaphrase the following passive verb forms. Give both possibilities, as indicated by the example.

vincitur: _____ is conquered   or _____ is being conquered

1. audītur

2. capitur

3. cognōscitur

4. regitur

■ Exercise 3

Circle a possible metaphrase for each verb.

1. adjuvātur   _____ has helped   _____ is helped

2. lavātur   _____ is being washed   _____ had washed

3. premitur   _____ is pursued   _____ was pursuing

4. impedītur   _____ is hindering   _____ is hindered

■ Exercise 4

Metaphrase the following, each of which includes an infinitive.

1. potest capī

2. potest capere

3. vult mittere

4. dēbet audīrī

5. solet cognōscere

Metaphrasing: The Prepositional Phrase with Ā/Ab

In lesson 4, the preposition *ā/ab* occurred with the meaning "from." However, in S6.2 *ā cane* means "by a dog," not "from a dog." There frequently occurs with the passive kernel a prepositional phrase with *ā/ab* plus a noun that has the semantic feature *animate*. Usually this prepositional phrase indicates "by whom" the action is done. It is metaphrased "(subject) is (passive verb)-ed by (animate noun in ablative)."

This prepositional phrase answers the Latin question *ā quō?* (by whom?) and is traditionally called *ablative of agent*. While the information as to the "agent" is here expressed by a modifier, and not by a kernel item, in the previous sentences in the active voice the "agent" was expressed by the subject of the kernel. Look at these examples.

In "the boy watches the dog," the subject "boy" is the agent.
In "the boy is watched by the dog," the agent is "dog," the noun in the prepositional phrase.

Even with a passive kernel, *ā/ab* plus the ablative of an animate noun may indicate *from* what person.

Another Adverbial Modifier: Noun in the Ablative without a Preposition

Two types of adverbial modifiers were introduced in lesson 4, i.e., adverbs and prepositional phrases. There is a third syntactic equivalent that is a *noun in the ablative without a preposition*.

Nouns in Latin never occur without inflectional morphemes for case; case is the main syntactic device in Latin. Case signals kernel functions: e.g., so far the nominative case signals the subject and the accusative case signals the direct object. Case also signals that a noun is a modifier. In lesson 4 the nouns in the prepositional phrases are in the ablative case. In this lesson nouns in the ablative without a preposition occur as adverbial modifiers.

English has no equivalent construction; the Latin noun in the ablative without a preposition must be preceded by a preposition in an English metaphrase.

The decision as to which preposition is appropriate in an English translation depends upon the interpretation. The interpretation in turn depends entirely on semantic features, both of the noun in the ablative and of the verb that is the head.

In the Latin sentences below nouns occur in the ablative case without prepositions. The English metaphrases of these nouns are italicized.

Mīles Rōmānus **gladiō** et **pīlō** pūgnat.
The Roman soldier fights *with sword* and *javelin*.
> gladium, gladiī, n.: sword
> pīlum, pīlī, n.: javelin

Mīles Rōmānus **aestāte** pūgnat, **hieme** nōn pūgnat.
The Roman soldier fights *in the summer*, he does not fight *in the winter*.
> aestās, aestātis, f.: summer
> hiems, hiemis, f.: winter

Mīles Rōmānus **victōriā** gaudet.
The Roman soldier rejoices *because of* the *victory*.
> victōria, victōriae, f.: victory

The nouns in the ablative in the first sentence, *gladiō* (sword) and *pīlō* (javelin), have the semantic feature *instrument*. This ablative is metaphrased with the prepositions "by/by means of" or "with." The nouns *ratiōne* and *impetū* in S6.3 (*Multitūdō nōn ratiōne dūcitur sed impetū*) are adverbial modifiers of this type. This use of the ablative answers the question *quō auxiliō?* (by what means?) and is traditionally called the *ablative of means*.

On the other hand, the nouns in the ablative in the second sentence, *hieme* (winter) and *aestāte* (summer), have the semantic feature *time*. Such an ablative is metaphrased with the prepositions "in," "at," or "on" (e.g., "in the spring," "at night," or "on that day"). This use of the ablative answers the question *quō tempore?* (at what time?) or *quandō?* (when?) and is traditionally called the *ablative of time when*.

In the third sentence, the verb *gaudet* (rejoices) allows the semantic interpretation of the noun in the ablative, *victōriā* (victory), as one expressing cause or reason. The metaphrase is "(subject) rejoices because of victory." This use of the ablative answers the question *quā dē causā?* (for what reason?). It is called *ablative of cause*.

Whether a noun in the ablative is to be interpreted as "means" or "cause" is sometimes not easily determined in either Latin or English because of the complex nature of the relationship between language and reality. There are some clues, however. Nouns in the ablative with the possible interpretation "cause" often occur with verbs that express emotion. An ablative with the possible semantic interpretation "means" occurs with verbs expressing action; by contrast, the ablative with the possible semantic interpretation "time" occurs with practically any verb.

In this situation, as in many more to come, it is better that readers/translators suspend judgment on a final metaphrase until they have examined the relevant *morphological, syntactic,* and *semantic* information, as well as information about the world of the author. Many of the difficulties that readers/translators encounter are quite legitimate particularly because information about semantic features and about the world of the author is not always readily available.

Summary of Semantic Categories Expressed by the Ablative Case with and without a Preposition

It is customary to speak of *case uses* with names derived from semantic categories. The corresponding question words are also listed. The following list of names for semantic categories covers the uses of the ablative introduced so far; it includes uses both with and without prepositions. Other uses of the ablative without a preposition will be introduced in later lessons.

Name	*Question Word*
accompaniment	quōcum?
agent	ā quō?
cause	quā dē causā?
manner	quō modō?
means or instrument	quō auxiliō?
place from where (also called separation)	quō ā/dē/ē locō? unde?
place where	quō in locō? ubi?
time when	quō tempore? quandō?

■ Exercise 5
Give the semantic category most nearly describing the italicized phrase.

1. The doctor treats the patient *with a new medicine*.

2. The doctor treats the patient *with gentleness*.

3. The doctor comes *with an assistant*.

4. The doctor treats the patient *in the home*.

5. The doctor treats the patient *at night*.

6. The doctor comes *from the office*.

7. The doctor is aided *by the assistant*.

8. The doctor is aided *by the computer*.

9. The doctor rejoiced *at the success*.

■ Exercise 6
Which of the prepositional phrases in exercise 5 would be expressed in Latin by a noun in the ablative *without* a preposition?

1.

2.

3.

4.

Which of the prepositional phrases in exercise 5 would be expressed in Latin by a prepositional phrase? And what would be the preposition for each?

1.

2.

3.

4.

5.

■ Exercise 7
Underline any item that is a *semantically* possible answer to the question provided.

1. Ā quō fēmina audītur?   ā culmine, ex harēnā, ā puerō

2. Quō auxiliō multitūdō dūcitur?   ā fēminā, īrā, cum cūrā

3. Quō modō multitūdō dūcitur?   cum cūrā, sine īrā, cum amīcō

4. Quō tempore occāsiō āmittitur? fortūnā, nocte, facile

5. Quā dē causā populus gaudet?   successū, numquam, in perīculō

■ Exercise 8
Fully identify each of the following (include part of speech). Look at the example.

    vidēre: verb—infinitive, active voice

1. mente

2. mittere

3. corpore

4. facilī

5. vincī

■ Exercise 9
Copy all modifiers from the Basic Sentences of this lesson onto this modifier chart. Name the semantic category of adverbial modifiers in the semantic information column.

| | | Syntactic Information | | | |
Modifier	Description*	Adverbial	Adjectival	Semantic Information	Head
6.1.					
6.1.					
6.2.					
6.2.					
6.2.					
6.2.					
6.3.					
6.3.					
6.3.					

*adjective, adverb, prepositional phrase, or noun in the ablative without a preposition.

Lesson Vocabulary

Nouns

aper, aprī, m.: boar
auxilium, auxiliī, n.: help, aid
canis, canis, m. & f.: dog
causa, causae, f.: reason, cause
impetus, impetūs, m.: impulse, attack
multitūdō, multitūdinis, f.: crowd, multitude
ratiō, ratiōnis, f.: reason
tempus, temporis, n.: time

Indeclinables
Adverbs
aegrē: with difficulty
facile: easily
saepe: often

Question Words

quā dē causā?: why? for what reason?
quandō?: when?
ā quō?: by whom?
quō auxiliō?: by what means?
quō tempore?: when? at what time?

Verbs

āmittō, āmittere: let go; lose
dūcō, dūcere: lead
mittō, mittere: send
offerō, offerre: offer
teneō, tenēre: hold; keep

Readings

Required

6.1. Nihil rēctē sine exemplō docētur aut discitur.—Columella
6.2. Antīquā veste pauper vestītur honestē.—Medieval
6.3. Vīnō forma perit, vīnō corrumpitur aetās.—Anon.
6.4. Amīcus certus in rē incertā cernitur.—Ennius
6.5. Nūtrītur ventō, ventō restinguitur ignis.—Ovid

Vocabulary

6.1. nihil, n. (indecl. noun): nothing
doceō, docēre: teach
exemplum, exemplī, n.: example
discō, discere: learn
aut (coord. conj.): or
6.2. antīquus, antīqua, antīquum: old, ancient
vestis, vestis, f.: clothing
pauper (pauperis): poor
vestiō, vestīre: clothe
honestē (adv.): honestly

6.3. forma, formae, f.: beauty
corrumpō, corrumpere: destroy, corrupt
aetās, aetātis, f.: youth; age
6.4. certus, certa, certum: certain, sure, true
incertus, incerta, incertum: uncertain, unsure
cernō, cernere: ascertain, identify
6.5. nūtriō, nūtrīre: nourish, feed
ventus, ventī, m.: wind
restinguō, restinguere: extinguish
ignis, ignis, m.: fire

Optional

6.6. Amphora sub veste numquam portātur honestē.—Medieval
6.7. Emitur sōlā virtūte potestās.—Claudian
6.8. Saepe malum petitur, saepe bonum āmittitur.—Anon.
6.9. Sapientia vīnō obumbrātur.—Pliny

Vocabulary

6.6. amphora, amphorae, f.: jug
sub (prep. + abl.): under
vestis, vestis, f.: clothing
portō, portāre: carry
honestē (adv.): honestly

6.7. emō, emere: buy, get
sōlus, sōla, sōlum: alone, only
virtūs, virtūtis, f.: goodness, worth
potestās, potestātis, f.: power
6.8. petō, petere: seek, look for
6.9. obumbrō, obumbrāre: overshadow

Latin Questions

Answer in Latin these questions on Basic Sentences and Readings. Note: the Latin question *quid patitur?* asks for a passive verb.

S6.1. Quid patitur facile occāsiō?

S6.2. Quantō ā cane tenētur aper?

Ā quō tenētur aper?

S6.3. Quō auxiliō multitūdō dūcitur?

R6.1. Quō modō nihil rēctē discitur?

Word Study: English Derivatives

From Lesson	**Latin**	**From Readings**	**Latin**
1. canine		1. annihilate	
2. impetuous		2. antiquity	
3. induce		3. discern	
4. magnify		4. disciple	
5. multitude		5. doctor	
6. produce		6. ignite	
7. rational		7. nutritious	
8. retain		8. ventilate	

Narrative Reading

The Fox and the Grapes

Vulpēs ēsuriēns et sitiēns in hortō errat. Subitō altā in vīneā ūvam dulcem cōnspicit et habēre maximē vult. Magnā cum spē salit, sed eam[1] tangere nōn potest. Deinde currit et altius[2] salit, sed ūvam capere nōn potest vulpēs. Tandem superbē discēdit et ait: "Quis ūvam acerbam edere vult? Nōn ego."[3]

Homō saepe dēspicit id[4] quod[4] capere nōn potest.

Notes

1. *eam:* pronoun, accusative singular, feminine, "this," "it"
2. *altius:* adverb, "higher"
3. *ego:* personal pronoun, nominative singular, "I"
4. *id quod:* "that which"; both are pronouns, accusative, singular, neuter

Vocabulary

acerbus, acerba, acerbum: sour
ait: _____ says
altus, alta, altum: high
cōnspiciō, cōnspicere: catch sight of, see
currō, currere: run
deinde (sentence connector): then
dēspiciō, dēspicere: despise
discēdō, discēdere: go away, depart
dulcis, dulce: sweet, luscious
edō, edere: eat
errō, errāre: wander
ēsuriēns (ēsurientis): hungry

hortus, hortī, m.: garden
maximē (adv.): very much
saliō, salīre: jump
sitiēns (sitientis): thirsty
subitō (adv.): suddenly
superbē (adv.): arrogantly
tandem (adv.): finally, at last
tangō, tangere: touch
ūva, ūvae, f.: grapes, bunch of grapes
vīnea, vīneae, f.: vine
vulpēs, vulpis, f.: fox

Derivatives from Narrative Reading

Latin

1. altitude
2. conspicuous
3. edible
4. error
5. horticulture
6. tangible

Summary Tasks

____ 1. Rewrite Basic Sentences 6.2 and 6.3 in the active voice.
____ 2. What syntactic expectation may be raised by an active verb but never by a passive verb?
____ 3. Which adjectives in Readings 6.6 through 6.9 have the syntactic function of kernel part rather than that of modifier?
____ 4. Write the paradigm (nominative, accusative, ablative singular) of these noun-adjective pairs.

      tempus, temporis (n.) + incertus, incerta, incertum
      aetās, aetātis (f.) + antīquus, antīqua, antīquum

____ 5. Copy from the Narrative Reading each *kernel item: verb* that includes a complementary infinitive.
____ 6. Write a cumulative metaphrase for Reading 6.6.

Lesson 7

Number and Number Agreement
Part of Speech: Pronoun

This lesson introduces *agreement* in *number* between noun and adjective and between subject and verb. The *plurals* of verbs and of first and second declension nouns and adjectives are presented. (The plurals of other declensions will occur in lesson 8.) This lesson also introduces the pronoun *is, ea, id*.

Basic Sentences

7.1. Magna dī[1] cūrant, parva neglegunt.—Cicero
    The gods take care of important things, but neglect the unimportant.
7.2. Ācta deōs numquam hūmāna fallunt.—Ovid
    Human deeds never escape the notice of the gods.
7.3. Crūdēlis lacrimīs pāscitur, nōn frangitur.—Publilius Syrus
    The cruel person is fed, not broken, by (another's) tears.

Note
1. *Dī* is a variant of *deī*.

Number and Number Agreement

Morphology: Nouns of First and Second Declensions

Examine these paradigms for the regular plural endings of nouns in the first and second declensions.

	First	Second, M	Second, N
Singular			
Nominative	**hōra**	**animus**	**cōnsilium**
Accusative	**hōram**	**animum**	**cōnsilium**
Ablative	**hōrā**	**animō**	**cōnsiliō**
Dative	hōrae	animō	cōnsiliō
Genitive	hōrae	animī	cōnsiliī
Plural			
Nominative	**hōrae**	**animī**	**cōnsilia**
Accusative	**hōrās**	**animōs**	**cōnsilia**
Ablative	**hōrīs**	**animīs**	**cōnsiliīs**
Dative	hōrīs	animīs	cōnsiliīs
Genitive	hōrārum	animōrum	cōnsiliōrum

■ Exercise 1

Identify the following by part of speech, case, and number. Use nominative, accusative, and ablative cases only.

1. fēminās

2. cōnsilia

3. cōnsilia

4. cūra

5. puerōs

6. virīs

7. vītae

8. amīcī

Morphology: Adjectives of First and Second Declensions

Examine the paradigms given for the singular and plural of first and second declension adjectives (*novus, -a, -um*).

	Masculine	Feminine	Neuter
Singular			
Nominative	**novus**	**nova**	**novum**
Accusative	**novum**	**novam**	**novum**
Ablative	**novō**	**novā**	**novō**
Dative	novō	novae	novō
Genitive	novī	novae	novī
Plural			
Nominative	**novī**	**novae**	**nova**
Accusative	**novōs**	**novās**	**nova**
Ablative	**novīs**	**novīs**	**novīs**
Dative	novīs	novīs	novīs
Genitive	novōrum	novārum	novōrum

■ Exercise 2

Fully identify the following ambiguous forms by part of speech, case, number, and gender. Disregard ambiguities with dative and genitive cases.

1. magnō

2. magnō

3. pūrīs

4. pūrīs

5. pūrīs

6. pulchrum

7. pulchrum

8. pulchrum

9. bona

10. bona

11. bona

Morphology: Verbs

The plural form of the verb in the third person *active* has the morpheme {nt}, and the plural of the verb in the third person *passive* has the morpheme {ntur}. Identify verbs by part of speech, person, number, and voice. Here are examples of the plural in each conjugation.

Conjugation	First Two Principal Parts	Third Person Plural	
		Active	Passive
First	amō, amāre	amant	amantur
Second	teneō, tenēre	tenent	tenentur
Third	āmittō, āmittere	āmittunt	āmittuntur
Third -*iō*	capiō, capere	capiunt	capiuntur
Fourth	audiō, audīre	audiunt	audiuntur

■ Exercise 3

Identify the Latin words by part of speech, person, number, and voice.

	Part of Speech	*Person*	*Number*	*Voice*
1. cūrantur				
2. vincit				
3. reguntur				
4. offerunt				
5. āmittitur				
6. sunt (pl. of est)				

Syntax

In Latin, a singular verb indicates that the subject of the kernel is singular because *a verb agrees with its subject in number*. Agreement between subject and verb can be seen in English in the third person singular only, e.g., "The girl swims," but "I/we/you/they swim."

A verb does *not* agree with a direct object. In S7.1 (*Magna dī cūrant*) the verb *cūrant* agrees with the plural subject *dī* just as in the sentence *Magnum dī cūrant*, where the direct object is singular instead of plural.

An adjective indicates which noun-head it modifies by agreeing with it in case, number, and gender. For example in S7.2 (*Ācta deōs numquam hūmāna fallunt*) the adjective *hūmāna* is nominative plural neuter so as to be in agreement with its noun-head *ācta*, which is nominative plural neuter.

■ Exercise 4

Metaphrase each of the following. Remember that every metaphrase must show a complete kernel. Look at the example.

canis virōs: dog _____s men

1. ā fonte magnō

2. in harēnīs

3. fēminās videt

4. ā puerīs capiuntur

5. Fortūna bonōs adjuvat.

6. magnās rēs

7. Puer cognōscit magna.

8. fēlīcitās

9. fēlīcem

10. cum amīcīs mittuntur

11. vīnum offerunt

12. possunt audīrī

Part of Speech: Pronoun[1]

As the Latin name indicates, pronouns may stand for nouns. The interrogative pronoun, e.g., *who?, what?*, asks a question, the answer to which is a noun or a personal pronoun such as *I, me, you, he, she, it*. This lesson introduces the *pronoun, is, ea, id*. The paradigm is as follows.

	Masculine	Feminine	Neuter
Singular			
Nominative	is	ea	id
Accusative	eum	eam	id
Ablative	eō	eā	eō
Dative	eī	eī	eī
Genitive	ejus	ejus	ejus
Plural			
Nominative	eī	eae	ea
Accusative	eōs	eās	ea
Ablative	eīs	eīs	eīs
Dative	eīs	eīs	eīs
Genitive	eōrum	eārum	eōrum

---

1. *Pronoun* is from Latin *prō nōmine* (in the place of a noun).

Syntax and Semantics

The most common English equivalent for *is, ea, id* without a noun-head is "he, she, it, they." As such *is, ea, id* is the equivalent of the personal pronoun of the third person, but it occurs far less often than the English personal pronoun. One of the reasons for this is that Latin can apply gapping where English must have at least a pronoun. The English translation for S2.3 (*Pecūnia nōn satiat avāritiam sed irrītat*) must include the pronoun "it," i.e., "Money does not satisfy greed but (it) inflames *it*." Latin does not need either pronoun.

When forms of *is, ea, id* occur with a noun-head, they stand for adjectives and have the syntax of adjectives.[1] The most common English equivalents for *is, ea, id* when so used are "this" and "that." For example, *ex eā harēnā* means "out of this/that arena," *eae fēminae* means "these/those women."

■ Exercise 5

Give a translation of each sentence. Look at the examples.

Quem puer amat?	Whom does the boy love?
Eam amat.	He loves her.
Eam fēminam amat.	He loves that lady.

1. Fēmina eum videt.

2. Fēmina eum locum videt.

3. Canis ab eō tenētur.

4. Puer cum eīs intrāre audet.

5. Quis eās audit?

6. Quis ea consilia cognōscit?

Lesson Vocabulary

Nouns
āctum, āctī, n.: deed, act
deus, deī, m.: god
fēlīcitās, fēlīcitātis, f.: success, prosperity, happiness
lacrima, lacrimae, f.: tear

Pronoun
is, ea, id: he, she, it; (pl.) they; this, that

Adjectives
crūdēlis, crūdēle: cruel
fēlix (fēlīcis)[1]: fortunate, happy, prosperous
hūmānus, hūmāna, hūmānum: human
multus, multa, multum: much; (pl.) many

Verbs
cūrō, cūrāre: care for
fallō, fallere: deceive
frangō, frangere: break
neglegō, neglegere: neglect
pāscō, pāscere: feed

Note
1. *Fēlix* (*fēlīcis*) represents *fēlix* as nominative in all three genders. The form *fēlīcis* is the genitive case and shows the stem *fēlīc-*. See also *absēns*, lesson 5.

---

1. The Latin word *nōmen* originally covered both nouns and adjectives. This may explain why pronouns stand for both nouns and adjectives.

Readings

Required

7.1. Tempore fēlīcī multī numerantur amīcī.—Medieval
7.2. In oculīs animus habitat.—Pliny
7.3. Generōsōs animōs labor nūtrit.—Seneca
7.4. Vēritās et virtūs vincunt.—Motto
7.5. Religiō deōs colit, superstitiō violat.—Seneca
7.6. Fēlīcitās multōs habet amīcōs.—Erasmus

Vocabulary

7.1. numerō, numerāre: count
7.2. oculus, oculī, m.: eye
    habitō, habitāre: live, dwell
7.3. generōsus, generōsa, generōsum: noble,
    nobly born
    labor, labōris, m.: toil
    nūtriō, nūtrīre: nourish

7.4. virtūs, virtūtis, f.: goodness, courage
7.5. religiō, religiōnis, f.: religion
    colō, colere: foster, cultivate
    superstitiō, superstitiōnis, f.: superstition
    violō, violāre: violate

Optional

7.7. Bēstia quaeque suōs nātōs cum laude corōnat.—Medieval
7.8. Tranquillās etiam naufragus horret aquās.—Ovid
7.9. Multī morbī cūrantur abstinentiā.—Celsus (?)
7.10. Litterae nōn dant pānem.—Medieval
7.11. Dīvitiae pariunt cūrās.—Medieval
7.12. Oculī amōrem incipiunt, cōnsuētūdō perficit.—Publilius Syrus

Vocabulary

7.7. bēstia, bēstiae, f.: beast
    quisque, quaeque, quodque (indef. pronoun & adj.): each (one), every(one)
    suus, sua, suum: one's own (his own, her own, its own, their own)
    nātus, nātī, m.: son
    laus, laudis, f.: praise
7.8. tranquillus, tranquilla, tranquillum: calm
    etiam: even
    naufragus, naufraga, naufragum: shipwrecked (person)
    horreō, horrēre: shudder at
7.9. morbus, morbī, m.: disease
    abstinentia, abstinentiae, f.: abstinence
7.10. littera, litterae, f.: letter; (pl.) literature
    dō, dare: give
    pānis, pānis, m.: bread
7.11. dīvitiae, dīvitiārum, f. pl.: riches, wealth
    pariō, parere: bring forth
7.12. oculus, oculī, m.: eye
    incipiō, incipere: begin
    cōnsuētūdō, cōnsuētūdinis, f.: custom, habit
    perficiō, perficere: complete, finish

Latin Questions

Answer in Latin these questions on Basic Sentences and Readings.

S7.1. Quid dī cūrant?

S7.2. Quālia ācta deōs numquam fallunt?

S7.3. Quō auxiliō crūdēlis nōn frangitur?

R7.1. Quō tempore multī amīcī numerantur?

   Quandō multī amīcī numerantur?

R7.5. Quōs superstitiō violat?

Word Study: English Derivatives

From Lesson	Latin	From Readings	Latin
1. action		1. enumerate	
2. deify		2. generous	
3. fallacy		3. habitation	
4. fragile		4. oculist	
5. negligible		5. invincible	

Narrative Reading

The Hare and the Tortoise

Testūdō, quod[1] ab aliīs animālibus[2] dērīdētur, leporem ad certāmen prōvocat. Lepus superbē rīdet et ait: "Cursus jam perficitur!" Alia animālia[3] autem cursum statuunt et vulpem faciunt jūdicem.[4] Vulpēs lātrātū sīgnum dat. Lepus et testūdō ex carcere prōcēdunt. Lepus summam celerī[5] pede harēnam lībat, sed testūdō tardō pede prōcēdit.

Lepus testūdinem longē post tergum relinquit. Mox gradum sistit, et testūdinem exspectat. Tandem somniculōsus jacet et dormit.

Intereā testūdō gradū tardō et cōnstantī prōcēdit. Leporem dormientem praeterit et ad mētam appropinquat. Subitō lepus ex somnō excitātur, sed nōn jam vincere potest. Trīstis ex campō discēdit. Vulpēs et alia animālia clāmant et victōrem laudant.

Celeritās et superbia cōnstantiā vincuntur.

Notes

1. *quod:* "because"
2. *animālibus:* a third declension noun, ablative plural
3. *alia animālia:* nominative plural
4. *vulpem . . . jūdicem:* two accusative nouns with *facit*. Translate "they make ＿＿＿
   ＿＿＿ ."
5. *celerī:* ablative singular

Vocabulary[1]

ad (prep. + acc.): to

ait: "_____ says"

alius, alia, aliud: other, another

appropinquō, appropinquāre: come near, approach

autem (sentence connector): but, however

campus, campī, m.: field

carcer, carceris, m.: the starting place

celer, celeris, celere: swift, fast

celeritās, celeritātis, f.: speed

certāmen, certāminis, n.: contest

clāmō, clāmāre: cry out

cōnstāns (cōnstantis): steady

cōnstantia, cōnstantiae, f.: steadiness

cursus, cursūs, m.: race

dērīdeō, dērīdēre: laugh at, deride

dō, dare: give

discēdō, discēdere: go away, depart

dormiēns (dormientis): sleeping

dormiō, dormīre: sleep

excitō, excitāre: arouse, wake up

exspectō, exspectāre: await, wait for

gradus, gradūs, m.: step

intereā (adv.): meanwhile

jaceō, jacēre: lie down

*jam (adv.): already, now

jūdex, jūdicis, m.: judge

lātrātus, lātrātūs, m.: a bark

laudō, laudāre: praise

lepus, leporis, m.: hare

lībō, lībāre: skim over

longē (adv.): far

mēta, mētae, f.: finish line

mox (adv.): soon

nōn jam (adv.): no longer

perficiō, perficere: finish

pēs, pedis, m.: foot

post (prep. + acc.): behind

praetereō, praeterīre: go past, pass

prōcēdō, prōcēdere: proceed

prōvocō, prōvocāre: challenge

relinquō, relinquere: leave

rīdeō, rīdēre: laugh

sīgnum, sīgnī, n.: signal, sign

sistō, sistere: halt, stop

somniculōsus, somniculōsa, somniculōsum: sleepy

somnus, somnī, m.: sleep

statuō, statuere: set up

subitō (adv.): suddenly

summus, summa, summum: highest, the top of

superbē (adv.): arrogantly

superbia, superbiae, f.: arrogance

tandem (adv.): finally, at last

tardus, tarda, tardum: slow

tergum, tergī, n.: back

testūdō, testūdinis, f.: tortoise

trīstis, trīste: sad

victor, victōris, m.: victor

Derivatives from Narrative Reading

Latin

1. adjacent

2. exclaim

3. gradual

4. provocation

5. relinquish

6. ridiculous

7. summit

8. tardy

---

1. Note to Students: Words from Readings and Narratives that occur three times are asterisked at the third appearance, and are not listed after that. These words are included in the General Vocabulary at the back of the textbook.

Summary Tasks

___ 1. Supply a morphologically and semantically appropriate subject for each of these verbs taken from the Reading Vocabulary of lesson 6: *docentur, discit, vestiuntur, docētur, cernunt.*

___ 2. Copy the kernels from Readings 7.1 through 7.6.

___ 3. Rewrite Basic Sentences 7.1 through 7.3, changing the subject from singular to plural or vice versa and making all other necessary changes.

___ 4. What syntactic expectation is raised by the first word in each of the Required Readings of this lesson?

___ 5. Write the singular and plural paradigm (nominative, accusative, ablative) of these noun-adjective pairs.

      virtūs, virtūtis (f.) + hūmānus, hūmāna, hūmānum

      opus, operis (n.) + magnus, magna, magnum

Lesson 8

Number and Number Agreement Continued
Cardinal Numbers

Basic Sentences

8.1. Parva levēs capiunt animōs.—Ovid
    Small things occupy lightweight minds.
8.2. Astra regunt hominēs, sed regit astra Deus.—Anon.
    The stars rule men, but God rules the stars.
8.3. Vulpēs nōn capitur mūneribus.—Medieval
    A fox is not caught by bribes.

Number and Number Agreement Continued

Morphology: Nouns of Third, Fourth, and Fifth Declensions

	Third	Third, n.	Fourth	Fifth
Singular				
Nominative	**fūr**	opus	**manus**	**rēs**
Accusative	**fūrem**	opus	**manum**	**rem**
Ablative	**fūre**	opere	**manū**	**rē**
Dative	fūrī	operī	manuī	reī
Genitive	fūris	operis	manūs	reī
Plural				
Nominative	**fūrēs**	opera	**manūs**	**rēs**
Accusative	**fūrēs**	opera	**manūs**	**rēs**
Ablative	**fūribus**	operibus	**manibus**	**rēbus**
Dative	fūribus	operibus	manibus	rēbus
Genitive	fūrum	operum	manuum	rērum

Third Declension I-Stem Nouns

The tendency to eliminate unnecessary differences in forms of words operates in all languages at all times. Nevertheless, some of these differences remain and exist in *irregular forms* that are remnants of an earlier stage in the language. An example of this is the presence of the *i-stem* nouns in Latin. Some third declension nouns have an *-ī* in certain case endings where other third declension nouns do not. For example, *animal* has *animālī* in the ablative singular (see the following paradigm), and the letter *i* also appears before the *a* in the nominative and accusative (as well as genitive) plural. The reader may also encounter the form *piscīs* in the accusative plural, where an accusative ending in *-ēs* was expected.

The beginning reader will sometimes misidentify some forms of these nouns. This, however, will not generally cause problems because other morphological and syntactic information is available in the sentence. It is not essential for readers to memorize which nouns are i-stem nouns but they must be ready to recognize them at all times.

Paradigms for three i-stem nouns are given here.

	Masculine	Neuter	Neuter
Singular			
Nominative	**piscis**	**animal**	**mare**
Accusative	**piscem**	**animal**	**mare**
Ablative	**pisce**	**animālī**	**marī**
Dative	piscī	animālī	marī
Genitive	piscis	animālis	maris
Plural			
Nominative	**piscēs**	**animālia**	**maria**
Accusative	**piscēs (-īs)**	**animālia**	**maria**
Ablative	**piscibus**	**animālibus**	**maribus**
Dative	piscibus	animālibus	maribus
Genitive	piscium	animālium	marium

Morphology: Adjectives of the Third Declension

In contrast to nouns, only a few of which are i-stem, most third declension adjectives are i-stems. This explains why the ablative singular ends in *-ī*.

	Masculine	Feminine	Neuter
Singular			
Nominative	**omnis**	**omnis**	**omne**
Accusative	**omnem**	**omnem**	**omne**
Ablative	**omnī**	**omnī**	**omnī**
Dative	omnī	omnī	omnī
Genitive	omnis	omnis	omnis
Plural			
Nominative	**omnēs**	**omnēs**	**omnia**
Accusative	**omnēs (-īs)**	**omnēs (-īs)**	**omnia**
Ablative	**omnibus**	**omnibus**	**omnibus**
Dative	omnibus	omnibus	omnibus
Genitive	omnium	omnium	omnium

	Masculine	Feminine	Neuter
Singular			
Nominative	**absēns***	**absēns**	**absēns**
Accusative	**absentem**	**absentem**	**absēns**
Ablative	**absentī**	**absentī**	**absentī**
Plural			
Nominative	**absentēs**	**absentēs**	**absentia**
Accusative	**absentēs (-īs)**	**absentēs (-īs)**	**absentia**
Ablative	**absentibus**	**absentibus**	**absentibus**

*See the appendix for complete paradigm of *absēns* (*absentis*).

■ Exercise 1

Fully identify each item. Include the part of speech. Also metaphrase each item.

	Identification	*Metaphrase*
1. hominēs		
2. hominēs		
3. rēs		
4. rēs		
5. rēs		
6. levēs		
7. levēs		
8. mūnus		
9. mūnus		
10. mūnera		
11. mūnera		

■ Exercise 2

The column on the left contains some of the predictable endings for the nominative, accusative, and ablative cases, in the singular and plural, of Latin nouns. Identify by case and number and, if neuter, by gender all predictable possibilities for each ending.

Case Ending	First	Second	Third	Fourth	Fifth
-ēs					
-a					
-īs					
-ōs					
-(ē/i)bus					
-us					
-um					

Optional: For each of the endings listed above, what possibilities exist that are *not* predictable?

■ Exercise 3

In the left-hand column are some adjective endings. Identify each as to what case, number, and gender it might signal in either group of adjectives. Use nominative, accusative, ablative only.

Ending	First and Second	Third
-e		
-ī		
-īs		
-a		

Cardinal Numbers

Latin *cardinal numbers* are indeclinable adjectives with the exception of the following numbers. (See these paradigms in the Appendix.)

ūnus, ūna, ūnum (one, I)
duo, duae, duo (two, II)
trēs, trēs, tria (three, III)

Numbers 4–10 and 100 are:

quattuor (four, IV)
quīnque (five, V)
sex (six, VI)
septem (seven, VII)
octō (eight, VIII)
novem (nine, IX)
decem (ten, X)
centum (one hundred, C)

The number *mīlle* (thousand) is indeclinable in the singular, but the plural *mīlia* is declined like the plural of *animal*. (The roman numeral is M.)

The question word that elicits numbers as answers is *quot?* (how many?).

Lesson Vocabulary

Nouns
animal, animālis, n.: animal
astrum, astrī, n.: star, constellation
mare, maris, n.: sea
mōs, mōris, m.: habit, custom; (pl.) morals, character

mūnus, mūneris, n.: gift
piscis, piscis, m.: fish
vulpēs, vulpis, f.: fox

Adjective
levis, leve: light, unstable

Numeral Adjectives

centum: 100

decem: 10

duo, duae, duo: 2

mīlle (pl. mīlia): 1,000

novem: 9

octō: 8

quattuor: 4

quīnque: 5

septem: 7

sex: 6

trēs, tria: 3

ūnus ūna, ūnum: 1

Question Word

quot?: how many?

Readings

Required

8.1. Stultī timent fortūnam, sapientēs ferunt.—Publilius Syrus

8.2. Fortēs Fortūna adjuvat.—Terence

8.3. Juppiter in caelīs, Caesar regit omnia terrīs.—Anon.

8.4. Aspiciunt oculīs superī mortālia jūstīs.—Ovid

8.5. Mōribus antīquīs stat rēs Rōmāna virīsque.—Ennius

8.6. Bonōs corrumpunt mōrēs congressūs malī.—Tertullian

8.7. In marī magnō piscēs capiuntur.—Anon.

Vocabulary

8.1. timeō, timēre: fear

sapiēns (sapientis): wise; (noun) wise person

ferō, ferre: endure

8.3. Juppiter, Jovis, m.: Jupiter, Jove (king of the gods)

caelum, caelī, n.: sky, heaven

Caesar, Caesaris, m.: Caesar

terra, terrae, f.: land, earth

8.4. aspiciō, aspicere: look at, see

oculus, oculī, m.: eye

superī, superōrum, m. pl.: those above, the gods

mortālis, mortāle: mortal, human

jūstus, jūsta, jūstum: just

8.5. antīquus, antīqua, antīquum: old, ancient

stō, stāre: stand

Rōmānus, Rōmāna, Rōmānum: Roman

8.6. corrumpō, corrumpere: corrupt

congressus, congressūs, m.: association (with people)

Optional

8.8. Omnia tempus revēlat.—Anon.

8.9. Vīna bibunt hominēs, animālia cētera fontēs.—Anon.

8.10. Ignis aurum probat, miseria fortēs virōs.—Anon.

8.11. Omnēs ūna manet nox.—Horace

8.12. Hōrae quidem cēdunt et diēs et mēnsēs et annī, nec praeteritum tempus umquam revertitur.—Cicero

8.13. Quid lēgēs sine mōribus vānae prōficiunt?—Horace

Vocabulary

8.8. revēlō, revēlāre: reveal, uncover

8.9. bibō, bibere: drink

     cēterī, cēterae, cētera (pl. adj.): the other, all other

8.10. ignis, ignis, m.: fire

     aurum, aurī, n.: gold

     probō, probāre: test, prove

     miseria, miseriae, f.: unhappiness, misery

8.11. maneō, manēre: await

8.12. quidem (intensifier): indeed, in fact, certainly

     cēdō, cēdere: go away

     mēnsis, mēnsis, m.: month

     annus, annī, m.: year

     nec (coord. conj.): and not, nor

     praeteritus, praeterita, praeteritum: past, gone by

     umquam (adv.): ever

     revertō, revertere: return

8.13. *lēx, lēgis, f.: law

     vānus, vāna, vānum: empty, vain

     prōficiō, prōficere: profit

Reminder: An asterisk (*) indicates the third time a word is used in Readings.

Latin Questions

S8.1. Quid levēs animōs capit?

S8.2. Quid deus regit?

S8.3. Quid nōn patitur vulpēs?

R8.5. Quālibus mōribus virīsque stat rēs Rōmāna?

R8.6. Quālēs mōrēs corrumpuntur?

Word Study: English Derivatives

From Lesson	Latin	From Readings	Latin
1. astronomy		1. antiquity	
2. decimal		2. celestial	
3. levity		3. congress	
4. millennium		4. immortal	
5. moral		5. superior	
6. percent		6. terrestrial	
7. remuneration		7. timid	
8. trilingual		8. virile	

Narrative Reading

Dē Asinō Parvō

Senex et fīlius parvō cum asinō in viā prōcēdunt. Mox duae puellae eōs cōnspiciunt. Ait ūna, "Ecce! Stultī hominēs habent asinum, sed pedibus prōcēdunt, nōn ab animālī vehuntur. Trēs asinī, nōn ūnus, prōcēdunt!" Tum fīlius in[1] asinum ascendit, et prōcēdunt, fīlius in asinō, pedibus pater.

Deinde eōs vident trēs senēs. Ait ūnus prō omnibus, "Ō tempora, Ō mōrēs! Ubi est pietās antīqua?" Magnō cum dolōre afficitur fīlius, et dēscendit, pedibusque prōcēdit. Pater in[1] asinum ascendit.

Deinde accūsant fēminae duae ūnā vōce patrem, quod[2] fīlius parvus tantum labōrem sustinet. Senex igitur fīlium quoque in[1] asinum impōnit. Et[3] pater et[3] fīlius in asinō sedent.

Mox autem viātor murmurat, "Asinus tam parvus est. Cūr hominēs ab asinō vehuntur? Cūr hominēs validī nōn ambulant? Cūr animal nōn portant?" Verbīs afficiuntur et[3] pater et[3] fīlius. Ambō[4] dēscendunt et animal parvum portant duo hominēs. Omnēs rīdent quod[2] hominēs tam stultī sunt.

Tandem pater, "Nihil," inquit, "ab omnibus probātur." Asinum igitur dēpōnunt et omnēs magnō gaudiō[5] pedibus prōcēdunt.

Notes

1. *in:* preposition with accusative noun, "onto ____"
2. *quod:* "because"
3. *et ____ et ____ :* "both ____ and ____"
4. *Ambō:* "both" (an irregular nominative plural form)
5. *magnō gaudiō:* Ablative of manner; *cum* is generally not expressed if the noun is modified by an adjective.

Vocabulary

accūsō, accūsāre: find fault with, accuse
afficiō, afficere: affect
*ait: "____ says" (introduces direct speech)
ambulō, ambulāre: walk
*antīquus, antīqua, antīquum: old, ancient
ascendō, ascendere: climb
asinus, asinī, m.: donkey
*autem (sentence connector): but, however
cōnspiciō, cōnspicere: see, look at
cūr?: why?
deinde (sentence connector): then, next
dēpōnō, dēpōnere: put down
dēscendō, dēscendere: climb down
dolor, dolōris, m.: grief
ecce (interjection): look!
fīlius, fīliī, m.: son
gaudium, gaudiī, n.: joy
igitur (sentence connector): therefore
impōnō, impōnere: put, set upon

inquit: "____ says" (introduces direct speech)
labor, labōris, m.: toil
mox (adv.): soon
murmurō, murmurāre: mumble
nihil (indecl. noun): nothing
pater, patris, m.: father
pēs, pedis, m.: foot
pietās, pietātis, f.: dutiful conduct toward gods, family, and country
portō, portāre: carry
prō (prep. + abl.): for, on behalf of
probō, probāre: approve
prōcēdō, prōcēdere: proceed
puella, puellae, f.: girl
quoque (indecl.): also
rīdeō, rīdēre: laugh
sedeō, sedēre: sit
senex, senis, m.: old man

sustineō, sustinēre: endure
tam (adv.): so
*tandem (adv.): finally, at last
tantus, tanta, tantum: so great, such great
tum (adv.): then
validus, valida, validum: strong

vehō, vehere: carry
verbum, verbī, n.: word
via, viae, f.: road
viātor, viātōris, m.: traveler
vōx, vōcis, f.: voice, word

Derivatives from Narrative Reading

Latin

1. ascend

2. duet

3. invalid

4. pedal

5. piety

6. probation

7. senile

8. vocal

Summary Tasks

____ 1. Name the kernel type of each kernel in the first paragraph of the Narrative Readings of lessons 7 and 8.
____ 2. Name the part of speech of each word in Basic Sentences 8.1 through 8.3.
____ 3. Rewrite Basic Sentences 5.1 through 5.4, changing the subject from singular to plural and vice versa, and making all necessary changes.
____ 4. Rewrite Readings 8.1 and 8.3 filling the gaps.
____ 5. Copy each adjective-noun construction in Readings 8.4 through 8.6.
____ 6. Rewrite Basic Sentence 6.2 putting the verb in the plural and making all necessary changes.
____ 7. Name the semantic feature(s) of the noun in the ablative in R8.3 *in caelīs,* R8.4 *oculīs,* R8.5 *mōribus.*
____ 8. Answer the following questions in Latin.
    a. Quot sunt septem et trēs?
    b. Quot sunt octō et duō?
    c. Quot sunt quattuor et quīnque?
    d. Quot sunt sex et duō?
____ 9. Write the singular and plural paradigm (nominative, accusative, ablative) of these noun-adjective pairs.
    a. astrum, astrī (n.) + omnis, omne
    b. mūnus, mūneris (n.) + parvus, parva, parvum
    c. vulpēs, vulpis (f.) + bonus, bona, bonum
    d. tempus, temporis (n.) + fēlīx (fēlīcis)
____ 10. Write a cumulative metaphrase for Reading 8.7. Remember to show two possibilities for *piscēs.*

Lesson 9

Principal Parts of Latin Verbs
The Present Perfective Tense

So far, verb listings in the vocabulary have included two *principal parts*, e.g., *amō, amāre*. From now on most verb listings will include four principal parts. This is the standard dictionary practice for verbs. English verbs, too, have principal parts. One can speak of the principal parts of English verbs in sets such as:

> take, took, taken
> rake, raked, raked
> make, made, made
> swim, swam, swum
> run, ran, run
> walk, walked, walked

A knowledge of such sets of principal parts is absolutely necessary for recognizing forms in the verb paradigm of any language. The *present perfective* verb forms introduced in this lesson are built from the third and fourth principal parts of the Latin verb.

Basic Sentences

9.1. Dīvīna nātūra dedit agrōs; ars hūmāna aedificāvit urbēs.—Varro
> Divine nature has given the fields; human skill has built the cities.

9.2. Ālea jacta est.—Suetonius (adapted)
> The die has been cast.

9.3. Caesar prō castrīs cōpiās prōdūxit et aciem īnstrūxit.—Caesar (adapted)
> Caesar led his troops forward before the camp and drew up a battle line.

Principal Parts of Latin Verbs

Latin verbs are grouped by conjugations, and the first two principal parts are regular and predictable within each conjugation. On the other hand, the third and fourth principal parts are not generally predictable except in regular verbs of the first and fourth conjugations. Third and fourth principal parts do, however, fall into patterns.

Here are examples of the four principal parts of some common Latin verbs.

amō, amāre, amāvī, amātus, -a, -um (love)
videō, vidēre, vīdī, vīsus, -a, -um (see)
regō, regere, rēxī, rēctus, -a, -um (rule)
capiō, capere, cēpī, captus, -a, -um (take)
audiō, audīre, audīvī, audītus, -a, -um (hear)

Principal parts show the stems of a verb. In Latin it is convenient to speak of three stems: the *imperfective* stem (from the first two principal parts), the *perfective active* stem (from the third principal part), and the stem of the *perfective passive participle* (from the fourth principal part). All of the verbs, both active and passive, in lessons 1 through 8 were built on the *imperfective* stem.

Morphology: Perfective Active Verb Forms

Dedit (has given) and *aedificāvit* (has built) in S9.1 and *prōdūxit* (led) and *īnstrūxit* (drew up) in S9.3 are verb forms built on the perfective active stem. The perfective active stem is found by removing the final *-ī* from the third principal part of the verb. This inflectional morpheme {ī} indicates first person singular, e.g., *dedī* (I have given). Look at the examples.

dō, dare, dedī, datus, -a, -um: perfective active stem = ded-
prōdūcō, prōdūcere, prōdūxī, prōductus, -a, -um: perfective active stem = prōdūx-

The morpheme {it} found with this stem represents the third person *singular*, active voice. The morpheme {ērunt} represents the third person *plural*, active voice.

dedit (he, she, it or <u>[noun]</u> has given)
dedērunt (they or <u>[noun]</u>s have given)

In general, the perfective active stem is formed in one of four ways, as illustrated. Only the first and third principal parts are listed.

(A)	(B)	(C)	(D)
amō/**amāvī**	regō/**rēxī**	videō/**vīdī**	dō/**dedī**
audiō/**audīvī**	scrībō/**scrīpsī**	capiō/**cēpī**	fallō/**fefellī**
teneō/**tenuī**			

Here is a summary of the characteristics of the perfective active stems in each column.

A: *-v-* or *-u-;* most verbs of the first and fourth conjugations are of this kind.
B: *-s-* or *-x-* (*x = gs,* or *cs;* thus *rēgsī* is spelled *rēxī*), mostly third conjugation verbs.
C: A change in the vowel and/or lengthening of the vowel of the root of the verb (like the change in English *run/ran, fight/fought*).
D: A reduplication of the first consonant of the verb root.

It is useful in memorizing principal parts of verbs to group them by conjugation and then to set up within each conjugation subgroups according to the third principal part. Learning by association often makes memorization more efficient. See the Vocabulary Appendix that follows the Lesson Vocabulary of this lesson for principal parts of all verbs in lessons 1 through 8.

■ Exercise 1

Write what characterizes *the third principal part* of each of these verbs. The example has been completed for you.

faciō, facere, fēcī   change and lengthening of vowel of root

1. cūrō, cūrāre, cūrāvī

2. neglegō, neglegere, neglēxī

3. capiō, capere, cēpī

4. habeō, habēre, habuī

5. videō, vidēre, vīdī

6. āmittō, āmittere, āmīsī

Morphology: Perfective Passive Verb Forms

Many verb forms in English are periphrastic[1] forms, i.e., they consist of more than one word: "has ____-ed," "has been ____-ed," etc. All perfective passive tenses in Latin are periphrastic verb forms.

Jacta est (has been cast) in S9.2 is a perfective passive verb built from the perfective passive participle and the verb *esse*. *Jacta* (cast) is a form of the participle *jactus, -a, -um* that occurs as the fourth principal part of the verb. *Est* and *sunt* are third person forms of the verb *sum, esse*.

The stem of a perfective passive participle ends in *-s* or *-t* and is found by removing the final *-us, -a, -um*. Look at the examples.

jaciō, jacere, jēcī, *jactus, -a, -um*: participle stem = *jact-*
premō, premere, pressī, *pressus, -a, -um*: participle stem = *press-*

The participle stem has become most productive in English derivatives, e.g., re*press*, com*press*. In contrast, no English derivatives are formed from the third principal part of Latin verbs.

The final morphemes of the participles, i.e., the regular *-us, -a, -um* ending of first and second declension adjectives, signal agreement in case, number, and gender with the subject of the kernel. For example, *jacta* agrees with *ālea*, a noun in the nominative singular feminine. If the subject were plural, i.e., *āleae*, the verb would be *jactae sunt*. Other examples are *canis pressus est* and *canēs pressī sunt*, or *animal pressum est* and *animālia pressa sunt*.

_____

1. In general, *periphrastic* means using several words where one would do; in grammar, using an auxiliary verb plus participle instead of a single inflected form.

■ Exercise 2
Underline the form of the perfective passive verb that agrees with the subject given.

1. canēs   audītus est, audītī sunt, audīta est

2. fēmina   audītus est, audītī sunt, audīta est

3. corpus   vīsus est, vīsa est, vīsum est

4. imitātiōnēs   vīsa est, vīsī sunt, vīsae sunt

5. animālia   captus est, capta est, capta sunt

Aspect

The difference between imperfective and perfective is a matter of *aspect*. *Perfective aspect* refers to *completedness; imperfective aspect* refers to *noncompletedness*. Consider these English examples.

> They took the exam.
> They have taken the exam.

Both of these events are considered to be completed events; therefore the Latin equivalents of these verbs would be formed from the perfective stem. Now read these examples.

> They take the exam.
> They are taking the exam.
> They were taking the exam.

The verbs in these sentences, if expressed in Latin, would all be formed from the imperfective stem. None of the events is considered to be a completed event. Although "were taking" indicates an event in the past, it does not indicate or stress completedness.

Just as Latin verbs show a contrast in aspect, i.e., imperfective or perfective, they also show a contrast in *time: past, present,* or *future*. Aspect and time together are often spoken of as *tense*. Latin verbs have six *tenses*.

Past Imperfective	Past Perfective
Present Imperfective	Present Perfective
Future Imperfective	Future Perfective

All of the verbs until lesson 26 are either present imperfective or present perfective in tense. In later lessons there will also be past and future imperfective and perfective tenses. Some of these verb tenses occur in Narrative Readings before lesson 26.

■ Exercise 3

For each of the verbs listed identify the *stem* as imperfective or perfective and the *voice* as active or passive. The principal parts of the verbs are provided.

amō, amāre, amāvī, amātus
audiō, audīre, audīvī, audītus
doceō, docēre, docuī, doctus
dūcō, dūcere, dūxī, ductus
premō, premere, pressī, pressus
videō, vidēre, vīdī, vīsus

	Stem	*Voice*
1. premitur		
2. pressit		
3. amātus est		
4. dūcunt		
5. amātur		
6. audīvērunt		
7. videt		
8. vīdit		
9. docet		
10. docuit		
11. audītae sunt		
12. dūcitur		
13. vīsa est		
14. amāvērunt		
15. dūxit		
16. audīvit		

The Present Perfective Tense

Latin verbs in the present perfective correspond either to English present perfective verbs, i.e., "has ____-ed" as in "has captured," "has heard," and "has seen" or to English "simple past" verbs, i.e., "____-ed" as in "captured," "heard," and "saw."

The verb in S9.2 (*Ālea jacta est*) is translated as an English present perfective, "The die has been cast." In another context, *jacta est* could be translated as "was cast," i.e., as a "simple past." According to tradition, as Caesar stood at the Rubicon River he announced (with the words *ālea jacta est*) his decision to cross the river that was the border between his province of Gaul and of Italy proper, and thereby to violate the Roman constitution. It is generally assumed, e.g., by Shakespeare, that Caesar here meant "The die has been cast" (i.e., "The die is now cast") and not "The die was cast."

In contrast, S9.3 (*Caesar cōpiās prō castrīs prōdūxit et aciem īnstrūxit*) is part of a *narrative account* of what Caesar did. *Caesar prōdūxit* is therefore translated "Caesar led," not "Caesar has led." Likewise *īnstrūxit* is "Caesar drew up," not "Caesar has drawn up." Most of the verb forms identified as present perfective tenses are parts of narrative accounts that tell of events as they happened in the past. The name *present perfective* does not accurately describe the "simple past" meaning; therefore it is helpful to have another name for the tense when it has this meaning; it will be referred to as the *narrative* tense in some discussions.

Present perfective is, however, an accurate description of the morphology of this tense in passive forms. For example, the compound form *jacta est* is put together from the *perfective* participle and *est*, a *present* time form.

It is interesting that ancient Greek, like English, has different forms to express the present perfective meaning and the simple past meaning. Why Latin has only one form is one of the many fascinating questions encountered in the historical study of language.

Form identification, whether of nouns or verbs, is only the first step in reading. To read and translate a form correctly, one must, as can be understood from this discussion, have other information also.

■ Exercise 4

Identify the forms of each of the verbs listed by completing the chart. Give an English equivalent of each verb. The principal parts are provided. Note: All verbs so far are *present imperfective* or *present perfective* tense.

audiō, audīre, audīvī, audītus (hear)
capiō, capere, cēpī, captus (take)
doceō, docēre, docuī, doctus (teach)
dūcō, dūcere, dūxī, ductus (lead)
sum, esse, fuī (be)

	Person/Number	*Tense*	*Voice*	*English Equivalent*
1. audītur				
2. ductus est				
3. dūcitur				
4. cēpit				
5. sunt				
6. capta est				
7. capitur				
8. fuērunt				
9. est				
10. docent				
11. docētur				
12. doctī sunt				

Lesson Vocabulary

Nouns
aciēs, aciēī, f.: battle line
ager, agrī, m.: field
ālea, āleae, f.: game of dice; a die
ars, artis, f.: skill, an art
Caesar, Caesaris, m.: Caesar
castra, castrōrum, n. (pl. only): camp
cōpia, cōpiae, f.: abundance; (pl.) troops, supplies
nātūra, nātūrae, f.: nature

Adjective
dīvīnus, dīvīna, dīvīnum: divine

Indeclinable
Preposition
prō (+ abl.): before, in front of; for, on behalf of

Verbs
aedificō, aedificāre, aedificāvī, aedificātus, -a, -um: build
dō, dare, dedī, datus, -a, -um: give
doceō, docēre, docuī, doctus, -a, -um: teach
īnstruō, īnstruere, īnstrūxī, īnstructus, -a, -um: draw up
jaciō, jacere, jēcī, jactus, -a, -um: throw, cast
prōdūcō, prōdūcere, prōdūxī, prōductus, -a, -um: lead forward

Vocabulary Appendix

Here are the principal parts of the verbs occurring in lessons 1 through 8. They are grouped within each conjugation according to the formation of the third principal part. Certain principal parts are left blank because they do not occur.

First Conjugation
ambulō, ambulāre, ambulāvī[1]
amō, amāre, amāvī, amātus, -a, -um
corōnō, corōnāre, corōnāvī, corōnātus, -a, -um
cūrō, cūrāre, cūrāvī, cūrātus, -a, -um
intrō, intrāre, intrāvī, intrātus, -a, -um
irrītō, irrītāre, irrītāvī, irrītātus, -a, -um
satiō, satiāre, satiāvī, satiātus, -a, -um
adjuvō, adjuvāre, adjūvī, adjūtus, -a, -um
lavō, lavāre, lāvī, lautus, -a, -um

Second Conjugation
dēbeō, dēbēre, dēbuī, dēbitus, -a, -um
habeō, habēre, habuī, habitus, -a, -um

teneō, tenēre, tenuī, tentus, -a, -um
videō, vidēre, vīdī, vīsus, -a, -um
audeō, audēre, ——, ausus, -a, -um[2]
soleō, solēre, ——, solitus, -a, -um[2]

Third Conjugation
alō, alere, aluī, altus, -a, -um
cognōscō, cognōscere, cognōvī, cognitus, -a, -um
cupiō, cupere, cupīvī, cupītus, -a, -um
pāsco, pāscere, pāvī, pāstus, -a, -um
vānēscō, vānēscere[1]
āmittō, āmittere, āmīsī, āmissus, -a, -um
dēfluō, dēfluere, dēflūxī[1]
dūcō, dūcere, dūxī, ductus, -a, -um

mittō, mittere, mīsī, missus, -a, -um

neglegō, neglegere, neglēxī, neglēctus,
 -a, -um

premō, premere, pressī, pressus, -a, -um

regō, regere, rēxī, rēctus, -a, -um

vīvō, vīvere, vīxī, vīctūrus, -a, -um[3]

agō, agere, ēgī, āctus, -a, -um

capiō, capere, cēpī, captus, -a, -um

faciō, facere, fēcī, factus, -a, -um

frangō, frangere, frēgī, frāctus, -a, -um

fugiō, fugere, fūgī, fugitūrus, -a, -um[3]

vincō, vincere, vīcī, victus, -a, -um

fallō, fallere, fefellī, falsus, -a, -um

Fourth Conjugation

audiō, audīre, audīvī, audītus, -a, -um

impediō, impedīre, impedīvī, impedītus,
 -a, -um

veniō, venīre, vēnī, ventūrus, -a, -um[3]

Irregular

offerō, offerre, obtulī, oblātus, -a, -um

pereō, perīre, periī/perīvī, peritūrus, -a, -um[3]

possum, posse, potuī

sum, esse, fuī, futūrus, -a, -um[3]

volō, velle, voluī

Notes

1. Some verbs such as *ambulō, vānēscō,* and *dēfluō* appear with only two or three principal parts because the others rarely or never occur.
2. Semideponent verbs: see lesson 20.
3. Intransitive verbs are listed with a fourth principal part ending in *-ūrus, -a, -um* instead of *-us, -a, -um.* This is so because intransitive verbs do not have a complete passive morphology. This form in *-ūrus* is an active form, the future active participle, which will be discussed in lesson 14.

Readings

Required

9.1. Incidit in[1] foveam quam[2] fēcit.—Anon.

9.2. Afflāvit Deus et dissipantur.—Motto on medal commemorating defeat of Spanish Armada.

9.3. Adam[3] prīmus homō[3] damnāvit saecula pōmō.—Medieval

9.4. Aelius est morbō correptus convaluitque.
 Ast medicum ut vīdit Simplicium, periit.—Parkhurst

Notes

1. *in:* prep. + acc. noun, "into _____"
2. *quam:* relative pronoun, accusative singular feminine, agreeing with *foveam,* translate "that"/"which"
3. *Adam . . . homō* is an example of one noun being in *apposition* to another, i.e., "Adam, the . . . man, . . ."

Vocabulary

9.1. incidō, incidere, incidī: fall (into)
 fovea, foveae, f.: pit

9.2. afflō, afflāre, afflāvī, afflātus, -a, -um: blow
 dissipō, dissipāre, dissipāvī, dissipātus, -a, -um: scatter

9.3. prīmus, prīma, prīmum: first
damnō, damnāre, damnāvī, damnātus, -a, -um: condemn
saeculum, saeculī, n.: generation
pōmum, pōmī, n.: apple

9.4. Aelius, Aeliī, m.: Aelius (a man's name)
morbus, morbī, m.: illness
corripiō, corripere, corripuī, correptus, -a, -um: seize
convalēscō, convalēscere, convaluī: get well
ast (coord. conj., variant of *at*): but
medicus, medicī, m.: doctor
ut (subord. conj.): when

Word Study: English Derivatives

From Lesson	Latin	From Readings	Latin
1. agriculture		1. convalescent	
2. copious		2. dissipated	
3. divinity		3. incident	
4. edifice		4. inflate	
5. injection		5. medical	
6. instruction		6. primitive	
7. natural		7. secular	

Narrative Reading

Juno's Jealousy

Of all the ancient heroes whose stories were told from one generation to the next, the one most popular at Rome was Hercules. Some of the stories about Hercules will be told in this and future lessons.

Herculēs, fīlius[1] Alcmēnae[2] et Jovis,[2] ōlim in Graeciā antīquā habitāvit. Jūnō, rēgīna[1] caelī,[2] Alcmēnam nōn amāvit, et īnfantem interficere voluit. Mīsit igitur duōs serpentēs saevōs. Serpentēs mediā nocte in cubiculum Alcmēnae[2] vēnērunt. In cubiculō Herculēs cum frātre dormiēbat.[3] Frāter in cūnīs, sed Herculēs in scūtō magnō cubābat.[3] Serpentēs jam appropinquāvērunt et scūtum mōvērunt. Itaque Herculēs ē somnō excitātus est.

Notes

Read the following notes carefully. The points discussed will occur again in other narratives.

1. *Herculēs, fīlius Alcmēnae et Jovis* (Hercules, the son of Alcmena and Jupiter). *Fīlius*, put next to *Herculēs*, is an example of one noun being in *apposition* to another, here to *Herculēs*. Likewise in line 1, *rēgīna* is in apposition to *Jūnō*, i.e., "Juno, queen of heaven."

2. *Alcmēnae, Jovis,* and *caelī* are nouns in the *genitive* singular. Translate these and other nouns identified as genitive by the prepositional phrase "of ____" until lesson 17, which describes the syntax of the genitive.

3. The morpheme {bă} in a verb form indicates the past imperfective tense. This tense indicates continued or repeated action in the past. It is here translated "was ____-ing." Other equivalents will appear later.

Vocabulary

Alcmēna, Alcmēnae, f.: Alcmena, mother of Hercules
appropinquō, appropinquāre, appropinquāvī: approach, draw near
caelum, caelī, n.: heaven
cubiculum, cubiculī, n.: bedroom
cubō, cubāre, cubāvī: lie down
cūnae, cūnārum, f. pl.: cradle
*dormiō, dormīre, dormīvī: sleep
excitō, excitāre, excitāvī, excitātus, -a, -um: arouse
fīlius, fīliī, m.: son
frāter, frātris, m.: brother
Graecia, Graeciae, f.: Greece
habitō, habitāre, habitāvī: live
igitur (sentence connector): therefore, and so
īnfāns, īnfantis, m. & f.: infant
interficiō, interficere, interfēcī, interfectus, -a, -um: kill
itaque (sentence connector): and so
Jūnō, Jūnōnis, f.: Juno, queen of the gods and wife of Jupiter
Juppiter, Jovis, m.: Jupiter, king of the gods and father of Hercules
medius, media, medium: middle of
moveō, movēre, mōvī, mōtus, -a, -um: move
ōlim (adv.): once upon a time
rēgīna, rēgīnae, f.: queen
saevus, saeva, saevum: fierce
scūtum, scūtī, n.: shield
serpēns, serpentis, m.: serpent, snake
somnus, somnī, m.: sleep

Derivatives from Narrative Reading

Latin

1. dormant

2. excitable

3. incubator

4. medium

5. regal

6. somnambulist

7. voluntary

Summary Tasks

___ 1. Copy each kernel from the Narrative Reading and name the kernel type. Be careful to fill gaps.

___ 2. Name the semantic feature(s) of these nouns in the ablative: R9.3 *pōmō*, R9.4 *morbō*.

___ 3. With the help of the Vocabulary Appendix rewrite Basic Sentences 7.1 and 7.2, putting the verb in the present perfective tense.

___ 4. How many kernels are there in R9.4?

___ 5. Write the ablative singular of all nouns in Review Lesson 2.

Review Lesson 2

Lesson Vocabulary

Nouns

aciēs, aciēī, f.: battle line
āctum, āctī, n.: deed, act
ager, agrī, m.: field
ālea, āleae, f.: game of dice; a die
animal, animālis, n.: animal
aper, aprī, m.: boar
ars, artis, f.: skill, an art
astrum, astrī, n.: star, constellation
auxilium, auxiliī, n.: help, aid
Caesar, Caesaris, m.: Caesar
canis, canis, m. & f.: dog
castra, castrōrum, n. (pl. only): camp
causa, causae, f.: reason, cause
cōpia, cōpiae, f.: abundance; (pl.) troops,
    supplies
deus, deī, m.: god
fēlīcitās, fēlīcitātis, f.: success, prosperity,
    happiness
impetus, impetūs, m.: impulse, attack
lacrima, lacrimae, f.: tear
mare, maris, n.: sea
mōs, mōris, m.: habit, custom; (pl.) morals,
    character
multitūdō, multitūdinis, f.: crowd, multitude
mūnus, mūneris, n.: gift
nātūra, nātūrae, f.: nature
piscis, piscis, m.: fish
ratiō, ratiōnis, f.: reason
tempus, temporis, n.: time
vulpēs, vulpis, f.: fox

Pronoun

is, ea, id: he, she, it; (pl.) they

Adjectives

crūdēlis, crūdēle: cruel
dīvīnus, dīvīna, dīvīnum: divine
fēlīx (fēlīcis): fortunate, happy, prosperous
hūmānus, hūmāna, hūmānum: human
levis, leve: light, unstable
multus, multa, multum: much; (pl.) many

Numeral Adjectives

centum: 100
decem: 10
duō, duae, duō: 2
mīlle (pl. mīlia): 1,000
novem: 9
octō: 8
quattuor: 4
quīnque: 5
septem: 7
sex: 6
trēs, tria: 3
ūnus, ūna, ūnum: 1

Indeclinables

Adverbs

aegrē: with difficulty
facile: easily
saepe: often

Preposition

prō (+ abl.): before, in front of; for,
    on behalf of

Question Words

ā quō?: by whom?
quā dē causā?: why? for what reason?
quandō?: when?
quō auxiliō?: by what means?
quō tempore?: when? at what time?
quot?: how many?

Verbs

aedificō, aedificāre, aedificāvī, aedificātus, -a, -um: build
āmittō, āmittere, āmīsī, āmissus, -a, -um: let go, lose
cūrō, cūrāre, cūrāvī, cūrātus, -a, -um: care for
dō, dare, dedī, datus, -a, -um: give
doceō, docēre, docuī, doctus, -a, -um: teach
dūcō, dūcere, dūxī, ductus, -a, -um: lead
fallō, fallere, fefellī, falsus, -a, -um: deceive
frangō, frangere, frēgī, frāctus, -a, -um: break
īnstruō, īnstruere, īnstrūxī, īnstrūctus, -a, -um: draw up
jaciō, jacere, jēcī, jactus, -a, -um: throw, cast, hurl
mittō, mittere, mīsī, missus, -a, -um: send
neglegō, neglegere, neglēxī, neglēctus, -a, -um: neglect
offerō, offerre, obtulī, oblātus, -a, -um: offer
pāscō, pāscere, pāvī, pāstus, -a, -um: feed
prōdūcō, prōdūcere, prōdūxī, prōductus, -a, -um: bring forth
teneō, tenēre, tenuī, tentus, -a, -um: hold, keep

Readings Vocabulary

From now on, there will be a section in Review Lessons that lists the vocabulary that has been marked by an asterisk (*) in the Readings and Narrative Readings of each group of lessons. Once words have appeared three times in the Readings or Narrative Readings, they are not listed again in the Readings. They are listed in the General Vocabulary at the end of this book.

ait: "_____ says" (introduces direct speech)
antīquus, antīqua, antīquum: old, ancient
autem (sentence connector): but, however; moreover
deinde (sentence connector): then, next
dormiō, dormīre, dormīvī: sleep; rest, be inactive
habitō, habitāre, habitāvī: live, dwell
itaque (sentence connector): and so
jam (adv.): already, now
lēx, lēgis, f.: law
rīdeō, rīdēre, rīsī, rīsus: laugh
tandem (adv.): finally, at last

Morphology Review

New Morphology: Lessons 6 through 9

noun: nominative, accusative, ablative plural
adjective: nominative, accusative, ablative plural
pronoun, *is, ea, id*: nominative, accusative, ablative, singular and plural

verb: third person singular, present imperfective, passive
third person plural, present imperfective, active and passive
third person singular and plural, present perfective, active and passive
passive infinitive
principal parts, perfective verb stems

Form Identification

Using the dictionary entries provided, identify the following forms and indicate the entry from which each is taken.

a. āctum, āctī, n.: deed, act
b. agō, agere, ēgī, āctus: do, act
c. āctiō, āctiōnis, f.: action, deed

1. āctus est _____
2. ēgērunt _____
3. agī _____
4. āctiō _____
5. agere _____
6. āctiōne _____
7. agitur _____
8. āctum _____
9. agunt _____
10. āctīs _____

Narrative Reading

Rānae Rēgem Petunt

Rānae in lātīs aquīs habitāvērunt; līberae sed nōn laetae erant.[1] Clāmōre magnō ā Jove petīvērunt rēgem.

Juppiter rīsit atque tigillum in[2] aquam mīsit, quod[3] magnō sonitū rānās terruit. Tigillum diū in aquā jacuit. Forte ūna ē rānīs prōtulit ex aquā caput, et suum rēgem spectāvit. Deinde aliās ēvocāvit. Rānae timōrem dēposuērunt et magnā celeritāte in[2] lignum ascendērunt. Maledīxērunt quod[4] tigillum erat[1] rēx inūtilis. Itaque ā Jove alium rēgem petīvērunt.

Tum Juppiter serpentem horribilem mīsit. Serpēns dente atrōcī rānās singulās rapuit. Rānae magnō cum timōre affectae sunt et vōcem etiam timor repressit. Tandem rānam fortem ad[5] Jovem mīsērunt. "Nōn jam," ait,[6] "rēgem rānae cupiunt. Subsidium petunt."

Juppiter, quod[4] rānae bonum rēgem (id est,[7] tigillum) nōn accēpērunt, subsidium recūsāvit, et serpentem nōn ēripuit.

Itaque rānae, quod[4] bonam fortūnam nōn tulērunt, nunc malam fortūnam pertulērunt.

Notes

1. *erant, erat:* past imperfective of *esse,* translate "were," "was"
2. *in* + noun in accusative case, translate "into, upon _____"
3. *quod:* relative pronoun, nominative singular, translate "which"
4. *quod:* subordinating conjunction, translate "because"
5. *ad* + noun in accusative case, translate "to _____"
6. *ait:* "_____ said"
7. *id est,* often abbreviated *i.e.:* "that is"

Vocabulary

accipiō, accipere, accēpī, acceptus, -a, -um: accept
afficiō, afficere, affēcī, affectus, -a, -um: affect
alius, alia, aliud: another, other
ascendō, ascendere, ascendī: climb
atrōx (atrōcis): cruel, fierce
caput, capitis, n.: head
celeritās, celeritātis, f.: speed
clāmor, clāmōris, m.: shout
*deinde (sentence connector): then
dēns, dentis, m.: tooth
dēpōnō, dēpōnere, dēposuī, dēpositus, -a, -um: put down, put aside
diū (adv.): for a long time
ēripiō, ēripere, ēripuī, ēreptus, -a, -um: take away, snatch away
etiam (intensifier): even
ēvocō, ēvocāre, ēvocāvī, ēvocātus, -a, -um: call out
ferō, ferre, tulī, lātus, -a, -um: suffer, bear
forte (adv.): by chance
*habitō, habitāre, habitāvī: live, dwell
horribilis, horribile: horrible
inūtilis, inūtile: not useful, useless
*itaque (sentence connector): and so, therefore
jaceō, jacēre, jacuī: lie
Juppiter, Jovis, m.: Jupiter, king of the gods
laetus, laeta, laetum: happy
lātus, lāta, lātum: broad, wide
līber, lībera, līberum: free
lignum, lignī, n.: wood, log
maledīcō, maledīcere, maledīxī, maledictus: curse; slander
nōn jam: no longer
nunc (adv.): now
perferō, perferre, pertulī, perlātus, -a, -um: bear, endure (to completion)
petō, petere, petīvī, petītus, -a, -um: seek
prōferō, prōferre, prōtulī, prōlātus, -a, -um: bring forth
rāna, rānae, f.: frog
rapiō, rapere, rapuī, raptus, -a, -um: snatch
recūsō, recūsāre, recūsāvī, recūsātus, -a, -um: refuse
reprimō, reprimere, repressī, repressus, -a, -um: suppress
rēx, rēgis, m.: king

*rīdeō, rīdēre, rīsī, rīsus, -a, -um: laugh
serpēns, serpentis, m. &. f.: serpent
singulus, singula, singulum: one at a time, one by one
sonitus, sonitūs, m.: sound
spectō, spectāre, spectāvī, spectātus, -a, -um: look at
subsidium, subsidiī, n.: help, aid
suus, sua, suum: his/her/its own, their own
terreō, terrēre, terruī, territus, -a, -um: frighten
tigillum, tigillī, n.: a small log
timor, timōris, m.: fear
tum (adv.): then
vōx, vōcis, f.: voice

Derivatives from Narrative Reading

Latin

1. aquarium

2. atrocious

3. benediction

4. convocation

5. dental

6. deposit

7. liberty

8. petition

9. subsidy

10. utility

■ Exercise: English to Latin Sentences
Following the structure of the Latin model sentences given, write a Latin translation of the English sentences. Keep the Latin word order.

1. Ā cane nōn magnō saepe tenētur aper. (S6.2)

   a. A bad thief is often caught by a small boy.

   b. Children are never neglected by a good mother.

   c. The wolf is being held by the good shepherd.

   d. Opportunity is never lost by a wise man.

2. Vulpēs nōn capitur mūneribus. (S8.3)

    a. A cruel person is not crushed by tears.

    b. The wise man is not being deceived by smooth speech.

    c. The frog is terrified by a loud sound.

3. Caesar cōpiās prō castrīs prōdūxit. (S9.3)

    a. The fox did not get the bunch of grapes.

    b. The shepherd caught the wolf.

4. Ālea jacta est. (S9.2)

    a. The thief has been caught by the woman.

    b. The thieves have been caught by the men.

Vocabulary

Nouns
boy: puer, puerī, m.
bunch of grapes: ūva, ūvae, f.
child: puer, puerī, m.
fox: vulpēs
frog: rāna, rānae, f.
man: vir
mother: māter, mātris, f.
opportunity: occāsiō
shepherd: pāstor, pāstōris, m.
sound: sonitus, sonitūs, m.
speech: ōrātiō, ōrātiōnis, f.
tear: lacrima
thief: fūr
wolf: lupus
woman: fēmina

Adjectives
bad: malus
cruel: crūdēlis
good: bonus
loud: magnus
small: parvus
smooth: blandus, blanda, blandum
wise: sapiēns (sapientis)

Indeclinables
by: ā/ab (prep.)
often: saepe (adv.)
never: numquam (adv.)
not: nōn (adv.)

Verbs
catch: capiō
crush: frangō
deceive: fallō
get: capiō
hold: teneō
lose: āmittō
neglect: neglegō
terrify: terreō, terrēre

Lesson 10

The Linking Kernel
The Factitive Kernel
Part of Speech: Pronoun

The number and nature of kernel types vary according to the theories of the person offering the description of a given language. The description in this course has been adopted with the practical needs of the reader in mind. It teaches the reader to expect one of eight kernel types, three of which have been studied so far. They are:

1. transitive active: subject—verb (active voice)—direct object
2. intransitive active: subject—verb (active voice)
3. passive: subject—verb (passive voice)

This lesson introduces the *linking* and the *factitive* kernel types.

Basic Sentences

10.1. Oculī sunt in amōre ducēs.—Propertius
         In love the eyes are the leaders.
10.2. Ars longa, vīta brevis.—Hippocrates (trans. from Greek)
         Art is long, life is short.
10.3. Necessitūdō etiam timidōs fortēs facit.—Sallust
         Necessity makes even the cowardly brave.

The Linking Kernel

Syntax

The linking kernel has a verb that patterns with a *complement* in the nominative case. This is in contrast to a transitive verb, which patterns with a direct object in the accusative case. A complement in the nominative is called a *subject complement* because it refers to the subject. Therefore, a linking kernel has items with these functions:

subject—verb (linking)—subject complement (nominative)

The list of verbs that occur in a linking kernel is short. The most frequently occurring are:

appellātur (is named, is called, *not* is called for, is summoned)
est (is, *not* exists)
fit (is made, becomes, *not* is done)
habētur (is considered, *not* is had)
tenētur (is considered)
vidētur (seems, *not* is seen)
vocātur (is named, *not* is called for, is summoned)

Notice that four of the verbs are passive in form. *Fit* looks active, but it substitutes throughout the language for the nonexistent passive of *facit*.

In S10.1 both *oculī* and *ducēs* are nouns in the nominative case. The verb *sunt* links the subject complement *ducēs* to the subject *oculī*. *Sunt* in this sentence can be replaced by *videntur, fīunt, tenentur, habentur, appellantur*. These verbs vary in the strength of the claim made about something or someone. For example, *oculī ducēs appellantur* is a linking kernel meaning "The eyes *are called* leaders." This is weaker than the sentence with *sunt*: "The eyes *are* leaders." The semantic notion of "linking" is most directly expressed by the verb *est* and other forms of *sum, esse*.

The subject complement in a linking kernel may be either a noun or an adjective. An adjective appears in *oculī sunt in amōre* caecī (from *caecus, caeca, caecum* [blind]) "Eyes are *blind* in love."

If a linking kernel has two nouns rather than a noun and an adjective, there may be syntactic ambiguity. This is so because there is no signal to show which noun is subject and which is subject complement. However, if the reader understands the context, a real ambiguity rarely occurs.

A sentence such as S10.2 (*Ars longa, vīta brevis*) is an example of the fact that in Latin and many other languages, but not in English, the linking verb often is understood but not expressed. Therefore, *ars longa* means "art is long."

Metaphrasing

In order to indicate that a linking verb is expected, it is convenient to show an equal sign in the verb slot. For example, *Caesar dux* can be metaphrased "Caesar ___=___s leader."

The verb *sum, esse* can now occur in two kernel types: a linking kernel, "_____ is _____ ," or an intransitive kernel, "_____ is/exists" or "there is _____ ." For example, *vīta brevis est* may, depending on the context, be "life is short" or "there is a short life."

■ Exercise 1
All nouns and adjectives in the kernels below function as kernel items, not as modifiers. Identify the kernels as passive or linking.

1. Fēmina fēlīx vidētur.

2. Fēmina vidētur.

3. Homō sapiēns tenētur.

4. Homō tenētur.

5. Puer appellātus est.

6. Puer Marcus appellātur.

The Factitive Kernel

Syntax

The factitive kernel has the same verbs (except *sum, esse*) as the linking kernel, but they are in the active voice and pattern with two accusatives that are in a semantic relationship of X = Y or X becomes Y. Read these English examples.

> They made a teacher treasurer. (i.e., the teacher "=/becomes" treasurer.)
> They consider the water pure. (i.e., the water "=/seems" pure.)
> They call the agreement a fraud. (i.e., the agreement "=/is called" a fraud.)

A factitive kernel has items with these functions:

> subject—verb—direct object—*object complement*

Just as the two nominatives in a linking kernel may be ambiguous as to function, so also the two accusatives in a factitive kernel may cause ambiguity. *Necessitūdō timidōs fortēs facit* has a factitive kernel and means either "Necessity makes the timid brave," or "Necessity makes the brave timid," according to the sense required by the context. The absence of a connector prevents this from meaning "A crisis produces timid *and* brave men."

It should be remembered that *facit* and the active form of the other verbs on the list above (see p. 98) also occur in simple transitive kernels. For example, *Necessitūdō fortēs facit* (Necessity makes brave people).

Metaphrasing

If one wishes to indicate clearly that two accusatives have raised the expectation of a factitive kernel, it is useful to metaphrase the two accusatives as "_____ (to be/become) _____ ." For example, *Caesarem ducem* can be metaphrased "_____ _____s Caesar (to be) leader," as in "They consider Caesar (to be) leader."

Kernel Information

Oculī sunt in amōre ducēs. (S10.1)

Item: Function	Item: Function	Item: Function	Kernel Type	Name
oculī: subj.	sunt: verb	ducēs: subj. compl.	linking	statement

Necessitūdō etiam timidōs fortēs facit. (S10.3)

Item: Function	Item: Function	Item: Function	Kernel Type	Name
necessitūdō: subj.	timidōs: dir. obj. fortēs: obj. compl.	facit: verb	factitive	statement

■ Exercise 2

Metaphrase each of the following sets of items according to the kernel type indicated. Signal a linking verb by the word *equal(s)* or the equal sign. Look at the example given.

	Kernel Type	Metaphrase
lupus virum	trans. active	Wolf _____s man.
1. vir lupus	linking	
2. vir lupus	linking	
3. īra sapientēs stultōs	factitive	
4. vir canem	trans. active	
5. dī hominēs	linking	
6. dī hominēs	linking	
7. dī hominēs	trans. active	
8. fortem timidum necessitūdō	factitive	

■ Exercise 3

Identify the kernels as transitive active or factitive.

1. Vir fēminam appellat.

2. Fēmina lupum crūdēlem habet.

3. Occāsiō facit fūrem.

4. Occāsiō fūrem philosophum facit.

5. Vīnum philosophus tenet.

6. Vīnum philosophus vītam tenet.

Part of Speech: Pronoun

In lesson 7 the pronoun *is, ea, id* was introduced. This pronoun belongs to a group called *demonstrative pronouns*. Two other demonstrative pronouns are *hic, haec, hoc* (this) and *ille, illa, illud* (that). *Hic* and *ille* have the same syntax as *is, ea, id*. If a form of *hic, haec, hoc* appears with a noun-head it must be translated as "this," e.g., *haec ratiō* means "this reason." Likewise, forms of *ille, illa, illud* must be translated as "that," e.g., *illa ratiō* means "that reason."

   Hic, haec, hoc without a noun-head can have various translations: "this one," "this man/woman/thing," or "he/she/it." *Ille, illa, illud* without a noun-head can be translated "that one," "that man/woman/thing," or "he/she/it." The paradigms are as follows.

	Masculine	Feminine	Neuter
Singular			
Nominative	**hic**	**haec**	**hoc**
Accusative	**hunc**	**hanc**	**hoc**
Ablative	**hōc**	**hāc**	**hōc**
Dative	huic	huic	huic
Genitive	hujus	hujus	hujus
Plural			
Nominative	**hī**	**hae**	**haec**
Accusative	**hōs**	**hās**	**haec**
Ablative	**hīs**	**hīs**	**hīs**
Dative	hīs	hīs	hīs
Genitive	hōrum	hārum	hōrum

	Masculine	Feminine	Neuter
Singular			
Nominative	**ille**	**illa**	**illud**
Accusative	**illum**	**illam**	**illud**
Ablative	**illō**	**illā**	**illō**
Dative	illī	illī	illī
Genitive	illīus	illīus	illīus
Plural			
Nominative	**illī**	**illae**	**illa**
Accusative	**illōs**	**illās**	**illa**
Ablative	**illīs**	**illīs**	**illīs**
Dative	illīs	illīs	illīs
Genitive	illōrum	illārum	illōrum

■ Exercise 4

Identify each of these demonstrative pronouns by case, number, and gender.

1. haec

2. haec

3. haec

4. ille

5. illōs

6. eā

7. ea

8. ea

9. ea

10. illā

■ Exercise 5
Metaphrase each of the following.

1. illa ars

2. illam

3. hōs ducēs

4. hī

5. illa castra

6. illa castra

Semantically, *hic* has the feature "near, in time or place" and *ille* has the feature "removed." They are similar to English "this" and "that," e.g., *haec domus* (this house [here]), but *illa domus* (that house [there]).

When *hic* and *ille* appear as a pair in a passage, *hic* can often be translated "the latter" and *ille* can be translated "the former."

Lesson Vocabulary

Nouns
dux, ducis, m.: leader
necessitūdō, necessitūdinis, f.: necessity
oculus, oculī, m.: eye

Pronouns
hic, haec, hoc: this; he, she, it, they; the latter
ille, illa, illud: that; he, she, it, they; the former

Adjectives
brevis, breve: short
longus, longa, longum: long
sapiēns (sapientis): wise
timidus, timida, timidum: timid

Indeclinable
Intensifier
etiam: even, also

Verbs
appellō, appellāre, appellāvī, appellātus, -a, -um: call; name
fīō, fierī, factus, -a, -um: be made, become, happen
vocō, vocāre, vocāvī, vocātus, -a, -um: call

Readings

Required

10.1. Celtae linguā Latīnā Gallī appellantur.—Caesar
10.2. Crūdēlem medicum intemperāns aeger facit.—Publilius Syrus
10.3. Īra furor brevis est.—Horace
10.4. Dē sapientī virō facit īra virum stultum.—Medieval
10.5. Omne initium est difficile.—Anon.

Vocabulary

10.1. Celtae, Celtārum, m. pl.: Celts
lingua, linguae, f.: tongue, language
Latīnus, Latīna, Latīnum: Latin
Gallī, Gallōrum, m. pl.: Gauls
10.2. *medicus, medicī, m.: doctor
intemperāns (intemperantis): intemperate
aeger, aegra, aegrum: sick
10.3. furor, furōris, m.: rage, madness
10.5. initium, initiī, n.: beginning
difficilis, difficile: difficult

Optional

10.6. Senectūs est morbus.—Terence (adapted)
10.7. Nōbilitās sōla est atque ūnica virtūs.—Juvenal
10.8. Fortūna caeca est.—Cicero (adapted)
10.9. In fugā foeda mors est; in victōriā, glōriōsa.—Cicero
10.10. Nihil sub sōle novum.—Ecclesiastes
10.11. Omnibus in rēbus gravis est inceptiō prīma.—Anon.

Vocabulary

10.6. senectūs, senectūtis, f.: old age
*morbus, morbī, m.: illness
10.7. nōbilitās, nōbilitātis, f.: nobility
sōlus, sōla, sōlum: only, alone
atque (coord. conj.): and
ūnicus, ūnica, ūnicum: one, sole
virtūs, virtūtis, f.: virtue
10.8. caecus, caeca, caecum: blind
10.9. fuga, fugae, f.: flight
foedus, foeda, foedum: disgraceful
mors, mortis, f.: death
victōria, victōriae, f.: victory
glōriōsus, glōriōsa, glōriōsum: glorious
10.10. nihil, n. (indecl. noun): nothing
sōl, sōlis, m.: sun
10.11. gravis, grave: hard
inceptiō, inceptiōnis, f.: beginning
prīmus, prīma, prīmum: first

Word Study: English Derivatives

From Lesson	**Latin**
1. appellation	
2. brief	
3. duke	
4. necessary	
5. ocular	

From Readings	**Latin**
1. difficult	
2. factitive	
3. initial	
4. linguist	
5. temperate	

Summary Tasks

____ 1. Name the five kernel types that have occurred so far.
____ 2. Name the syntactic functions you expect to be filled in a factitive kernel.
____ 3. Name the syntactic functions you expect to be filled in a linking kernel.
____ 4. Copy the kernels of all Readings in this lesson.
____ 5. Copy each adjective-noun construction in R10.1, 10.3, 10.4, 10.5.
____ 6. What expectations are raised by the first word in R10.4 and 10.5?

Lesson 11

Dependent Clauses
Dependent Clauses as Adverbial Modifiers

So far, whenever there has been a sentence with more than one clause, the clauses have been connected to each other in one of two ways.

1. by a connector such as *et*, as in *Fūrem fūr cognōscit et lupum lupus,* or
2. by a comma, as in *Prūdēns cum cūrā, stultus sine cūrā vīvit*

In sentences such as these, the clauses are *coordinate clauses,* that is, they are on the same level. This lesson introduces sentences in which the clauses are *not* on the same level; one is a *dependent clause.*

Basic Sentences

11.1. Hominēs, dum docent, discunt.—Seneca
      People learn while they teach.
11.2. Ut fragilis glaciēs, interit īra morā.—Ovid
      Anger dies down with time just as perishable ice melts.
11.3. Postquam Crassus carbō factus, Carbō crassus factus est.—Terence
      After Crassus became ashes, Carbo became fat (i.e., rich).
      (Crassus was the name of a rich man; his heir's name was Carbo. After Crassus died and was cremated, Carbo became rich.)

Dependent Clauses

S11.1 (*Hominēs, dum docent, discunt*) is an example of a sentence that has clauses that are *not* all on the same level, i.e., they are not all equal. Such sentences have a *main clause,* e.g., *hominēs discunt,* and one or more *dependent clauses,* e.g., *dum docent.*

Note: Main clauses are also called *independent clauses* and dependent clauses are also called *subordinate clauses.*

An understanding of the different semantic and syntactic roles and relationships of dependent clauses is as important for the reader as an understanding of the basic kernel. Only with this understanding can one learn to read the prose of an author such as Cicero, one of whose sentences may cover a whole page and may include numerous clauses dependent upon each other and upon the main clause.

This lesson introduces dependent clauses that function as adverbial modifiers. These are marked by *subordinating conjunctions.* Because of their role in marking clauses, subordinating conjunctions will be referred to as *clause markers* in this course.

Subordinating Conjunctions

The number of subordinating conjunctions is not very large. In English they come first in the dependent clause. In Latin, however, they do not always come first in the clause. One or more words of the clause may precede them.

Several of the most common Latin clause markers, e.g., *ut* and *cum,* have more than one English equivalent and therefore set up a variety of semantic expectations for the dependent clause. Here is a partial list of clause markers. Additional English equivalents of these, as well as additional clause markers, will be introduced in later lessons.

Latin Word	*English Equivalent*
cum	when
dum	while
postquam	after
quia	because
quod	because
sī	if
ubi	when
ubi	where
ut	when
ut	as

■ Exercise 1
Circle all clause markers and underline the dependent clauses in this English version of a well-known ancient fable.

The Lion and the Mouse

While a lion was sleeping in his den one day, a mischievous mouse ran across the outstretched paw and up the royal nose of the king of beasts and awakened him. The mighty beast, as he clapped his paw upon the frightened little creature, almost made an end of him.

"Please," squealed the mouse, "don't kill me. If you will forgive me this time, I'll never forget it; a day may come when I may do you a good turn to repay your kindness." The lion, because he was amused by such a thought, let him go.

Not long afterward the lion, while he was ranging the forest for his prey, was caught in a net placed by hunters to catch him. He let out a loud roar and the mouse heard it, and because he recognized the voice of his former benefactor and friend, he ran to the spot and saw him lying tangled in the net of ropes.

"Well, your majesty," said the mouse, "I know you didn't believe me when I promised to return your kindness, but here is my chance." And because he began immediately to nibble at the net, the lion was soon able to crawl out of the hunters' snare and be free.

Dependent Clauses as Adverbial Modifiers

Syntax

The Basic Sentences and Readings in this lesson consist of a main clause and one or more dependent clauses, each with a clause marker. The dependent clauses, *dum docent* and *ut fragilis glaciēs* ∅ = *interit* (from S11.1 and 11.2), have a kernel of their own and the main clause is complete without them. They are syntactically equivalent to other adverbial modifiers, e.g., prepositional phrases or adverbs. The dependent clause in the sentence "People learn *while they teach*" corresponds syntactically to prepositional phrases such as "from teaching" or "by teaching" in the simple sentences "People learn from teaching" or "People learn by teaching."

Note: In contrast to the term *simple sentence*, the term *complex sentence* is often used for a sentence that has dependent clauses.

The position of the adverbial clause within the sentence is relatively free. It may come before or after the main clause or it may interrupt it. Moreover, it may interrupt another dependent clause. The only restriction universal to all languages is that the interrupting clause must be completed before the interrupted clause continues to its own completion. The main clause may *not* interrupt a dependent clause.

Possible
Hominēs, *dum docent*, discunt.
Dum docent, hominēs discunt.
Hominēs discunt, *dum docent*.

Not Possible
Dum, hominēs discunt, *docent*.

Semantics

The semantic categories of adverbial clauses correspond to those of other adverbial modifiers. Some of the clause markers clearly indicate one category, others have several possible interpretations.

A clause with the marker *quod* (because) or *quia* (because) expresses cause. Traditionally it is called a *causal clause;* for example, *Hominēs*, quod *docent*, discunt (People learn *because* they teach). These clauses answer the question *cūr?* (why?).

Sī (if) indicates that the clause expresses a condition; for example, *Hominēs*, sī *docent*, discunt (People learn *if* they teach). The *sī* clause traditionally is called a *conditional clause*. The question word for a conditional clause is *quā condiciōne?* (under what condition?).

Postquam (after) as in S11.3 indicates that the clause expresses time. Clauses expressing time traditionally are called *temporal clauses*. In S11.3 the *postquam* clause is a temporal clause.

Ut (as, when) is the most common clause marker in Latin and *ut* clauses have a number of possible meanings and interpretations. This lesson introduces *ut* in *clauses of comparison* and in *temporal clauses*. It is not always easy to determine the semantic category. Consider, for example, *Hominēs*, ut *docent*, discunt.

Comparative: People learn *just as* they teach (i.e., in the same manner as).
Temporal: People learn *when* they teach.

Ubi marks a *clause of place* (where) or a *temporal clause* (when). *Ubi* (when) could replace *postquam* in S11.3. *Dum* in S11.1 marks a *temporal clause*.

Ø or the Gap

Any item, whether kernel part or modifier, may be gapped across clause boundaries. For example, *Hominēs, dum docent, discunt* equals *Hominēs, dum Ø = hominēs docent, discunt*.

Kernel Information

Dependent clauses appear in the following way on a kernel chart. M/D represents main or dependent clause. The last column gives the traditional grammatical name or label of the construction or clause, e.g., statement, question, temporal clause, conditional clause, etc. Lessons to this point have included only statements or questions.

Clause Marker	Item: Function	Item: Function	Item: Function	Kernel Type	M/D	Name
—	hominēs: subject	discunt: verb	—	IA	M	statement
dum	Ø = hominēs: subject	docent: verb	—	IA	D	temporal clause

■ Exercise 2
Copy the kernels from S11.2 (*Ut fragilis glaciēs, interit īra morā*).

Clause Marker	Item: Function	Item: Function	Item: Function	Kernel Type	M/D	Name
1.						
2.						

■ Exercise 3
Copy all modifiers from the Basic Sentences of this lesson onto this modifier chart. Complete the chart. Include semantic information about adverbial modifiers. S11.1 is provided as an example.

Sentence Number	Modifier	Description	Syntactic Information		Semantic Information	Head
			Adverbial	Adjectival		
11.1.	dum docent	dependent cl.	X		temporal	discunt
11.2.						
11.2.						
11.2.						
11.3.						

Metaphrasing

A clause marker stands at the beginning of a clause in English, although this is not always so in Latin.

Because any metaphrase begins with the expectation of a main kernel, i.e., "_____ _____s ± _____," an adverbial clause generally follows. The position of the clause in the final translation depends on other considerations, such as content, style, and emphasis. Look at the cumulative metaphrase of S11.1.

Hominēs, dum docent, discunt.

Item	Part of Speech and Form	Syntactic Information	Cumulative Metaphrase
hominēs	noun: nominative, plural	kernel item: subject	People _____ ± _____ .
dum	subordinating conjunction	clause marker	People _____ ± _____ while _____ _____s ± _____ .
docent	verb: third plural, active	kernel item: verb	People _____ ± _____ while _____s teach ± _____ .
discunt	verb: third plural, active	kernel item: verb	People learn ± _____ while _____s teach ± _____ .

The final metaphrase is "People learn while ∅ = people teach."

Possible translations: "People learn while they teach."
"People, while they teach, learn."
"While they teach, people learn."

■ Exercise 4

Metaphrase each of the following in the context of a complete sentence. Follow the example.

dum īra: _____ _____s ± _____ while anger _____s ± _____ .
 or While anger _____s ± _____ , _____ _____s ± _____ .

1. cum fēminīs

2. cum fēminās

3. postquam Caesar prōdūxit

4. puer canisque

5. ut fortūna

6. ut fortūna

7. ab illō fonte

■ Exercise 5

Complete each sentence by underlining the word or words that could fill the blank.

1. Dī parva neglegunt ____ parva levēs capiunt animōs: dum, magnō, sed, omnem

2. Hominēs ____ saepe dūcuntur: fortūnam, ratiōne, ā stultō, illōs

3. ____ ars longa, vīta brevis est: ab, ut, facere, cum

4. Natūra ____ habētur: ubi, crūdēlis, agrōs, dīvīna

■ Exercise 6

Two original passages from Julius Caesar's famous account of the Gallic War are given. They show how one Latin sentence may include a number of coordinate and dependent clauses and how one clause may interrupt another.

Circle each clause marker and put a number over it. Put the same number over the verb that is a kernel item *in that same clause.* Caution: These passages include much that has not yet been studied in this course, and a translation should not be attempted.

1. Exiguā parte aestātis reliquā, Caesar, (etsī)¹ in hīs locīs, (quod)² Gallia ad septentriōnēs vergit,² mātūrae sunt¹ hiemēs, tamen in Britanniam proficīscī contendit, quia omnibus ferē Gallicīs bellīs hostibus nostrīs inde subministrāta auxilia intellegēbat et, sī tempus annī ad bellum gerendum dēficeret, tamen magnō sibi ūsuī fore arbitrābātur, sī modo īnsulam adīsset.

2. Caesar questus quod cum in continentem lēgātīs missīs pācem ab sē petīssent bellum sine causā intulissent, īgnōscere imprūdentiae dīxit obsidēsque imperāvit.

Lesson Vocabulary

Nouns
Carbō, Carbōnis, m.: Carbō
carbō, carbōnis, m.: charcoal
condiciō, condiciōnis, f.: condition
Crassus, Crassī, m.: Crassus
glaciēs, glaciēī, f.: ice
mora, morae, f.: delay

Adjectives
crassus, crassa, crassum: fat, gross
fragilis, fragile: fragile, easily broken

Indeclinables
Subordinating Conjunctions
cum: when
dum: while

postquam: after
quia: because
quod: because
sī: if
ubi: when, where
ut: when, as

Question Words
cūr?: why?
quā condiciōne?: under what condition?

Verbs
discō, discere, didicī: learn
intereō, interīre, interiī: perish, die

Readings

Required

11.1. Ut vēr dat flōrem, studium sīc reddit honōrem.—Medieval
11.2. Sua multī āmittunt, cupidē dum aliēna appetunt.—Anon.
11.3. Sī caecus caecum dūcit, ambō cadunt.—Anon.
11.4. Thāida Quīntus amat. Quam Thāida? Thāida luscam.
      Ūnum oculum Thāis nōn habet; ille duōs.—Martial
11.5. Nēmō . . . patriam quia magna est amat, sed quia sua.—Seneca
11.6. Dum fēlēs dormit, mūs gaudet.—Medieval

Vocabulary

11.1. vēr, vēris, n.: spring
    flōs, flōris, m.: flower
    studium, studiī, n.: study
    sīc (adv.): thus, so
    reddō, reddere, reddidī, redditus, -a, -um: give back, return
    honor, honōris, m.: esteem, honor
11.2. suus, sua, suum: (in this sentence) "their own"
    cupidē (adv.): eagerly
    aliēnus, aliēna, aliēnum: belonging to another
    appetō, appetere, appetīvī, appetītus, -a, -um: grasp at, seek
11.3. caecus, caeca, caecum: blind
    ambō, ambae, ambō: both
    cadō, cadere, cecidī, cāsūrus, -a, -um: fall
11.4. Thāida: accusative of the Greek name Thāis
    quam Thāida?: "which Thais?"
    luscus, lusca, luscum: one-eyed
11.5. nēmō, nēminis, m. & f.: no one
    patria, patriae, f.: country, homeland
11.6. fēlēs, fēlis, f.: cat
    mūs, mūris, m. & f.: mouse
    gaudeō, gaudēre: rejoice, play

Optional

11.7. Mulier rēctē olet, ubi nihil olet.—Plautus
11.8. Saepe potēns justum premit ut rapidus lupus agnum.—Anon.
11.9. Dum vītant stultī vitia, in contrāria currunt.—Horace
11.10. Tua rēs agitur, pariēs cum proximus ārdet.—Horace
    (Note: *agitur* here means "is in danger")

Vocabulary

11.7. mulier, mulieris, f.: woman
    nihil (indecl.): not at all
    oleō, olēre, oluī: smell

11.8. potēns (potentis): powerful
jūstus, jūsta, jūstum: just
rapidus, rapida, rapidum: grabby, greedy, swift
*agnus, agnī, m.: lamb

11.9. vītō, vītāre, vītāvī, vītātus, -a, -um: avoid, evade
contrārius, contrāria, contrārium: opposite
currō, currere, cucurrī: run

11.10. tuus, tua, tuum: your own
pariēs, parietis, m.: wall
proximus, proxima, proximum: nearby, next
ārdeō, ārdēre, ārsī: burn, be in flames

Latin Questions

S11.1. Quō tempore hominēs discunt?

S11.3. Quālis Carbō factus est?

R11.1. Quō modō studium reddit honōrem?

R11.3. Quā condiciōne ambō cadunt?

R11.5. Cūr homō patriam amat?

Word Study: English Derivatives

From Lesson	Latin	From Readings	Latin
1. carbon		1. alien	
2. disciple		2. ambiguous	
3. discipline		3. appetite	
4. docile		4. Florida	
5. fragment		5. florist	
6. glacier		6. olfactory	
7. ire		7. patriotic	
8. moratorium		8. studious	

Narrative Reading

Hercules and the Serpents

Note: Before reading this story, review the Narrative in lesson 9.

Iphiclēs, frāter Herculis,[1] magnā vōce exclāmāvit; at Herculēs, puer fortis parvīs manibus serpentēs statim cēpit collaque magnā vī compressit. Serpentēs ā puerō interfectae sunt. Māter Alcmēna, ubi clāmōrem audīvit, patrem Amphytriōnem ē somnō excitāvit. Pater, postquam lūmen accendit et gladium rapuit, ad puerōs properāvit. In cubiculō rem mīram vīdit; Herculēs enim rīdēbat[2] et serpentēs mortuās mōnstrābat.[2]

Notes
1. *Herculis:* genitive case, "of Hercules"
2. *rīdēbat, mōnstrābat:* past imperfective tense with the morpheme {bă}, translate "was
   _____-ing"

Vocabulary
accendō, accendere, accendī, accēnsus, -a, -um: light, apply fire to
Amphytriō, Amphytriōnis, m.: Amphitrion (father of Hercules)
at (coordinating conjunction): but
clāmor, clāmōris, m.: cry, shout
collum, collī, n.: neck
comprimō, comprimere, compressī, compressus, -a, -um: press hard
cubiculum, cubiculī, n.: bedroom
enim (sentence connector): for
*excitō, excitāre, excitāvī, excitātus, -a, -um: wake, rouse
exclāmō, exclāmāre, exclāmāvī, exclāmātus, -a, -um: cry out
*frāter, frātris, m.: brother
gladius, gladiī, m.: sword
Herculēs, Herculis, m.: Hercules
*interficiō, interficere, interfēcī, interfectus, -a, -um: kill
Iphiclēs, Iphiclis, m.: Iphicles
lūmen, lūminis, n.: light, lamp
māter, mātris, f.: mother
mīrus, mīra, mīrum: amazing, wonderful
mōnstrō, mōnstrāre, mōnstrāvī, mōnstrātus, -a, -um: show
mortuus, mortua, mortuum: dead
pater, patris, m.: father
properō, properāre, properāvī, properātus, -a, -um: hasten, hurry
*rapiō, rapere, rapuī, raptus, -a, -um: seize, grab
*serpēns, serpentis, f.: snake
somnus, somnī, m.: sleep
statim (adv.): immediately
vīs (irreg. noun, abl. sing. *vī*): force, strength
vōx, vōcis, f.: voice, shout

Derivatives from Narrative Reading

Latin

1. auditorium

2. evidence

3. excited

4. exclaim

5. gladiator

6. illuminate

7. incendiary

8. miracle

Summary Tasks

_____ 1. Copy the sames connected by coordinating conjunctions in Basic Sentences 5.4, 6.3, 8.2, 9.3. See exercise 3 in lesson 2.

_____ 2. Complete a modifier chart (see exercise 3) for all the modifiers in these Readings: 11.1, 11.3, 11.5, 10.1, 10.4, 7.1, 7.2, 4.1, 4.2, 4.3, 4.4, 4.5.

_____ 3. What is the minimum number of kernels you must expect if the sentence contains a clause marker?

_____ 4. Name the part of speech to which clause markers belong.

_____ 5. Describe the adverbial modifiers that have occurred so far in this course.

_____ 6. Copy into your notebook, on a page labeled Clause Markers, all subordinating conjunctions together with the traditional names for the clauses which they introduce. Add to this list throughout the course.

Lesson 12

Adverbial Accusatives with Prepositions
Adverbial Accusatives without Prepositions

So far nouns in the accusative case have been kernel items in transitive and factitive kernels. In this lesson nouns and adjectives in the accusative case occur also as adverbial modifiers with and without prepositions.

Basic Sentences

12.1. Cōgitur ad lacrimās oculus, dum cor dolet intus.—Werner
   The eye is forced to tears while the heart aches inside.
12.2. Noctēs atque diēs patet jānua.—Vergil *Aeneid*
   The door stands open day and night. (Here *jānua* is the door to the underworld, i.e., to death.)
12.3. Multum lacrimās verba inter singula fundit.—Vergil *Aeneid*
   He weeps a great deal between every word. (Aeneas describes the emotions of Helenus, another exile from Troy, upon their unexpected reunion after many years of separation.)

Adverbial Accusatives with Prepositions

Here is a list of prepositions that pattern with an object in the accusative case. Words marked with an asterisk (*) may occur also as adverbs; see Lesson Vocabulary for meanings.

ad	to, toward (with verbs of motion), at (with other verbs)
ante*	in front of (with nouns of place), before (with nouns of time)
contrā*	against
extrā	outside of
in	into, onto
inter	between, among
intrā	within
ob	against, because of
per	through
post*	behind (with nouns of place), after (with nouns of time)
praeter	in addition to, except
prope	near
propter	because of
sub	under
super*	above, over
suprā*	above, over
trāns	across

Syntax

In S12.1 (*Cōgitur ad lacrimās oculus, dum cor dolet intus*) the main kernel is *cōgitur oculus*. This passive kernel is complete. The noun in the accusative *lacrimās* is not a kernel item, but is in the prepositional phrase *ad lacrimās*. Phrases consisting of preposition + accusative are adverbial modifiers, just like phrases consisting of preposition + ablative. There are, of course, two other adverbial modifiers in the sentence. The *dum* clause is a subordinate adverbial clause and *intus* is an adverb.

Semantics and Metaphrasing

The only prepositions + accusative that warrant special attention are *ad*, *ante* and *post*, *in* and *sub*. *Ad* is best metaphrased as "to _____" or "toward _____" in the environment of verbs with the semantic feature *motion*. In other environments it is best metaphrased as "at _____ ."

Ante and *post* are metaphrased "in front of _____" and "behind _____ ," respectively, with a noun that has the semantic feature *place*. With a noun with the semantic feature *time*, they are metaphrased as "before _____" and "after _____ ," respectively.

Metaphrasing the preposition *in* presents a different problem. Phrases consisting of *in* with the accusative appear with verbs that have the semantic feature *motion* and answer the question *quem ad locum?* or *quō?* (to/into what place?). A phrase consisting of *in* with the ablative answers the question *quō in locō?* or *ubi?* (at/in what place?). The common practice in English of using *in* and *on* for *into* and *onto* obscures this distinction.

The semantic difference between *sub* + the ablative and *sub* + the accusative does not show in English. For example, in English "somebody is swimming under the bridge" is ambiguous. In Latin, *sub* with the accusative indicates that the swimmer *is going to* a place under the bridge, but *sub* with the ablative indicates that he *is in* a place under the bridge.

Adverbial Accusatives without Prepositions

Syntax

In S12.2 (*Noctēs atque diēs patet jānua*) the kernel is *patet jānua*. This intransitive kernel is complete; the nouns *noctēs* and *diēs* are not kernel items but are adverbial accusatives *without* a preposition. *Multum* in S12.3 (*Multum lacrimās verba inter singula fundit*) is also accusative and an adverbial modifier. The kernel $\emptyset = Helenus\ lacrimās\ fundit$ is complete and *verba inter singula* is a prepositional phrase.

In the Required Readings there are several adverbial accusatives without prepositions. In R12.4 (*Domum reductus est Publius Scīpiō*) the kernel *reductus est Publius Scīpiō* is complete; therefore *domum* is an adverbial accusative. *Rōmam* in R12.5 is also an adverbial accusative; *elephantōs* is the direct object of the kernel.

Semantics

Noctēs and *diēs* have the semantic feature *time*. These and other time expressions, when used adverbially, answer the question *quam diū?* (how long?), for example, *multōs diēs* (for many days) and *multōs annōs* (for many years). Such expressions are traditionally named *accusative of time how long* or *accusative of duration of time*. Note the contrast with *ablative of time when*.

Multum (much) is an example of a small group of expressions, all with the semantic feature *degree*. They answer the question *quantum?* (how much/to what degree?). Other such expressions are as follows.

> nihil (not at all)
> plūrimum (very much, greatly)
> plūs (more)
> tantum (so much)

Another group of adverbial accusatives without prepositions contains selected expressions with the semantic feature *place;* they answer the question *quem ad locum?* (to what place/where to?). These expressions include proper names of cities, e.g., *Rōmam* and small islands, but not generic words such as *urbs* (city), *mōns* (mountain), etc. In addition to *domum* (home/homeward) as in R12.4, the words *rūs* (to the country) and *humum* (to the ground) are adverbial accusatives.

■ Exercise 1

Identify the italicized words as adverbial accusative or as a kernel item (direct object).

	Adverbial Accusative		
	with Prep.	without Prep.	Direct Object
1. Herculēs trāns *mare* Rōmam vēnit.	_____	_____	_____
2. Herculēs trāns mare *Rōmam* vēnit.	_____	_____	_____
3. Vir *multōs diēs* trāns mare fūgit.	_____	_____	_____
4. Puer *multa animālia* Rōmam dūxit.	_____	_____	_____
5. Helenus *multum* doluit.	_____	_____	_____
6. Hostēs *Rōmam* capere nōn potuērunt. (hostis, hostis "enemy")	_____	_____	_____

■ Exercise 2

Identify each of the italicized indeclinable words as adverb, preposition, or subordinating conjunction (clause marker). Then metaphrase each set of words in the context of a complete sentence.

	Identification	*Metaphrase*
1. *ante* urbem		
2. *ante* māter		
3. *saepe* puerum		
4. *cum* amīcus		
5. *cum* amīcō		
6. *sine* īrā		
7. *semper* multī		
8. *postquam* nox		
9. *post* mōram		
10. *post* nox		

Lesson Vocabulary

Nouns

annus, annī, m.: year
cor, cordis, n.: heart
domus, domūs, f.: home
jānua, jānuae, f.: door
nihil (indecl. noun), n.: nothing
Rōma, Rōmae, f.: (city of) Rome
urbs, urbis, f.: city
verbum, verbī, n.: word

Adjectives

singulī, singulae, singula: single
tantus, tanta, tantum: so great a,
    of such a size

Indeclinables
Adverbs

ante: before, previously
contrā: on the contrary, in turn
multum: much, greatly
nihil: not at all
plūrimum: very much, greatly
plūs: more
post: afterward
super: above; moreover, besides
suprā: above, over
tantum: so much, only

Prepositions

ad (+ acc.): to, toward
ante (+ acc.): in front of; before
contrā (+ acc.): against
extrā (+ acc.): outside of
in (+ acc.): into, onto
inter (+ acc.): between, among
intrā (+ acc.): within
ob (+ acc.): against; because of
per (+ acc.): through
post (+ acc.): behind; after
praeter (+ acc.): in addition to; except
prope (+ acc.): near
propter (+ acc.): because of
sub (+ acc., abl.): under
super (+ acc.): above, over
suprā (+ acc.): above, over
trāns (+ acc.): across

Coordinating Conjunction

atque: and

Question Words

quam diū?: how long?
quantum?: how greatly?
quō? quem ad locum?: where (to)?
    to what place?

Verbs

cōgō, cōgere, coēgī, coāctus, -a, -um: force, compel
doleō, dolēre, doluī: grieve
fundō, fundere, fūdī, fūsus, -a, -um: pour
pateō, patēre, patuī: stand open

Readings

Required

12.1. Inter caecōs rēgnat luscus.—Anon.
12.2. Post calamitātem memoria alia est calamitās.—Publilius Syrus
12.3. Silent . . . lēgēs inter arma.—Cicero
12.4. Domum reductus est Publius Scīpiō.—Eutropius
12.5. Curius Rōmam quattuor elephantōs dūcit.—Eutropius

Vocabulary

12.1. caecus, caeca, caecum: blind
    rēgnō, rēgnāre, rēgnāvī, rēgnātus, -a, -um: reign, rule
    luscus, lusca, luscum: one-eyed
12.2. calamitās, calamitātis, f.: disaster
    memoria, memoriae, f.: memory
    alius, alia, aliud: other, another
12.3. sileō, silēre, siluī: be silent
    arma, armōrum, n. pl.: arms, weapons
12.4. redūcō, redūcere, redūxī, reductus, -a, -um: lead back
12.5. elephantus, elephantī, m.: elephant

Optional

12.6. Post jactūram quis nōn sapit?—Anon.
12.7. Interdum stabulum reparātur post grave damnum.—Medieval
12.8. Equus parātur ad bellum, sed ā Dominō victōria datur.—Proverbs

Vocabulary

12.6. jactūra, jactūrae, f.: loss
    sapiō, sapere, sapīvī: be wise
12.7. interdum (adv.): sometimes
    stabulum, stabulī, n.: stable
    reparō, reparāre, reparāvī, reparātus, -a, -um: repair
    gravis, grave: heavy, serious
    damnum, damnī, n.: loss
12.8. equus, equī, m.: horse
    parō, parāre, parāvī, parātus, -a, -um: prepare, get ready
    bellum, bellī, n.: war
    Dominus, Dominī, m.: Lord, God
    victōria, victōriae, f.: victory

Latin Questions

S12.1. Quid patitur oculus?

S12.1. Quō cōgitur oculus?

S12.2. Quam diū patet jānua?

S12.3. Quantum lacrimās Helenus fundit?

R12.4. Quō Scīpiō reductus est?

R12.5. Quem ad locum Curius elephantōs dūcit?

Word Study: English Derivatives

From Lesson	Latin	From Readings	Latin
1. cogent		1. alias	
2. condolence		2. alibi	
3. janitor		3. belligerent	
4. patent		4. equestrian	
5. refund		5. intermission	
6. singular		6. postdate	
7. verbal		7. postpone	
8. verbose		8. reparation	

Narrative Reading

Herculēs Adulēscēns

Herculēs adulēscēns in urbe Thēbīs habitāvit. Rēx Creōn magnīs honōribus Herculem decorāvit; fīliam suam eī[1] in mātrimōnium dedit. Post paucōs annōs Herculēs in furōrem incidit, atque līberōs suōs occīdit. Post breve tempus reductus est ad sānitātem, sed propter illud crīmen magnō dolōre affectus est. Itaque ad ōrāculum Delphicum properāvit. Ibi sacerdōs, postquam cōnsilium cēpit, Herculem mīsit ad rēgem Eurystheum. Multōs annōs in servitūte ab Eurystheō Herculēs tenēbātur.[2] Eurystheus duodecim labōrēs eī[3] imperāvit. Sīc Herculēs tantum crīmen expiāre potuit.

Notes
1. *eī:* pronoun, dative case, "to him"
2. *tenēbātur:* past imperfective passive; the morpheme {bǎ} indicates action repeated or continuous in past time; translate "was held"
3. *eī:* pronoun, dative case, "upon him"

Vocabulary

adulēscēns (adulēscentis): young; as a noun, m. & f., young man, young woman

*afficiō, afficere, affēcī, affectus, -a, -um: affect

Creōn, Creōnis, m.: Creon, king of Thebes

crīmen, crīminis, n.: crime

decorō, decorāre, decorāvī, decorātus, -a, -um: decorate, honor

Delphicus, Delphica, Delphicum: Delphic, of Delphi (a city in Greece)

*dolor, dolōris, m.: grief, sorrow

duodecim (indecl. numeral adj.): twelve

expiō, expiāre, expiāvī, expiātus, -a, -um: atone for, make amends for

fīlia, fīliae, f.: daughter

furor, furōris, m.: madness, rage

honor, honōris, m.: honor

ibi (adv.): there, in that place

imperō, imperāre, imperāvī, imperātus, -a, -um: impose, order

incidō, incidere, incidī: fall into

*labor, labōris, m.: toil, work

līberī, līberōrum, m. pl.: children

mātrimōnium, mātrimōniī, n.: marriage

occīdō, occīdere, occīdī, occīsus, -a, -um: kill

ōrāculum, ōrāculī, n.: oracle

paucī, paucae, pauca (pl. only): few

properō, properāre, properāvī: hasten

redūcō, redūcere, redūxī, reductus, -a, -um: bring back, lead back

rēx, rēgis, m.: king

sacerdōs, sacerdōtis, m. & f.: priest, priestess (as in this Narrative Reading)

sānitās, sānitātis, f.: sanity

servitūs, servitūtis, f.: slavery

sīc: thus, so, in this way

tantus, tanta, tantum: such great, so great

Thēbae, Thēbārum, f. pl.: Thebes (a city in Greece)

Derivatives from Narrative Reading

Latin

1. accidental

2. adolescent

3. annual

4. criminal

5. decorate

6. imperative

7. matrimony

8. multiply

Summary Tasks

____ 1. Describe the adverbial modifiers that have occurred so far in this course.

____ 2. Copy the kernels of the Basic Sentences of this lesson.

____ 3. Rewrite the verbs in the present perfective tense: R12.1, 12.2, 12.3, 12.5.

____ 4. Copy the adverbial modifiers that occur in the Narrative Reading of this lesson and give the traditional name of each one.

____ 5. Copy into your notebook, on a page labeled Prepositions + Accusative, all the prepositions in this lesson. Add to this list throughout the course.

____ 6. Write the paradigm, singular and plural (nominative, accusative, ablative) of these noun-adjective pairs:

a. hic, haec, hoc + verbum, verbī, n.

b. ille, illa, illud + urbs, urbis, f.

c. is, ea, id + annus, annī, m.

Lesson 13

Relative Pronouns
Relative Clauses as Adjectival Modifiers
Relative Clauses as Noun Equivalents

There are three types of dependent clauses: adverbial, adjectival, and noun (also called nominal). Lesson 11 introduced clauses as adverbial modifiers. This lesson introduces *relative clauses* as *adjectival modifiers* and as *noun equivalents*. The clause markers in these are *relative pronouns*.

Basic Sentences

13.1. Condidit urbem Rōmulus quam ex nōmine suō Rōmam vocāvit.—Eutropius
   Romulus founded a city which he called Rome from his own name.
13.2. Nīl agit exemplum, lītem quod līte resolvit.—Horace
   An explanation which answers one question by asking another accomplishes nothing.
13.3. Cito fit quod dī volunt.—Petronius
   What the gods want happens quickly.
13.4. Semper inops quīcumque cupit.—Claudian
   Whoever wants more is always poor.

Relative Pronouns

Morphology

The relative pronoun in English has the following forms: who, whom, whose, which, that. The relative pronoun in Latin has the following paradigm.

	Masculine	Feminine	Neuter
Singular			
Nominative	quī	quae	quod
Accusative	quem	quam	quod
Ablative	quō	quā	quō
Dative	cui	cui	cui
Genitive	cujus	cujus	cujus
Plural			
Nominative	quī	quae	quae
Accusative	quōs	quās	quae
Ablative	quibus	quibus	quibus
Dative	quibus	quibus	quibus
Genitive	quōrum	quārum	quōrum

Relative Clauses as Adjectival Modifiers

Syntax

Most relative clauses are syntactic equivalents of adjectives in that they both modify noun-heads. The two-kernel complex sentence "The teacher needs the chart which is new," corresponds to the one-kernel simple sentence, "The teacher needs the new chart." The relative clause "which is new" and the adjective "new" both modify the noun "chart," and can substitute for each other.

■ Exercise 1
Rewrite, on the basis of the model provided, each of the following sentences.

He needs the *old edition:* He needs the edition *which is old.*

1. I love *green apples.*

2. *Green apples* make me sick.

3. She is disturbed by *loud music.*

4. The remarks of the *new teacher* are interesting.

Like any adjectival modifier, the adjectival relative clause has a noun-head. It is outside the relative clause but inside the main clause. The noun-head is called the *antecedent* of the relative pronoun.

A relative clause, like any clause, has a kernel and, possibly, modifiers. The relative pronoun may be a kernel item or a modifier in the relative clause as indicated by its case. Compare the relative pronouns in these sentences.

1. Vir *quem fēmina videt* gladiātor est.
   The man *whom the woman sees* is a gladiator.
2. Vir *quī ā fēmina vidētur* gladiātor est.
   The man *who is seen by the woman* is a gladiator.
3. Vir *ā quō fēmina vidētur* gladiātor est.
   The man *by whom the woman is seen* is a gladiator.

The relative clause is italicized in each sentence. In sentence 1 the pronoun *quem* (whom) in the accusative case is the direct object of *videt* in the relative clause. In sentence 2 the pronoun *quī* (who) in the nominative case is the subject of *vidētur* in the relative clause. In sentence 3 the pronoun *quō* in the ablative case is the object of the preposition in the prepositional phrase *ā quō.* This is an adverbial modifier in the relative clause. The antecedent in each sentence is *vir* (man).

Relative pronouns, like all pronouns, take their gender and number from the noun that they replace. For the reader, this means that the relative pronoun in an adjectival clause will have the same number and gender as the antecedent. The reader should not expect the case of the antecedent and relative pronoun to be the same. In S13.1 *quam* is accusative and direct object of the factitive kernel. In the relative clause of S13.2 *lītem quod līte resolvit,* the pronoun *quod* is nominative and subject of the transitive kernel.

■ Exercise 2

Circle the English and Latin relative pronouns. Underline the relative clause in each English and Latin sentence. Follow the example.

Rōmulus, ā ⓠuō urbs condita est, urbem amāvit.

Rōmulus, by ⓦhom a city was founded, loved the city.

1. Rōmulus urbem quam condidit amāvit.

   Romulus loved the city which he founded.

2. Urbs Rōma vocāta est ā Rōmulō quī urbem condidit.

   The city was called Rome by Romulus who founded the city.

3. Rōmulus urbem quae condita est amāvit.

   Romulus loved the city which was founded.

4. Urbs quam Rōmulus condidit Rōma vocāta est.

   The city which Romulus founded was called Rome.

■ Exercise 3

Identify the case, number, and gender of the antecedent and of the relative pronoun in the Latin sentences in exercise 2.

1. urbem

   quam

2. Rōmulō

   quī

3. urbem

   quae

4. urbs

   quam

Note: Although a metaphrase for the sentence *Rōmulus urbem quam condidit amāvit* is "Romulus loved the city which he founded," idiomatic English prefers "Romulus loved the city he founded." English can delete the relative pronoun if it is the direct object of its own clause; Latin can not.

Kernel Information

The relative pronoun is a kernel item of its own clause if it is the subject or direct object. Whether it is or is not a kernel item, a relative pronoun is *always* a clause marker.

■ Exercise 4

Copy all kernels of sentences 2, 3, and 4 in exercise 2. Sentence 1 is used as an example.

Clause Marker	Item: Function	Item: Function	Item: Function	Kernel Type	M/D	Name
1. —	Rōmulus: subject	urbem: dir. obj.	amāvit: verb	TA	M	statement
1. quam	quam: dir. obj.	condidit: verb	Ø = Rōmulus: subject	TA	D	rel. cl.
2.						
2.						
3.						
3.						
4.						
4.						

Now list the sentences in which the relative pronoun is a kernel part. _____

Metaphrasing

In contrast to adverbial clauses, the position of adjectival relative clauses in English is not free, but restricted by the rules of English word order. Adjectival relative clauses follow their noun-head, i.e., their antecedent. In English the relative pronoun starts the clause regardless of whether it is a kernel part or an adverbial modifier. This is not so in Latin, as can be seen in the word order of the relative clause in S13.2 *lītem quod līte resolvit*, where a word belonging to the relative clause precedes the clause marker *quod*. Look at the metaphrase example.

Rōmulus quem Rōmānī amāvērunt Rōmam condidit.

Item	Part of Speech and Form	Syntactic Information	Cumulative Metaphrase
Rōmulus	noun: nom., sing., m.	subject	Romulus ____s ± ____ .
quem	rel. pro.: acc., sing., m.	clause marker and direct object	Romulus whom (subject) (verb)s ____s ____.
Rōmānī	noun: nom., pl., m.	subject	Romulus whom the Romans (verb) ____s ± ____ .
amāvērunt	verb: third, pl., pres. perf., act.	verb	Romulus whom the Romans loved ____s ± ____ .
Rōmam	noun: acc., sing., f.	direct object	Romulus whom the Romans loved ____s Rome.
condidit	verb: third, sing., pres. perf., act.	verb	Romulus whom the Romans loved founded Rome.

Important: Note that in English the relative pronoun comes first in its own clause, even if it is a direct object in that clause. This is a notable exception to the English subject—verb—object word order.

■ Exercise 5

Metaphrase these items in the context of a complete sentence. Treat these as antecedent—relative pronoun pairs. Put parentheses around each relative clause and label each of the blanks in the relative clause.

　　　　mātrem quae: _____ _____s the mother (who <u>(verb)</u>s ± <u>(direct object)</u>)

1. māter quam

2. ā mātre quae

3. mātrem quam

4. māter ā quā

5. patrem quem

6. pater quem

7. pater ā quō

8. ā patre quī

Morphology: The Interrogative Adjective

Both English and Latin have interrogative adjectives as well as interrogative pronouns (see lesson 3 and Appendix p. 401). The interrogative adjective in English is "which _____ ?" or "what _____ ?" as in "*What book* does the teacher want?"

　　The paradigm of the interrogative adjective in Latin looks like that of the relative pronoun. An adjectival relative clause is elicited by the interrogative adjective plus noun-head. For example, in English, "Which man is the gladiator?" can be answered by "The man whom the woman sees." In Latin *Quī vir gladiātor est?* can be answered by *Vir quem fēmina videt.*

　　Many of the Latin question words consist of the interrogative adjective plus noun-head:

　　quō tempore?
　　quō ā/dē/ē locō?
　　quem ad/in locum?
　　quō modō?
　　quā condiciōne?

Relative Clauses as Noun Equivalents

Not all relative clauses function as adjectival modifiers. Some of them, like adjectives, have no definite noun-head, either expressed or understood, and are therefore the syntactic equivalent of nouns. They are called *noun relative clauses*. Semantically, the absence of a noun-head means the absence of definiteness. For this reason they are sometimes also called *indefinite relative clauses*. Consider these sentences in English.

1. *Whoever helped the children* will get the reward.
2. The girl *who helped the children* will get the reward.

In the first sentence, the clause "whoever helped the children" is a noun relative clause that functions as the subject of "will get the reward." On the other hand, the clause "who helped the children" in the second sentence is not a kernel item but is an adjectival modifier of the noun-head "girl."

To the question "Who will get the reward?" the answer for sentence 1 is "whoever helped the children." The answer to the same question for sentence 2 is "the girl who helped the children." Semantically, the answer for the first sentence has the feature *indefiniteness* and the answer for the second has the feature *definiteness*. Compare these sentences.

Quī labōrem nōn fugit fortis est. (Whoever doesn't shun work is strong.)

The *qu-* clause in this sentence functions as subject of the main kernel, just as the *wh-* clause does in English.

Puer quī labōrem nōn fugit fortis est. (The boy who doesn't shun work is strong.)

The *qu-* clause in this sentence is an adjectival relative clause modifying the noun-head *puer*. In S13.3, *quod dī volunt* is a noun relative clause functioning as the subject of the main verb *fit. Quod* is the direct object in its own clause.

Indefinite Pronouns

Morphemes such as {soever} and {ever} on the English pronoun *whosoever* and *whatever* overtly indicate indefiniteness. In Latin {cumque} as in *quīcumque, quaecumque, quodcumque* is the most common morpheme for indefiniteness. In S13.4, therefore, the reader knows from morphological information that the clause *quīcumque cupit* is a noun clause, here functioning as subject of the sentence.

■ Exercise 6
Underline the noun relative clause in each English sentence. Identify the clause as subject or direct object of the main kernel.

1. Who steals my purse steals trash.

2. Many people dislike what they don't understand.

3. Whoever wins will be praised.

4. I will take my boots and whatever I need for hiking.

Kernel Information

Since the noun relative clause is the syntactic equivalent of a noun, the whole clause is to be treated as a single item in the main kernel. Like all dependent clauses it has a clause marker and kernel of its own as well.

From now on, kernel charts will include a column for indicating whether a dependent clause is an adjectival, adverbial, or noun clause. Look at the next chart for an example.

Quī labōrem nōn fugit fortis est.

Clause Marker	Item: Function	Item: Function	Item: Function	Kernel Type	M/D	Adj./Adv./ Noun	Name
quī	quī: subject	labōrem: dir. obj.	fugit: verb	TA	D	noun	noun rel. cl.
	quī labōrem fugit: subject	fortis: subj. compl.	est: verb	Lkg.	M	—	statement

■ Exercise 7

Copy the kernels from these sentences.

1. Semper inops quīcumque cupit. (There is a ∅ = *est* in the main clause.)
2. Citō fit quod dī volunt.

Clause Marker	Item: Function	Item: Function	Item: Function	Kernel Type	M/D	Adj./Adv./ Noun	Name
1.							
1.							
2.							
2.							

Note: In many readings the pronoun *is, ea, id* will occur with an indefinite relative clause. This corresponds to the indefinite *he, she, that,* etc., in English. For example, "*He who* steals my purse steals trash," or "Many people dislike *that which* they don't understand."

Lesson Vocabulary

Nouns

exemplum, exemplī, n.: example
līs, lītis, f.: quarrel, lawsuit
māter, mātris, f.: mother
nīl (contracted form of *nihil*), n.: nothing
nōmen, nōminis, n.: name
pater, patris, m.: father
Rōmulus, Rōmulī, m.: Romulus

Pronouns

quī, quae, quod: who, which, that
quīcumque, quaecumque, quodcumque
    (indef. pronoun): whoever, whatever, whichever

Adjectives
inops (inopis): poor, helpless
quī, quae, quod?: which? what?
suus, sua, suum: his/her/its own, their own

Indeclinable
Adverb
cito: quickly

Question Words
quī, quae, quod?: which? what?

Verbs
condō, condere, condidī, conditus, -a, -um:
    found, establish
resolvō, resolvere, resolvī, resolūtus,
    -a, -um: resolve

Readings

Required

13.1. Condidit urbem Rōmulus quam ex nōmine suō Rōmam vocāvit. Centum senēs ēlēgit
      quōs senātōrēs nōminavit propter senectūtem.—Eutropius
13.2. Nōn convalēscit planta quae saepe trānsfertur.—Seneca
13.3. Quī prō innocente dīcit, satis est ēloquēns.—Publilius Syrus
13.4. Ā lacū Lemannō, quī in flūmen Rhodanum īnfluit, ad montem Jūram, quī Sēquanōs ab
      Helvētiīs dīvidit, Caesar mūrum perdūcit.—Caesar (adapted)
13.5. Damnant stultī quod nōn intellegunt.—Anon.
13.6. Quī quod vult dīcit, quod nōn vult saepius audit.—Werner

Vocabulary

13.1. senex, senis, m.: old man
      ēlegō, ēlegere, ēlēgī, ēlēctus, -a, -um: pick out, choose
      senātor, senātōris, m.: senator
      nōminō, nōmināre, nōminavī, nōminātus, -a, -um: name
      senectūs, senectūtis, f.: old age
13.2. convalēscō, convalēscere, convaluī: get well
      planta, plantae, f.: plant
      trānsferō, trānsferre, trānstulī, trānslātus, -a, -um: transfer
13.3. innocēns (innocentis): innocent
      dīcō, dīcere, dīxī, dictus, -a, -um: speak, say
      satis (adv.): enough
      ēloquēns (ēloquentis): eloquent
13.4. lacus, lacūs, m.: lake
      lacus Lemannus: Lake Geneva
      Rhodanus, Rhodanī, m.: the Rhone
      īnfluō, īnfluere, īnflūxī: flow into
      mōns, montis, m.: mountain
      Jūra, Jūrae, f.: Jura (a mountain range)
      Sēquanī, Sēquanōrum, m. pl.: Sequanians, a people of Gaul
      Helvētiī, Helvētiōrum, m. pl.: Helvetians, a people of Gaul
      dīvidō, dīvidere, dīvīsī, dīvīsus, -a, -um: separate
      mūrus, mūrī, m.: wall
      perdūcō, perdūcere, perdūxī, perductus, -a, -um: lead through, bring
13.5. damnō, damnāre, damnavī, damnātus, -a, -um: condemn
      intellegō, intellegere, intellēxī, intellēctus, -a, -um: understand
13.6. dīcō, dīcere, dīxī, dictus, -a, -um: speak, say
      saepius (adv.): quite often

Optional

13.7. Lāta est porta et spatiōsa, quae dūcit ad perditiōnem, et multī sunt quī intrant.—New
   Testament
13.8. Quī capit, capitur.—Anon.
13.9. Fēlīciter sapit quī perīculō aliēnō sapit.—Plautus
13.10. Nōn omnēs quī habent citharam sunt citharoedī.—Varro
13.11. Ubi jūdicat quī accūsat, vīs, nōn lēx, valet.—Publilius Syrus

Vocabulary

13.7. lātus, lāta, lātum: wide, broad
   porta, portae, f.: gate
   spatiōsus, spatiōsa, spatiōsum: spacious, large
   perditiō, perditiōnis, f.: destruction, perdition
   intrō, intrāre, intrāvī, intrātus, -a, -um: enter
13.9. sapiō, sapere, sapīvī: be wise
   aliēnus, aliēna, aliēnum: another's
13.10. cithara, citharae, f.: lyre, harp, lute
   citharoedus, citharoedī, m.: lyre player
13.11. jūdicō, jūdicāre, jūdicāvī, jūdicātus, -a, -um: judge
   accūsō, accūsāre, accūsāvī, accūsātus, -a, -um: accuse
   vīs, f.: force
   valeō, valēre, valuī: be strong, be effective, prevail

Latin Questions

S13.1. Quam urbem Rōmulus condidit?

S13.2. Quod exemplum nīl agit?

S13.3. Quid cito fit?

S13.4. Quis semper inops est?

R13.2. Quae planta nōn convalēscit?

R13.5. Quid stultī damnant?

Word Study: English Derivatives

From Lesson	Latin	From Readings	Latin
1. exemplary		1. elect	
2. litigation		2. influence	
3. maternal		3. intelligent	
4. nominate		4. loquacious	
5. paternal		5. mountain	
6. resolve		6. satisfy	

Narrative Reading

Prīmus Labor: Leō Nemaeus

Prope Mycēnās in silvā vīxit leō quī vallem Nemaeam īnfestam faciēbat[1] et perīculōsam. In silvam quam leō incolēbat[1] Herculēs statim iter fēcit. Mox leōnem invēnit et arcum intendit; ejus[2] pellem quae maximē dēnsa erat[1] sagittae nōn trājēcērunt. Tum clāvam magnam Herculēs rapuit et leōnem percussit. Sed frūstrā. Dēnique suīs manibus collum cēpit et magnā vī pressit. Post breve tempus bēstia exanimāta est. Pellem leōnis[2] Herculēs dētrāxit quam posteā prō veste gerēbat.[1] Corpus mortuum ad Eurystheum, quī tantā fortitūdine territus est, portāvit. Sed cēterī, ubi dē morte leōnis[2] audīvērunt, laetī fuērunt.

Notes

1. past imperfective verbs: *faciēbat* (was making), *incolēbat* (inhabited), *erat* (was), and *gerēbat* (wore)
2. *ejus, leōnis:* genitive case, translate "its" or "his," "of the lion"

Vocabulary

arcus, arcūs, m.: bow
bēstia, bēstiae, f.: beast, monster
cēterī, cēterae, cētera: the others, all the others
clāva, clāvae, f.: club
collum, collī, n.: neck
dēnique (adv.): finally
dēnsus, dēnsa, dēnsum: thick
dētrahō, dētrahere, dētrāxī, dētractus, -a, -um: drag off
exanimō, exanimāre, exanimāvī, exanimātus, -a, -um: strangle
fortitūdō, fortitūdinis, f.: bravery, courage
frūstrā (adv.): in vain
gerō, gerere, gessī, gestus, -a, -um: wear
incolō, incolere, incoluī: inhabit
īnfestus, īnfesta, īnfestum: unsafe
intendō, intendere, intendī, intentus, -a, -um: stretch
inveniō, invenīre, invēnī, inventus, -a, -um: find
iter, itineris, n.: journey
laetus, laeta, laetum: glad
leō, leōnis, m.: lion
maximē (adv.): very
mors, mortis, f.: death
mortuus, mortua, mortuum: dead
*mox (adv.): soon
Mycēnae, Mycēnārum, f. pl.: Mycenae (a city in Greece)
Nemaeus, Nemaea, Nemaeum: Nemean, of Nemea (a city in Greece)
pellis, pellis, f.: skin
percutiō, percutere, percussī, percussus, -a, -um: strike hard
perīculōsus, perīculōsa, perīculōsum: dangerous
portō, portāre, portāvī, portātus, -a, -um: carry
posteā (adv.): afterward, then
sagitta, sagittae, f.: arrow

silva, silvae, f.: forest
statim (adv.): immediately
terreō, terrēre, terruī, territus, -a, -um: frighten
trājiciō, trājicere, trājēcī, trājectus, -a, -um: pierce
vallēs, vallis, f.: valley
vestis, vestis, f.: clothing
*vīs (irreg. noun, abl. sing. *vī*), f.: force

Derivatives from Narrative

Latin

1. attractive

2. corpuscle

3. extend

4. frustration

5. inanimate

6. invention

7. percussion

8. projectile

Summary Tasks

_____ 1. Label all relative clauses in Readings 13.1 through 13.6 as noun clauses or adjectival modifiers.

_____ 2. Underline all relative pronouns in the Narrative Reading and put brackets around the relative clauses.

_____ 3. What is the minimum number of clauses a sentence must have if the sentence contains a relative pronoun?

_____ 4. Translate into Latin these sentences:
   a. Whoever teaches learns. (S11.1)
   b. They teach whoever wants to learn.
   c. The father whom they teach learns.
   d. The father who teaches learns.

_____ 5. Rewrite the items in exercise 5 in the plural.

_____ 6. Give one possible answer in Latin to each of the Latin question words on page 118.

_____ 7. Copy and identify by case and number all relative pronouns that occur in the first two paragraphs of Eutropius, Battle of Cannae, page 374.

Review Lesson 3

Lesson Vocabulary

Nouns

annus, annī, m.: year
Carbō, Carbōnis, m.: Carbo
carbō, carbōnis, m.: charcoal
condiciō, condiciōnis, f.: condition
cor, cordis, n.: heart
Crassus, Crassī, m.: Crassus
domus, domūs, f.: home
dux, ducis, m.: leader
exemplum, exemplī, n.: example
glaciēs, glaciēī, f.: ice
jānua, jānuae, f.: door
līs, lītis, f.: quarrel, lawsuit
māter, mātris, f.: mother
mora, morae, f.: delay
necessitūdō, necessitūdinis, f.: necessity
nihil (indecl. noun), n.: nothing
nīl (indecl. noun), n.: nothing
nōmen, nōminis, n.: name
oculus, oculī, m.: eye
pater, patris, m.: father
Rōma, Rōmae, f.: (city of) Rome
Rōmulus, Rōmulī, m.: Romulus
urbs, urbis, f.: city
verbum, verbī, n.: word

Pronouns

hic, haec, hoc: this; he, she, it, they;
  the latter
ille, illa, illud: that; he, she, it, they;
  the former
quī, quae, quod (rel. pronoun): who, which,
  that
quīcumque, quaecumque, quodcumque:
  whoever, whatever, whichever

Adjectives

brevis, breve: short
crassus, crassa, crassum: fat
fragilis, fragile: fragile, easily broken
inops (inopis): poor, helpless
longus, longa, longum: long
quī, quae, quod? (interrogative adj.): which?
  what?
sapiēns (sapientis): wise
singulī, singulae, singula: single
suus, sua, suum: his/her/its own, their own
tantus, tanta, tantum: so great a, of such
  a size
timidus, timida, timidum: timid

Indeclinables

Adverbs

ante: before, previously
cito: quickly
contrā: on the contrary, in turn
multum: much, greatly
nihil: not at all
plūrimum: very much, greatly
plūs: more
post: afterward
super: above; moreover, besides
suprā: above, over
tantum: so much, only

Prepositions

ad (+ acc.): to, toward
ante (+ acc.): in front of; before
contrā (+ acc.): against
extrā (+ acc.): outside of
in (+ acc.): into, onto

inter (+ acc.): between, among
intrā (+ acc.): within
ob (+ acc.): against; because of
per (+ acc.): through
post (+ acc.): behind; after
praeter (+ acc.): in addition to; except
prope (+ acc.): near
propter (+ acc.): because of
sub (+ acc., abl.): under
super (+ acc.): above, over
suprā (+ acc.): above, over
trāns (+ acc.): across

Intensifier
etiam: even, also

Coordinating Conjunction
atque: and

Subordinating Conjunctions
cum: when
dum: while
postquam: after
quia: because
quod: because
sī: if
ubi: when; where
ut: when; as

Question Words
cūr?: why?
quā condiciōne?: under what condition?
quam diū?: how long?
quantum? (interrogative adv.): how greatly?
quī, quae, quod? (interrogative adj.):
    which? what?
quō? quem ad locum?: to what place?
    where (to)?

Verbs
appellō, appellāre, appellāvī, appellātus, -a, -um: call; name
cōgō, cōgere, cōēgī, cōāctus, -a, -um: force, compel
condō, condere, condidī, conditus, -a, -um: found, establish
discō, discere, didicī: learn
doleō, dolēre, doluī: grieve
fīō, fīerī, factus, -a, -um: be made, become, happen
fundō, fundere, fūdī, fūsus, -a, -um: pour
intereō, interīre, interiī: perish, die
pateō, patēre, patuī: stand open
resolvō, resolvere, resolvī, resolūtus, -a, -um: resolve
vocō, vocāre, vocāvī, vocātus, -a, -um: call

Readings Vocabulary

afficiō, afficere, affēcī, affectus, -a, -um: affect
agnus, agnī, m.: lamb
appropinquō, appropinquāre, appropinquāvī: approach, draw near
bēstia, bēstiae, f.: beast
discēdō, discēdere, discessī: go away, depart
dolor, dolōris, m.: grief
excitō, excitāre, excitāvī, excitātus, -a, -um: arouse
frāter, frātris, m.: brother
interficiō, interficere, interfēcī, interfectus, -a, -um: kill, do away with
labor, labōris, m.: toil, hardship
laetus, laeta, laetum: happy
maximē (adv.): very much
medicus, medicī, m.: physician
morbus, morbī, m.: disease

mox (adv.): soon
occīdō, occīdere, occīdī, occīsus, -a, -um: kill
pēs, pedis, m.: foot
quoque (adv.): also
rapiō, rapere, rapuī, raptus, -a, -um: seize, grab
serpēns, serpentis, f.: snake, serpent
sōlus, sōla, sōlum: alone, the only
stō, stāre, stetī: stand
subitō (adv.): suddenly, abruptly
vīs (irreg. noun), f.: force, violence; power

Morphology Review

New Morphology: Lessons 10 through 13

pronouns: nominative, accusative, ablative, singular and plural of *hic, ille,* the relative pronoun and indefinite pronoun

Form Identification

    a. fragilis, fragile: fragile, easily broken
    b. frangō, frangere, frēgī, frāctus: break
    c. frāctūra, frāctūrae, f.: break, fracture

1. fragilī   _____

2. frāctūrae   _____

3. frāctī sunt   _____

4. frāctās   _____

5. frangere   _____

6. frāctūrās   _____

7. fragilēs   _____

8. frēgit   _____

Narrative Reading

Androclēs et Leō

Ōlim in Circō Maximō sedēbant[1] multī hominēs spectāculum spectantēs[2] in quō gladiātōrēs contrā bēstiās pūgnābant.[1] Gladiātōrēs gladiōs et alia arma habēbant.[1] Tandem omnia animālia occīdērunt et ex harēnā discessērunt. Mox ūnus homō sōlus, quī nūlla arma habuit, harēnam intrāvit. Magnus leō, quī in harēnam ex aliā portā vēnit, ad hominem miserum celeriter accurrit, cum subitō stetit et ad pedēs hominis[3] dēcubuit. Omnēs spectātōrēs inter sē[4] rogābant[1]: "Cūr leō hominem nōn occīdit?"

Homō miser, Androclēs nōmine, in harēnā apud imperātōrem et spectātōrēs fābulam mīram nārrāvit. Multōs annōs servus fuerat.⁵ Tandem ex vīllā dominī³ crūdēlis³ fūgit et in antrum vēnit. Dum dormit, magnus leō quoque in antrum vēnit. Leō ad Androclem appropinquāvit et pedem, quī sanguinem fundēbat,¹ mōnstrāvit. Androclēs inter digitōs pedis³ magnam spīnam vīdit quam extrāxit. Pedem cūrāvit et diū leō cum Androcle in antrō habitāvit.

Post multōs diēs mīlitēs Rōmānī Androclem cēpērunt et ad dominum crūdēlem trāxērunt, quī eum ad urbem dūxit et in harēnam mīsit. Mīlitēs posteā magnum quoque leōnem quī cum Androcle habitāverat⁵ cēpērunt et eum dūxērunt ad urbem ubi in harēnam missus est. Sed leō Androclem nōn occīdit quod eum amāvit.

Omnēs spectātōrēs, postquam fābulam mīram audīvērunt, maximē laetī fuērunt et imperātor lībertātem et Androclī⁶ et leōnī⁶ dedit.

Saepe Androclēs, medicus leōnis,³ cum leōne, hominis³ amīcō, in viīs ambulāvit, ubi spectātōrēs eōs magnā cum dēlectātiōne spectāvērunt.

Notes

1. *sedēbant, pugnābant, habēbant, rogābant, fundēbat:* past imperfective, translate "was/were _____-ing" or "_____-ed"
2. *spectantēs:* verbal adjective, "watching, looking at"
3. *hominis, dominī crūdēlis, pedis, leōnis, hominis:* genitive singular, "of the _____" or "_____'s"
4. *inter sē:* "among themselves"; translate "one another"
5. *fuerat, habitāverat:* past perfective tense, "had been," "had lived"
6. *Androclī, leōnī:* dative case, "to (the) _____"

Vocabulary

accurrō, accurrere, accurrī: run to
ambulō, ambulāre, ambulāvī: walk
antrum, antrī, n.: cave
*appropinquō, appropinquāre, appropinquāvī: approach
apud (prep. + acc.): in the presence of, among
arma, armōrum, n. pl.: weapons
*bēstia, bēstiae, f.: beast
celeriter (adv.): quickly
circus, circī, m.: circus
dēcumbō, dēcumbere, dēcubuī: lie down
dēlectātiō, dēlectātiōnis, f.: pleasure, delight
digitus, digitī, m.: finger
*discēdō, discēdere, discessī: go away, depart
diū (adv.): for a long period of time
dominus, dominī, m.: master
extrahō, extrahere, extrāxī, extractus, -a, -um: draw out, extract
fābula, fābulae, f.: story
gladius, gladiī, m.: sword
habeō, habēre, habuī: have
imperātor, imperātōris, m.: emperor, commander
*laetus, laeta, laetum: happy
leō, leōnis, m.: lion

lībertās, lībertātis, f.: freedom
*maximē (adv.): very
maximus, maxima, maximum: largest, biggest
mīles, mīlitis, m.: soldier
mīrus, mīra, mīrum: wonderful, strange
miser, misera, miserum: miserable, unhappy
mōnstrō, mōnstrāre, mōnstrāvī, mōnstrātus, -a, -um: show
nārrō, nārrāre, nārrāvī, nārrātus, -a, -um: tell
nūllus, nūlla, nūllum: none
*occīdō, occīdere, occīdī, occīsus, -a, -um: kill
ōlim (adv.): once upon a time
*pēs, pedis, m.: foot
porta, portae, f.: door, gate
posteā (adv.): afterward
pūgnō, pūgnāre, pūgnāvī: fight
quod (subord. conj.): because
*quoque (adv.): also
rogō, rogāre, rogāvī, rogātus, -a, -um: ask
Rōmānus, Rōmāna, Rōmānum: Roman
sanguis, sanguinis, m.: blood
sedeō, sedēre, sēdī: sit
servus, servī, m.: slave
*sōlus, sōla, sōlum: alone, only
spectāculum, spectāculī, n.: spectacle, performance
spectātor, spectātōris, m.: spectator
spectō, spectāre, spectāvī, spectātus, -a, -um: watch
spīna, spīnae, f.: thorn
*stō, stāre, stetī: stand
*subitō (adv.): suddenly
trahō, trahere, trāxī, tractus, -a, -um: drag, draw
via, viae, f.: street, road
vīlla, vīllae, f.: country home, villa

Derivatives from Narrative Reading

Latin

1. ambulatory

2. concurrent

3. digit

4. dominate

5. imperial

6. incumbent

7. interrogative

8. military

9. narrative

Latin

10. pugnacious

11. refuge

12. subtract

■ Exercise 1: English to Latin Sentences
Following the Latin models, translate the English sentences into Latin.

1. Necessitūdō etiam timidōs fortēs facit. (S10.3)

   Good clothes make even sad people happy.

2. Noctēs atque diēs patet jānua. (S12.2)

   Rome stood for many years.

3. Leō quī cum Androcle habitāvit in harēnam missus est.

   The slave who lived with the lion was captured and dragged into the city.

4. Hominēs, dum docent, discunt. (S11.1)

   The gods neglect unimportant things, while they take care of the important things.

5. Oculī sunt in amōre ducēs. (S10.1)

   Large ships seem small in the ocean.

Vocabulary

Nouns
city: urbs
clothes: vestis, vestis, f.
god: deus
lion: leō, leōnis, m.
ocean: mare
Rome: Rōma
ship: nāvis, nāvis, f.
slave: servus, servī, m.
year: annus

Pronoun
who: quī

Adjectives
good: bonus
happy: laetus, laeta, laetum
important: magnus
large: magnus
many: multī

sad: trīstis, trīste
small: parvus
unimportant: parvus

Indeclinables
even: etiam (intensifier)
in: in (prep.)
into: in (prep.)
while: dum (subord. conj.)
with: cum (prep.)

Verbs
capture (take): capiō
drag: trahō, trahere, trāxī, tractus, -a, -um
live: habitō, habitāre, habitāvī
make: faciō
neglect: neglegō
seem: vidērī (videntur)
stand: stō, stāre, stetī
take care of: cūrō

■ Exercise 2: Latin Questions

Write a Latin answer to each of the following questions based on the story of Androcles and the Lion.

1. Ubi spectātōrēs Rōmānī sedēbant?

2. Quod spectāculum spectātōrēs spectābant?

3. Apud quōs Androclēs fābulam mīram nārrāvit?

4. Quam diū Androclēs fuit servus?

5. Quandō leō in antrum vēnit?

6. Quem in locum Androclēs et leō missī sunt?

7. Cūr Androclēs ā leōne nōn occīsus est?

8. Quandō spectātōrēs maximē laetī fuērunt?

Lesson 14

The Participle: A Non-Finite Verb Form
Participial Clause as Adjectival Modifier

Lesson 9 introduced the perfective passive and future active participles. This lesson introduces the *imperfective active participle*. So far, the perfective passive participle has been used with the verb *sum, esse* to form finite verbs such as *amātus est* "_____ has been/was loved" and *victī sunt* "_____s have been/were conquered." This lesson introduces participles without *sum, esse* as the verbs of *participial clauses*.

Basic Sentences

14.1. Invādunt urbem somnō vīnōque sepultam.—Vergil
> They invade the city overwhelmed by wine and sleep. (Aeneas describes how the Greeks who had entered Troy in the wooden horse open the city gates from the inside at night and let their comrades into the city.)

14.2. Stēlla facem dūcēns multā cum lūce cucurrit.—Vergil
> A star drawing a trail of fire plunged in brilliant light. (Aeneas describes how, on the night in which Troy fell, he and his father got new hope upon seeing a meteor.)

14.3. Vōx audīta perit, littera scrīpta manet.—Anon.
> The spoken word vanishes but the written letter remains.

The Participle: A Non-Finite Verb Form

Verb forms that can be identified for person are *finite verb forms*. For example, *vincō* "I conquer" is identified as first person but *vincit* "he, she, it conquers" is identified as third person (see lesson 18). So far, all verbs, with the exception of infinitives, have been finite. Infinitives (from the Latin word for "not-finite") and *participles* are *non-finite verb forms*. They are not identified for person. They do, however, have such verb properties as voice and aspect.

Participles also have the adjective properties: case, number, and gender. They are therefore usually described as *verbal adjectives*.

Morphology: The Perfective Passive Participle

This participle has the morpheme {t} or {s} plus the endings of first and second declension adjectives. Example: *audītus, -a, -um* (having been heard) from the verb *audiō, audīre, audīvī, audītus, -a, -um*.

	Masculine	Feminine	Neuter
Singular			
Nominative	**audītus**	**audīta**	**audītum**
Accusative	**audītum**	**audītam**	**audītum**
Ablative	**audītō**	**audītā**	**audītō**
Dative	audītō	audītae	audītō
Genitive	audītī	audītae	audītī
Plural			
Nominative	**audītī**	**audītae**	**audīta**
Accusative	**audītōs**	**audītās**	**audīta**
Ablative	**audītīs**	**audītīs**	**audītīs**
Dative	audītīs	audītīs	audītīs
Genitive	audītōrum	audītārum	audītōrum

■ Exercise 1

Underline and identify by case, number, and gender all words that *look like* perfective passive participles.

1. parātae

2. cāsūs

3. scrīptā

4. occāsiō

5. acceptīs

6. āctiō

7. falsam

8. āctī

9. crēditōs

10. trīste

11. sitis

12. grātiam

13. imposita

14. sepultam

15. montēs

16. territa

17. permōtī

18. hostēs

19. jactō

20. āmissum

Morphology: The Imperfective Active Participle

This participle is built on the imperfective stem of the verb and has the morpheme {nt} (except in the nominative singular), plus the endings of third declension adjectives. It has, therefore, the same forms as the third declension adjective *absēns* except in the ablative singular.[1] Example: *audiēns* (*audientis*) (hearing) from *audiō, audīre, audīvī, audītus, -a, -um.*

	Masc. & Fem.	Neut.
Singular		
Nominative	**audiēns**	**audiēns**
Accusative	**audientem**	**audiēns**
Ablative	**audiente** (or -ī)	**audiente** (or -ī)
Dative	audientī	audientī
Genitive	audientis	audientis
Plural		
Nominative	**audientēs**	**audientia**
Accusative	**audientēs**	**audientia**
Ablative	**audientibus**	**audientibus**
Dative	audientibus	audientibus
Genitive	audientium	audientium

Here are other examples.

amāns (amantis) from amō, amāre, amāvī, amātus, -a, -um
docēns (docentis) from doceō, docēre, docuī, doctus, -a, -um
regēns (regentis) from regō, regere, rēxī, rēctus, -a, -um
capiēns (capientis) from capiō, capere, cēpī, captus, -a, -um

■ Exercise 2
Underline and identify by case, number, and gender all the words that *look like* imperfective active participles.

1. ventōs

2. cadentia

3. inventus

4. hostibus

5. ruēns

6. grātia

7. moenia

8. lātrante

9. vēritāte

10. laudantēs

11. parant

12. dīcentibus

---

1. The ablative, when used as an adjective, usually has the form ending in *-ī*, but there is a great deal of free variation.

Participial Clause as Adjectival Modifier

Syntax

The previous lesson introduced the relative clause as an adjectival modifier. This lesson introduces the *participial clause* as another type of adjectival modifier.

As said above, participles are usually described as *verbal adjectives*. *Adjective* means that, just like adjectives, participles modify a noun-head with which they agree in case, number, and gender. Examples from the Basic Sentences show this agreement.

> S14.1. *urbem sepultam:* both noun-head and participle are accusative singular feminine
> S14.2. *stēlla dūcēns:* both noun-head and participle are nominative singular feminine
> S14.3. *vōx audīta:* both noun-head and participle are nominative singular feminine
> S14.3. *littera scrīpta:* both noun-head and participle are nominative singular feminine

Verbal means that, just like finite verbs in a finite clause, participles function as verbs in a non-finite kernel. The noun-head functions as the subject of the kernel no matter what function it has in the main clause. In S14.1 (*Invādunt urbem vīnō somnōque sepultam*), the participle *sepultam* (overwhelmed, buried) modifies *urbem* (city), the direct object in the main clause. Both are accusative, singular, feminine. Within the participial clause *urbem* functions as the subject and *sepultam* functions as the verb. That *urbem* and *sepultam* are in a subject-verb relationship might seem strange, especially since no subject so far has been in a case other than the nominative. But it is only with finite verbs that the reader must expect a subject in the nominative.

The participle may have adverbial modifiers. *Sepultam* is modified by *somnō vīnōque*, ablatives of means.

An imperfective active participle may have a direct object. In S14.2 (*Stēlla facem dūcēns multā cum lūce cucurrit*), the noun-head *stēlla* is subject, *facem* is direct object, and *dūcēns* is the verb of the participial clause. *Stēlla* is also subject of the main kernel. This use of the participle has also been called *participium conjunctum*.

The most common word order pattern within a participial clause in prose writing is that which is found in the Basic Sentences. That is, the noun-head and the participle mark the beginning and end of the clause. Be prepared to find other patterns, however.

■ Exercise 3
Underline each participle in the sentences below, write the name of the participle on the line, and draw an arrow to the noun-head/subject of each participle.

Vōx ab hominibus <u>audīta</u> perit.   <u>perfective passive participle</u>

1. Fēmina amīcum semper currentem videt. _____

2. Puer canēs ā virō captōs videt. _____

3. Māter amīcum vocāns virum videt. _____

4. Ā cane semper currente vir premitur. _____

Kernel Information

The presence of a participle means the presence of at least two kernels, a main kernel, as in all sentences, and the non-finite dependent kernel. Although the participial clause is dependent, it has *no* clause marker in Latin. Only dependent clauses with finite verbs have clause markers. As a reminder that the participial kernel is dependent, though without a clause marker, it is useful to put a Ⓟ in the clause marker column.

Note: From now on indicate in the kernel chart whether a kernel is finite (F) or non-finite (NF). This is the last kernel-chart heading that will be included in the description of clauses taught in this course. All clauses to be introduced from now on can be described under these headings. The kinds of information over which a reader must have conscious or subconscious control in order to be successful are represented in these headings. The information is of course interrelated and may be processed in virtually any order.

Stēlla facem dūcēns magnā cum lūce cucurrit.

Clause Marker	Item: Function	Item: Function	Item: Function	Kernel Type	F/NF	M/D	Adj./Adv./ Noun	Name
Ⓟ	stēlla: subj.	facem: dir. obj.	dūcēns: verb	TA	NF	D	adj.	participial clause
—	stēlla: subj.	cucurrit: verb	—	IA	F	M	—	statement

■ Exercise 4

Complete the chart for these two sentences:

1. Māter amīcum vocāns virum videt.
2. Puer canēs ā virō captōs videt.

Clause Marker	Item: Function	Item: Function	Item: Function	Kernel Type	F/NF	M/D	Adj./Adv./ Noun	Name
1.								
1.								
2.								
2.								

Metaphrasing: The Perfective Passive Participle

A participle is metaphrased immediately *after* its noun-head in order to show its verb role. The metaphrase of a perfective passive participle is:

"(noun-head) having been _____-ed."

vōx audīta: voice having been heard _____s ± _____ .
litteram scrīptam: _____ _____s letter having been written.
ā mātre vīsā: _____ is _____-ed by the mother having been seen.
pater audītus: the father having been heard _____s ± _____ .
canēs ā virō captōs: _____ _____s dogs having been captured/caught by the man.

Beginning students must be sure to use the metaphrase "_____ having been _____-ed" in order to avoid confusion with other English verb forms in -ed. However, in final translations the perfective passive participle is expressed most often simply as "_____-ed" rather than "having been _____-ed." The translation of *sepultam* in S14.1 is "overwhelmed," not "having been overwhelmed." Likewise, the translation of the last example above would most often be "_____ _____s the dogs captured by the man."

Furthermore, in translations participles without modifiers usually are placed in the customary adjective position before the noun-head, e.g., "the *written* letter remains" instead of "the letter *written/having been written* remains" (S14.3). Learners must avoid this word order inversion, however, until they are certain that the participle has no modifiers of its own. *Vident canēs ā virō captōs* is not "They see the captured by the man dogs," or "They see the captured dogs by the man," but "They see the dogs captured by the man."

Metaphrasing: The Imperfective Active Participle

The imperfective active participle is metaphrased immediately *after* its noun-head also. This metaphrase is:

"(noun-head) _____-ing."

stēlla facem dūcēns: a star leading a light _____s ± _____ .
māter fīliam vocāns: a mother calling her daughter _____s ± _____ .
mātrem fīliam vocantem: _____ _____s a mother calling her daughter.
ā cane domum currente: _____ is being _____-ed by a dog running home.

Beginning students must be sure to use the metaphrase "(noun-head) _____-ing" in order to avoid confusion with other English verb forms in -ing.

This participle, too, can be placed immediately before its noun-head in a final translation if it has neither an object nor a modifier, e.g., *ā cane currente:* "_____ is _____-ed by a running dog."

Participles and Relative Time

A *perfective participle* describes an event as a *preceding* event, i.e., as having happened *prior* to the time of the verb in the main clause.

The *imperfective participle* describes an event as being *simultaneous* or *concurrent* with the time of the verb in the main clause.

Note on the *future active participle:* Lesson 9 introduced the future active participle as the fourth principal part of intransitive verbs, e.g., *pereō, perīre, periī, peritūrus, -a, -um.* Although future active participles do not appear in the principal parts of other verbs, most verbs have a future active participle ending in -*ūrus, -a, -um* and built on what looks like the stem of the perfective passive participle. For example, *audītūrus, -a, -um* is the future active participle and *audītus, -a, -um* is the perfective passive participle of *audiō, audīre, audīvī, audītus, -a, -um.*

The *future active participle* is metaphrased "(noun-head) about to _____ ," and describes an event as *following* the time of the verb in the main clause.

māter fīliam vocātūra: the mother about to call her daughter _____s _____ .

This participle has the same syntax as the other participles but it occurs rarely in participial clauses. However, combined with the infinitive *esse,* it forms a future infinitive that is somewhat more common. (Lesson 24 will describe this.)

■ Exercise 5

Metaphrase each of the following participle clauses in the context of a complete sentence. For the purposes of this exercise treat the first noun in each set as the noun-head of the participle and treat any other words as part of the participial clause.

1. mātrem vocātam

2. puerōs ab amīcō audītōs

3. vir cum cūrā doctus

4. puer saepe scrībēns

5. fēminam patrem audientem

6. ā virō saepe currente

7. vēritāte victā

8. virōs fugientēs

9. lupum captum

10. deus magna neglegēns

11. vōcem ā fēminā audītam

12. Juppiter omnia regēns

■ Exercise 6

Each of the following sentences contains a participial form. Indicate by a check whether the participial form is used as part of a finite verb (the perfective passive) or as participle. Metaphrase each sentence. Two examples are provided.

Sentence	Part of Finite Verb	Participle	Metaphrase
Ālea jacta est.	✔		The die has been cast.
Occāsiō neglēcta āmittitur.		✔	An opportunity having been neglected is lost.
1. Littera scrīpta manet.			
2. Vēritās nōn victa est.			
3. Lupus ā virō vīsus fugit.			
4. Urbēs arte hūmānā aedificātae sunt.			

■ Exercise 7
All of the following words look like perfective participles, but they are not. Identify each word by part of speech and write the dictionary listing.

1. fēlīcitās

2. senātus

3. stultus

4. crassus

■ Exercise 8
All of the following words look like imperfective active participles, but they are not. Identify each word by part of speech and write the dictionary listing.

1. mentem

2. absentibus

3. sapientia

Lesson Vocabulary

Nouns
fax, facis, f.: torch, light, flame
littera, litterae, f.: a letter of the alphabet; (usually pl.) a letter, dispatch; literature
lūx, lūcis, f.: light
somnus, somnī, m.: sleep
stēlla, stēllae, f.: star
vōx, vōcis, f.: voice, cry, utterance

Verbs[1]
currō, currere, cucurrī, cursūrus, -a, -um: run, hasten
invādō, invādere, invāsī, invāsus, -a, -um: enter, attack
maneō, manēre, mānsī, mānsūrus, -a, -um: remain, stay
scrībō, scrībere, scrīpsī, scrīptus, -a, -um: write
sepeliō, sepelīre, sepelīvī, sepultus, -a, -um: bury

Note
1. From now on, the fourth principal part of verbs will be listed in the masculine only (*-us*).

Narrative Reading

The Second Labor: Hercules Kills the Hydra

Herculēs, ab Eurystheō jussus, cum amīcō Īolāō, ad lacum Lernaeum contendit in quō Hydra habitābat.[1] Hydra fuit mōnstrum, quod novem capita habuit. Prīmum Herculēs, arcum intendēns, sagittās mīsit quae pellem mōnstrī[2] nōn trājēcērunt. Deinde, collum laevā

manū prehendēns, novem capita dextrā manū abscīdere incēpit. Sed frūstrā! Nova capita,
duo prō capite singulō, statim crēscēbant.[1] Tum postrēmō hērōs cōnsilium novum cēpit. Cum
amīcō arborēs succīdit et, postquam ignis ex lignīs factus est, facibus ārdentibus magnō cum
labōre colla ussit. Nova capita ex hīs collīs nōn jam[3] crēscere incipiēbant.[1] Hydra interfecta
est, et sanguine mōnstrī[2] Herculēs sagittās suās mortiferās fēcit.

Notes

1. past imperfective verbs, translate *habitābat* "lived," *crēscēbant* "began to grow,"
   incipiēbant "began, were beginning"
2. *mōnstrī:* genitive case, "of the monster"
3. *nōn jam:* "no longer"

Vocabulary

abscīdō, abscīdere, abscīdī, abscīsus: cut away, cut off
arbor, arboris, f.: tree
arcus, arcūs, m.: bow
ārdeō, ārdēre, ārsī: burn
caput, capitis, n.: head
*collum, collī, n.: neck
contendō, contendere, contendī: stretch vigorously, hasten
crēscō, crēscere, crēvī, crētus: grow, increase
dexter, dextra, dextrum: right
frūstrā (adv.): in vain
hērōs, hērōis, m.: hero, a demi-god
Hydra, Hydrae, f.: Hydra, a water monster
*ignis, ignis, m.: fire
incipiō, incipere, incēpī, inceptus: begin (+ inf.), undertake
intendō, intendere, intendī, intentus: bend, aim
jubeō, jubēre, jussī, jussus: order
lacus, lacūs, m.: lake
laevus, laeva, laevum: left
Lernaeus, Lernaea, Lernaeum: of Lerna, Lernaean
lignum, lignī, n.: wood
mōnstrum, mōnstrī, n.: monster
mortifer, mortifera, mortiferum: death bringing, deadly
pellis, pellis, f.: skin, hide
*portō, portāre, portāvī, portātus: carry
postrēmō (adv.): finally
prehendō, prehendere, prehendī, prehēnsus: grasp, seize
*prīmum (adv. acc.): at first
sagitta, sagittae, f.: arrow
sanguis, sanguinis, m.: blood
*statim (adv.): immediately
succīdō, succīdere, succīdī, succīsus: cut down
trājiciō, trājicere, trājēcī, trājectus: pierce
*tum (adv.): then
ūrō, ūrere, ussī, ustus: burn, sear

Word Study: English Derivatives

From Lesson	Latin		**From Narrative Reading**	Latin
1. audible			1. arcade	
2. invasion			2. ardent	
3. lucid			3. comprehend	
4. occur			4. decide	
5. postscript			5. dexterity	
6. remainder			6. injection	
7. sepulcher			7. recipient	
8. stellar			8. trajectory	

Summary Tasks

_____ 1. Write a cumulative metaphrase of S14.3.

_____ 2. Write the paradigm, singular and plural (nominative, accusative, ablative), of these noun and participle pairs: *stēlla currēns, exemplum manēns, vōx audīta.*

_____ 3. Rewrite the items in exercise 5 by changing each noun-head from singular to plural or vice versa, and making all necessary changes.

_____ 4. Copy the kernels of all participle clauses in the Narrative Reading.

_____ 5. Enter onto a modifier chart from the Narrative Reading all adverbial modifiers in the ablative, with or without a preposition.

_____ 6. Write the Latin for these two sentences.

    a. They see the star which is falling.

    b. They see the falling star.

    (fall: *cadō, cadere*)

Lesson 15

The Ablative Absolute: Participial Clause as Adverbial Modifier

Lesson 11 introduced adverbial clauses with a finite verb; this lesson introduces an adverbial clause called the *ablative absolute* with a non-finite verb. This is a participial clause.

Basic Sentences

15.1. Fortūnā fortēs adjuvante, perīculum vincitur.—Motto
     With Fortune aiding the brave, peril is overcome.

15.2. Caesar, obsidibus acceptīs, exercitum in Bellovacōs dūcit.—Caesar
     Caesar, after he has accepted hostages (= with hostages having been accepted), leads the army into the territory of the Bellovaci.

The Ablative Absolute: Participial Clause as Adverbial Modifier

Syntax and Semantics

The word *ablative* in the name ablative absolute is descriptive in that the subject (noun-head) of the participial clause and the participle are both in the ablative case. The ablative absolute is never the object of a preposition.

In the Basic Sentences, *fortūnā fortēs adjuvante* and *obsidibus acceptīs* are ablative absolute clauses; each has a subject in the ablative, *fortūnā* and *obsidibus,* and a participle, *adjuvante* and *acceptīs. Fortēs* is the direct object of *fortūnā adjuvante.*

Ablative absolutes are the equivalent of finite dependent clauses and often have the semantic interpretation *time, condition,* or *cause.* Thus, e.g., *fortūnā fortēs adjuvante* can be interpreted as:

> ubi fortūna fortēs adjuvat *"when* Fortune aids the brave,"
> sī fortūna fortēs adjuvat *"if* Fortune aids the brave," or
> quod fortūna fortēs adjuvat *"because* Fortune aids the brave."

As the name *absolute* (meaning "detached") indicates, this construction is not part of another clause but is a separate clause. The ablative absolute and the main clause in a sentence do not, as a rule, have a noun in common. The subject in the ablative absolute clause is almost always expressed and the participle is usually found nearby.

On the other hand, even without a participle, two nouns in the ablative or one noun and an adjective in the ablative may have to be read as an ablative absolute. For example, *Caesare cōnsule* means "with Caesar being consul" or "while Caesar is/was consul." *Caesare* is the subject and *cōnsule* the subject complement of a linking kernel formed by the ablative absolute. There is no participle because the verb *sum, esse* has neither an imperfective participle nor a perfective participle. Other examples are:

> Caesare duce "with Caesar ∅ = being the leader" (noun + noun), and
> Caesare invītō "with Caesar ∅ = being reluctant" (noun + adjective).

■ Exercise 1
Underline all possible ablative absolutes.

1. opera ācta

2. vōce audītā

3. virīs victīs

4. ā virīs victīs

5. vēritāte victus

6. corde dolente

7. magnā cum cūrā

8. fēminā vōcem audiente

9. cum fēminīs fugientibus

10. stēllā facem dūcente

Kernel Information

Any kernel type may occur in an ablative absolute. In a transitive kernel there is a direct object in the accusative. In a linking kernel there is a subject complement in the ablative (see *Caesare duce* above).

■ Exercise 2
Copy the kernels from these sentences, following the example.

> Fortūnā fortēs adjuvante, perīculum vincitur.

1. Caesar, obsidibus acceptīs, exercitum in Bellovacōs dūcit.
2. Rōmulō duce, urbs Rōma condita est.

Clause Marker	Item: Function	Item: Function	Item: Function	Kernel Type	F/NF	M/D	Adj./Adv./ Noun	Name
Ⓟ	fortūnā: subj.	fortēs: dir. obj.	adjuvante: verb	TA	NF	D	adv.	abl. abs.
	perīculum: subj.	vincitur: verb	—		P	F	M	—	statement
1.								
1.								
2.								
2.								

Metaphrasing

If the participle is imperfective active the metaphrase for the ablative absolute is:

"with <u>(noun-head)</u> <u>(participle)</u>-ing ± <u>(object)</u> , _____ _____s ± _____ ."

             ablative absolute   main clause

corde dolente: "with the heart grieving, _____ _____s ± _____ ."
stēllā facem dūcente: "with a star drawing a trail of fire, _____ _____s ± _____ ."

If the participle is perfective passive the metaphrase for the ablative absolute is:

"with <u>(noun-head)</u> having been <u>(participle)</u>-ed, _____ _____s ± _____ ."

             ablative absolute   main clause

virīs victīs: "with men having been conquered, _____ _____s ± _____ ."

Although an ablative absolute is metaphrased by "with" and a non-finite clause, a translation often uses a clause marker and a finite clause, as can be seen in the examples following. Notice that the exact nature of the semantic relationship between the ablative absolute and the rest of the sentence is not stated in Latin and is not expressed in a metaphrase. It is only in a finite clause that the relationship is expressed.

> *Fonte fluente, flūmen crēscit.*
> Metaphrase: "With the spring flowing, the river increases." Possible translations:
>   "Because/since/when/while/if the spring is flowing, the river increases."
>
> *Fonte neglēctō, flūmen nōn crēscit.*
> Metaphrase: "With the spring having been neglected, the river does not increase."
>   Possible translations: "Because/since/when/after the spring has been neglected, the river does not increase."

An ablative absolute containing an imperfective active participle usually answers the question *quā condiciōne?* (under what condition?). An ablative absolute with a perfective passive participle usually answers the question *quō factō?* (with what [having been] done?).

■ Exercise 3
Metaphrase the ablative absolutes from exercise 1 in the context of a complete sentence.

1.

2.

3.

4.

5.

■ Exercise 4
Complete each sentence by underlining the word or words that could fill the blank.

1. ____ urbs Rōma condita est: Rōmulō duce, ā Rōmulō duce, Rōmulus dux

2. ____ hominēs regentia regit deus: astra, astrum, astrīs

3. Lacrimīs ____ pāscentibus, timidī fortēs fiunt: crūdēlēs, ā crūdēlī, crūdēlem

4. Stēlla ____ multī vident magna est: quae, quam, ā quā

■ Exercise 5
The following passage is from the Life of Hannibal by the Roman author C. Nepos,
a contemporary of Julius Caesar.

The italicized words are noun-heads in a participial clause or in an ablative absolute.
Find each participle, circle it, and draw an arrow to its noun-head.

⟨Hannibal⟩ hāc *pūgnā* pūgnātā Rōmam profectus *nūllō* resistente in propinquīs urbī

montibus morātus est. Cum aliquot ibi diēs castra habuisset et Capuam reverterētur,

Q. Fabius Māximus, dictātor Rōmānus, in agrō Falernō eī sē objēcit. ∅=*Hannibal* hīc

clausus locōrum angustiīs noctū sine ūllō dētrīmentō exercitūs sē expedīvit Fabiōque,

callidissimō imperātōrī, dedit verba. Namque obductā *nocte sarmenta* in cornibus

juvencōrum dēligāta incendit ejusque generis *multitūdinem* māgnam dispālātam immīsit. Quō

repentīnō *vīsū* objectō tantum terrōrem injēcit exercituī Rōmānōrum ut ēgredī extrā vāllum

nēmō sit ausus. Hanc post *rem* gestam nōn ita multīs diēbus *M. Minucium Rūfum* dolō

prōductum in proelium fugāvit. *Ti. Semprōnium Gracchum* in īnsidiās inductum sustulit.

(Nepos *Hannibal* 5.2)

Lesson Vocabulary

Nouns
Bellovacī, Bellovacōrum, m. pl.: the Bellovaci, a people of Gallia Belgica
exercitus, exercitūs, m.: army
flūmen, flūminis, n.: river
obses, obsidis, m. & f.: hostage

Question Words
quō factō?: with what (having been) done?

Verbs
accipiō, accipere, accēpī, acceptus: accept, receive
crēscō, crēscere, crēvī, crētus: grow, increase
fluō, fluere, flūxī: flow

Narrative Reading

Other Labors of Hercules

Hydrā occīsā, Eurystheus, timōre perterritus, Herculem[1] jussit cervum quendam[2] reportāre.[1] Hic cervus, quī cornua aurea, aereōs pedēs gessit, celerrimē[3] cucurrit. Herculēs, ubi in silvīs cervum vīdit, summīs vīribus currere incēpit, neque tempus ad quiētem relīquit. Tandem, postquam tōtum annum cucurrit, bēstiam cursū exanimātam captāvit et vīvam ad rēgem Eurystheum reportāvit.

Hōc tertiō labōre cōnfectō, Eurystheus aliōs labōrēs imperāvit in quibus Herculēs cēpit animālia quae hominēs laesērunt. In quārtō labōre Herculēs summā difficultāte aprum laqueō implicātum ad rēgem dūxit. In sextō labōre deā Minervā adjuvante, avēs Stymphālidēs, quae rostrīs ātrōcibus acūtīsque unguibus hominēs oppressērunt et multōs dēvorāvērunt, sagittīs mortiferīs dēlēvit. Hīs avibus interfectīs, Herculēs in septimō labōre bovem, magnā difficultāte captum, vīvum ex īnsūlā Crētā ad Graeciam rettulit. Quō[4] factō, octāvum labōrem Herculēs suscēpit. Equōs Diomēdis,[5] quī carne hūmānā vīxērunt, superāvit et eōs ad Eurystheum dūxit.

Quīntus labor autem mente, nōn vīribus, cōnfectus est. Herculēs stabula rēgis Augēae, quae trīgintā annōs nōn lauta erant,[6] pūrgāvit. Duōbus flūminibus per stabula conversīs, Herculēs opus ūnō diē facile cōnfēcit.

Notes

1. *Herculem . . . reportāre:* accusative with infinitive, direct object of *jussit*
2. *quendam:* adjective, accusative singular masculine, "a certain"
3. *celerrimē:* adverb, superlative degree, "very fast"
4. *quō factō:* "with this having been done, whereupon." After a period or semicolon the relative pronoun is preferred to the demonstrative. In this position the relative is called a *connecting relative*.
5. *Diomēdis:* genitive case, "of Diomedes"
6. *lauta erant:* past perfective passive, "had been cleaned, washed"

Vocabulary

acūtus, acūta, acūtum: sharp
aereus, aerea, aereum: of bronze
ātrōx (ātrōcis): frightful, savage
Augēas, Augēae, m.: Augeas (a king in the south of Greece)
aureus, aurea, aureum: golden, of gold
avis, avis, f.: bird
bōs, bovis, m. & f.: ox, bull
carō, carnis, f.: flesh
cervus, cervī, m.: deer
cōnficiō, cōnficere, cōnfēcī, cōnfectus: complete, finish
convertō, convertere, convertī, conversus: turn
cornū, cornūs, n.: horn
cursus, cursūs, m.: running
dēleō, dēlēre, dēlēvī, dēlētus: destroy
dēvorō, dēvorāre, dēvorāvī, dēvorātus: devour
equus, equī, m.: horse

exanimō, exanimāre, exanimāvī, exanimātus: (in passive) be exhausted
gerō, gerere, gessī, gestus: have, wear
imperō, imperāre, imperāvī, imperātus: order, impose
implicō, implicāre, implicāvī, implicātus: entangle, catch
*incipiō, incipere, incēpī, inceptus: begin
jubeō, jubēre, jussī, jussus: order
laedō, laedere, laesī, laesus: harm, injure
laqueus, laqueī, m.: noose, trap
neque (coord. conj.): nor, and not
octāvus, octāva, octāvum: eighth
opprimō, opprimere, oppressī, oppressus: overpower, overwhelm
perterreō, perterrēre, perterruī, perterritus: thoroughly frighten
pūrgō, pūrgāre, pūrgāvī, pūrgātus: clean
quārtus, quārta, quārtum: fourth
quiēs, quiētis, f.: rest, sleep
quīntus, quīnta, quīntum: fifth
referō, referre, rettulī, relātus: carry back, bring back
relinquō, relinquere, relīquī, relictus: leave
reportō, reportāre, reportāvī, reportātus: carry back
*rēx, rēgis, m.: king
rōstrum, rōstrī, n.: beak
*sagitta, sagittae, f.: arrow
septimus, septima, septimum: seventh
sextus, sexta, sextum: sixth
silva, silvae, f.: forest
stabulum, stabulī, n.: stable
Stymphālis, Stymphālidis: adj. of Stymphalus (a lake)
summus, summa, summum: highest, greatest
superō, superāre, superāvī, superātus: overcome, conquer
suscipiō, suscipere, suscēpī, susceptus: undertake
tertius, tertia, tertium: third
timor, timōris, m.: fear
tōtus, tōta, tōtum: all, whole, entire
trīgintā (indecl. numeral adj.): thirty
unguis, unguis, m.: claw, talon
vīvus, vīva, vīvum: alive

Word Study: English Derivatives

From Lesson	Latin		From Narrative Reading	Latin
1. acceptable			1. carnivorous	
2. adjutant			2. delete	
3. fortify			3. implication	
4. fortunate			4. incision	
5. invincible			5. invert	
6. obsession			6. lesion	
7. perilous			7. oppressive	
8. reception			8. relic	
9. reduce			9. rostrum	

Summary Tasks

____ 1. Give the syntactic names for the constructions *hydrā occīsā* and *bēstiam exanimātam* that occur in the Narrative Reading, lesson 15.

____ 2. In the Narrative Reading for lesson 14, find and copy two examples of a periphrastic verb form.

____ 3. Give the final metaphrase for the first three words in each sentence of paragraph 1, Narrative Reading.

____ 4. Identify the part of speech and form of each word in S15.1.

____ 5. Name the syntactic function of each word in S15.1.

____ 6. Copy each finite verb in the Basic Sentences of lessons 14 and 15, and change the aspect from imperfective to perfective or vice versa.

Review Lesson 4

Lesson Vocabulary

Nouns

Bellovacī, Bellovacōrum, m. pl.: the Bellovaci, a people of Gallia Belgica
exercitus, exercitūs, m.: army
fax, facis, f.: torch, light, flame
flūmen, flūminis, n.: river
littera, litterae, f.: a letter of the alphabet; (usually pl.) a letter, dispatch; literature
lūx, lūcis, f.: light
obses, obsidis, m. & f.: hostage
somnus, somnī, m.: sleep
stēlla, stēllae, f.: star
vōx, vōcis, f.: voice, cry, utterance

Question Words

quō factō?: with what (having been) done?

Verbs

accipiō, accipere, accēpī, acceptus: accept, receive
crēscō, crēscere, crēvī, crētus: grow, increase
currō, currere, cucurrī, cursūrus: run, hasten
fluō, fluere, flūxī: flow
invādō, invādere, invāsī, invāsus: enter, attack
maneō, manēre, mānsī, mānsūrus: remain, stay
scrībō, scrībere, scrīpsī, scrīptus: write
sepeliō, sepelīre, sepelīvī, sepultus: bury

Readings Vocabulary

arcus, arcūs, m.: bow
ascendō, ascendere, ascendī, ascēnsus: climb, mount
cēterī, cēterae, cētera: the others, the rest
collum, collī, n.: neck
cōnspiciō, cōnspicere, cōnspexī, cōnspectus: see, look at
fīlia, fīliae, f.: daughter
ignis, ignis, m.: fire
incipiō, incipere, incēpī, inceptus: begin
intendō, intendere, intendī, intentus: stretch, bend; intend
jubeō, jubēre, jussī, jussus: order

leō, leōnis, m.: lion
pellis, pellis, f.: skin, animal hide
petō, petere, petīvī, petītus: seek, look for
portō, portāre, portāvī, portātus: carry
prīmum (adv.): at first
rēx, rēgis, m.: king
sagitta, sagittae, f.: arrow
statim (adv.): immediately
tum (adv.): then

Morphology Review

New Morphology: Lessons 14 and 15

verb, participles: perfective passive, imperfective active, future active

Form Identification

    a. vōx, vōcis, f.: voice, cry, utterance
    b. vocō, vocāre, vocāvī, vocātus: call, invite
    c. vocābulum, vocābulī, n.: word
    d. vōcālis, vōcāle: vocal

1. vōcis   _____
2. vocābulī   _____
3. vōce   _____
4. vocātīs   _____
5. vocante   _____
6. vōcāle   _____
7. vocantibus   _____
8. vocābulīs   _____
9. vocāre   _____
10. vōcālēs   _____

Narrative Reading

The Ninth and Tenth Labors of Hercules

Octāvō labōre cōnfectō, Eurystheus Herculem[1] Hippolytae[2] zōnam ā fīliā suā petītam capere[1] jussit. Hippolyta quae erat[3] rēgīna Amāzonum,[2] fēminārum[2] bellicōsārum,[2] zōnam trādere voluit; itaque Herculēs vēla dare parābat.[3] Cēterae Amāzonēs autem ā Jūnōne commōtae impetum in Herculis[2] nāvēs fēcērunt. Herculēs, cum hīs fēminīs pūgnāre coāctus, facile vīcit et, zōnā captā, ad urbem Mycēnās rediit.

Hōc labōre cōnfectō, Herculēs bovēs Gēryonis[2] capere jussus est. Gēryon erat[3] gigās triplicī[4] corpore,[4] quī in longinquā Hispāniā habitābat.[3] Quod iter erat[3] tam longum, Herculēs, ut fāma est, deō Apolline adjuvante, in crātērā aureā vēlum dedit. Pelle leōnis[2] prō vēlō intentā, brevī tempore in Hispāniam pervēnit.

Herculēs, postquam montem ascēndit, bovēs ā pāstōre magnō[4] corpore[4] et ā cane bicipitī custōdītōs cōnspexit. Hic canis, ferōciter lātrāns, in Herculem impetum fēcit, sed Herculēs, quī magnā cum fortitūdine pūgnābat,[3] et canem et pāstōrem clāvā mox occīdit. Jam ā Gēryone ad pūgnam prōvocātus est et, arcum intendēns, ūnam sōlam sagittam per triplica corpora gigantis[2] mīsit. Gēryone occīsō, prīmō crātēram auream Apollinī[5] reddidit, deinde bovēs per Eurōpam ad Graeciam dūcere coepit. Tandem, post aliās rēs gestās, Herculēs magnō itinere dēfessus in urbem Mycēnās pervēnit.

Notes

1. *Herculem . . . capere:* accusative with infinitive, object of *jussit*
2. *Hippolytae, Amāzonum, fēminārum bellicōsārum, Herculis, Gēryonis, leōnis, gigantis:* genitive case, translate "of _____"
3. *parābat, erat, habitābat, pūgnābat:* past imperfective verbs, translate *parābat* "was _____-ing," *erat* "was," *habitābat* "_____-ed," *pūgnābat* "was _____-ing"
4. *triplicī corpore, magnō corpore:* descriptive ablative. An ablative noun modified by an adjective may be used to modify another noun. As the equivalent of an adjective, this phrase answers the question *quālis? quāle?*
5. *Apollinī:* dative case, "to Apollo"

Vocabulary

Amāzonēs, Amāzonum, f. pl.: Amazons
Apollo, Apollinis, m.: Apollo (a Greek god)
*arcus, arcūs, m.: bow
*ascendō, ascendere, ascendī, ascēnsus: climb
aureus, aurea, aureum: of gold, golden
autem (sentence connector): but, however
bellicōsus, bellicōsa, bellicōsum: warlike
biceps (bicipitis): two headed, with two heads
bos, bōvis, m. & f.: cow
*cēterī, cēterae, cētera: the others, the rest
clāva, clāvae, f.: club
coepī, coepisse, coeptus (a defective verb): begin
commoveō, commovēre, commōvī, commōtus: move deeply, alarm
cōnficiō, cōnficere, cōnfēcī, cōnfectus: finish, complete
*cōnspiciō, cōnspicere, cōnspēxī, cōnspectus: catch sight of, see
crātēra, crātērae, f.: bowl
custōdiō, custōdīre, custōdīvī, custōdītus: guard
dēfessus, dēfessa, dēfessum: tired, exhausted
fāma, fāmae, f.: report, story, rumor
ferōciter (adv.): fiercely
*fīlia, fīliae, f.: daughter
fortitūdō, fortitūdinis, f.: strength, courage, bravery
gerō, gerere, gessī, gestus: do, make, carry on
Gēryon, Gēryonis, m.: Geryon
gigās, gigantis, m.: giant

Hispānia, Hispāniae, f.: Spain
*intendō, intendere, intendī, intentus: stretch, spread
iter, itineris, n.: journey
*jubeō, jubēre, jussī, jussus: order
*leō, leōnis, m.: lion
longinquus, longinqua, longinquum: far away
mōns, montis, m.: mountain
nāvis, nāvis, f.: ship
octāvus, octāva, octāvum: eighth
parō, parāre, parāvī, parātus: prepare, get ready
pāstor, pāstōris, m.: shepherd
*pellis, pellis, f.: skin, hide
perveniō, pervenīre, pervēnī: arrive
*petō, petere, petīvī, petītus: seek, ask for
prīmō (adv.): at first
prōvocō, prōvocāre, prōvocāvī, prōvocātus: call forth, challenge
pūgna, pūgnae, f.: fight, battle
pūgnō, pūgnāre, pūgnāvī: fight
reddō, reddere, reddidī, redditus: give back, return
redeō, redīre, rediī: come back, return
rēgīna, rēgīnae, f.: queen
tam (adv.): so
trādō, trādere, trādidī, trāditus: give over, hand over
triplex (triplicis): threefold, triple
vēlum, vēlī, n.: sail
vēlum dare: to set sail
zōna, zōnae, f.: belt

Derivatives from Narrative Reading

Latin

1. ascend
2. commotion
3. corps
4. crater
5. custodian
6. ferocious
7. impetuous
8. intervene
9. itinerary
10. provoke
11. triplicate
12. zone

■ Exercise 1: English to Latin Sentences

Using these Latin sentences as models, translate the following English sentences into Latin. Each Latin sentence should have one participle.

1. Littera scrīpta manet. (S14.3)
2. Fortūnā fortēs adjuvante, perīculum vincitur. (S15.1)
3. Herculēs, arcum intendēns, sagittās ēmīsit. (based on Narrative Reading)
4. Hydrā occīsā, Eurystheus quārtum labōrem imperāvit. (based on Narrative Reading)

a. An arrow shot into the air does not return. (1)

b. Because a god was helping, Hercules began the journey. (2)

c. A god, taking care of important things, neglects unimportant things. (3)

d. When the ninth labor was finished, Hercules undertook three other difficult labors. (4)

Vocabulary

Nouns
air: aura, aurae, f.
arrow: sagitta
god: deus
Hercules: Herculēs, Herculis, m.
journey: iter, itineris, n.
labor: labor

Adjectives
difficult: difficilis, difficile
important: magnus
ninth: nōnus, nōna, nōnum
other: alius, alia, aliud
three: trēs
unimportant: parvus

Indeclinables
into: in (prep.)
not: nōn (adv.)

Verbs
begin: coepī, coepisse, coeptus
finish: cōnficiō, cōnficere, cōnfēcī, cōnfectus
help: adjuvō
neglect: neglegō
return: redeō, redīre, rediī
shoot: ēmittō, ēmittere, ēmīsī, ēmissus
take care of: cūrō
undertake: suscipiō, suscipere, suscēpī, susceptus

■ Exercise 2: Latin Questions

Write a Latin answer to each of the following questions on the Narrative Reading.

1. Quis Hippolytae zōnam cupīvit?

2. Quā condiciōne Herculēs ex terrā Amāzonum exīre parābat?

3. Quis Amāzonēs commōvit?

4. Quō factō Herculēs ad urbem Mycēnās rediit?

5. Quandō Herculēs bovēs Gēryonis cōnspexit?

6. Quid agēns canis impetum in Herculem fēcit?

7. Quō auxiliō Herculēs canem et pāstōrem occīdit?

8. Quō factō Herculēs crātēram auream Apollinī reddidit?

Lesson 16

The Dative Case
Kernels with Nouns in the Dative
Nonkernel Occurrences of Nouns in the Dative

Nouns in the dative case can be expected as kernel items in two new kernel types that are introduced in this lesson. However, most nouns in the dative are not kernel items. These nonkernel datives can theoretically be expected in any sentence and, like nouns in the ablative, have a variety of semantic roles.

   A noun in the dative is never the object of a preposition, but it can almost always be metaphrased as object of a preposition, usually "to" or "for." (Reminder: Any discussion regarding nouns applies also to pronouns and adjectives used as nouns.)

Basic Sentences

16.1. Sōlitūdō placet Mūsīs, urbs est inimīca poētīs.—Petrarch (?)
   Solitude pleases the Muses; the city is unfriendly to poets.
16.2. Hōc tempore nūlla cīvitās Athēniēnsibus auxiliō fuit praeter Plataeēnsēs.—Nepos
   At this time no state was of help to the Athenians except the people of Plataea.
   (This refers to the Battle of Marathon in 490 B.C.)
16.3. Inopī beneficium bis dat quī dat celeriter.—Publilius Syrus
   Whoever confers a benefit quickly on a poor person confers it twice.
16.4. Impōnit fīnem sapiēns et rēbus honestīs.—Juvenal
   The wise person puts a limit even on honorable undertakings.

The Dative Case

Morphology

The dative case is in boldface in the paradigms. Examples of nouns by declension are given. For the dative case of adjectives and pronouns see model paradigms in previous lessons or in the Appendix.

	First	Second	Third	Fourth	Fifth
Singular					
Nominative	hōra	animus	fūr	manus	rēs
Accusative	hōram	animum	fūrem	manum	rem
Ablative	hōrā	animō	fūre	manū	rē
Dative	**hōrae**	**animō**	**fūrī**	**manuī**	**reī**
Genitive	hōrae	animī	fūris	manūs	reī
Plural					
Nominative	hōrae	animī	fūrēs	manūs	rēs
Accusative	hōrās	animōs	fūrēs	manūs	rēs
Ablative	hōrīs	animīs	fūribus	manibus	rēbus
Dative	**hōrīs**	**animīs**	**fūribus**	**manibus**	**rēbus**
Genitive	hōrārum	animōrum	fūrum	manuum	rērum

■ Exercise 1

Fully identify each of the following nouns and adjectives. Include part of speech. Give all possibilities.

1. vōcī _____

2. exercituī _____

3. vītā _____

4. perīculō _____

5. occāsiō _____

6. multīs _____

7. omnī _____

8. omne _____

9. lūce _____

10. lūcī _____

Kernels with Nouns in the Dative

Nouns in the dative can be expected as kernel items in two kernel types, the *special intransitive* and the *special linking*.

Syntax: The Special Intransitive Kernel

A dative in the environment of certain intransitive verbs is for the reader the equivalent of the accusative direct object of transitive verbs. In S16.1, *placet* is one such verb that patterns with a dative, here *Mūsīs*. *Placet* + *Mūsīs* is equivalent to the transitive verb *dēlectat* + accusative *Mūsās* in *Sōlitūdō dēlectat Mūsās;* both sentences mean "Solitude pleases the Muses."

It is practical, therefore, to consider this dative as a kernel item with the same function as an object in the accusative. This kernel type is called the *special intransitive kernel*. The label *direct object* is traditionally reserved for the accusative with transitive verbs; use the label *dative object* for datives in special intransitive kernels. Semantically, a dative object is an animate or abstract noun.

Here is a list of *special intransitive verbs*, i.e., verbs which regularly raise the expectation of a dative object.

> crēdō, crēdere, crēdidī (trust, rely on, *but not* entrust)
> faveō, favēre, fāvī (favor, offer favor to)
> noceō, nocēre, nocuī (harm, do harm to, injure)
> parcō, parcere, pepercī (spare, be lenient to)
> pāreō, pārēre, pāruī (obey, be obedient to)
> placeō, placēre, placuī (please, be pleasing to)
> resistō, resistere, restitī (resist, oppose, offer resistance to)
> serviō, servīre, servīvī (serve, help, offer service to)

Sentence 16.1 (*Sōlitūdō placet Mūsīs*) would be given on a kernel chart in this way:

Clause Marker	Item: Function	Item: Function	Item: Function	Kernel Type	F/NF	M/D	Adj./Adv./ Noun	Name
—	sōlitūdō: subject	placet: verb	Mūsīs: dative obj.	spec. intr.	F	M	—	statement

Syntax: The Special Linking Kernel

Lesson 10 introduced the linking kernel with a noun or adjective in the nominative case as subject complement. Occasionally this role may be filled by a noun in the dative. Only a few nouns commonly occur in this role. In S16.2 *auxiliō* is one such noun. Others are *honōrī* (honor, distinction), *impedīmentō* (hindrance), *salūtī* (health, safety), and *ūsuī* (advantage).

Note: These dative complements have sometimes been called *datives of purpose*.

The English sentence "This is an advantage" may be expressed in Latin as *Hoc ūsuī est* where *ūsuī* is in the dative case, not the nominative case. It might help to consider that "This is an advantage to you" may be restated as "This is to your advantage" or "This is for your advantage." Look at this sentence as given on the kernel chart.

Hoc ūsuī est.

Clause Marker	Item: Function	Item: Function	Item: Function	Kernel Type	F/NF	M/D	Adj./Adv./ Noun	Name
—	hoc: subject	ūsuī: dative complement	est: verb	spec. lkg.	F	M	—	statement

The sentence can be metaphrased in this way.

> Hoc: this ____s ± ____ .
> ūsuī: this ____s ± ____ for an advantage.
> est: this is for an advantage.
>
> Metaphrase: "This is (for) an advantage."
> Translation: "This is an advantage."

Note: The dative complement may also fill one of the complement slots in a factitive kernel. For example, *Caesar legiōnēs praesidiō relinquit.* (Caesar is leaving the legions as [for] a protection.)

■ Exercise 2

Copy the kernel items and write a translation for each of these sentences.

1. Pecūnia salūtī nōn est.

2. Bonus animus in malā rē magnō auxiliō est.

3. Successus nōn semper honōrī est.

4. Cui Fortūna favet multōs amīcōs habet.

Clause Marker	Item: Function	Item: Function	Item: Function	Kernel Type	F/NF	M/D	Adj./Adv./ Noun	Name
1.								
2.								
3.								
4.								
4.								

Final Translation

1.

2.

3.

4.

Nonkernel Occurrences of Nouns in the Dative

Nouns in the dative that are not part of the kernel may occur in any sentence. In certain environments, such nonkernel datives can be expected regularly; however, they may also occur without any special signal in the environment.

A dative that occurs without any special signal in the environment generally designates the person (less often the thing) to whom the sentence refers or is of interest. The name commonly used to describe it is *dative of reference*.

Fugit hōra. (Time flies.)
Omnibus hōra fugit. (Time flies *for everybody*.)

The specific syntactic information conveyed by a dative such as *omnibus* in *omnibus hōra fugit* is not as easily understood as that of other modifiers studied so far. It is clear that it is not an adjectival modifier and adverbial modifier may be too narrow a description when the dative seems to modify or expand the whole sentence. Nevertheless, for the purposes of the beginning student of Latin it is convenient to consider nonkernel datives as adverbial modifiers.

When the *dative of reference* occurs in a sentence which has a linking kernel with a *dative complement* (*dative of purpose*), the name *double dative* is frequently used to label this combination of datives.

> Bonus animus *magnō auxiliō omnibus* est. (Good courage is *of great help for all*. or *For all people*, good courage is a *great help*.)

In S16.2 *nūlla cīvitās Athēniēnsibus auxiliō fuit*, *auxiliō* is the dative complement and *Athēniēnsibus*, an animate noun, is the dative of reference.

Specific Environments for the Dative

This section presents some specific environments where the nonkernel dative may be expected *regularly*. These uses of the dative are traditionally named according to individual characteristics of the environment.

1. *Dative with* est. When *est* is not a linking verb but is the so-called existential *est*, i.e., "_____ exists," or "there is _____ ," the dative signals the person to whom something belongs. It is therefore called the *dative of possession*.

> *Cui* liber est? (*To whom* does the book belong?)
> *Virō* liber est, nōn *puerō*. (The book belongs *to the man*, not *the boy*.)

Note: All the compounds of the verb *sum, esse* except *absum, abesse* (be away, be apart) set up the expectation of a dative.

> adsum, adesse: be present (to/for _____) / help (_____)
> dēsum, dēesse: be lacking (to _____) / fail (_____)

2. *Dative with verbs meaning "give," "tell," "show," "offer."* The dative signals the *indirect object*, i.e., the person to whom somebody gives, tells, etc., something. These verbs include:

> dīcō, dīcere, dīxī, dictus (say, tell, speak)
> dō, dare, dedī, datus (give)
> mōnstrō, mōnstrāre, mōnstrāvī, mōnstrātus (show)
> nārrō, nārrāre, nārrāvī, nārrātus (tell, relate, narrate)
> offerō, offerre, obtulī, oblātus (offer)

> *Cui* occāsiō aegrē offertur? (*To whom* is opportunity offered with difficulty?)
> *Hominī* occāsiō aegrē offertur. (Opportunity is offered *to a person* with difficulty.)

In S16.3 *inopī* is the indirect object with *dat*.

3. *Dative with compound verbs.* The dative serves as an expansion item with many verbs that are compounded with prefixes. These prefixes include *ad-, ante-, com-, in-, ob-, post-, prae-, pro-*, and *sub-*, as in these compounds of *pōnō:*

> appōnō (put [accusative] toward/next to [dative])
> antepōnō (put [accusative] before [dative])
> oppōnō (put [accusative] against [dative] , etc.)

In S16.4 *rēbus honestīs* fulfills the expectation raised by the verb *impōnit*. This dative use is simply called *dative with compound verb*.

4. *Dative with adjectives.* The dative patterns with certain adjectives of fitness, nearness, likeness, inclination, and their opposites. These include *amīcus* and *inimīcus*, *aptus, cārus, grātus, proximus, similis* and *dissimilis*. This dative use is called *dative with adjectives*.

In S16.1 *poētīs* patterns with the adjective *inimīca*.

It is impossible to identify a noun in the dative by morpheme except in the dative singular of the third and fourth declension, where the morpheme {ī} is unambiguous. However, when the morpheme is ambiguous one should consider these suggestions.

  a. Examine the environment of a could-be dative with both syntactic and semantic considerations in mind.

  b. Remember that a noun with the semantic category *animate* is more likely to be a dative than an ablative, except in an ablative absolute or after a preposition.

  c. Examine any modifying adjective to see if its form is unambiguous.

Example: *Frātrēs frātribus similēs sunt: frātribus* is probably a dative because *frāter* has the category *animate* and because *similis* belongs on the list of adjectives that pattern with a dative.

Example: *Deō volente: Deō* is probably ablative because the modifier *volente* is definitely ablative.

■ Exercise 3

Complete the chart for the following sentences. The first sentence is given as an example.

	Word in Dative or Ablative	Criteria/Signals from Syntax or Semantics	Case in This Sentence
1. Frātrēs frātribus similēs sunt.	frātribus	*similēs* is on the "dative with adjectives" list	dative
2. Urbs poētīs nōn placuit.			
3. Vulpēs piscibus inimīcae sunt.			
4. Patre vīsō, puer laetus est.			
5. Haec rēs impedīmentō fuit.			
6. Noctēs atque diēs patet jānua hominibus.			
7. Occāsiō populō offertur aegrē.			
8. Timidī nōn pūgnant cum fortibus.			
9. Fīnis philosophō opus corōnāvit.			
10. Timidī fortibus auxilium nōn dedērunt.			
11. Mātrī pecūnia est.			
12. Lupus timōrem virō injēcit.			

■ Exercise 4

Write a metaphrase for each sentence in exercise 3.

1.

2.

3.

4.

5.

6.

7.

8.

9.

10.

11.

12.

Lesson Vocabulary

Nouns

beneficium, beneficiī, n.: kindness, favor, service
cīvitās, cīvitātis, f.: state; citizenship
honor, honōris, m.: honor, distinction
impedīmentum, impedīmentī, n.: hindrance
Mūsa, Mūsae, f.: a Muse
poēta, poētae, m.: poet
salūs, salūtis, f.: health, safety
sōlitūdō, sōlitūdinis, f.: loneliness, solitude
ūsus, ūsūs, m.: advantage, use; practice

Adjectives

aptus, apta, aptum: fitting, suitable
Athēniēnsēs, Athēniēnsium: (people) of Athens
cārus, cāra, cārum: dear
dissimilis, dissimile: not like
grātus, grāta, grātum: pleasing, agreeable
honestus, honesta, honestum: honorable, respectable
inimīcus, inimīca, inimīcum: unfriendly, hostile
nūllus, nūlla, nūllum: no
Plataeēnsēs, Plataeēnsium: Plataeans; people of Plataea
proximus, proxima, proximum: nearest, next
similis, simile: similar, like

Indeclinables

Adverbs

bis: twice

celeriter: quickly

Intensifier

et (shortened form of etiam): even

Verbs

adsum, adesse, adfuī: be present, be at hand

crēdō, crēdere, crēdidī: trust, rely on

dēsum, dēesse, dēfuī: be lacking, fail

dīcō, dīcere, dīxī, dictus: say, tell, speak; call, name

faveō, favēre, fāvī: favor, offer favor to

impōnō, impōnere, imposuī, impositus: place upon, impose

iniciō, inicere, injēcī, injectus: throw on or into

mōnstrō, mōnstrāre, mōnstrāvī, mōnstrātus: show

nārrō, nārrāre, nārrāvī, nārrātus: tell, relate, narrate

noceō, nocēre, nocuī: harm, do harm to

parcō, parcere, pepercī: spare, be lenient to

placeō, placēre, placuī: please, be pleasing to

resistō, resistere, restitī: resist, offer resistance to

serviō, servīre, servīvī: serve, help, offer service to

Readings

Required

16.1. Cui Fortūna favet multōs amīcōs habet.—Anon.

16.2. Inopiae dēsunt multa; avāritiae omnia.—Publilius Syrus

16.3. Deus superbīs resistit; humilibus autem dat grātiam.—I Peter

16.4. Bonus vir nēmō est nisī quī bonus est omnibus.—Publilius Syrus

16.5. Sōl omnibus lūcet.—Petronius

16.6. Nūllī est hominī perpetuum bonum.—Plautus

Vocabulary

16.2. inopia, inopiae, f.: neediness

16.3. superbus, superba, superbum: lofty, haughty

humilis, humile: humble, lowly

grātia, grātiae, f.: favor, kindness, grace

16.4. nēmō, nēminis, m. & f.: no one

nisī (subord. conj.): except, unless

16.5. sōl, sōlis, m.: sun

lūceō, lūcēre, lūxī: shine

16.6. perpetuus, perpetua, perpetuum: perpetual, everlasting

Optional

16.7. Maximō perīculō custōdītur quod multīs placet.—Publilius Syrus

16.8. Mulier quae multīs nūbit multīs nōn placet.—Publilius Syrus

16.9. Gaudēns gaudentī, flēns flentī, pauper egentī, prūdēns prūdentī, stultus placet īnsipientī.—Werner

16.10. Nēmō līber est quī corporī servit.—Seneca

16.11. Deō, Rēgī, Patriae.—Motto

16.12. Suum cuique pulchrum est.—Cicero

16.13. Verbum sapientī sat est.—Anon.

16.14. Immodicīs brevis est aetās et rāra senectūs.—Martial

16.15. Nīl hominī certum est.—Ovid

Vocabulary

16.7. maximus, maxima, maximum: greatest
*custōdiō, custōdīre, custōdīvī, custōdītus: guard

16.8. mulier, mulieris, f.: woman
nūbō, nūbere, nūpsī: marry

16.9. gaudeō, gaudēre: rejoice, be glad
fleō, flēre, flēvī: weep
pauper (pauperis): poor
egeō, egēre, eguī: be needy (with abl. or gen. as its complement)
īnsipiēns (īnsipientis): foolish

16.10. nēmō, nēminis, m. & f.: no one
līber, lībera, līberum: free

16.11. patria, patriae, f.: country, homeland

16.12. quisque, quidque: each one

16.13. sat (indecl.): enough

16.14. immodicus, immodica, immodicum: immoderate
aetās, aetātis, f.: lifetime
rārus, rāra, rārum: rare, unusual
*senectūs, senectūtis, f.: old age

16.15. *certus, certa, certum: certain, sure

Word Study: English Derivatives

From Lesson	Latin	From Readings	Latin
1. beneficial		1. favorable	
2. credence		2. humility	
3. date		3. perpetuate	
4. dative		4. resistance	
5. inimical		5. solar	
6. opulent		6. superb	
7. placid		7. translucent	
8. solitary			

Narrative Reading

The Eleventh Labor: The Golden Apples

Part 1

Decimō labōre cōnfectō, Eurystheus Herculī ūndecimum labōrem imposuit. Herculēs aurea pōma ex hortō Hesperidum[1] reportāre dēbuit. Hesperidēs erant nymphae pulchrae, quibus haec pōma ā Jūnōne commissa erant.[2] Aliī hominēs, aurī[3] cupiditāte inductī, pōma auferre sine successū temptāverant.[2] Rēs difficillima[4] erat. Nam hortus, in quō pōma erant, altō mūrō circumdatus est. Dracō, cui fuērunt centum capita et quī numquam dormīvit, portam hortī[3] custōdīvit. Praetereā situs hortī[3] erat Herculī omnīnō ignōtus. Herculēs, quamquam opus erat difficillimum,[4] cōnstituit tamen Eurystheō pārēre. Multa itinera per multās terrās fēcit, sed dē situ hortī[3] nihil invenīre potuit. Tandem in longinquam terram pervēnit, quae Ōceanō proxima erat. In illō locō Atlantem, gigantem ingentis[3] corporis,[3] quī caelum umerīs sustinēbat, invēnit. Ab eō Herculēs auxilium petīvit. Quod Atlās erat pater Hesperidum,[1] situm hortī[3] cognōvit et Herculī prōdesse voluit, sed dracōnem maximē timuit. Herculēs autem, sagittā trāns mūrum trājectā, dracōnem statim interfēcit. Deinde negōtium caelum sustinendī[5] suscēpit, dum Atlās abest.

Herculēs reditum Atlantis[3] plūrēs diēs exspectāvit, neque ūllam fāmam dē reditū ejus[6] audīvit. Tandem, longā morā commōtus, eum cum tribus pōmīs redeuntem vīdit. Atlās autem pōma Herculī nōn dedit, quod ipse Eurystheō ea trādere volēbat. Hoc Herculī nōn placuit, quī novum cōnsilium cēpit. Atlās, ut Herculēs rogāvit, pondus caelī[3] recēpit, dum Herculēs pulvīnum umerīs suīs impōnit. Deinde Herculēs pōma cēpit et, magnīs gratiīs Atlantī actīs, ad Graeciam iter facere properāvit.

Notes

1. *Hesperidum:* genitive plural of *Hesperidēs;* translate "of the Hesperides"
2. *commissa erant,* past perfective passive, "had been _____-ed"; *temptāverant,* past perfective active, "had _____-ed"
3. *aurī, hortī, ingentis corporis, Atlantis, caelī:* genitive singular, translate "of _____"
4. *difficillimus, -a, -um:* superlative adjective, "very _____"
5. *sustinendī:* a gerund, genitive case, translate "of _____-ing"
6. *ejus:* genitive case of *is, ea, id,* translate "his"

Vocabulary

absum, abesse, āfuī: be away from, be absent
alius, alia, aliud: another, other
altus, alta, altum: high
Atlās, Atlantis, m.: Atlas (giant who carried the sky on his shoulders)
auferō, auferre, abstulī, ablātus: carry away, remove
aureus, aurea, aureum: of gold, golden
aurum, aurī, n.: gold
caelum, caelī, n.: sky
caput, capitis, n.: head
circumdō, circumdare, circumdedī, circumdatus: surround
committō, committere, commīsī, commissus: entrust
commoveō, commovēre, commōvī, commōtus: alarm
cōnficiō, cōnficere, cōnfēcī, cōnfectus: achieve, finish
cōnstituō, cōnstituere, cōnstituī, cōnstitūtus: decide

cupiditās, cupiditātis, f.: desire, wish
decimus, decima, decimum: tenth
difficilis, difficile: difficult
dormiō, dormīre, dormīvī, dormītus: sleep
dracō, dracōnis, m.: dragon
exspectō, exspectāre, exspectāvī, exspectātus: wait for, look for
fāma, fāmae, f.: report, rumor
gigās, gigantis, m.: giant
grātiae, grātiārum, f. pl.: thanks
hortus, hortī, m.: garden
ignōtus, ignōta, ignōtum: unknown
indūcō, indūcere, indūxī, inductus: lead on, influence
ingēns (ingentis): huge, enormous
inveniō, invenīre, invēnī, inventus: discover
ipse, ipsa, ipsum (intensive pronoun): him/her/itself, themselves
iter, itineris, n.: journey
longinquus, longinqua, longinquum: far away
mūrus, mūrī, m.: wall
nam (sentence connector): for
negōtium, negōtiī, n.: task
neque (coord. conj.): nor, and not
omnīnō (adv.): entirely
pāreō, pārēre, pāruī: (+ dat. obj.) obey
perveniō, pervenīre, pervēnī: arrive at, come to
plūrēs, plūrium (pl. only): quite a number, several
pōmum, pōmī, n.: apple
pondus, ponderis, n.: weight
porta, portae, f.: gate
praetereā (adv.): moreover, in addition, besides
*properō, properāre, properāvī, properātus: hurry, hasten
prōsum, prōdesse, prōfuī: be useful, be a help to
pulvīnus, pulvīnī, m.: cushion, pillow
quamquam (subord. conj.): although
recipiō, recipere, recēpī, receptus: take back
reditus, reditūs, m.: return
reportō, reportāre, reportāvī, reportātus: carry back
rogō, rogāre, rogāvī, rogātus: ask
situs, situs, m.: location
suscipiō, suscipere, suscēpī, susceptus: undertake
sustineō, sustinēre, sustinuī, sustentus: hold up
tamen (adv.): nevertheless
temptō, temptāre, temptāvī, temptātus: try, attempt
terra, terrae, f.: land
*timeō, timēre, timuī: fear, be afraid of
trādō, trādere, trādidī, trāditus: hand over
*trājiciō, trājicere, trājēcī, trājectus: hurl, shoot
ūllus, ūlla, ūllum: any
umerus, umerī, m.: shoulder
undecimus, undecima, undecimum: eleventh

The Eleventh Labor: The Golden Apples

Part 2

Herculēs ad Graeciam rēctā viā nōn rediit. Prīmum Libyam trānsiit, ubi Antaeus gigās viātōrēs cum ipsō pūgnāre coēgit; hōc modō eōs interfēcit. Nōn sōlum erat Antaeus validus perītusque āthlēta, sed, quotiēns terram tetigit, vīrēs eī refectae sunt. Herculēs, quod Antaeum viātōribus nōn jam nocēre voluit, eum ad pūgnam prōvocāvit. Pūgna erat longa et difficilis; māter Tellūs auxiliō Antaeō erat. Tandem Herculēs Antaeum altum super terram sustulit; costās compressit et frēgit. Hōc modō Antaeō nōn pepercit, sed eī mortem effēcit. Antaeō interfectō, Herculēs ad Graeciam rūrsus prōcessit, et post longum tempus in urbem Mycēnās pervēnit, ubi Eurystheō aurea pōma trādidit.

Vocabulary

altus, alta, altum: high
āthlēta, āthlētae, m.: athlete
*aureus, aurea, aureum: of gold, golden
comprimō, comprimere, compressī, compressus: press together, squeeze
costa, costae, f.: rib
difficilis, difficile: difficult
efficiō, efficere, effēcī, effectus: bring about, cause
gigās, gigantis, m.: giant
ipse, ipsa, ipsum (intensive pronoun): him/her/itself, themselves
mors, mortis, f.: death
nōn jam: no longer
perītus, perīta, perītum: experienced, trained
pōmum, pōmī, n.: apple
*prōvocō, prōvocāre, prōvocāvī, prōvocātus: challenge
pūgna, pūgnae, f.: battle
*pūgnō, pūgnāre, pūgnāvī, pūgnātus: fight
quotiēns (subord. conj.): as often as, every time that
rēctus, rēcta, rēctum: direct, straight
redeō, redīre, rediī, reditūrus: return
reficiō, reficere, refēcī, refectus: restore, renew
rūrsus (adv.): again
sōlus, sōla, sōlum: alone, only
sufferō, sufferre, sustulī, sublātus: hold up
tangō, tangere, tetigī, tāctus: touch
Tellūs, Tellūris, f.: Earth; Mother Earth (a goddess)
terra, terrae, f.: land
tollō, tollere, sustulī, sublātus: lift up, raise
trādō, trādere, trādidī, trāditus: hand over
trānseō, trānsīre, trānsiī: go across
validus, valida, validum: strong
*via, viae, f.: road, way
*viātor, viātōris, m.: traveler

Derivatives from Narrative Reading

Part 1	Latin	Part 2	Latin
1. approximate		1. direct	
2. commission		2. experience	
3. constitution		3. innocent	
4. impose		4. procession	
5. negotiate		5. refectory	
6. situated		6. repression	
7. sustain		7. viaduct	

Summary Tasks

_____ 1. Write the paradigm, singular and plural (nominative, accusative, ablative, dative), of these noun-participle pairs.
  a. ūsus impositus
  b. beneficium placēns
  c. Mūsa poētīs favēns

_____ 2. Copy and name all datives that occur in Readings 16.1 through 16.6.

_____ 3. Copy from the Narrative Reading, part 1, all complementary infinitives together with the finite verb that they complement.

_____ 4. Bracket in the Narrative Reading, part 2, all finite dependent clauses.

_____ 5. Write the Latin for:
  a. Hercules saw them.
  b. Hercules did not spare them.

_____ 6. Copy from the first ten lines of the Narrative Reading, part 1, all nouns that could be either ablative or dative.

Lesson 17

The Genitive Case
Noun in the Genitive as Adjectival Modifier

It should be clear by now that the same case has different roles according to the semantic or syntactic environment. This is true also of the *genitive* case that is introduced in this lesson.

Just like the dative, the genitive may be a kernel part, i.e., complement in a linking kernel. Likewise, there are special intransitive verbs that pattern with an object in the genitive. Both are rare and, therefore, are *not* introduced here. This lesson introduces the genitive as *adjectival modifier*.

It is important to note that the genitive case is the only inflected case in the English noun system; it is marked by apostrophe + s (singular) or by an apostrophe (plural), e.g., girl's, girls'. It is often called the *possessive* case.

Basic Sentences

17.1. Imāgō animī vultus; indicēs oculī.—Cicero
       The face is a vague reflection of the spirit; the eyes are the clear indicators.
17.2. Jūstitia omnium est domina et rēgīna virtūtum.—Cicero (adapted)
       Justice is the mistress and queen of all the virtues.

The Genitive Case

Morphology

See model paradigms of nouns, adjectives, and pronouns in previous lessons or in the Appendix for the complete morphology of these parts of speech. The genitive singular of a noun is already known, since it is part of the dictionary listing. Examples of nouns in the genitive singular and plural, by declension, are:

	First	Second	Third	Fourth	Fifth
Singular Genitive	hōrae	animī	fūris piscis	manūs	reī
Plural Genitive	hōrārum	animōrum	fūrum piscium (i-stem)	manuum	rērum

176

Noun in the Genitive as Adjectival Modifier

Syntax

The most common role of the genitive is to modify another noun. The syntactic information conveyed by this genitive is *adjectival modifier*. Example: *imāgō animī* (reflection of the spirit), where *imāgō* (in the nominative) is the noun-head and *animī* (in the genitive) is the adjectival modifier.

If there is more than one noun in the clause, as in S17.1, there may be ambiguity as to which noun is the noun-head for the genitive. Generally, there is no syntactic signal to indicate the direction of modification. The reader should assume that it goes with the nearest noun with which it makes a sensible combination. In the spoken language, the direction of modification is indicated by intonation and pauses. Thus in S17.1 a pause would occur after *animī,* not after *imāgō.*

Caution: Although the genitive is an adjectival modifier, it does *not agree* with its noun-head in case, number, or gender as adjectives do.

■ Exercise 1
Underline each noun or adjective in the genitive and draw an arrow to the noun-head that it modifies.

1. Imāgō animī vultus; indicēs ∅ = animī oculī.

2. Jūstitia omnium est domina et rēgīna virtūtum.

Metaphrasing

It is safest to metaphrase the genitive after its noun-head as "(noun-head) of (noun in genitive) ." In a translation some genitives may appear before the noun-head as nouns with apostrophes, e.g., *imāgō animī:* "reflection of the spirit" = "*spirit's* reflection."

There are a variety of possible semantic relationships between noun-head and noun in the genitive. For example, in the phrase "the portrait of Anna," Anna may be the owner of the painting, the painter, or the person painted. Traditionally, the following labels have been used to describe the semantic relationships between the genitive and its noun-head.

a. *possessive* genitive: "the portrait of Anna" = the painting owned by Anna
b. *subjective* genitive: "the portrait of Anna" = Anna painted it
c. *objective* genitive: "the portrait of Anna" = someone painted Anna's portrait
d. *partitive* genitive: "some of the portraits" = some *part* of the whole number of paintings

This is similar to "case uses" that label, e.g., the semantic relationships of nouns in the ablative without a preposition to their environment (see lesson 6).

The genitive of the relative pronoun should be translated "whose," not "of whom." Thus, *puerī quōrum amīcī vēnērunt* is translated "the boys whose friends have arrived _____ ± _____ ."

■ Exercise 2
Which of the following can be expressed with an -'s form?

1. lots of candy

2. love of truth

3. truth of love

4. property of the people

5. people of property

6. writer of a story

7. story of a writer

8. the oldest of the sisters

The genitive can also be a *genitive of description,* as in this example from the Narrative Reading of lesson 16: *Atlantem, gigantem ingentis corporis, invēnit* (He found Atlas, a giant of huge body).

It is not always possible or necessary to specify a particular semantic relationship between noun-head and noun in the genitive. The "_____ of _____" format is most efficient under these circumstances.

■ Exercise 3
Write the paradigms of the following sets of words.

	magnum opus	*quī vir*	*ratiō bona*	*ea rēs*
Singular				
Nominative				
Accusative				
Ablative				
Dative				
Genitive				
Plural				
Nominative				
Accusative				
Ablative				
Dative				
Genitive				

■ Exercise 4

Metaphrase each of the following in the context of a complete sentence.

1. vultus ejus virī

2. nōmen Rōmulī

3. pater cujus fīlia adest

4. omnium imāginēs deōrum

5. vōcem hujus puerī

6. fēminās quārum vōcēs audiuntur

Lesson Vocabulary

Nouns

domina, dominae, f.: mistress
imāgō, imāginis, f.: image, likeness
index, indicis, m.: indicator, sign; informer
jūstitia, jūstitiae, f.: justice
rēgīna, rēgīnae, f.: queen
virtūs, virtūtis, f.: excellence; courage; goodness; virtue
vultus, vultūs, m.: appearance, face

Readings

Required

17.1. Tōtus mundus deōrum est immortālium templum.—Seneca
17.2. Discordia ōrdinum venēnum est urbis.—Q. Capitolinus
17.3. Nēmō mortālium omnibus hōrīs sapit.—Pliny the Elder
17.4. Quī pingit flōrem, flōris nōn pingit odōrem.—Werner
17.5. Jūcunda memoria est praeteritōrum malōrum.—Cicero
17.6. Condidit urbem Rōmulus quam ex nōmine suō Rōmam vocāvit. Centum senēs
    ēlēgit quōrum cōnsiliō omnia ēgit et quōs senātōrēs nōminānit propter
    senectūtem.—Eutropius
17.7. Calamitās virtūtis occāsiō est.—Seneca

Vocabulary

17.1.   tōtus, tōta, tōtum: whole, entire
        mundus, mundī, m.: world
        immortālis, immortāle: immortal
        templum, templī, n.: temple

17.2. discordia, discordiae, f.: lack of harmony, discord
      ordō, ordinis, m.: order, rank
17.3. mortālis, mortāle: mortal
      *sapiō, sapere, sapīvī: know, have knowledge of
17.4. pingō, pingere, pīnxī, pictus: draw, paint
      flōs, flōris, m.: flower
      odor, odōris, m.: smell, odor
17.5. jūcundus, jūcunda, jūcundum: pleasant
      memoria, memoriae, f.: remembrance, memory
      praeteritus, praeterita, praeteritum: past
17.6. *senex, senis, m.: old man
      ēlegō, ēlegere, ēlēgī, ēlēctus: choose, select
      senātor, senātōris, m.: senator
17.7. calamitās, calamitātis, f.: misfortune, calamity

Optional

17.8. Rōma caput mundī.—Lucan
17.9. Salūs populī suprēma lēx.—Legal
17.10. Nōn scrībit, cujus carmina nēmō legit.—Martial
17.11. Bonus animus in malā rē dīmidium est malī.—Plautus
17.12. Rērum hūmānārum domina Fortūna.—Cicero
17.13. Māter artium necessitās.—Anon.
17.14. Patria . . . commūnis est omnium parēns.—Cicero

Vocabulary
17.8. *caput, capitis, n.: head
      mundus, mundī, m.: world
17.9. suprēmus, suprēma, suprēmum: highest, most important
17.10. carmen, carminis, n.: song, poem
      legō, legere, lēgī, lēctus: read
17.11. dīmidium, dīmidiī, n.: half
17.13. *necessitās, necessitātis, f.: necessity
17.14. *patria, patriae, f.: country, homeland
      commūnis, commūne: common, shared
      parēns, parentis, m. & f.: parent

Word Study: English Derivatives

From Lesson	Latin	From Readings	Latin
1. dominion		1. calamity	
2. imagine		2. condiment	
3. indicate		3. discordant	
4. justice		4. jocund	
5. regiment		5. mortality	
6. virtuous		6. mundane	

Narrative Reading

Twelfth Labor: Hercules Goes to the Underworld

Aureīs pōmīs ad Eurystheum relātīs, ūnus labor relinquēbātur,[1] quī difficillimus[2] duodecim labōrum erat.[1] Nam Eurystheus Herculem[3] trahere[3] Cerberum jussit ex Orcō, Plūtōnis rēgnō, ex quō nēmō umquam redierat.[4] Praetereā Cerberus mōnstrum erat,[1] cui erant[1] tria capita serpentibus saevīs cīncta. Herculēs tamen imperia rēgis Eurystheī perficere mātūrāvit. "Nūllum opus," sibi[5] inquit, "Herculī difficile est!"

Itaque in Lacōniam iter fēcit. Hīc erat[1] spēlunca quae aditum ad Orcum dedit. Auxiliō Mercuriī et Minervae Herculēs sine morā ad Orcum dēscendit et mox ad rīpam flūminis Stygis pervēnērunt. Quod in hōc flūmine nūllus pōns erat,[1] umbrae mortuōrum trāns-vehēbantur[6] ā Charonte quī cum parvā scaphā ad rīpam exspectābat.[6] Herculēs nāvem statim cōnscendit, sed Charon propter magnum pondus Herculis scapham solvere nōlēbat.[6] Tandem minīs Herculis territus Charon eum trāns flūmen trādūxit.

Postquam flūmen Stygem trānsiit, Herculēs ab Mercuriō et Minervā dēductus in sēdem Plūtōnis vēnit. Plūtō eum benīgnē excēpit, et facultātem quam ille petēbat[6] libenter dedit. "Sed," inquit Plūtō, "necesse est Cerberum sine armīs capere et auferre, et posteā in Orcum redūcere." Statim Herculēs Cerberum nōn sine magnō perīculō prehendit et summō cum labōre ad urbem Eurystheī trāxit. Quō[7] factō, Eurystheus maximē territus Herculem[3] mōnstrum sine morā in Orcum redūcere jussit.

Sīc contrā omnium opīniōnem illī duodecim labōrēs quōs Eurystheus jusserat[4] intrā duodecim annōs cōnfectī sunt et Herculēs tandem servitūte līberātus magnō cum gaudiō ad urbem Thēbās rediit.

Notes
1. *relinquēbātur; erat, erant:* past imperfective, translate "was left"; "was, were"
2. *difficillimus, -a, -um:* "very difficult"
3. *Herculem:* accusative, with infinitive *trahere,* object of *jussit* (see lesson 23)
4. *redierat, jusserat:* past perfective, translate "had returned," "had ordered"
5. *sibi:* reflexive pronoun, dative case, "to himself"
6. *trānsvehēbantur, exspectābat, nōlēbat, petēbat:* past imperfective tense, showing *continued* and *repeated* or *customary* action; translate "were accustomed to be carried across," "waited," "did not want," "was seeking"
7. *quō:* a connecting relative, "this"; see note on Narrative Reading, lesson 15

Vocabulary
aditus, aditūs, m.: access, approach
*arma, armōrum, n. pl.: weapons
auferō, auferre, abstulī, ablātus: carry away
benīgnē (adv.): kindly
Cerberus, Cerberī, m.: Cerberus (a dog who guarded the entrance to the Underworld)
Charon, Charontis, m.: Charon (ferryman of the Underworld)
cingō, cingere, cīnxī, cīnctus: encircle, surround
*cōnficiō, cōnficere, cōnfēcī, cōnfectus: finish, achieve
cōnscendō, cōnscendere, cōnscendī: go aboard
dēdūcō, dēdūcere, dēdūxī, dēductus: conduct
dēscendō, dēscendere, dēscendī: descend

*difficilis, difficile: difficult

excipiō, excipere, excēpī, exceptus: receive

exspectō, exspectāre, exspectāvī, exspectātus: wait

facultās, facultātis, f.: opportunity

gaudium, gaudiī, n.: joy

hīc (adv.): here

imperium, imperiī, n.: command

inquit: "―― says"

*iter, itineris, n.: journey

Lacōnia, Lacōniae, f.: Laconia (the area around Sparta in ancient Greece)

libenter (adv.): gladly, willingly

līberō, līberāre, līberāvī, līberātus: set free, free

mātūrō, mātūrāre, mātūrāvī: hasten

Mercurius, Mercuriī, m.: Mercury (one of the twelve Olympian gods and goddesses)

minae, minārum, f. pl.: threats

Minerva, Minervae, f.: Minerva (one of the twelve Olympian gods and goddesses)

mōnstrum, mōnstrī, n.: monster

*mortuus, mortua, mortuum: dead, belonging to the dead

nam (sentence connector): for

nāvis, nāvis, f.: ship

necesse (indecl. adj.): necessary

nōlō, nōlle, nōluī: be unwilling, not wish

opīniō, opīniōnis, f.: opinion, expectation

Orcus, Orcī, m.: the Underworld

*perficiō, perficere, perfēcī, perfectus: make or do thoroughly, carry out

*perveniō, pervenīre, pervēnī: arrive

Plūtō, Plūtōnis, m.: Pluto (king of the Underworld, brother of Jupiter)

*pōmum, pōmī, n.: apple

pondus, ponderis, n.: weight

pōns, pontis, m.: bridge

posteā (adv.): afterward

praetereā (adv.): besides (this)

prehendō, prehendere, prehendī, prehēnsus: seize, grasp

*redeō, redīre, rediī: go back, return

*redūcō, redūcere, redūxī, reductus: lead back, bring back

referō, referre, rettulī, relātus: bring back, carry back

rēgnum, rēgnī, n.: kingdom

*relinquō, relinquere, relīquī, relictus: leave behind

rīpa, rīpae, f.: bank, shore

saevus, saeva, saevum: fierce

scapha, scaphae, f.: small boat, skiff

sēdēs, sēdis, f.: seat, dwelling place

servitūs, servitūtis, f.: slavery

sīc (adv.): so, in this manner

solvō, solvere, solvī, solūtus: loosen, set sail

spēlunca, spēluncae, f.: cave

Styx, Stygis, f.: Styx (the chief river of the Underworld)

*summus, summa, summum: greatest

tamen (adv.): nevertheless
*terreō, terrēre, terruī, territus: be frightened, terrified
Thēbae, Thēbārum, f. pl.: Thebes (a city in Greece)
trādūcō, trādūcere, trādūxī, trāductus: carry across, bring over
trahō, trahere, trāxī, trāctus: drag, pull
trānseō, trānsīre, trānsiī: go across
trānsvehō, trānsvehere, trānsvēxī, trānsvectus: carry across
umbra, umbrae, f.: ghost
umquam (adv.): ever

Derivatives from Narrative Reading

Latin

1. capital

2. descend

3. distracted

4. efficient

5. menace

6. ponderous

7. recipient

8. relate

9. solution

10. succinct

11. transit

12. vehicle

Summary Tasks

____ 1. Copy all genitives plus noun-heads from Readings 17.1 through 17.7.
____ 2. Write the genitive plural for all nouns in the Review Lesson 5 list.
____ 3. Copy all kernels, finite and non-finite, from the third paragraph of the Narrative Reading.
____ 4. Copy all adverbial modifiers from the same paragraph.

Review Lesson 5

Lesson Vocabulary

Nouns
beneficium, beneficiī, n.: kindness, favor, service
cīvitās, cīvitātis, f.: state; citizenship
domina, dominae, f.: mistress
honor, honōris, m.: honor, distinction
imāgō, imāginis, f.: image, likeness
impedīmentum, impedīmentī, n.: hindrance
index, indicis, m.: indicator, sign; informer
jūstitia, jūstitiae, f.: justice
Mūsa, Mūsae, f.: a Muse
poēta, poētae, m.: poet
rēgīna, rēgīnae, f.: queen
salūs, salūtis, f.: health, safety
sōlitūdō, sōlitūdinis, f.: loneliness, solitude
ūsus, ūsūs, m.: advantage, use; practice
virtūs, virtūtis, f.: excellence; courage; goodness; virtue
vultus, vultūs, m.: appearance, face

Adjectives
aptus, apta, aptum: fitting, suitable
Athēniēnsēs, Athēniēnsium: (people) of Athens
cārus, cāra, cārum: dear
dissimilis, dissimile: not like, unlike
grātus, grāta, grātum: pleasing, agreeable
honestus, honesta, honestum: honorable, respectable
inimīcus, inimīca, inimīcum: unfriendly, hostile
nūllus, nūlla, nūllum: no
Plataeēnsēs, Plataeēnsium: Plataeans; people of Plataea
proximus, proxima, proximum: nearest, next
similis, simile: similar, like

Indeclinables
Adverbs
bis: twice
celeriter: quickly

Intensifier
et (shortened form of etiam): even

Verbs

adsum, adesse, adfuī: be present, be at hand
crēdō, crēdere, crēdidī: trust, rely on
dēsum, dēesse, dēfuī: be lacking, fail
dīcō, dīcere, dīxī, dictus: say, tell, speak; call, name
faveō, favēre, fāvī: favor, offer favor to
impōnō, impōnere, imposuī, impositus: place upon, impose
iniciō, inicere, injēcī, injectus: throw on or into
mōnstrō, mōnstrāre, mōnstrāvī, mōnstrātus: show
nārrō, nārrāre, nārrāvī, nārrātus: tell, relate, narrate
noceō, nocēre, nocuī: harm, do harm to
parcō, parcere, pepercī: spare, be lenient to
pāreō, pārēre, pāruī: obey, be obedient to
placeō, placēre, placuī: please, be pleasing to
resistō, resistere, restitī: resist, offer resistance to
serviō, servīre, servīvī: serve, help, offer service to

Readings Vocabulary

arma, armōrum, n. pl.: weapons
aureus, aurea, aureum: golden, of gold
bōs, bovis, m. & f.: ox, bull
caput, capitis, n.: head
certus, certa, certum: certain, sure
cōnficiō, cōnficere, cōnfēcī, cōnfectus: finish, achieve
custōdiō, custōdīre, custōdīvī, custōdītus: guard
difficilis, difficile: difficult
iter, itineris, n.: journey
mōnstrum, mōnstrī, n.: monster, beast
mortuus, mortua, mortuum: dead
necessitās, necessitātis, f.: necessity
patria, patriae, f.: country, fatherland
perficiō, perficere, perfēcī, perfectus: complete, finish, bring to an end
perveniō, pervenīre, pervēnī: arrive
pōmum, pōmī, n.: fruit, apple
properō, properāre, properāvī, properātus: hasten
prōvocō, prōvocāre, prōvocāvī, prōvocātus: call forth, challenge
pūgnō, pūgnāre, pūgnāvī, pūgnātūrus: fight
redeō, redīre, rediī, reditūrus: go back, return
redūcō, redūcere, redūxī, reductus: lead back, bring back
relinquō, relinquere, relīquī, relictus: leave behind, abandon
sapiō, sapere, sapīvī: be wise
senectūs, senectūtis, f.: old age
senex, senis, m.: old man
sōl, sōlis, m.: sun
summus, summa, summum: greatest, best, highest
superbus, superba, superbum: proud, haughty

terreō, terrēre, terruī, territus: frighten; be frightened
timeō, timēre, timuī: fear
trājiciō, trājicere, trājēcī, trājectus: throw across, pierce
via, viae, f.: road, way
viātor, viātōris, m.: wayfarer, traveler

Morphology Review

New Morphology: Lessons 16 and 17

noun: dative and genitive, singular and plural
adjective: dative and genitive, singular and plural
pronoun: dative and genitive, singular and plural

Form Identification

    a. serviō, servīre, servīvī: serve, help, offer service to
    b. servus, servī, m.: slave, servant
    c. servitūdō, servitūdinis, f.: slavery, servitude

1. servō   _____
2. servīvī   _____
3. servitūdinem   _____
4. servōrum   _____
5. servitūdō   _____
6. servitūdine   _____
7. servum   _____
8. servitūdinī   _____
9. serviō   _____
10. servīs   _____

Note to the Student

Although you are only halfway through this course, you have learned enough about the structure of the Latin sentence and about the form of its words to be able to observe and perhaps appreciate the system as it works in the hands of the poet Vergil. It is in the nature of great poetry in any language that its creators sometimes push the system to its limits, but without violating it. In practical terms this may mean that, just as in English poetry, word order patterns may be rather different from those used in colloquial speech. Nevertheless, if the language is to be understood, the writer must not violate the basic principles of his language.

Vergil's poetry represents the most classical realization of the possibilities of Latin. There are many elements of his style that contribute to the sum of the poetic impact. Some of them can be observed with the knowledge of structure already at your disposal. Among them are: Vergil's use of the variety of word orders possible in the kernel, in modification structures, and in the position of clause markers and connectors; also his use of the possibilities of gapping.

You know that all decisions begin with form identification, i.e., that each word as it appears must be identified for its possible part of speech and description. Once you have this information you can begin forming expectations regarding kernels, modification structures, and connectors. Here are some examples of observations to be made on the first few lines of the text that follows.

In line 1 there are two complete kernels, one finite—*spēlunca fuit*—and one non-finite—∅ = *spēlunca submōta*. *Vastō,* identifiable as adjective in the dative or ablative, singular, masculine or neuter, raises the expectation of a noun-head. This is fulfilled, after the participle *submōta,* by *recessū,* a noun in the ablative, resolving the case ambiguity of *vastō.* Such an ambiguity and such a separation of adjective and noun-head is, as you know, well within the Latin system.

In line 2 the system seems to the beginning reader to be pushed to extremes. The clause marker *quam* appears late in its clause and it also separates the head *faciēs* from the adjectival modifier *dīra.* Again, if you remember that the clause marker need not start the clause in Latin and that the adjective need not precede the noun-head, this is quite manageable.

You can observe that the *-que* in line 3 seems to connect its clause with the previous clause, but this expectation has to be changed when you meet the *-que* in line 4, for the two *-que*'s are in a "both . . . and" relationship.

In lines 6–7 you have a kernel without an expressed subject. The rules of gapping provide an explanation for this.

Proceed through this passage as well as other passages, paying careful attention to words and structures according to the Latin system, forming expectations as a Roman reader would, and changing them as the environment suggests. By and by you will understand more and more of the text and you will become a real reader of classical Latin.

Narrative Reading

Hercules and the Giant Cacus

Reread in Review Lesson 4 the story of Hercules' adventure with the giant Geryon before you go on with this Narrative Reading.

In the eighth book of his epic poem, Vergil, the best known of all Roman poets, tells of another adventure of Hercules. He does so because Hercules was the only hero from Greek mythology who had come to Italy and who was worshiped at Rome. Vergil explains in the *Aeneid* the origin of that worship.

Aeneas, a refugee from Troy, has arrived at the future site of Rome, where he finds the Arcadians and their king Evander celebrating the worship of Hercules. Aeneas is invited to join in the festivities, after which Evander tells how Hercules saved his people from the monster Cacus and was thereafter worshiped by them. Here is a part of the story as told by Evander.

Hīc spēlunca fuit, vastō submōta recessū
sēmihominis Cācī faciēs[1] quam[2] dīra tenēbat,
sōlis inaccessam[3] radiīs; semperque recentī
caede tepēbat humus, foribusque adfīxa[3] superbīs
5 ōra[1] virum[4] trīstī pendēbant pallida tābō.
Huic mōnstrō Volcānus erat pater; illius[5] ātrōs
ōre vomēns ignēs magnā sē[6] mōle ferēbat.[7]
Attulit[8] et nōbīs[9] aliquandō optantibus aetās[8]
auxilium adventumque deī.[10] Nam maximus ultor,[10]
10 tergeminī nece Gēryonae[11] spoliīsque superbus,
Alcīdēs[12] aderat taurōsque hāc victor[13] agēbat
ingentēs, vallemque bovēs amnemque tenēbant.

Of course Hercules succeeded in killing the monster Cacus. For students who wish to read how this was accomplished, the story is continued as Optional Reading in lessons 19, 20, and 21.

Notes

1. *faciēs, ōra:* used figuratively, a part for the whole
2. The clause marker *quam* appears in the middle of its own clause.
3. *inaccessam:* the head is *quam = spēlunca; adfīxa:* head is *ōra*
4. *virum:* alternate form of *virōrum*
5. *illius = Volcānī,* genitive, "his"
6. *sē:* accusative pronoun, "himself"
7. *ferēbat:* the Ø subject is *mōnstrum*
8. Notice the "bookend" word order *Attulit . . . aetās.*
9. *et nōbīs: et:* "also, even"; *nōbīs:* personal pronoun, dative plural, "to us"
10. *deī, ultor:* both refer to Hercules (*Alcīdēs* in line 11)
11. *Gēryonae:* cf. Narrative Reading in Review Lesson 4
12. *Alcīdēs:* a name for Hercules; Hercules is referred to by various names denoting his ancestry or a place; Alceus was his grandfather.
13. *victor:* "as victor"

Vocabulary

adferō, adferre, attulī, adlātus: bring (to)
adfīgō, adfīgere, adfīxī, adfīxus: fasten to
adventus, adventūs, m.: arrival
aetās, aetātis, f.: time
aliquandō (adv.): at last, at some time or other
amnis, amnis, m.: river
āter, ātra, ātrum: black
*bōs, bovis, m. & f.: ox, bull
caedēs, caedis, f.: killing, slaughter
dīrus, dīra, dīrum: horrible
faciēs, faciēī, f.: face
foris, foris, f.: door, entrance
hāc (adv.): this way
hīc (adv.): here, in this place

humus, humī, m.: ground, earth

inaccessus, inaccessa, inaccessum: inaccessible

ingēns (ingentis): huge, enormous

maximus, maxima, maximum: very great, greatest

mōlēs, mōlis, f.: mass, bulk

*mōnstrum, mōnstrī, n.: monster, beast

nam (sentence connector): for (in explanation)

nex, necis, f.: slaughter, death

optō, optāre, optāvī, optātus: wish for, long for

ōs, ōris, n.: mouth

pallidus, pallida, pallidum: pale

pendeō, pendēre, pependī: hang

radius, radiī, m.: ray

recēns (recentis): fresh, recent

recessus, recessūs, m.: recess, a going back

sēmihomō, sēmihominis, m.: half-man

*sōl, sōlis, m.: sun

spēlunca, spēluncae, f.: cave

spolium, spoliī, n.: booty, spoils

submoveō, submovēre, submōvī, submōtus: move under, hide

*superbus, superba, superbum: proud, haughty

tābum, tābī, n.: decayed blood

taurus, taurī, m.: bull

tepeō, tepēre, tepuī: be warm

tergeminus, tergemina, tergeminum: three-bodied

trīstis, trīste: dreadful

ultor, ultōris, m.: avenger

vallis, vallis, f.: valley

vastus, vasta, vastum: vast, deep

victor, victōris, m.: conqueror, victor

vomō, vomere, vomuī: pour forth, vomit

Derivatives from Narrative Reading

Latin

1. advent

2. dire

3. face

4. humus

5. impending

6. intercession

7. maximum

8. recession

9. superb

10. tepid

■ Exercise: English to Latin Sentences

Using the following Latin sentences or parts of sentences as models, translate the English sentences into Latin.

1. Inopī beneficium bis dat quī dat celeriter. (S16.3)
2. Sōlitūdō placet Mūsīs, urbs est inimīca poētīs. (S16.1)
3. Nūlla cīvitās Athēniēnsibus auxiliō fuit. (S16.2)
4. Impōnit fīnem sapiēns et rēbus honestīs. (S16.4)
5. Nūllī est hominī perpetuum bonum. (R16.6)
6. Imāgō animī vultus. (S17.1)

a. The king told his friend the story (told the story to his friend). (1)

b. The monster injured the people (human beings). (2)

c. The cave of the monster was near the river. (2 and 6)

d. The monster fastened the heads of human beings to the doors of the cave. (4 and 6)

e. The monster has Vulcan as his father. (5)

f. The arrival of a god was of great benefit to the people. (3 and 6)

Vocabulary

Nouns

arrival: adventus, adventūs, m.
benefit (use): ūsus, ūsūs, m.
cave: spēlunca, spēluncae, f.
door: foris, foris, f.
father: pater
friend: amīcus
god: deus
head: caput
human beings (people): hominēs
king: rēx
monster: mōnstrum
river: flūmen
story: fābula, fābulae, f.
Vulcan: Vulcānus, Vulcānī, m.

Adjectives

great: magnus
near: proximus
this: hic, haec, hoc

Verbs

fasten: adfīgō, adfīgere, adfīxī, adfīxus
has: sum, esse (with dat.)
injure: noceō
tell: nārrō, nārrāre, nārrāvī, nārrātus
was: sum, esse (erat)

Stem List

One of the most effective tools for enlarging one's vocabulary in Latin and English is a list of morphemes such as is found in the back of this textbook under the label *Stem List*. This is so because the same stems occur in many different words belonging to different parts of speech. A knowledge of the basic meanings of stems, combined with an awareness of how words are put together, enables one to guess the general meaning of unknown words.

For example, readers who know that {pōn} means "put/place" and who know preposi-tions can guess that the Latin verb *dēpōnō* means "put down," and that *impōnō* means "place in or upon." They can also guess at the general meanings of *appōnō* (*ad* + *pōnō*), *antepōnō, interpōnō, oppōnō* (*ob* + *pōnō*), *postpōnō, suppōnō* (*sub* + *pōnō*), and *trānspōnō*.

They can likewise guess at the general meanings of words built on the morpheme {posit}, which is the variant of {pōn}. Such words include *oppositiō, oppositiōnis,* and *interpositiō, interpositiōnis.*

A stem such as {rēg} can also occur with a variety of suffixes as in *rēgina, rēginae,* and *rēgnum, rēgnī.*

Variations in spelling of stems or prefixes are explained on page 383.

Listed below (and in later review lessons and in the Plautus selections) are words whose stems are useful to know. Write each of them under the appropriate stem in the Stem List. Also give the dictionary listing and meaning of each word entered. All words occur within the lesson.

For example, enter *adsum, adesse* under the stem *es* (to be) with the meaning "to be near or present."

Words for Stem List

1. adsum, adesse

2. amīcus

3. beneficium

4. dēsum, dēesse

5. impōnit

6. inimīca

7. placet

8. rēgīna

Lesson 18

Personal Pronouns
Persons of the Verb in the Active Voice

All verbs in previous lessons have been identified as *third person* singular or plural; all pronouns so far, e.g., *he, she, it* and *they,* have had a third person referent: boy, girl, money, books, etc. This lesson introduces verbs identified as *first* and *second person* singular and plural, and the personal pronouns for the first person (*I, me, we, us*) and the second person (*you*).

Basic Sentences

18.1. Caecī . . . ducem quaerunt; nōs sine duce errāmus.—Seneca
    Blind persons look for a guide; we are going astray without (even looking for) a guide.

18.2. Ex ōre tuō tē jūdicō.—Anon.
    I judge you from your own speech (from your own mouth).

18.3. Vēnī, vīdī, vīcī.—Suetonius (attributed to Caesar)
    I came, I saw, I conquered.

18.4. Effugere nōn potes necessitātēs; potes vincere.—Seneca
    You can not run away from necessary things; you can conquer them.

Personal Pronouns

Morphology

	First Person		Second Person	
Singular				
Nominative	ego	} I	tū	
Accusative	mē		tē	
Ablative	mē	} me	tē	} you
Dative	mihi		tibi	
Genitive	meī		tuī	
Plural				
Nominative	nōs	} we	vōs	
Accusative	nōs		vōs	
Ablative	nōbīs		vōbīs	} you
Dative	nōbīs	} us	vōbīs	
Genitive	nostrum, nostrī*		vestrum, vestrī*	

*The forms *nostrum* and *vestrum* are used partitively; the forms *nostrī* and *vestrī* are chiefly used objectively (see lesson 17 for these genitive uses).

Third Person (review lesson 7)

	Masc.	Fem.	Neut.	
Singular				
Nominative	is	ea	id	} he, she, it
Accusative	eum	eam	id	
Ablative	eō	eā	eō	
Dative	eī	eī	eī	} him, her, it
Genitive	ejus	ejus	ejus	
Plural				
Nominative	eī	eae	ea	} they
Accusative	eōs	eās	ea	
Ablative	eīs	eīs	eīs	
Dative	eīs	eīs	eīs	} them
Genitive	eōrum	eārum	eōrum	

Alternatives for a third person pronoun that have already occurred are forms of *hic* and *ille*.

■ Exercise 1

Identify the case, number, and, where appropriate, gender. (Give gender for *is, ea, id* only.) Some words have several possibilities.

1. tē _____

2. tū _____

3. nōbīs _____

4. mē _____

5. ejus _____

6. id _____

7. ego _____

8. eārum _____

Syntax and Metaphrasing

The personal pronouns of the first and second persons do not occur as adjectival modifiers in either Latin or English. But, as said in lesson 7, Latin pronouns of the third person can occur also as adjectival modifiers. They must then be metaphrased as "this ____" or "that ____" and not as "he," "she," "it," or "they."

■ Exercise 2

Metaphrase each of the following in the structural context of a sentence.

1. ā mē

2. mē

3. eam

4. eam fēminam

5. tibi

6. is

7. is fūr

8. tū

9. mēcum[1]

10. vōbīscum[1]

Note

1. The preposition *cum* is appended to the pronouns *mē, tē, nōbīs, vōbīs;* thus, *mēcum* instead of *cum mē.* This is also true of the reflexive pronoun in the next lesson and of the interrogative pronoun already introduced.

Persons of the Verb in the Active Voice

Latin indicates person of the verb by the ending of the verb; English indicates person by a pronoun in the first and second persons and by a noun or pronoun in the third person.

Morphology

There are two sets of person endings in the active voice. One is called *active voice* set of person endings. This set is as follows. Look also at the example of a first conjugation verb.

	Endings	
	Singular	Plural
First person	-m, -ō	-mus
Second person	-s	-tis
Third person	-t	-nt

Here is this set of endings used in the present imperfective tense of the first conjugation.

	First	
	Singular	Plural
First person	laudō (I praise)	laudāmus (we praise)
Second person	laudās (you praise)	laudātis (you [all] praise)
Third person	laudat (he/she/it praises)	laudant (they praise)

The active voice set of person endings for sample verbs of other conjugations is as follows.

	Second		Third		Third -iō		Fourth	
	Singular	Plural	Singular	Plural	Singular	Plural	Singular	Plural
First person	videō	vidēmus	regō	regimus	capiō	capimus	audiō	audīmus
Second person	vidēs	vidētis	regis	regitis	capis	capitis	audīs	audītis
Third person	videt	vident	regit	regunt	capit	capiunt	audit	audiunt

Note: Because the morphemes for first and second persons resemble morphemes of other parts of speech, beginning readers are faced with problems of morphological ambiguity. Careful attention to the stem morpheme will usually resolve such morphological ambiguities.

Irregular verbs are those whose forms differ in some way from the great bulk of verbs. Irregular verbs are common words; otherwise speakers of the language would have regularized them. Here are the most common irregular verbs in Latin.

	Singular	Plural	Singular	Plural	Singular	Plural	Singular	Plural
First person	sum	sumus	possum	possumus	ferō	ferimus	volō	volumus
Second person	es	estis	potes	potestis	fers	fertis	vīs	vultis
Third person	est	sunt	potest	possunt	fert	ferunt	vult	volunt

	Singular	Plural	Singular	Plural	Singular	Plural	Singular	Plural
First person	nōlō	nōlumus	mālō	mālumus	eō	īmus	fīō	—
Second person	nōn vīs	nōn vultis	māvīs	māvultis	īs	ītis	fīs	—
Third person	nōn vult	nōlunt	māvult	mālunt	it	eunt	fit	fīunt

■ Exercise 3
Identify the person and number of each verb.

1. dūcimus

2. fertis

3. it

4. adsum

5. premō

6. impōnimus

7. servīs

8. accipiunt

9. volō

10. crēdis

11. audīmus

12. currunt

13. placētis

14. īs

Morphology

The other set of person endings is the *present perfective active* set of endings. The endings of the third person singular and plural of the present perfective, active voice, were introduced in lesson 9, e.g., *laudāvit* and *laudāvērunt*. The third principal part of most verbs shows the first person singular, e.g., *laudāvī*. Listed here is the complete paradigm for all persons, singular and plural, for the present perfective active set of endings, plus an example is given.

	Endings	
	Singular	Plural
First person	-ī	-imus
Second person	-istī	-istis
Third person	-it	-ērunt
		(-ēre)

	Present Perfective Active			
	Singular		Plural	
First person	laudāvī	(I praised)*	laudāvimus	(we praised)
Second person	laudāvistī	(you praised)	laudāvistis	(you [all] praised)
Third person	laudāvit	(he/she/it praised)	laudāvērunt	(they praised)
			(laudāvēre)	

*Or "have/has praised."

All verbs, both regular and so-called irregular, are regular in the perfective aspect. Here are the irregular verbs in the present perfective tenses.

	Singular	Plural	Singular	Plural	Singular	Plural	Singular	Plural
First person	fuī	fuimus	potuī	potuimus	tulī	tulimus	voluī	voluimus
Second person	fuistī	fuistis	potuistī	potuistis	tulistī	tulistis	voluistī	voluistis
Third person	fuit	fuērunt	potuit	potuērunt	tulit	tulērunt	voluit	voluērunt

	Singular	Plural	Singular	Plural	Singular	Plural	Singular	Plural
First person	nōluī	nōluimus	māluī	māluimus	iī	iimus	factus sum*	factī sumus
Second person	nōluistī	nōluistis	māluistī	māluistis	iistī	iistis	factus es	factī estis
Third person	nōluit	nōluērunt	māluit	māluērunt	iit	iērunt	factus est	factī sunt

*The perfective of *fīō* uses passive voice forms.

■ Exercise 4

Identify the person, number, tense, and voice of each verb. Translate each verb. This list includes both present imperfective and present perfective verbs.

	Identification	*Translation*
1. dūximus		
2. dūcimus		
3. fers		
4. tulistī		
5. premis		
6. pressērunt		
7. accipit		
8. accēpit		
9. audīvimus		
10. audīvit		
11. fuistī		
12. fuī		
13. vīdit		
14. videt		
15. es		
16. cēpistis		

Syntax and Metaphrasing

Verb inflections indicate agreement with a referent. This referent is:

First person singular: ego (I)
First person plural: nōs (we)

Second person singular: tū (you)
Second person plural: vōs (you [all])

The referent for the third person is a noun or a pronoun. In Latin, these referents are very often ∅, especially in connected speech. In Basic Sentences 18.2 through 18.4 no pronoun appears as subject in the Latin. In S18.1, the *nōs* seems to be there in order to show an emphatic contrast with the *caecī* of the first clause.

Beginning readers of Latin often have a problem with third person verbs because they cannot assign a pronoun until they have identified the referent from the context.

■ Exercise 5

Translate each of these verbs, giving as subject all possible English personal pronouns. Just as is true in English, certain Latin verbs usually have a subject with either the feature *animate* or *nonanimate*.

1. dūcunt

2. laudāvērunt

3. audīmus

4. videt

5. quaeritis

6. est

7. cupiō

8. fluit

■ Exercise 6

Expand each sentence with a possible Latin pronoun as subject.

1. _____ cognōscimus nihil.

2. _____ cognōscit nihil.

3. _____ cognōscitis nihil.

4. _____ cognōscis nihil.

5. _____ cognōscō nihil.

6. _____ occāsiōnem vult.

7. _____ occāsiōnem vīs.

8. _____ occāsiōnem volō.

9. _____ occāsiōnem volumus.

10. _____ occāsiōnem vultis.

■ Exercise 7

Supply the correct form of the verb to agree with the subject.

1. corōnāre   Nōs nātōs cum laude _____ .

2. nocēre   Tū omnibus miserīs _____ .

3. regere   Dī omnia in caelō _____ .

4. capere   Ego in harēnā cōnsilium _____ .

5. velle   Nōs laudem _____ .

6. esse   Nōs firmāmentum reī pūblicae _____ .

7. esse   Vōs firmāmentum reī pūblicae _____ .

■ Exercise 8

Identification of nouns naturally becomes more complicated when they are seen in contrast with verbs. Identify the following, first by part of speech, then by case and number for nouns, or person and number for verbs.

1. effugis

2. capiō

3. vīvō

4. aprīs

5. regit

6. canis

7. vitiō

8. operis

Note Regarding Unknown Vocabulary and Metaphrasing

It will happen increasingly often in the second half of this course that you will recognize the morphology and the syntax of a word or words, but will not recall or be given the meaning. This need not prevent you from continuing the metaphrase. You often can guess the meaning or, if not, you can at least show by a "blank" where or how the word fits into English structure. Use a Latin dictionary to check your conclusions.

Lesson Vocabulary

Nouns
necessitās, necessitātis, f.: necessity
ōs, ōris, n.: mouth, face

Pronouns
ego, meī: I, me
nōs, nostrum: we, us
tū, tuī: you
vōs, vestrum: you (pl.)

Adjectives
caecus, caeca, caecum: blind
meus, mea, meum: my, mine[1]
noster, nostra, nostrum: our[1]
tuus, tua, tuum: your (sing.)[1]
vester, vestra, vestrum: your (pl.)[1]

Verbs

effugiō, effugere, effūgī: escape

eō, īre, iī (īvī), itūrus: go

errō, errāre, errāvī: wander, err

ferō, ferre, tulī, lātus: bring, carry, endure

jūdicō, jūdicāre, jūdicāvī, jūdicātus: judge

laudō, laudāre, laudāvī, laudātus: praise

mālō, mālle, māluī: prefer

nōlō, nōlle, nōluī: not wish, be unwilling

quaerō, quaerere, quaesīvī, quaesītus: look for, search for, ask

Note

1. possessive adjectives

Readings

Required

18.1. Nōs . . . beātam vītam in animī sēcūritāte pōnimus.—Cicero

18.2. Cōgitō, ergō sum.—Descartes

18.3. Certa mittimus dum incerta petimus.—Plautus

18.4. Animum dēbēs mūtāre, nōn caelum.—Seneca

18.5. Mē lūmen, vōs umbra regit.—Sundial inscription

18.6. Ego sum rēx Rōmānus et suprā grammaticam.—Sigismund the First

Vocabulary

18.1. beātus, beāta, beātum: blessed, happy

sēcūritās, sēcūritātis, f.: security

pōnō, pōnere, posuī, positus: put, place

18.2. cōgitō, cōgitāre, cōgitāvī, cōgitātus: think

ergō (adv.): therefore

18.3. incertus, incerta, incertum: uncertain, not sure

18.4. mūtō, mūtāre, mūtāvī, mūtātus: change

*caelum, caelī, n.: heaven, sky

18.5. lūmen, lūminis, n.: light, daylight

*umbra, umbrae, f.: shadow (of death)

18.6. *Rōmānus, Rōmāna, Rōmānum: Roman

grammatica, grammaticae, f.: grammar, philology

Optional

Paraphrasis means "paraphrase," a restatement in different form. The paraphrases in these readings are generally easier to read and therefore help in understanding the original text.

18.7. "Yes, I like him, but. . . ."

> Difficilis, facilis, jūcundus, acerbus es īdem.
> Nec tēcum possum vīvere nec sine tē.—Martial

18.8. You're not a real success, says Martial, until you have made some enemies.

> Laudat, amat, cantat nostrōs mea Rōma libellōs,
> mēque sinūs omnēs, mē manus omnis habet.
> Ecce rubet quīdam, pallet, stupet, ōscitat, ōdit.
> Hoc volō. Nunc nōbīs carmina nostra placent.—Martial

Paraphrasis: Tōta Rōma carmina Mārtiālis celebrat, dīligit, recitat; libellī ejus in omnī gremiō et omnī manū sunt. Nōndum Mārtiālis contentus est. Subitō autem aspicit quendam invidum ejus carmina legentem. Fit faciēs rubida, deinde pallida; stat sine mōtū; ōs aperītur; Mārtiālem perōdit. Hoc est quod Mārtiālis vult: nunc versūs eī jūcundī sunt, quod ille invidiā cruciātur.

18.9. Whereas a modern author's work appears in book form, Roman poetry was often heard in public recitation.

> Quem recitās, meus est, Ō Fīdentīne, libellus;
> sed male cum recitās, incipit esse tuus.—Martial

Paraphrasis: Meus libellus est, nōn tuus, quem tū recitās. Sed cum tū male recitās, vidētur esse vērē tuus libellus.

18.10. This is well known in English as "I do not love thee, Doctor Fell," etc.

> Nōn amō tē, Sabidī, nec possum dīcere quā rē.
> Hoc tantum possum dīcere: Nōn amō tē.—Martial

Paraphrasis: Ō Sabidī, tē nōn dīligō, nec ratiōnem odiī hujus reddere possum. Hanc ūnam ratiōnem dare possum: Nōn tē dīligō.

Vocabulary

18.7. jūcundus, jūcunda, jūcundum: sweet, agreeable
   īdem, eadem, idem: the same
   acerbus, acerba, acerbum: bitter, disagreeable
   nec (coord. conj.): nor; *nec . . . nec:* neither . . . nor

18.8. cantō, cantāre, cantāvī, cantātus: sing, recite
   libellus, libellī, m.: little book
   sinus, sinūs, m.: fold, pocket
   ecce (interjection): look! behold!
   rubeō, rubēre, rubuī: blush, turn red
   quīdam, quaedam, quiddam: a certain person, a certain thing
   palleō, pallēre, palluī: turn pale
   stupeō, stupēre, stupuī: be stunned
   ōscitō, ōscitāre, ōscitāvī, ōscitātus: gape
   ōdī, ōdisse (a defective verb): hate
   nunc (adv.): now
   carmen, carminis, n.: poem

18.9. recitō, recitāre, recitāvī, recitātus: recite
Fīdentīnus, Fīdentīnī, m.: Fidentinus (a man's name; *Fīdentīne* is in the vocative case, the case used to address someone directly)
libellus, libellī, m.: little book

18.10. Sabidius, Sabidiī, m.: Sabidius (a man's name; *Sabidī* is in the vocative case, the case used to address someone directly)
tantum (adv.): only

Word Study: English Derivatives

From Lesson	Latin	From Readings	Latin
1. erratic		1. beatitude	
2. inquiry		2. certainty	
3. judgment		3. cogitate	
4. oral		4. debtor	
5. potential		5. secure	

Summary Tasks

____ 1. Write the forms for all persons, singular and plural, present imperfective and perfective of *laudō, quaerō, ferō*.

____ 2. Copy the kernels for Readings 18.1 through 18.6.

____ 3. Rewrite each verb in exercise 4, changing it from singular to plural, or vice versa.

____ 4. Name the syntactic function of each noun or pronoun in Readings 18.4, 18.5, and 18.6.

Lesson 19

Persons of the Verb in the Passive Voice
The Reflexive Pronoun
The Intensive Pronoun

Lesson 6 introduced passive voice forms of the present imperfective tense, e.g., *laudātur* and *laudantur*. Lesson 9 introduced passive voice forms of the present perfective, e.g., *laudātus, -a, -um est* and *laudātī, -ae, -a sunt*. This lesson introduces the first and second persons, singular and plural, of the passive voice. The lesson also introduces the reflexive pronoun and the intensive pronoun.

Basic Sentences

19.1. Trahimur omnēs studiō laudis.—Cicero
      We are all pulled by our desire for praise.
19.2. Quī sēsē accūsat ipse, ab aliō nōn potest.—Publilius Syrus
      Whoever himself accuses himself, can not be accused by another.

Persons of the Verb in the Passive Voice

There is only one set of person endings for the passive voice in Latin; these occur only on imperfective verb forms. Passive verbs in the perfective are periphrastic, where the forms of *sum* indicate person.

Morphology

The *imperfective passive* set of endings is as follows.

| | Endings | |
	Singular	Plural
First person	-or, -r	-mur
Second person	-ris (-re)*	-minī
Third person	-tur	-ntur

    *The ending *-re* occurs as an alternate
    to *-ris* mostly in poetry.

Here is this set of endings used in the present imperfective tense of the first conjugation.

	First Conjugation	
	Singular	Plural
First person	laudor (I am [being] praised)	laudāmur (we are [being] praised)
Second person	laudāris (you are [being] praised)	laudāminī (you are [being] praised)
Third person	laudātur (he/she/it is [being] praised)	laudantur (they are [being] praised)

Sample verbs of other conjugations include the following. Note: Most irregular verbs do not have passive morphology.

	Second		Third		Third -iō		Fourth	
	Singular	Plural	Singular	Plural	Singular	Plural	Singular	Plural
First person	videor	vidēmur	regor	regimur	capior	capimur	audior	audīmur
Second person	vidēris	vidēminī	regeris	regiminī	caperis	capiminī	audīris	audīminī
Third person	vidētur	videntur	regitur	reguntur	capitur	capiuntur	audītur	audiuntur

■ Exercise 1

Identify the person and number of each verb. Translate each verb.

	Identification	*Translation*
1. dūcimur		
2. audīris		
3. vinciminī		
4. capimur		
5. regeris		
6. neglegitur		
7. cūrāminī		
8. frangitur		

Morphology

The present perfective tense in the passive is periphrastic; it consists of the perfective passive participle and forms of the verb *sum*. Remember that forms of *sum* in this context must be translated as "was" or "has been," not as "am, is, are."

The complete paradigm of the passive voice of the *present perfective* tense is as follows:

	Singular	Plural
First person	laudātus, -a, -um sum (I was/have been praised)	laudātī, -ae, -a sumus (we were/have been praised)
Second person	laudātus, -a, -um es (you were/have been praised)	laudātī, -ae, -a estis (you were/have been praised)
Third person	laudātus, -a, -um est (he/she/it was/has been praised)	laudātī, -ae, -a sunt (they were/have been praised)

■ Exercise 2

Identify the person, number, tense, and voice of each verb. Translate each verb, giving two English equivalents of each verb.

	Person/Number	Tense	Voice	Translations
1. ductī sumus				
2. dūcimur				
3. audītae estis				
4. victī sunt				
5. dūcor				
6. neglēctus sum				
7. audīta es				
8. audīmur				
9. vīsa sunt				
10. capiminī				

The Reflexive Pronoun

Both Latin and English distinguish between the pronouns in such pairs of sentences as:

Puella *sē* videt in pictūrā. (The girl sees *herself* in the picture.)

Puella *eam* videt in pictūrā. (The girl sees *her* in the picture.)

"Herself" in the first sentence is an example of a *reflexive pronoun,* which "reflects" back to the subject "girl." "Her" in the second sentence is a *personal pronoun,* which does not "reflect" back to the subject "girl" but refers to another person.

Morphology

The reflexive pronoun looks like the personal pronoun in the first and second persons.

Reflexive	Videō *mē*. (I see *myself*.)	Vidēs *tē*. (You see *yourself*.)
Personal	Vidēs *mē*. (You see *me*.)	Videō *tē*. (I see *you*.)

The third person reflexive pronoun has a form of its own that is the same for singular and plural, and for all three genders.

Accusative	sē, *or* sēsē
Ablative	sē, *or* sēsē
Dative	sibi
Genitive	suī

Puella *sē* videt. (The girl sees *herself*.)
Puellae *sē* vident. (The girls see *themselves*.)

Puer *sē* videt. (The boy sees *himself*.)
Puerī *sē* vident. (The boys see *themselves*.)

Animal *sē* videt. (The animal sees *itself*.)
Animālia *sē* vident. (The animals see *themselves*.)

In English the reflexive pronoun ends with the morpheme {self}. The third person reflexive pronoun is translated as "himself, herself, itself" or "themselves" to agree with its referent, i.e., the subject of the verb. The *sēsē* in S19.2 is translated "himself" to agree with the subject *quī*, which is masculine and singular.

Note: In S19.2, "be accused" is a passive infinitive. In Latin it is *accūsārī*, which is gapped here. The morphology of passive infinitives is given in lesson 6, page 54, and in the Appendix. This morphology should be reviewed before doing the following exercise.

■ Exercise 3
Write a metaphrase of these sentences.

1. Mē videō.

2. Mē vidēre possum.

3. Mē vidēre nōn potest.

4. Vidērī nōn possumus.

5. Audīrī ā nōbīs nōn vultis.

6. Capī dēbent.

■ Exercise 4
Write a metaphrase of these sentences, each of which has a personal or reflexive pronoun.

1. Sē lavant.

2. Puer sē lavat.

3. Fēminae sē lavant.

4. Fēmina tē lavat.

5. Mē accūsō.

6. Eōs accūsāmus.

7. Vōs accūsat.

8. Sē accūsant.

The adjective *suus, -a, -um* was introduced in S13.1 (*Condidit urbem Rōmulus quam ex nōmine suō Rōmam vocāvit*). *Suus, -a, -um* is a *reflexive adjective*. Although the referent of *suō* is *Rōmulus*, the subject of the sentence, it agrees in case, number, and gender with its noun-head *nōmine*.

■ Exercise 5
Write a metaphrase of these sentences.

1. Pater fīliās suās amat.

2. Māter fīliam suam amat.

3. Puer videt mātrem suam.

4. Puella frātrēs suōs videt.

5. Puerī cum amīcō suō currunt.

The Intensive Pronoun

The intensive pronoun *ipse, ipsa, ipsum* puts special emphasis on the noun or pronoun with which it agrees. For examples look at these metaphrases.

vir *ipse*	the man *himself* _____s ± _____ , *or*
	the *very* man _____s ± _____
feminam *ipsam*	_____ _____s the woman *herself, or*
	_____ _____s the *very* woman
ducēs *ipsōs*	_____ _____s the leaders *themselves, or*
	_____ _____s the *very* leaders (about whom they were speaking)

As a pronoun *ipse, ipsa, ipsum* can occur without another noun, e.g., *ipse effūgit* means "he *himself* escaped."

Morphology

	Masculine	Feminine	Neuter
Singular			
Nominative	ipse	ipsa	ipsum
Accusative	ipsum	ipsam	ipsum
Ablative	ipsō	ipsā	ipsō
Dative	ipsī	ipsī	ipsī
Genitive	ipsīus	ipsīus	ipsīus
Plural			
Nominative	ipsī	ipsae	ipsa
Accusative	ipsōs	ipsās	ipsa
Ablative	ipsīs	ipsīs	ipsīs
Dative	ipsīs	ipsīs	ipsīs
Genitive	ipsōrum	ipsārum	ipsōrum

Metaphrasing

The intensive pronoun in English has the morpheme {self}, just as the reflexive pronoun does. It is helpful in metaphrasing to place the intensive pronoun immediately after the noun or pronoun with which it agrees, no matter where it is in Latin. In S19.2, the intensive pronoun *ipse* is separated from *quī,* the pronoun with which it agrees.

■ Exercise 6
Write a metaphrase of these sentences.

1. Vir sē videt.

2. Vir ipse videt puellam.

3. Vir ipse sē videt.

4. Vir videt puellam ipsam.

5. Puella ipsa sē videt.

6. Puellae ipsae tē vident.

7. Puella tē ipsum videt.

8. Vir ā puellīs ipsīs vidētur.

■ Exercise 7
Given the following dictionary entries, fully identify each item. Include the part of speech. Metaphrase each in the context of a complete sentence.

    laus, laudis, f.: praise, glory, fame
    laudātor, laudātōris, m.: praiser (one who praises)
    laudō, laudāre, laudāvī, laudātus: praise

1. laudātās _____

2. laudās _____

3. laudēs _____

4. laudātor _____

5. laudor _____

6. laudātōre _____

7. laudāre _____

8. laudī   _____

9. laudārī   _____

10. laudāvī   _____

Lesson Vocabulary

Nouns

laus, laudis, f.: praise, glory, fame
puella, puellae, f.: girl
studium, studiī, n.: eagerness, zeal; study

Adjectives

alius, alia, aliud¹: another, other

Pronouns

ipse, ipsa, ipsum: -self, e.g., myself, yourself, himself, etc.
sē², sē, sibi, suī: himself, herself, itself, themselves

Verbs

accūsō, accūsāre, accūsāvī, accūsātus: accuse
trahō, trahere, trāxī, tractus: drag, draw, pull

Notes

1. See Special Adjectives in lesson 20 for morphology.
2. acc., abl., dat., gen. cases (no nom.)

Readings

Required

19.1. Omnia mūtantur, nōs et mūtāmur in illīs.
19.2. Nōn sibi, sed patriae.—Motto
19.3. Bis vincit quī sē vincit in victōriā.—Publilius Syrus
19.4. Haec in nostrōs fabricāta est machina mūrōs.—Vergil
    (Note: from the passage in Vergil's _Aeneid_ describing the horse that has been set outside the walls of Troy, later to be known as the Trojan Horse.)
19.5. Gallia est omnis dīvīsa in partēs trēs.—J. Caesar
    (Note: These famous words open the first chapter of Julius Caesar's _Commentary on the Gallic War_. In this chapter Caesar describes the geography, not the history, of Gaul. Therefore, the words are properly translated as "All Gaul is divided into three parts," rather than "All Gaul was divided." Under this circumstance _est_ is a linking verb with the complement _dīvīsa_. Kernels with a linking verb and a participle as complement are quite common in English.)

Vocabulary

19.1. *mūtō, mūtāre, mūtāvī, mūtātus: change

19.3. *victōria, victōriae, f.: victory

19.4. fabricō, fabricāre, fabricāvī, fabricātus: build, construct

   machina, machinae, f.: machine, device

   *mūrus, mūrī, m.: wall

19.5. Gallia, Galliae, f.: Gaul

   dīvidō, dīvidere, dīvīsī, dīvīsus: divide

   pars, partis, f.: part, section

Word Study: English Derivatives

From Lesson	Latin	From Readings	Latin
1. abstract		1. commute	
2. accusation		2. conviction	
3. alien		3. division	
4. distract		4. fabrication	
5. laudatory		5. immutable	
6. student		6. intramural	
7. suicide		7. patriot	
8. tractor		8. victorious	

Narrative Reading

Hercules and the Giant Cacus, Part 2

The wicked and crafty Cacus, attracted by the beautiful cattle grazing in the valley, stole eight of the finest ones. These he dragged by their tails into his cave, so that the direction of their footprints would deceive anyone searching for them. Meanwhile, as Hercules prepared the herd for departure, the cattle objected with loud bellowings, and filled the whole grove with their complaints.

> Reddidit ūna boum vōcem vastōque sub antrō
> mūgiit et Cācī spem custōdīta[1] fefellit.
> Hīc[2] vērō Alcīdēs . . . .
> . . . . rapit arma manū nōdīsque gravātum
> 5   rōbur, et āëriī cursū petit ardua montis.
> Tum prīmum nostrī[3] Cācum vīdēre[4] timentem
> turbātumque oculīs; fugit[5] īlicet ōcior[6] Eurō[6]
> spēluncamque petit; pedibus timor addidit ālās.

Notes

1. *custōdīta:* the head is *ūna (boum)*
2. *hīc* (adv.): at this point, now

3. *nostrī:* "our people"
4. *vīdēre = vīdērunt*
5. *fugit:* the Ø subject is *Cācus*
6. *ōcior Eurō:* translate "swifter than the southeast wind"

Vocabulary

addō, addere, addidī: add
āërius, āëria, āërium: of the air, lofty, high
āla, ālae, f.: wing
antrum, antrī, n.: cave
arduum, arduī, n.: height, a steep place
*cursus, cursūs, m.: running, race; course
custōdiō, custōdīre, custōdīvī, custōdītus: guard
gravō, gravāre, gravāvī, gravātus: make heavy, burden
īlicet (adv.): immediately
*mōns, montis, m.: mountain
mūgiō, mūgīre, mūgiī: bellow, moo
nōdus, nōdī, m.: knot
reddō, reddere, reddidī: give back, return
rōbur, rōboris, n.: wooden club
*spēlunca, spēluncae, f.: cave
*timor, timōris, f.: fear
turbō, turbāre, turbāvī, turbātus: disturb
vastus, vasta, vastum: huge, vast
vērō (adv.): but, indeed

Derivatives from Narrative Reading

Latin

1. aerial

2. arduous

3. course

4. nodule

Summary Tasks

___ 1. List all adjective-noun pairs from the Narrative Reading of lesson 19.
___ 2. Find four morphologically ambiguous forms in Readings 19.1 through 19.4, identify
the possibilities, choose the correct one, and describe the evidence.
___ 3. Complete the sentence: The endings of verbs indicate ___ , ___ , and ___ .

Lesson 20

Deponent Verbs
Demonstrative Pronouns
Special Adjectives

Certain verbs introduced in this lesson show an unusual distribution of active and passive forms and meanings. They are called *deponent* verbs and *semideponent* verbs.

The lesson also introduces two more demonstrative pronouns and a group of special adjectives.

Basic Sentences

20.1. Nōn omnēs eadem mīrantur amantque.—Horace
People do not all love and admire the same things.
20.2. Ubi lībertās cecidit, audet līberē nēmō loquī.—Publilius Syrus
When liberty has fallen, no one dares to speak freely.

Deponent Verbs

Morphology

All finite forms of *deponent* verbs are passive in form but active in meaning. In S20.1 *mīrantur* does *not* mean "____s are admired" but "____s admire." Both *mīrantur* and *amant* are active in meaning.

Note: Deponent verbs are remnants of an earlier stage of the language during which a full set of verb forms had not only active and passive voice but a third voice. This third voice looked much like the passive but was nearer to the active in meaning. A few frequently used verbs survived as deponents only, though no special meaning has survived. They are therefore to be translated as any other verb in the active voice. It is interesting to note that many Greek verbs have all three voices.

All three participles of deponent verbs are active in meaning. The perfective participle is passive in form and the imperfective and future participles are active in form. Here are the participles of the verb *sequor, sequī, secūtus* (follow).

Imperfective	sequēns (sequentis) (following)
Perfective	secūtus, secūta, secūtum (having followed)
Future	secūtūrus, secūtūra, secūtūrum (about to follow)

The imperfective infinitive, like the finite forms, is passive in form and active in meaning. The imperfective infinitive of *sequor* is *sequī* (to follow).

Principal Parts of Deponent Verbs

The three forms listed as principal parts of deponent verbs are equivalent to the first three principal parts of regular verbs, but are passive in form: for example, *imitor* (I imitate), *imitārī* (to imitate), *imitātus sum* (I have imitated).

> imitor, imitārī, imitātus sum (imitate)
> īrāscor, īrāscī, īrātus sum (be angry)
> loquor, loquī, locūtus sum (speak)
> mentior, mentīrī, mentītus sum (lie)
> mīror, mīrārī, mīrātus sum (admire, love)
> morior, morī, mortuus sum (die)
> moror, morārī, morātus sum (delay)
> nāscor, nāscī, nātus sum (be born)
> patior, patī, passus sum (suffer, endure)
> sequor, sequī, secūtus sum (follow)
> ūtor, ūtī, ūsus sum (use)
> vereor, verērī, veritus sum (fear, respect)

Principal Parts of Semideponents

Semideponents (literally, "partial deponents") occur in several varieties. Four common semideponents are given here.

> audeō, audēre, ausus sum (dare)
> fīō, fierī, factus sum (become) (used as the passive of *faciō*)
> gaudeō, gaudēre, gāvīsus sum (rejoice, be glad)
> soleō, solēre, solitus sum (be accustomed)

Syntax

Deponent verbs occur in any kernel type except the passive kernel. In fact, the appearance of an accusative with a "passive" verb form is usually an indication that the verb is a deponent. For example, in S20.1 *eadem* indicates that *mīrantur* is a deponent. The semideponents *audeō* and *soleō* belong on the list of verbs with which a complementary infinitive is expected. Thus, in S20.2, *loquī* is a complementary infinitive.

■ Exercise 1
Complete each sentence by underlining the word or words that could fill the blank, and give a final metaphrase of each sentence.

1. Fūr pecūniam semper _____.   amat, mīrātur, amantur

2. Vēritātem nōn _____.   timeor, vereor, timeō

3. Homō fortūnam _____ dēbet.   patī, ferre, ferrī

■ Exercise 2

To which conjugation does each of the following deponent verbs belong? Use the list of principal parts if necessary.

1. loquī

2. mentītur

3. morāris

4. verita est

5. sequimur

■ Exercise 3

Complete the paradigms. First person singulars are given.

	Singular	Plural	Singular	Plural
First person	loquor		mentior	
Second person				
Third person				

	Singular	Plural	Singular	Plural
First person	vereor		locūtus, -a, -um sum	
Second person				
Third person				

■ Exercise 4

Write all three participles of the verbs and give an English equivalent of each.

1. loquor _____

2. vereor _____

3. imitor _____

■ Exercise 5

Identify each of these verbs as passive or deponent. Translate each verb.

	Identification	Translation
1. patimur		
2. capimur		
3. mentīris		
4. mittitur		

5. loquiminī _____

6. sequitur _____

7. quaeriminī _____

8. amantur _____

9. imitāris _____

10. patiminī _____

■ Exercise 6

Copy the kernels of Basic Sentences 18.2, 18.4, 19.1, 19.2, 20.1, and 20.2 onto the kernel chart.

Clause Marker	Item: Function	Item: Function	Item: Function	Kernel Type	F/NF	M/D	Adj./Adv./ Noun	Name
1.								
2.								
3.								
4.								
5.								
6.								
7.								
8.								
9.								
10.								

Demonstrative Pronouns

There are two more demonstrative pronouns: *īdem, eadem, idem* and *iste, ista, istud*.

Īdem is formed from *is, ea, id* and the morpheme {dem} that means "same." For example: *vir īdem* (the same man). See the Appendix, page 400, for the complete paradigm. Note the various sound changes, as in *eundem* (*eum* + *dem*).

Iste is declined like *ille, illa, illud*. This pronoun contrasts with *hic* and *ille* in that it indicates that which is near the person spoken to. For example, *vir iste* means "that man (near to *you*)."

Special Adjectives

The following ten adjectives—*ūnus, tōtus, sōlus, ūllus, uter, alter, neuter, nūllus, uterque,* and *alius*—have the same paradigm as first and second declension adjectives *except* that the dative singular has the morpheme {ī} and the genitive singular has {īus}. Their complete dictionary entries are as follows.

> alter, altera, alterum: one (of two), the other one
> alius, alia, aliud: other, another; *aliī . . . aliī:* some . . . others
> neuter, neutra, neutrum: neither
> nūllus, nūlla, nūllum: none, no
> sōlus, sōla, sōlum: alone, the only
> tōtus, tōta, tōtum: whole
> ūllus, ūlla, ūllum: any
> ūnus, ūna, ūnum: one
> uter, utra, utrum?: which (of two)?
> uterque, utraque, utrumque: (usually singular) each (of two)

Lesson Vocabulary

Nouns
lībertās, lībertātis, f.: freedom
nēmō, nēminis, m. & f.: no one

Pronouns
īdem, eadem, idem: the same
iste, ista, istud: that (near you), that of yours

Adjectives
alter, altera, alterum: one (of two),
    the other one
līber, lībera, līberum: free
neuter, neutra, neutrum: neither
sōlus, sōla, sōlum: alone, the only
tōtus, tōta, tōtum: whole
ūllus, ūlla, ūllum: any
uter, utra, utrum?: which (of two)?
uterque, utraque, utrumque: (usually
    singular) each (of two)

Verbs
cadō, cadere, cecidī, cāsūrus: fall
dīco, dīcere, dīxī, dictus: say, tell, speak;
    call, name
gaudeō, gaudēre, gāvīsus: rejoice, be glad
imitor, imitārī, imitātus: imitate
īrāscor, īrāscī, īrātus: be angry
loquor, loquī, locūtus: say, speak, tell
mentior, mentīrī, mentītus: lie, tell a lie
mīror, mīrārī, mīrātus: admire, love
morior, morī, mortuus: die
nāscor, nāscī, nātus: be born
patior, patī, passus: suffer, endure; allow
sequor, sequī, secūtus: follow
timeō, timēre, timuī: fear
ūtor, ūtī, ūsus (+ abl.): use
vereor, verērī, veritus: fear, respect

Readings

Required

20.1. Multī fāmam, cōnscientiam paucī verentur.—Pliny
20.2. Dum loquor, hōra fugit.—Ovid
20.3. Rōma locūta est; causa fīnīta est.—Anon.

20.4. Prōgredimur quō dūcit quemque voluntās.—Lucretius

20.5. Nōn quia difficilia sunt, nōn audēmus; sed quia nōn audēmus, difficilia sunt.—Seneca

20.6. Saepe solet fīlius similis esse patrī.—Werner

Vocabulary

20.1. fāma, fāmae, f.: rumor, fame

cōnscientia, cōnscientiae, f.: conscience

paucī, paucae, pauca: few

20.3. causa, causae, f.: case

fīniō, fīnīre, fīnīvī, fīnītus: bring to an end; come to an end

20.4. prōgredior, prōgredī, prōgressus: go forth

quō (adv.): where, to whatever place

*quisque, quaeque, quodque: each one

voluntās, voluntātis, f.: desire, will

20.5. difficilis, difficile: difficult

20.6. *fīlius, fīliī, m.: son

Optional

20.7. Fortune hunters were common in Rome.

> Petit Gemellus nūptiās Marōnillae
> et cupit et īnstat et precātur et dōnat.
> Adeōne pulchra est? Immō foedius nīl est.
> Quid ergō in illā petitur et placet? Tussit.—Martial 1.10

Paraphrasis: Gemellus Marōnillam in mātrimōnium dūcere vult, et urget et rogat et eī mūnera dat. Estne Marōnilla tam pulchra? Ex contrāriō, nēmō tam foeda est. Quid igitur in eā Gemellus amat? Quod tussī labōrat et tantum brevī vīvere potest. Gemellus avārus pecūniam ejus cupit.

20.8. Labienus has no rival.

> Sē sōlum Labiēnus amat, mīrātur, adōrat:
>   nōn modō sē sōlum, sē quoque sōlus amat.—Joannes Audoenus

Vocabulary

20.7. Gemellus, Gemellī, m.: Gemellus (a man's name)

nūptiae, nūptiārum, f. pl.: marriage

Marōnilla, Marōnillae, f.: Maronilla (a woman's name)

īnstō, īnstāre, īnstitī: insist

precor, precārī, precātus: beg

dōnō, dōnāre, dōnāvī, dōnātus: give presents

adeō (adv.): to such a degree, so

immō (sentence connector): on the contrary

foedus, foeda, foedum: ugly

ergō (sentence connector): therefore, then

tussiō, tussīre, tussīvī: cough

Paraphrasis:

tussis, tussis, f.: a cough

labōrō, labōrāre: labor, suffer

20.8. Labiēnus, Labiēnī, m.: Labienus (a man's name)
adōrō, adōrāre, adōrāvī, adōrātus: adore
nōn modō (adv. phrase): not only

Word Study: English Derivatives

From Lesson	**Latin**	**From Readings**	**Latin**
1. accidental		1. assimilate	
2. admirable		2. filial	
3. audacity		3. ingredient	
4. colloquial		4. insolent	
5. consequence		5. patrician	
6. identical		6. patricide	
7. liberty		7. paucity	
8. patient		8. progress	

Narrative Reading

Hercules and the Giant Cacus, Part 3

Cacus quickly reached the entrance to his cave and shut himself inside; in his excitement he broke the chains which lowered the huge rock that closed the entrance. Hercules was soon there looking all around, gnashing his teeth and hot with anger. Three times he tried without success to pull out the huge rock; but since the rock and chains had been designed by the god Vulcan, he had to give up. Then he saw a sharp pointed rock projecting above the peak of the Aventine mountain, rising against the back of the cave and leaning toward the river. This he shook and loosened from its foundations; then he gave it a powerful thrust, and the great rock fell into the river and stopped the course of the stream.

> At specus et Cācī dētēcta appāruit ingēns
> rēgia et umbrōsae penitus patuēre[1] cavernae.
> Ergō īnspērātā dēprēnsum[2] lūce repente
> inclūsumque[2] cavō saxō (atque īnsuēta rudentem)
> 5 dēsuper Alcīdēs tēlīs premit, omniaque arma
> advocat et rāmīs vastīsque molāribus īnstat.
> Ille autem, neque[3] enim fuga[4] jam[3] super[5] ūlla perīclī,[6]
> faucibus ingentem fūmum, mīrābile dictū,[7]
> ēvomit involvitque domum cālīgine caecā.

Notes

1. *patuēre = patuērunt*
2. *dēprēnsum, inclūsum:* ∅ head is *Cācum*
3. *neque . . . jam:* "and no longer"
4. *fuga:* subject with ∅ verb *est*
5. *super:* adverb with ∅=*est*, means "is over and above," = "is left"
6. *perīclī = perīculī*, genitive case modifies *fuga*
7. *mīrābile dictū:* "wonderful to tell about"

Vocabulary

advocō, advocāre, advocāvī, advocātus: summon, call to one's aid
appāreō, appārēre, appāruī: appear
*at (coord. conj.): but
cālīgō, cālīginis, f.: fog, darkness
caverna, cavernae, f.: cavern, cave
cavus, cava, cavum: hollow
dēprendō, dēprendere, dēprendī, dēprēnsus: catch
dēsuper (adv.): from above
dētegō, dētegere, dētēxī, dētēctus: uncover, expose
enim (sentence connector): for
ergō (sentence connector): therefore
ēvomō, ēvomere, ēvomuī, ēvomitum: vomit forth
faucēs, faucium, f. pl.: throat, jaws
fuga, fugae, f.: flight
fūmus, fūmī, m.: smoke
inclūdō, inclūdere, inclūsī, inclūsus: enclose
*ingēns (ingentis): huge, enormous
īnspērātus, īnspērāta, īnspērātum: unexpected, unhoped for
īnstō, īnstāre, īnstitī: press on, attack
īnsuētus, īnsuēta, īnsuētum: unaccustomed
involvō, involvere, involvī, involūtus: envelop, wrap
molāris, molāris, m.: millstone, a large stone
penitus (adv.): far within
rāmus, rāmī, m.: branch (of a tree)
rēgia, rēgiae, f.: palace
repente (adv.): suddenly
rudō, rudere, rudīvī, rudītus: roar
saxum, saxī, n.: rock
specus, specūs, m.: cave
tēlum, tēlī, n.: weapon
umbrōsus, umbrōsa, umbrōsum: shady, dark
*vastus, vasta, vastum: huge, vast

Derivatives from Narrative Reading

Latin

1. apparent

2. cavity

3. conclusion

4. desperation

5. detect

6. fume

7. miraculous

8. molar (tooth)

9. ramification

10. revolve

Summary Tasks

____ 1. Rewrite Reading 20.1, filling the gaps.

____ 2. Complete the sentence: A verb form that looks passive is sure to be a deponent
  if _____ .

____ 3. Copy all participles together with their noun-heads from the Narrative Reading, lines
  1–4.

____ 4. Copy all coordinating conjunctions together with the sames that they connect from
  the Narrative Reading, lines 1–4.

____ 5. Write a cumulative metaphrase of Reading 20.4.

Lesson 21

The Verbal Noun: Infinitive

So far an infinitive has occurred as complementary infinitive and has therefore been part of the verb of the kernel. Complementary infinitives have been expected with a limited number of verbs such as *potest, cupit,* and *vult* (see lesson 3).

On the other hand, infinitives are not always part of the verb of the kernel. In certain environments presented in this lesson an infinitive is a *verbal noun* functioning as subject or complement in a kernel. Lesson 22 will introduce another verbal noun, the gerund, that fills other noun functions.

Basic Sentences

21.1. Et monēre et monērī proprium est vērae amīcitiae.—Cicero

Both to advise and to be advised is appropriate to real friendship.

21.2. Difficile est longum subitō dēpōnere amōrem.—Catullus

It is difficult to give up long-standing love abruptly.

21.3. Labōrāre est ōrāre.—Motto

To work is to pray.

21.4.   Juvat īre et Dōrica castra

dēsertōsque vidēre locōs lītusque relictum.—Vergil *Aeneid*

It was[1] pleasant to go out and to see the Greek camp and the deserted stations and the abandoned shore. (Aeneas gives Queen Dido a vivid description of the events preceding the fall of Troy.)

Note

1. In lively narrative the present imperfective tense is sometimes used in Latin of an action already completed. This is sometimes called the *historical present*.

The Verbal Noun: Infinitive

Syntax

Infinitives may occur as subject or complement of a linking kernel. This is called the *verbal noun* use of infinitives. In S21.1, the infinitives *monēre* and *monērī* are verbal nouns used as subject of the verb *est*. An infinitive so used has properties of both nouns and verbs. As a noun it is neuter by gender; hence *proprium*, the subject complement, is neuter by agreement. As a verb it has voice: *monēre* is active voice and *monērī* is passive voice. Another verb property is in evidence in S21.2, where the infinitive *dēpōnere* has a direct object, *longum amōrem*.

In S21.3, one verbal noun is subject and the other is the subject complement of the kernel.

Note: It is important to observe that the infinitive as verbal noun generally does not have a subject of its own. Also, verbal nouns of transitive verbs often appear without direct objects, e.g., *monēre* in S21.1. Both of these characteristics contribute to the view of verbal nouns as being abstract in terms of their semantic features. For these reasons, the infinitive as verbal noun generally is not entered as a verb onto a kernel chart. If it were entered, the infinitive kernel of S21.2 could read as follows: *dēpōnere:* verb; *amōrem:* dir. obj. (no subject).

An infinitive functioning as a verbal noun is also to be expected with certain verbs such as:

> decet (is fitting/suitable)
> juvat (is pleasing, pleases, delights)
> licet (is allowed/possible)
> oportet (is necessary)
> placet (is pleasing, pleases)
> concēditur (is allowed)

In S21.4, *īre . . . relictum* is the subject of the verb *juvat*. The final metaphrase might therefore be "To go . . . is pleasing." As this metaphrase shows, *juvat,* as well as the other verbs in the list, is the semantic equivalent of a linking verb plus complement.

Note: Verbs such as those in this list have traditionally been labeled as *impersonal verbs* when the subject is an infinitive. The use of *it* preceding the verbs in translations, e.g., "it is pleasing to go," reflects this impersonal label. An example of *placet* not used impersonally is found in S16.1, *Sōlitūdō placet Mūsīs* (Solitude pleases the Muses), where the subject *sōlitūdō* is a noun, not an infinitive.

Kernel Information

Difficile est longum subitō dēpōnere amōrem.
Juvat īre et Dorica castra dēsertōsque vidēre locōs lītusque relictum.

Clause Marker	Item: Function	Item: Function	Item: Function	Kernel Type	F/NF	M/D	Adj./Adv./ Noun	Name
—	difficile: subj. compl.	est: verb	dēpōnere amōrem: subj.	Lkg.	F	M	—	statement
—	juvat: verb	īre . . . relictum: subj.		IA	F	M	—	statement

Metaphrasing

The infinitive as verbal noun has several possible metaphrases. The following examples are all metaphrases of *Monēre est proprium.*

1. Most simply it is metaphrased as a "to _____" form in subject position, i.e., "to advise is proper."

2. Frequently the "to _____" form is put immediately after the complement, i.e., "it is proper to advise." This position is called *extraposition* because the "to _____" appears to be outside of the kernel.

3. The Latin infinitive as verbal noun can be metaphrased by an English gerund, i.e., "____-ing," as in "advising is proper."

■ Exercise 1
Write three metaphrases for each of the following sentences.

1. Difficile est dēpōnere amōrem.

2. Juvat Dōrica castra vidēre.

3. Placet laudārī ab amīcō.

4. Et amāre et amārī proprium est hominibus.

■ Exercise 2
Copy the kernels onto the kernel chart.

1. Multōs timēre dēbet crūdēlis.
2. Errāre hūmānum est.
3. Fūrem fūr cognōscere potest.
4. Licet nēminī contrā patriam dūcere exercitum.

Clause Marker	Item: Function	Item: Function	Item: Function	Kernel Type	F/NF	M/D	Adj./Adv./ Noun	Name
1.								
2.								
3.								
4.								

■ Exercise 3
Label each infinitive as *complementary infinitive* or *verbal noun* and write a final metaphrase for each sentence from exercise 2.

1.

2.

3.

4.

Lesson Vocabulary

Nouns
amīcitia, amīcitiae, f.: friendship
lītus, lītoris, n.: shore, beach

Adjectives
difficilis, difficile: difficult
Dōricus, Dōrica, Dōricum: Doric, Greek
proprius, propria, proprium: appropriate, proper
vērus, vēra, vērum: true, real

Indeclinables
Adverb
subitō: abruptly, suddenly

Connector
et . . . et: both . . . and

Verbs
concēdō, concēdere, concessī, concessus: allow; give up, yield
decet, decēre, decuit (impers.): is fitting/suitable[1]
dēpōnō, dēpōnere, dēposuī, dēpositus: lay aside
dēserō, dēserere, dēseruī, dēsertus: leave, desert
juvō, juvāre, jūvī, jūtus: help; please; (impers.) delights
labōrō, labōrāre, labōrāvī, labōrātus: work
licet, licēre, licuit (impers.): is allowed/possible
moneō, monēre, monuī, monitus: advise, warn
oportet, oportēre, oportuit (impers.): is necessary
ōrō, ōrāre, ōrāvī, ōrātus: pray, beg, beseech
relinquō, relinquere, relīquī, relictus: leave behind, abandon

Note
1. Impersonal verbs are listed in the dictionary with the third person singular in the first and third principal parts.

Readings

Required

21.1. Nēmō . . . regere potest nisī quī et regī.—Seneca
21.2. Dulce et decōrum est prō patriā morī.—Horace
21.3. Stultum est querī dē adversīs ubi culpa est tua.—Publilius Syrus
21.4. Multōs timēre dēbet quem multī timent.—Publilius Syrus
21.5. Miserum est mortem cupere nec posse morī.—Anon.
21.6. Omnia mors poscit; lēx est, nōn poena, perīre.—Seneca

Vocabulary

21.1. nisi (subord. conj.): except; if not, unless
21.2. *dulcis, dulce: sweet, pleasant
        decōrus, decōra, decōrum: proper
21.3. queror, querī, questus: complain
        adversus, adversa, adversum: unfavorable, adverse
        culpa, culpae, f.: fault
21.5. miser, misera, miserum: wretched, miserable
        *mors, mortis, f.: death
21.6. poscō, poscere, poposcī: demand
        poena, poenae, f.: punishment

Optional

21.7. Et facere et patī fortia Rōmānum est.—Livy
21.8. Sōlem . . . ē mundō tollere videntur quī amīcitiam ē vītā tollunt.—Cicero
21.9. Stultum facit Fortūna quem vult perdere.—Publilius Syrus
21.10. Nōn sentīre mala sua nōn est hominis,[1] et nōn ferre, nōn est virī.[1]—Seneca
21.11. Ars est cēlāre artem.—Anon.
21.12. Aliud est scrībere epistulam, aliud historiam, aliud amīcō, aliud omnibus.—Pliny

Note

1. Genitive used as complement of *esse,* translate "(characteristic) of _____ ."

Vocabulary

21.8. mundus, mundī, m.: world
        tollō, tollere, sustulī, sublātus: take away
21.9. perdō, perdere, perdidī, perditus: destroy
21.10. sentiō, sentīre, sēnsī, sēnsus: feel, perceive
21.11. cēlō, cēlāre, cēlāvī, cēlātus: hide
21.12. aliud . . . aliud: one . . . another
        epistula, epistulae, f.: letter
        historia, historiae, f.: history

Word Study: English Derivatives

From Lesson	Latin	From Readings	Latin
1. admonish		1. adversity	
2. adoration		2. culpable	
3. concession		3. decorum	
4. decent		4. misery	
5. derelict		5. mortuary	
6. laboratory		6. penal	
7. license		7. penalty	
8. verify		8. querulous	

Narrative Reading

Hercules and the Giant Cacus, Part 4

Cacus has vomited out smoke and filled the cave with a blinding fog.

>   Nōn tulit[1] Alcīdēs animīs sēque ipse per ignem
>   praecipitī jēcit saltū, quā[2] plūrimus[3] undam
>   fūmus agit nebulāque ingēns specus aestuat ātrā.
>   Hīc[4] Cācum in tenebrīs incendia vāna vomentem
>   5 corripit[5] in nōdum complexus, et angit inhaerēns
>   ēlīsōs oculōs et siccum[6] sanguine guttur.
>   Panditur extemplō foribus domus ātra revulsīs
>   abstractaeque bovēs abjūrātaeque rapīnae
>   caelō ostenduntur, pedibusque īnfōrme cadāver
> 10 prōtrahitur.

Notes

1. *tulit:* Ø direct object "this" referring to Cacus's defensive measures
2. *quā:* clause marker, "where"
3. *plūrimus:* superlative adjective, "the most"
4. *hīc:* adverb, "at this point, now"
5. *corripit:* Ø subject *Alcīdēs*
6. *siccum sanguine:* translate after *guttur* (see lesson 14)

Vocabulary

abjūrō, abjūrāre, abjūrāvī, abjūrātus: deny on oath
abstrahō, abstrahere, abstrāxī, abstractus: drag away
aestuō, aestuāre, aestuāvī: seethe, burn
angō, angere, anxī: squeeze
āter, ātra, ātrum: black
cadāver, cadāveris, n.: corpse
complector, complectī, complexus: embrace, enfold
corripiō, corripere, corripuī, correptus: seize
ēlīdō, ēlīdere, ēlīsī, ēlīsus: cause to protrude, strike (squeeze) out
extemplō (adv.): immediately
foris, foris, f.: door, entrance
fūmus, fūmī, m.: smoke
guttur, gutturis, n.: throat
incendium, incendiī, n.: fire, flame
īnformis, īnforme: shapeless
inhaereō, inhaerēre, inhaesī, inhaesus: cling to
nebula, nebulae, f.: cloud
nōdus, nōdī, m.: knot
ostendō, ostendere, ostendī, ostentus: show
pandō, pandere, pandī, pānsus: spread open
praeceps (praecipitis): headlong
prōtrahō, prōtrahere, prōtrāxī, prōtractus: drag forth, drag out
rapīna, rapīnae, f.: robbery

revellō, revellere, revellī, revulsus: tear away
saltus, saltūs, m.: leap, jump
*sanguis, sanguinis, n.: blood
siccus, sicca, siccum: dry
specus, specūs, m.: cave
tenebrae, tenebrārum, f. pl.: darkness
vānus, vāna, vānum: empty, useless
vomō, vomere, vomuī, vomitus: spew forth, vomit

Derivatives from Narrative Reading

Latin

1. adhere
2. collision
3. complex
4. convulsion
5. desiccated
6. insulting
7. nebulous
8. precipitant

Epilogue

The English poet Dryden, who translated the *Aeneid,* ends Evander's story with these lines:

> The wondering neighborhood, with glad surprise,
> Behold his shagged breast, his giant size,
> His mouth that flames no more, and his extinguished eyes.
> From that auspicious day, with rites divine,
> We worship at the hero's holy shrine.

The hero's holy shrine was the Ara Maxima (the Greatest Altar) that stood in Rome in the Forum Boarium (the Cattle Market) in the valley between the Aventine and Palatine hills, where Hercules had found such fine pasturage for his cattle. The worship of Hercules at the Ara Maxima continued throughout the pagan history of Rome. Hercules became almost a patron saint who would help his worshippers overcome the numerous difficulties of life.

Summary Tasks

____ 1. Write all kernels for Readings 21.1, 21.4, and 21.5.
____ 2. Complete the sentence: A complementary infinitive together with another verb fills the kernel function ____ ; the infinitive as verbal noun fills the kernel function ____ or ____ .
____ 3. Metaphrase in three different ways Reading 21.2.
____ 4. Complete the sentence: A verb is labeled "impersonal" when ____ .
____ 5. Copy adjective-noun pairs, including participles and noun-heads, from the Narrative Reading. Label the participles.

Review Lesson 6

Lesson Vocabulary

Nouns
amīcitia, amīcitiae, f.: friendship
laus, laudis, f.: praise, glory, fame
lībertās, lībertātis, f.: freedom
lītus, lītoris, n.: shore, beach
necessitās, necessitātis, f.: necessity
nēmō, nēminis, m. & f.: no one
ōs, ōris, n.: mouth, face
puella, puellae, f.: girl
studium, studiī, n.: eagerness, zeal; study

Pronouns
ego, meī: I, me
īdem, eadem, idem: the same
ipse, ipsa, ipsum: self, e.g., myself, yourself, himself, etc.
iste, ista, istud: that (near you), that of yours
nōs, nostrum: we, us
sē, sē, sibi, suī: himself, herself, itself, themselves
tū, tuī: you
vōs, vestrum: you (pl.)

Adjectives
alius, alia, aliud: another, other
alter, altera, alterum: one (of two), the other
caecus, caeca, caecum: blind
difficilis, difficile: difficult
Dōricus, Dōrica, Dōricum: Doric
līber, lībera, līberum: free
meus, mea, meum: my, mine
neuter, neutra, neutrum: neither
noster, nostra, nostrum: our
proprius, propria, proprium: appropriate, proper
sōlus, sōla, sōlum: alone, the only
tōtus, tōta, tōtum: whole, entire
tuus, tua, tuum: your (sing.)
ūllus, ūlla, ūllum: any
uter, utra, utrum: which (of two)?
uterque, utraque, utrumque: (usually sing.) each (of two)

vērus, vēra, vērum: true, real
vester, vestra, vestrum: your (pl.)

Indeclinables
Adverb
subitō: suddenly, abruptly

Connector
et . . . et: both . . . and

Verbs
accūsō, accūsāre, accūsāvī, accūsātus: accuse
cadō, cadere, cecidī, cāsūrus: fall
concēdō, concēdere, concessī, concessus: allow; give up, yield
decet, decēre, decuit (impers.): is fitting/suitable
dēpōnō, dēpōnere, dēposuī, dēpositus: lay aside
dēserō, dēserere, dēseruī, dēsertus: leave, desert
dīcō, dīcere, dīxī, dictus: say, tell, speak; call, name
effugiō, effugere, effūgī: escape
eō, īre, iī (īvī), itūrus: go
errō, errāre, errāvī: wander, err
ferō, ferre, tulī, lātus: bring, carry, endure
gaudeō, gaudēre, gavīsus: rejoice, be glad
imitor, imitārī, imitātus: imitate
īrāscor, īrāscī, īrātus: be angry
jūdicō, jūdicāre, jūdicāvī, jūdicātus: judge
juvō, juvāre, jūvī, jūtus: help; please; (impers.) delights
labōrō, labōrāre, labōrāvī, labōrātus: work
laudō, laudāre, laudāvī, laudātus: praise
licet, licēre, licuit (impers.): is allowed/possible
loquor, loquī, locūtus: say, speak, tell
mālō, mālle, māluī: prefer
mentior, mentīrī, mentītus: lie, tell a lie
mīror, mīrārī, mīrātus: admire, love
moneō, monēre, monuī, monitus: advise, warn
morior, morī, mortuus: die
nāscor, nāscī, nātus: be born
nōlō, nōlle, nōluī: not wish, be unwilling
oportet, oportēre, oportuit (impers.): is necessary
ōrō, ōrāre, ōrāvī, ōrātus: pray, beg, beseech
patior, patī, passus: suffer, endure, allow
quaerō, quaerere, quaesīvī, quaesītus: look for, search for, ask
relinquō, relinquere, relīquī, relictus: leave behind, abandon
sequor, sequī, secūtus: follow
timeō, timēre, timuī: fear
trahō, trahere, trāxī, tractus: drag, draw, pull
ūtor, ūtī, ūsus: use (+ abl.)
vereor, verērī, veritus: fear, respect

Readings Vocabulary

at (coord. conj.): but
caelum, caelī, n.: heaven, sky
cursus, cursūs, m.: running, race; course
dulcis, dulce: sweet
fīlius, fīliī, m.: son
ingēns (ingentis): huge
mōns, montis, m.: mountain
mors, mortis, f.: death
mūrus, mūrī, m.: wall
mūtō, mūtāre, mūtāvī, mūtātus: change
quisque, quaeque, quodque: each one, everyone
Rōmānus, Rōmāna, Rōmānum: Roman
sanguis, sanguinis, n.: blood
spēlunca, spēluncae, f.: cave
timor, timōris, m.: fear, dread
umbra, umbrae, f.: shadow, shade
vastus, vasta, vastum: huge
victōria, victōriae, f.: victory

Morphology Review

New Morphology: Lessons 18 through 21

pronouns: personal
            reflexive
            intensive
            demonstrative
special adjectives
verbs: all person forms, singular and plural, present imperfective and present perfective,
    active and passive
deponent verbs

Form Identification

    a. mīror, mīrārī, mīrātus: admire, love
    b. mīrus, mīra, mīrum: wonderful
    c. mīrābilis, mīrābile: wonderful

1. mīrābilī   _____
2. mīrāta est   _____
3. mīrābilis   _____
4. mīra   _____
5. mīrāminī   _____

6. mīrābilia   _____

7. mīrāris   _____

8. mīrārī   _____

9. mīrātae sumus   _____

10. mīrī   _____

■ Exercise: English to Latin Sentences
Using the Latin sentences as models, translate the English sentences into Latin.

1. Ex ōre tuō tē jūdicō. (S18.2)
2. Effugere nōn potes necessitātēs; potes vincere. (S18.4)
3. Trahimur omnēs studiō laudis. (S19.1)
4. Quī sēsē accūsat ipse, ab aliō nōn potest. (S19.2)
5. Nōn omnēs eadem mīrantur amantque. (S20.1)
6. Difficile est longum subitō dēpōnere amōrem. (S21.2)
7. Juvat īre et Dōrica castra dēsertōsque vidēre locōs lītusque relictum. (S21.4)

   a. You are able to judge me from my speech. (1, 2)

   b. You are all influenced by the necessities of life. (3)

   c. Whoever judges himself, is able to judge others. (4)

   d. We do not all follow and praise the same leaders. (5)

   e. It is easy to admire the brave. (6)

   f. It is a pleasure to go and to change (one's) environment. (7)

Vocabulary

Nouns
environment: locus, locī
leader: dux
life: vīta
necessity: necessitās
speech: ōs

Pronouns
himself: sē
me: ego
whoever: quī

Adjectives
all: omnis
brave: fortis
easy: facilis
my: meus
other: alius
same: īdem

Indeclinables
from: ex (prep. + abl.)
not: nōn (adv.)

Verbs
admire: mīror
be, is: sum
be able, can: possum
change: mūtō
follow: sequor
go: eō, īre
influence: trahō
it is pleasing: placet
judge: jūdicō
praise: laudō

Stem List

Enter the following words in the Stem List found in the back of this book. Also add dictionary listings for each word entered.

1. amīcitiae	8. effugere	15. morior	22. sequor
2. amōrem	9. eō	16. ōrāre	23. trahimur
3. audet	10. ferō	17. ōre	24. ūtor
4. cecidit	11. juvat	18. patior	25. vēnī
5. concēditur	12. loquī	19. potes	26. vīcī
6. dēpōnere	13. mīrantur	20. quaerunt	27. vīdī
7. dīcō	14. monēre	21. relictum	28. volō

Lesson 22

The Verbal Noun: Gerund

Each infinitive as verbal noun in the English sentence *"To work is to pray"* can be replaced by the other type of verbal noun, the *gerund,* e.g., *"Working is praying."* This cannot occur in Latin where the infinitive and the gerund each have different noun functions. Latin gerunds function only as modifiers.

Basic Sentences

22.1. Hominis mēns discendō alitur et cōgitandō.—Cicero
        The mind of man is nourished by learning and thinking.
22.2. Timendī causa est nescīre.—Seneca
        Not knowing is the cause of fearing.

The Verbal Noun: Gerund

Morphology

The *gerund* is built from the imperfective stem of the verb. The characteristic morpheme is {nd}. The Latin gerund has active voice only, in contrast to the infinitive, which has both active and passive voices.

The case endings are those of second declension neuter nouns. They occur in the singular only. The gerund is the same for verbs of all conjugations as can be seen in the examples.

	First	Second	Third	Third -iō	Fourth
Nominative	—	—	—	—	—
Accusative	ad amandum	ad videndum	ad regendum	ad capiendum	ad audiendum
Ablative	amandō	videndō	regendō	capiendō	audiendō
Dative	amandō	videndō	regendō	capiendō	audiendō
Genitive	amandī	videndī	regendī	capiendī	audiendī

■ Exercise 1
Underline any form that looks like a gerund and identify its case.

1. agendī

2. agentī

3. tenendīs

4. mittendī

5. mittendus

6. capientī

7. capiendī

8. laudātō

9. laudandō

10. amanda

Syntax and Metaphrasing

The Latin gerund does not occur as subject, complement, or direct object in a kernel. It functions only as an adjectival or adverbial modifier and occurs in the accusative case with *ad,* or in the ablative, dative, and genitive cases. In S22.1, *discendō* and *cōgitandō* are gerunds in the ablative without a preposition. They have the case use "ablative of means."

Semantically, all gerunds are abstract and, like other abstract nouns, commonly express "means" or "cause" in the ablative case.

Most gerunds with the final morpheme {ō} are ablatives since a dative gerund seldom occurs.

Although the gerund, like the infinitive as verbal noun, may have a direct object (see Reading 22.2), generally it is not entered onto a kernel chart.

All gerunds must be metaphrased "_____-ing." *Discendō* and *cōgitandō* in S22.1 are metaphrased "by *learning* and *thinking*."

The preposition *ad* plus a gerund in the accusative expresses purpose, e.g., *ad audiendum* (for [the purpose of] hearing). Likewise a gerund in the genitive case followed by the ablative *causā* expresses purpose, e.g., *audiendī causā* (for [the purpose of] hearing). In S22.2, *causa* is in the nominative and therefore does not set up a purpose expression.

Learners must be very careful to discriminate between the metaphrase of the imperfective active participle and the gerund because both end in -ing in English. The critical difference between the two is that the participle is metaphrased "(noun-head) _____-ing" but the gerund is metaphrased "_____-ing."

■ Exercise 2

Identify each *-ing* word as a participle or gerund. For each participle draw an arrow to its noun-head.

1. I see the horse running in the field.

2. She was tired of swimming.

3. They were frightened by the shouting.

4. The person advising us was a friend of ours.

5. We sent him for the purpose of buying the book.

6. She was awakened by the baby crying loudly.

■ Exercise 3

Enter all gerunds (with prepositions, if present) onto this chart.

Sentence	Item	Syntactic Information*	Head
1. Populus resistit ad vincendum.	ad vincendum	adv. mod.	resistit
2. Cōgitandō cōgitāre discimus.			
3. Timor est sēnsus timendī.			
4. Puer manet ad loquendum.			

*Adverbial or adjectival modifier.

■ Exercise 4

Metaphrase each of the following.

1. artem vīvendī: _____ _____ s the art of living.

2. vincendī causā

3. studium discendī

4. ad regendum

5. loquendō

6. Aper currit ad effugiendum.

7. Aper currit effugiendī causā.

8. Scrībendō scrībere discunt.

9. Timor est sēnsus timendī.

10. Cōgitandō cōgitāre discunt.

■ Exercise 5

Identify each italicized word as imperfective or perfective participle or as gerund. Metaphrase each set of words in the context of a complete sentence.

	Identification	*Metaphrase*
1. hostēs *victōs*		
2. ad canem *effugientem*		
3. ad *effugiendum*		
4. causa *sequendī*		
5. *sequendī* causā		
6. puerō *sequentī*		
7. puerī ab amīcō *laudātī*		
8. *laudandō*		

■ **Exercise 6**

These words all look like gerunds but some are not. With the aid of the dictionary entries, identify each word.

> dēscendō, dēscendere, dēscendī
> fundō, fundere, fūdī, fūsus
> tendō, tendere, tetendī, tentus

1. fundō _____

2. fundendō _____

3. tendō _____

4. tendendī _____

5. dēscendī _____

6. dēscendendī _____

7. tetendī _____

Lesson Vocabulary

Nouns

hostis, hostis, m.: enemy
sēnsus, sēnsūs, m.: sensation, feeling
timor, timōris, m.: fear, dread

Verbs

cōgitō, cōgitāre, cōgitāvī, cōgitātus: think, consider
nesciō, nescīre, nescīvī: not know, be ignorant of

Readings

Required

22.1. Nīl agentī diēs longus est.—Seneca
22.2. Nihil agendō hominēs male agere discunt.—Marcus Cato
22.3. Legendī semper occāsiō est, audiendī nōn semper.—Pliny the Younger
22.4. Breve . . . tempus aetātis; satis est longum ad bene honestēque vīvendum.—Cicero
22.5. An old man waiting for the doctor complains:

> Lumbī sedendō, oculī spectandō dolent,
> manendō medicum.—Plautus

Vocabulary[1]
22.2. male (adv.): badly
22.3. *legō, legere, lēgī, lēctus: read
22.4. *aetās, aetātis, f.: youth, age, period of life
　　　 *satis (adv.): enough
　　　 bene (adv.): well
22.5. lumbus, lumbī, m.: loins
　　　 *sedeō, sedēre, sēdī: sit

Optional

Note: No vocabulary will be given for the Optional Readings in the remaining lessons. If you do them without your instructor, use a Latin dictionary as needed.

Using a Latin dictionary in preparing these readings is sometimes quite difficult, since the dictionary gives many meanings for a word and you need to pick the one that fits best with the total meaning of the sentence.

In previous reading vocabularies only the most appropriate meaning of a word was given; therefore, there were few decisions for you to make about the meaning of a particular word.

22.6. See Plautus Selection to Be Read after Lesson 22 (p. 349).
22.7. Ōrātor est vir bonus, dīcendī perītus.—Cato
22.8. Vigilandō, agendō, bene cōnsulendō prospera omnia *cēdunt.—Sallust
22.9. Ūnus homō nōbīs cūnctandō restituit rem.²—Ennius
22.10. Nūlla causa *jūsta cuiquam esse potest contrā patriam arma capiendī.—Cicero (adapted)
22.11. Ut ad cursum *equus, ad arandum bōs, ad indāgandum canis, *sīc homō ad duās rēs, ad intellegendum et ad agendum, est nātus.—Cicero (adapted)

Notes

1. An asterisk (*) indicates the third time a word is used in Readings.
2. Said of Quintus Fabius Maximus, victor over Hannibal, and afterward given the surname of Cūnctātor. Why?

Word Study: English Derivatives

From Lesson	Latin	From Readings	Latin
1. alimony		1. agility	
2. cogitation		2. audience	
3. disciplinary		3. illegible	
4. hostile		4. malevolent	
5. mental		5. nihilism	
6. omniscient		6. remain	
7. science		7. satisfaction	
8. sensuous		8. sedentary	

Summary Tasks

____ 1. Complete the sentence: The gerund does/does not function as a kernel part because ____ .

____ 2. Identify by part of speech all words in Readings 22.1 through 22.5.

____ 3. Write the ablative gerund of all third conjugation verbs listed in the Vocabulary Appendix of lesson 9.

Lesson 23

Dependent Clauses as Kernel Items
Non-Finite Noun Clauses
The Objective Infinitive: A Non-Finite Noun Clause
The Indirect Statement: A Non-Finite Noun Clause

Dependent Clauses as Kernel Items

One characteristic of both English and Latin is that one sentence can be *embedded* into another as a kernel item. This process can be repeated endlessly. For example, the direct statement "the soldiers are building a bridge" can be embedded into the sentence "Caesar said it." The result of such embedding is the sentence "Caesar said that the soldiers were building a bridge." This process can be repeated, e.g., "the general heard that Caesar said that the soldiers were building a bridge," or "they know that the general heard that Caesar said that . . . ," and so on. The same is true for direct questions, which can be embedded endlessly.

Every one of the clauses in such a sentence except the last one embedded is a *governing clause*. Every one except the main clause is a *dependent* or *embedded clause*.

The dependent clauses in Latin introduced so far have been adverbial or adjectival modifiers with one exception, the relative clause as noun equivalent. This lesson and future lessons will introduce a number of dependent clauses that are always noun clauses.[1] All of these noun clauses are kernel items, not modifiers. The clauses introduced in this lesson are the *objective infinitive construction* and the *indirect statement*. Both of these are non-finite; all other noun clauses are finite.

Basic Sentences

23.1. Caesar mīlitēs pontem facere jubet/jussit.
      Caesar orders/ordered soldiers to build a bridge.
23.2. Caesar dīcit mīlitēs pontem facere.
      Caesar says that soldiers are building a bridge.
23.3. Caesar dīxit mīlitēs pontem facere.
      Caesar said that soldiers were building a bridge.

---

1. Since lesson 13, relative clauses that function as nouns have been identified on a kernel chart as noun clauses. This practice should be continued.

Non-Finite Noun Clauses

Dependent clauses in previous lessons have been both finite and non-finite. The finite are those with a finite verb and a subject in the nominative. The non-finite are those with a participle and a noun-head (as subject) in any case.

The clauses of this lesson are non-finite: the verb is an infinitive and the subject is a noun or pronoun in the accusative case. For this reason they traditionally are referred to as *accusative with infinitive* constructions. They have *no clause marker* in Latin.

The Objective Infinitive: A Non-Finite Noun Clause

Syntax and Semantics

An *accusative with infinitive* may be expected in kernels with verbs that are related semantically to "ordering," "wishing," etc. *Jubeō* in S23.1 is one such verb. Other verbs with this general semantic notion include:

cōgō (force)
moneō (advise, warn)
postulō (demand)
prohibeō (prevent)
vetō (forbid)
nōlō (not wish)
volō (wish)

Traditionally, such a noun clause is called the *objective infinitive* construction.

Grammarians do not agree among themselves on the description of an item such as *mīlitēs* in S23.1. Is it associated more closely with the governing verb, in this case *jubet/jussit* (as its object), or with the dependent infinitive, in this case *facere* (as its subject)? For the purpose of learning to read Latin, however, it is advisable to consider *mīlitēs* as subject for the verb *facere*. In this sentence the whole noun clause *mīlitēs pontem facere* is the object of *jubet/jussit*. Which of two accusatives in such a clause is the subject and which is the direct object of the infinitive is not a matter of Latin syntax but of other considerations, including semantics and context.

Kernel Information

Caesar mīlitēs pontem facere jussit.

Clause Marker	Item: Function	Item: Function	Item: Function	Kernel Type	F/NF	M/D	Adj./Adv./ Noun	Name
—	Caesar: subj.	mīlitēs pontem facere: dir. obj.	jussit: verb	TA	F	M	—	statement
①	mīlitēs: subj.	pontem: dir. obj.	facere: verb	TA	NF	D	noun	obj. inf. clause

Note: By analogy with Ⓟ for participle clauses, it might be helpful to the beginner to indicate an infinitive clause by an Ⓘ in the Clause Marker column. This is a reminder that the clause is dependent even though there is no clause marker.

Metaphrasing

The objective infinitive construction does not have a clause marker in either Latin or English. The objective infinitive in English is marked by *to* as in "to build."

■ Exercise 1

Underline the non-finite noun clause in each sentence. Then copy the finite and non-finite kernels for sentences 1 and 2 on the kernel chart.

1. Nēmō mīlitēs currere cōgit.
2. Volumus tē eum sequī.
3. Vōs venīre vetō.
4. Quis jubet puerōs labōrāre?

Clause Marker	Item: Function	Item: Function	Item: Function	Kernel Type	F/NF	M/D	Adj./Adv./ Noun	Name
1.								
2.								
3.								
4.								

■ Exercise 2

Write a final metaphrase of each sentence in exercise 1.

1.

2.

3.

4.

The Indirect Statement: A Non-Finite Noun Clause

Syntax and Semantics

Another *accusative with infinitive* occurs with governing verbs that are related semantically to "saying," "thinking," or "perceiving." This non-finite noun clause is called an *indirect statement*.

In S23.2, *mīlitēs pontem facere* is an indirect statement; it functions as direct object of *dīcit*. The direct statement would be *mīlitēs pontem faciunt*. That is,

Direct statement: Mīlitēs pontem faciunt. (The soldiers are building a bridge.)
Indirect statement: Caesar dīcit *mīlitēs pontem facere*. (Caesar says *that the soldiers are building a bridge.*)

Verbs that raise the expectation of an indirect statement are related semantically to "saying," "thinking," "perceiving," etc.[1] *Dīcit* in S23.2 is one such verb. Others include:

arbitror (think)
audiō (hear)
cognōscō (recognize, learn)
dīcō (say)
nārrō (narrate, talk)
negō (deny, say . . . not)
putō (think)
sciō (know)
scrībō (write)
sentiō (feel, perceive)
videō (see, perceive)

Kernel Information

Caesar dīcit mīlitēs pontem facere.

Clause Marker	Item: Function	Item: Function	Item: Function	Kernel Type	F/NF	M/D	Adj./Adv./ Noun	Name
—	Caesar: subj.	dīcit: verb	mīlitēs pontem facere: dir. obj.	TA	F	M	—	statement
①	mīlitēs: subj.	pontem: dir. obj.	facere: verb	TA	NF	D	noun	ind. st.

Metaphrasing

In contrast to the Latin infinitives studied so far, *the infinitive in an indirect statement is expressed as a finite verb* in English. It is *not* to be expressed as a "to _____" form. Look at S23.2, *Caesar dīcit mīlitēs pontem facere.*

   Correct: Caesar says *that* the soldiers *are building* a bridge.
   Incorrect: Caesar says the soldiers to build a bridge.

No clause marker introduces an indirect statement in classical Latin. In English an indirect statement is commonly introduced by the clause marker "that," although it is not obligatory. In order to become familiar with the indirect statement, and to avoid confusion with other constructions, learners should always insert the clause marker "that" before the indirect statement.
   Note: A reflexive pronoun as subject of an indirect statement in Latin clearly indicates that the subject of the indirect statement and the subject of the governing verb have the same referent. Since English uses a personal pronoun and not a reflexive pronoun in this

---

1. The traditional label for this list of verbs is *verba dīcendī et sentiendī.*

construction the relationship in English is not clear. (See reflexive pronouns, lesson 19.) For example, *Puella* **sē** *esse in pictūrā cōgitat* (The girl thinks that *she* is in the picture).

■ Exercise 3
Underline the non-finite noun clause in each sentence. Then copy the finite and non-finite kernels for sentences 1 and 2 onto the kernel chart.

1. Audīmus eum litterās scrībere.
2. Pater puellās ā puerīs laudārī dīcit.
3. Puerī sē labōrāre dīcunt.
4. Tē mentīrī sciō.

Clause Marker	Item: Function	Item: Function	Item: Function	Kernel Type	F/NF	M/D	Adj./Adv./ Noun	Name
1.								
1.								
2.								
2.								

■ Exercise 4
Write a final metaphrase of each sentence in exercise 3.

1.

2.

3.

4.

Infinitives built on the imperfective stem, just like participles built on the imperfective stem, express time *simultaneous* with, i.e., at the same time as, that of the governing verb.

Caesar *dīcit* mīlitēs pontem *facere*. (Caesar *says* that the soldiers *are building* a bridge.)
Caesar *dīxit* mīlitēs pontem *facere*. (Caesar *said* that the soldiers *were building* a bridge.)

Notice that in these examples the infinitive *facere* is metaphrased as "are building" with *dīcit* (says), but as "were building" with *dīxit* (said). This shift is necessary for grammatical correctness in English, but does not always happen in present-day speech. There is no meaning difference between "are building" and "were building." Both show the same time relative to that of the governing verb. Shifts such as these occur also in Latin and will be introduced in later lessons.

■ Exercise 5
Write a final metaphrase of each of the following sentences. Remember to express the proper relative time.

1. Pater puerum ab amīcō adjuvārī dīcit.

2. Pater puerum ab amīcō adjuvārī dīxit.

3. Scīvī eōs multa scrībere.

4. Sciō eōs multa scrībere.

■ Exercise 6
Using the dictionary entries provided, identify the following forms and indicate the entry from which each one comes.

    a. sentiō, sentīre, sēnsī, sēnsus
    b. sēnsus, sēnsūs, m.
    c. sententia, sententiae, f.
    d. sententiōsus, sententiōsa, sententiōsum

1. sēnsūs _____

2. sententiam _____

3. sententiōsam _____

4. sēnsōs _____

5. sēnsērunt _____

6. sentientem _____

7. sentīrī _____

8. sēnsibus _____

9. sententiōsī _____

10. sentiendī _____

Lesson Vocabulary

Nouns
mīles, mīlitis, m.: soldier
pōns, pontis, m.: bridge

Verbs
arbitror, arbitrārī, arbitrātus: think
jubeō, jubēre, jussī, jussus: order
nārrō, nārrāre, nārrāvī, nārrātus: tell, relate, narrate
negō, negāre, negāvī, negātus: deny, say . . . not
prohibeō, prohibēre, prohibuī, prohibitus: prevent, hinder, keep from
putō, putāre, putāvī, putātus: consider, think
sciō, scīre, scīvī, scītus: know
sentiō, sentīre, sēnsī, sēnsus: feel, perceive
vetō, vetāre, vetuī: forbid, prohibit

Readings

Required

23.1. Victōrem ā victō superārī saepe vidēmus.—Dionysius Cato

23.2. Nēmō doctus umquam . . . mūtātiōnem cōnsiliī incōnstantiam dīxit esse.—Cicero

23.3. Atque equidem Teucrum meminī Sīdōna venīre
   fīnibus expulsum patriīs, nova rēgna petentem.—Vergil *Aeneid* 1.619

23.4. Quod mē dīxī velle vōbīs dīcere, dīcam.—Plautus

Vocabulary

23.1. victor, victōris, m.: victor
    superō, superāre, superāvī, superātus: overcome, conquer

23.2. *umquam (adv.): ever
    mūtātiō, mūtātiōnis, f.: change
    incōnstantia, incōnstantiae, f.: inconsistency

23.3. equidem (intensifier): indeed, truly
    Teucer, Teucrī, m.: Teucer (a Trojan prince)
    meminī, meminisse: remember
    Sīdōna: an accusative form "to Sidon" (a town in Phoenicia)
    expellō, expellere, expulsī, expulsus: drive out, exile
    patrius, patria, patrium: ancestral, native
    rēgnum, rēgnī, n.: kingdom

23.4. dīcam: "I will say"

Optional

23.5. Plautus Selection to Be Read after Lesson 23 (page 352)

23.6. Dīcis amōre tuī bellās *ardēre puellās,
       quī *faciem sub aquā, Sexte, natantis habēs.—Martial 2.87
    Paraphrasis: Dīcis puellās pulchrās tē ad īnsāniam amāre. Crēdere hoc difficile est: nam
    tū habēs tālem vultum quālem sub aquā natāns, id est, *pallidum et turgidum.

23.7. "Omnēs," inquit Alexander, "jūrant esse mē Jōvis fīlium, sed vulnus hoc hominem mē
    esse clāmat."—Seneca

23.8. Haec tua est amīca, quam mihi
    tē amāre dīxistī?—Plautus

Word Study: English Derivatives

From Lesson	Latin		From Readings	Latin
1. arbitration			1. constant	
2. military			2. counsel	
3. narrative			3. doctrine	
4. negative			4. expulsion	
5. pontoon			5. final	
6. prohibition			6. insuperable	
7. reputation			7. predict	
8. sentimental			8. victorious	

Summary Tasks

—— 1. Copy from the list of Basic Sentences in the appendix of this book all infinitives between lessons 18 and 23 and name the infinitive use.

—— 2. Embed the second Basic Sentence of lessons 1 through 8 as an indirect statement after *dīcit/dīxit*.

—— 3. Name all verb lists that have occurred so far according to semantic or syntactic criteria (e.g., special intransitive verbs, etc.).

—— 4. Complete this series in English and translate into Latin: "I say that I know many things," "you say that you know many things," etc. Express all pronouns in the Latin.

Lesson 24

Relative Time in the Indirect Statement

Man in Western civilization is often said to be preoccupied with time. It is certainly true that time plays a prominent role in the verb system of Latin. Time, as it goes by, usually is divided into past, present, and future time. On the other hand there is *relative time,* denoting whether one event happens before, at the same time as, or after another event.

Back-shift is introduced in order to explain the different English metaphrases of a given Latin infinitive.

Basic Sentences

24.1. Caesar mīlitēs pontem fēcisse dīcit.
     Caesar says that the soldiers have built a bridge.
24.2. Caesar mīlitēs pontem factūrōs (esse) dīcit.
     Caesar says that the soldiers will build a bridge.
24.3. Victōrem ā victō superātum esse saepe vidēmus.—Dionysius Cato (adapted)
     We often see that the victor has been overcome by the vanquished one.

Relative Time in the Indirect Statement

The infinitives in the previous lessons were all built on the *imperfective* stem. This lesson presents the *perfective infinitive* and the *future infinitive.* In an indirect statement each of these infinitives indicates a different *relative* time.

Morphology: Latin Infinitives

	Imperfective	*Perfective*	*Future*
Active	amāre	amāvisse	amātūrus, -a, -um esse
	vidēre	vīdisse	vīsūrus, -a, -um esse
	regere	rēxisse	rēctūrus, -a, -um esse
	audīre	audīvisse	audītūrus, -a, -um esse
	esse	fuisse	futūrus, -a, -um esse
Passive	amārī	amātus, -a, -um esse	—
	vidērī	vīsus, -a, -um esse	—
	regī	rēctus, -a, -um esse	—
	audīrī	audītus, -a, -um esse	—
	—	—	—

The *perfective active infinitive* has as a signal the morpheme {isse} on the perfective active stem (from the third principal part of the verb).

The *perfective passive infinitive* is a periphrastic form consisting of the perfective passive participle plus *esse*. Note: the *esse* is omitted in many sentences.

The *future active infinitive* is also a periphrastic form consisting of the future active participle (signaled by the morpheme {ūr}) plus the word *esse,* which is frequently omitted. (The English word *future* is derived from *futūrus, -a, -um,* the future participle of the Latin verb *esse.*)

The future passive infinitive is rare and need not be learned at this time.

Syntax

The participle part of the perfective passive and the future active infinitives shows agreement in case, number, and gender with the subject of the infinitive, i.e., with the noun in the accusative. In S24.2, *factūrōs* agrees with *mīlitēs;* in S24.3, *superātum* agrees with *victōrem.*

■ Exercise 1

Complete the chart in order to identify the infinitives. Number 1 has been given as an example.

Infinitive	Imperfective/ Perfective/Future	Active Voice/ Passive Voice
1. captōs esse	perfective	passive voice
2. laudārī		
3. vincere		
4. laudātūrum esse		
5. cēpisse		
6. laudātam esse		
7. vīcisse		
8. vincī		
9. ferre		
10. lāta esse		

Relative Time

As said in lesson 23, imperfective infinitives express time simultaneous with (at the same time as) that of the governing verb. See S23.3 for an example.

Perfective infinitives express time preceding (time before) that of the governing verb. There are several English translations that indicate "time before." For example, in S24.1, the perfective infinitive *fēcisse* could be translated as "built," "have built," or even "had built." In S24.3, "we" are reporting on something that happened, has happened, or even had happened before the time of the governing verb *vidēmus.*

Future infinitives express time following (time after) that of the governing verb. *Factūrōs esse* in S24.2 describes that which will happen after the time of the governing verb *dīcit.*

■ Exercise 2

On the basis of the morphology of the infinitive in each of these sentences, mark whether the event described by the indirect statement (the accusative plus infinitive construction) happens/happened *before*, at the *same time as*, or at a *time after* the time of the governing verb.

Sentences	Indirect Statement		
	Time Before	Same Time	Time After
1. Dīcō fūrem fūrem cognōscere.	————	————	————
2. Crēdunt gladiātōrem cōnsilium cēpisse.	————	————	————
3. Crēdidērunt gladiātōrem cōnsilium cēpisse.	————	————	————
4. Dīxērunt gladiātōrem leōnem captūrum esse.	————	————	————
5. Negāmus īram fuisse magnam.	————	————	————
6. Dīxit eōs ducem sequī.	————	————	————
7. Nārrāvit piscem ā puellā captum esse.	————	————	————
8. Audīvistis puerum leōnem vīdisse.	————	————	————

Metaphrasing

Compare these sentences:

> Caesar mīlitēs pontem fēcisse dīcit. (Caesar *says* that the soldiers *have built* a bridge.)
> Caesar mīlitēs pontem fēcisse dīxit. (Caesar *said* that the soldiers *had built* a bridge.)

The change from *have built* to *had built* while the Latin infinitive remains the same is another example of the shift mentioned in lesson 23. In current descriptions of languages, the term for this phenomenon is *back-shift*.

The description of the term *back-shift* is this: when the time meaning of the governing verb is changed into the past, e.g., "says" to "said," there is a corresponding back-shift in the dependent verb, but without any change in meaning. In the example, "has built" after "says" is back-shifted to "had built" after "said." The shift from "are building" in S23.2 to "were building" in S23.3 is another example of back-shift.

Back-shift affects finite verbs only, not infinitives, in both Latin and English. Thus, in the two example sentences above, *fēcisse*, an infinitive, remains the same with *dīcit* and *dīxit*. However, because the English demands a finite verb, the metaphrase is "have built" after "says," but "had built" after "said."

Back-shift as it applies to Latin will be discussed in lesson 30.

■ Exercise 3

Write a metaphrase of each sentence found in exercise 2.

1.

2.

3.

4.

5.

6.

7.

8.

Reminder: The infinitive as a verbal noun is never translated as a finite verb. The imperfective infinitive as verbal noun is translated as "to ____" or "to be ____-ed," the perfective infinitive as "to have ____-ed" or "to have been ____-ed." For example:

Infinitive as verbal noun: Temptāvisse sat est. (To have tried is enough.)
Infinitive in indirect statement: Sē temptāvisse negat. (He denies that he tried.)

■ Exercise 4
Write a metaphrase of each of the following.

1. a. Dīxī vēritātem vincere.

   b. Dīxī vēritātem victūram esse.

   c. Dīxī vēritātem vīcisse.

2. a. Dīcis amīcum rem quaesīvisse.

   b. Dīcis amīcum rem quaesītūrum.

   c. Dīcis amīcum rem quaerere.

3. a. Dīcimus occāsiōnem facile āmittī.

   b. Dīcimus occāsiōnem facile āmissam.

4. a. Dīxit longum esse iter.

   b. Dīxit longum fore* iter.

   c. Dīxit longum fuisse iter.

   *Fore is an alternate form of futūrus, -a, -um esse.

Lesson Vocabulary

Noun

victor, victōris, m.: victor, conqueror

Verb

superō, superāre, superāvī, superātus: overcome, surpass

Readings

Required

24.1. Posse patī voluī nec mē temptā'sse negābō.—Ovid
(Notes: *temptā'sse = temptāvisse*
negābō, translate "I will deny")
24.2. Crās tē vīctūrum, crās dīcis, Postume, semper.—Martial
(Note: *Postume* is the man's name, Postumus, in the vocative case, which is used to address the person spoken to; see lesson 28.)
24.3. Dīmidium factī est coepisse.—Ausonius
24.4. Atque hoc poētae faciunt in comoediīs:
omnīs rēs gestās esse Athēnīs dīcunt.—Plautus
(Note: *Athēnīs*, "in Athens")
24.5. Aut hīc est aut hīc adfore āctūtum autumō.—Lucilius

Vocabulary

24.1. *nec (coord. conj.): nor, and not
temptō, temptāre, temptāvī, temptātus: attempt, try
24.2. crās (adv.): tomorrow
vīctūrus, -a, -um: from *vīvō* (not from *vincō*)
24.3. dīmidium, dīmidiī, n.: half
factum, factī, n.: deed, action
coepī, coepisse: begin
24.4. comoedia, comoediae, f.: comedy
*gerō, gerere, gessī, gestus: do, carry on
24.5. aut (coord. conj.): or; aut . . . aut: either . . . or
hīc (adv.): here
āctūtum (adv.): instantly, immediately
adfore: future infinitive of *adsum*
autumō, autumāre, autumāvī, autumātus: assert, affirm, say

Optional

24.6. Plautus Selection to Be Read after Lesson 24 (page 354)
24.7. Spērat adulēscēns diū sē vīctūrum.—Seneca
24.8. Nō'sse volunt omnēs, mercēdem *solvere nēmō.—Juvenal (adapted)
(Note: *nō'sse = nōvisse*)

24.9. Carthāginī erat quidem ingēns terror et Scīpiōnem ipsam Carthāginem repente
adgressūrum crēdēbant.—Livy

24.10. Prīmus ibi ante omnēs magnā comitante catervā
Lāocoōn ardēns summā dēcurrit ab arce,
et procul: "ō miserī, quae tanta īnsānia, cīvēs?
crēditis āvectōs hostīs? aut ūlla putātis
dōna carēre dolīs Danaum?"—Vergil *Aeneid*

24.11. Putō hodiē quod ego dīxī per jocum
id ēventūrum esse sērium.—Plautus

24.12. The following lines are adapted from Tacitus' *Annals*, one of the source books for
I, Claudius. Augustus is about to die; young Agrippa is supposed to succeed him, but
Livia wants her son Tiberius to become emperor.

> Postquam aderat fīnis (∅=Augustī), paucī bona lībertātis cūrāre,[1] aliī bellum
> timēre,[1] aliī bellum cupere.[1]

People said many things, e.g., that

> Agrippam nōn aetāte neque experientiā tantō operī pārem ∅=esse; Tiberium
> Nērōnem mātūrum annīs esse, sed multa indicia saevitiae et arrogantiae exhibēre.
> Intereā gravēscere[1] valētūdō Augustī, et quīdam Liviam suspectābant.

Then Augustus dies, Agrippa is murdered, and Tiberius succeeds. This is, according
to Tacitus, the beginning of servitude.

> at Rōmae[2] ruere[1] in servitium cōnsulēs, patrēs, equitēs.

24.13. Factum id esse hic nōn negat . . . et deinde
factūrum autumat.—Terence
(Note: *Factūrum* with ∅·*esse* is a future infinitive in an accusative with infinitive construction with the verb *autumat*. The infinitive's time, relative to that of the governing
verb, is in the future, that is, *after* the time of the governing verb.)

Notes

1. There is a kernel variant where the subject is in the nominative case and the verb is in the
infinitive form. The infinitive, called the *historical infinitive,* substitutes for a past imperfective finite verb (see lesson 27). This kernel variant occurs in vivid descriptions.
Here the subject of *cūrāre* is *paucī;* of *timēre* and *cupere* it is *aliī;* of *gravēscere* it is
valētūdō; and of *ruere* it is *cōnsulēs, patrēs, equitēs.*
2. *Rōmae:* locative case, "at Rome"

Word Study: English Derivatives

From Readings	Latin		From Readings	Latin
1. attempt			5. patience	
2. comedian			6. possible	
3. fact			7. procrastinate	
4. negation			8. suggest	

Summary Tasks

___ 1. Embed Basic Sentences 9.1, 9.2, 9.3, and 14.2 as indirect statements after *dīcit*.

___ 2. In the Plautus Selection for Lesson 24 (p. 354), copy and name the infinitives in lines 20–24.

___ 3. Change the aspect of the governing verb of each sentence in exercise 4 and give a metaphrase for each sentence thus changed.

___ 4. Write all infinitives for these verbs: *sum, arbitror, agō*.

Review Lesson 7

Lesson Vocabulary

Nouns

hostis, hostis, m. & f.: enemy
mīles, mīlitis, m.: soldier
pōns, pontis, m.: bridge
sēnsus, sēnsūs, m.: sensation, feeling
timor, timōris, m.: fear, dread
victor, victōris, m.: victor, conqueror

Verbs

arbitror, arbitrārī, arbitrātus: think
cōgitō, cōgitāre, cōgitāvī, cōgitātus: think, consider
jubeō, jubēre, jussī, jussus: order
nārrō, nārrāre, nārrāvī, nārrātus: tell, relate, narrate
negō, negāre, negāvī, negātus: deny, say . . . not
nesciō, nescīre, nescīvī: not know, be ignorant of
postulō, postulāre, postulāvī, postulātus: demand
prohibeō, prohibēre, prohibuī, prohibitus: prevent, hinder, keep from
putō, putāre, putāvī, putātus: consider, think
sciō, scīre, scīvī, scītus: know
sentiō, sentīre, sēnsī, sēnsus: feel, perceive
superō, superāre, superāvī, superātus: overcome, surpass
vetō, vetāre, vetuī: forbid, prohibit

Readings Vocabulary

aetās, aetātis, f.: youth, age, period of life
ārdeō, ārdēre, ārsī: burn
cēdō, cēdere, cessī, cessūrus: grant; go, proceed
equus, equī, m.: horse
faciēs, faciēī, f.: face
gerō, gerere, gessī, gestus: do, carry on, carry
jūstus, jūsta, jūstum: just
legō, legere, lēgī, lēctus: read; choose
nec (coord. conj.): and not, nor
pallidus, pallida, pallidum: pale
satis (adv., also indecl. adj., noun): enough
sedeō, sedēre, sēdī: sit
sīc (adv.): thus, so

solvō, solvere, solvī, solūtus: loose, destroy
umquam (adv.): ever

Morphology Review

New Morphology: Lessons 22 through 24

verb: gerund
     infinitives—perfective active and passive, future active

Form Identification

    a. victor, victōris, m.: conqueror, victor
    b. victōria, victōriae, f.: victory
    c. victōriōsus, victōriōsa, victōriōsum: victorious
    d. vincō, vincere, vīcī, victus

1. vincendum _____
2. victōriōsum _____
3. victum _____
4. vincentem _____
5. victūrum _____
6. vīcisse _____
7. victa esse _____
8. victōrī _____
9. victōria _____
10. victōriōsa _____

■ Exercise: English to Latin Sentences
Using the Latin sentences as models, translate the English sentences into Latin.

1. Hominis mēns discendō alitur et cōgitandō. (S22.1)
2. Caesar mīlitēs pontem facere jussit. (S23.1)
3. Caesar mīlitēs pontem facere dīcit. (S23.2)
4. Caesar mīlitēs pontem facere dīxit. (S23.3)
5. Victōrem ā victō superātum esse vidēmus. (S24.3)

    a. The body is fed by eating and drinking. (1)

    b. The man ordered his girlfriend to prepare dinner. (2)

    c. The girlfriend thinks that the brother is the husband. (3)

    d. The girlfriend said that dinner was being prepared. (4)

    e. The parasite knows that dinner has been prepared. (5)

Vocabulary

Nouns

body: corpus
brother: frāter
dinner: prandium, prandiī, n.
girlfriend: amīca
man, husband: vir
parasite: parasītus, parasītī, m.

Verbs

drink: bibō, bibere, bibī
eat: edō, edere, ēdī, ēsus
feed: alō
is: sum
know: sciō
order: jubeō
prepare: adparō, adparāre, adparāvī, adparātus
say: dīcō
think (believe): crēdō

Stem List

Enter the following words in the Stem List found in the back of this book. Also add
dictionary listings for each word entered.

1. alitur
2. audīvimus
3. jubet
4. jussit
5. nescīre
6. prohibeō

7. sciō
8. scrībere
9. sēnsus
10. sentit
11. victor
12. vident

Lesson 25

Comparison in Terms of Unequalness
Comparison in Terms of Equalness

All people like to describe one thing in relation to another in terms of their equalness or unequalness, i.e., they make comparisons. This lesson introduces *comparison* that is expressed through adjectives and adverbs.

Basic Sentences

25.1. Melior est canis vīvus leōne mortuō.—Ecclesiastes
      A live dog is better than a dead lion.
25.2. Intolerābilius nihil est quam fēmina dīves.—Juvenal
      Nothing is more intolerable than a rich female.
25.3. Omnium Gallōrum fortissimī sunt Belgae.—Caesar
      Of all the Gauls the bravest are the Belgians.
25.4. Nihil tam cito redditur quam ā speculō imāgō.—Seneca
      Nothing is given back as fast as a reflection from a mirror.

Comparison in Terms of Unequalness

This part of the lesson introduces comparison in terms of the unequalness of items as expressed through adjectives and adverbs. Many adjectives and adverbs in Latin and in English are inflected to show degree, e.g., "bigger" shows *comparative degree* and "biggest" shows *superlative degree*. "Big" is said to show *positive degree*.

Morphology

Latin adjectives in the positive degree are either first and second declension or third declension, but in the *comparative* degree they all have third declension case endings and in the *superlative* degree they all have first and second declension endings.

    Here is the paradigm of the comparative degree of the adjective *pūrus, -a, -um*. The {iōr} morpheme added to the stem signals the comparative degree. The case endings are those of the third declension. Notice that the ablative singular ends in *-e;* comparative adjectives are not *i*-stem adjectives.

	Masc. & Fem.	Neut.
Singular		
Nominative	pūrior	pūrius
Accusative	pūriōrem	pūrius
Ablative	pūriōre	pūriōre
Dative	pūriōrī	pūriōrī
Genitive	pūriōris	pūriōris
Plural		
Nominative	pūriōrēs	pūriōra
Accusative	pūriōrēs	pūriōra
Ablative	pūriōribus	pūriōribus
Dative	pūriōribus	pūriōribus
Genitive	pūriōrum	pūriōrum

Adjectives with the morpheme {issim} added to the stem signal the superlative degree. The case endings are those of first and second declension adjectives, e.g., pūr*issim*us, pūr*issim*a, pūr*issim*um from pūrus, -a, -um and fort*issim*us, fort*issim*a, fort*issim*um from fortis, -e.

The comparative and superlative adjectives have corresponding adverbs. For example:

Prīmus sapiēns *honestē* vīvit. (The first wise man lives *decently*.)
Secundus *honestius* vīvit. (The second lives *more decently*.)
Tertius *honestissimē* vīvit. (The third lives *most decently*.)

The comparative of the adverb, e.g., *honestius*, ends in *-ius* and looks like the nominative/accusative of the neuter gender of the comparative adjective. The superlative of the adverb, e.g., *honestissimē*, has the adverb morpheme {ē}.

■ Exercise 1
Underline all forms that could be comparative adverbs or adjectives.

1. longiōra
2. breviōrem
3. victor
4. pulchrior
5. lātius

6. lātus
7. negōtium
8. opera
9. illīus
10. ulterius

A few adjectives have stem variations in their comparative and superlative degrees, as in English "good, better, best." The most common *irregular adjectives* are:

Positive Degree	*Comparative Degree*	*Superlative Degree*
bonus, -a, -um (good)	melior, melius (better)	optimus, -a, -um (best)
magnus, -a, -um (big)	major, majus (bigger)	maximus, -a, -um (biggest)
malus, -a, -um (bad)	pejor, pejus (worse)	pessimus, -a, -um (worst)
multus, -a, -um (much/many)	plūrēs, plūra (pl.) (more)	plūrimus, -a, -um (most)
parvus, -a, -um (small)	minor, minus (smaller, less)	minimus, -a, -um (smallest, least)

In addition, adjectives that end in -er are compared like *pulcher, pulchrior, pulcherrimus*. Six adjectives in -*lis* (*facilis, difficilis, similis, dissimilis, gracilis, humilis*) are compared like *facilis, facilior, facillimus*. Other adjectives in -*lis*, e.g., *crūdēlis, nōbilis*, etc., have the -*issimus* superlative, as in *crūdēlissimus, nōbilissimus*, etc.

■ Exercise 2
Write the paradigm, singular and plural, of these noun plus comparative adjective pairs.

Singular

Nominative   auxilium minus (parvus, -a, -um)   rēs similior (similis, -e)

Accusative

Ablative

Dative

Genitive

Plural

Nominative

Accusative

Ablative

Dative

Genitive

■ Exercise 3
Write the paradigm, singular and plural, of these noun plus superlative adjective pairs.

Singular

Nominative   rēx fortissimus   maximus pōns

Accusative

Ablative

Dative

Genitive

Plural

Nominative

Accusative

Ablative

Dative

Genitive

Syntax of the Comparative

An adjective or adverb in the comparative degree raises the expectation of two items being compared. Thus, in the English version of S25.1 the comparative phrase "better than" sets up a comparison between "a live dog" and "a dead lion."

In Latin, the item to which comparison is being made, here *leōne mortuō,* can be in the ablative. This ablative use in the environment of a comparative is labeled *ablative of comparison.*[1]

Instead of finding an ablative of comparison in the environment of a comparative, the reader may instead find a *quam* clause containing the item to which comparison is being made. *Quam* in this environment is a connector meaning "than." The compared word in the *quam* clause is in the same case as the other compared word. S25.1 can therefore be expressed also as *Melior est canis vīvus quam leō mortuus* ($\emptyset$ = *est bonus*). There is extensive gapping in both Latin and English in such comparative clauses; the adjective is almost always gapped.

Note: If there is a comparative adjective but there are not two items to be compared, the comparative indicates one of two situations: (1) moderate intensification of the adjective, or (2) the second item must be understood from the context. In the first situation, the complete sentence *Melior est canis* could mean "The dog is *rather good*," or "The dog is *quite good*," or "The dog is *pretty good*."

■ Exercise 4

Rewrite each sentence showing the comparison without using *quam.* Write a final metaphrase of each sentence.

1. Nihil intolerābilius quam fēmina dīves.

2. Mīles amīcior quam dux est.

3. Vōx audīta brevior est quam verbum scrīptum.

4. Canis timidus longius quam canis fortis lātrat.
   (*lātrat:* "_____ barks")

5. Piscis captus melior quam piscis vīvus est.

Syntax of the Superlative

An adjective or adverb in the superlative degree raises the expectation of a noun in the genitive denoting the whole with which a part is being compared, i.e., of a partitive genitive. For example, in S25.3, *omnium Gallōrum* is the whole of which the Belgians are the bravest part. If there is no genitive, the superlative expresses great intensification, e.g., *vīta brevissima est* "life is *very* short," or "life is *exceedingly* short."

---

1. This ablative may be understood historically as expressing the semantic notion of "place/point from which."

■ Exercise 5

Write a metaphrase of each of the following sentences.

1. Aper timidissimus est.

2. Aprō timidior est canis.

3. Aper timidius vīvit quam canis.

4. Virō stultior fēmina est.

5. Vir stultior fēminā est.

6. Fēminā vir stultior est.

7. Puer sapientior rēge est.

8. Rēge sapientior puer est.

9. Puerō sapientior rēx est.

10. Lupus fortior est.

11. Lupī fortissimī sunt.

12. Lupī fortissimē canēs petunt.

13. Fōns pūrior flūmine est.

14. Fonte pūrius flūmen est.

15. Fōns pūrius flūmine fluit.

16. Flūmine pūrior fōns est.

17. Mātre pulchrior fīlia est.

18. Māter pulchrior fīliā est.

Comparison in Terms of Equalness

In the pairs of words listed below, the words on the right have occurred as question words. When paired with those on the left, the pairs function as *correlatives* and compare two items as being equal. The *qu-* words, in addition to being modifiers, are also clause markers in this environment. Extensive gapping can be expected in correlative clauses.

Correlatives

tālis	(such)	. . . quālis	(as)	
tantus	(as great)	. . . quantus	(as)	
tot	(as many)	. . . quot	(as)	
totiēns	(as often)	. . . quotiēns	(as)	
tam	(as/so)	. . . quam	(as)	
eō	(the ____-er)	. . . quō	(the ____-er)	
tantō	(the ____-er)	. . . quantō	(the ____-er)	
ibi	(there)	. . . ubi	(where)	
ita	(in the same way)	. . . ut	(as)	

Note that English *as* corresponds to various Latin words.

In S25.4 (*Nihil tam cito redditur quam ā speculō imāgō*), the words *tam* and *quam* are correlatives. The speed with which *nihil* and *imāgō* are given back is what is being compared.

■ Exercise 6

Pick from the list of correlatives the pair of words that would be used in a Latin translation of the following sentences.

1. The book is there, where you put it yesterday.

2. He comes here as often as he can.

3. She has as many friends as anyone I know.

4. Their courage was such as to inspire us all.

5. He is as great as he is famous.

■ Exercise 7

Underline all *qu-* words that function in these sentences as correlatives. Remember that *qu-* words may also be relative or interrogative pronouns or connectors.

1. Nihil est intolerābilius quam fēmina dīves.

2. Fēmina quam quaerimus abiit.

3. Haec fēmina nōn tam pulchra est quam illa.

4. Quam fēminam mīrāris?

5. Quot amīcī cōnsulem secūtī sunt?

6. Tot hominēs adfuērunt quot numquam vīdimus anteā.

7. Quālem aedem emere vultis?

8. Tālem aedem, quālem emere vultis, numquam vīdimus.

9. Meus servus numquam tāle fēcit quāle tū mihi.

10. Omne ita parātum est ut jussistī.

■ Exercise 8
Write a metaphrase of sentences 2, 3, and 4 in exercise 7.

2.

3.

4.

Lesson Vocabulary

Nouns
aedēs, aedium, f. pl.: house
Belgae, Belgārum, m. pl.: the Belgians
Gallus, Gallī, m.: a Gaul
leō, leōnis, m.: lion
plūs, plūris, n.: more
speculum, speculī, n.: mirror

Adjectives
dīves (dīvitis): rich
gracilis, gracile: graceful
humilis, humile: humble, lowly
intolerābilis, intolerābile: intolerable
major, majus: greater, bigger
maximus, maxima, maximum: greatest,
  biggest
melior, melius: better
minimus, minima, minimum: least, smallest
minor, minus: less, smaller
mortuus, mortua, mortuum: dead
nōbilis, nōbile: noble
optimus, optima, optimum: best
pejor, pejus: worse
pessimus, pessima, pessimum: worst
plūrēs, plūra (pl.): more
plūrimus, plūrima, plūrimum: most
tālis, tāle: such, of such a kind
vīvus, vīva, vīvum: alive, living

Indeclinables
Adjective
tot: so many

Adverbs
ibi: there
ita: thus, so
tam: so
totiēns: so often

Connector
quam: than; (as a correlative) as

Correlatives
eō . . . quō (+ comp.): the _____-er . . .
  the _____-er
ibi . . . ubi: there . . . where
ita . . . ut: in the same way . . . as
tālis . . . quālis: such . . . as
tam . . . quam: as . . . as
tantō . . . quantō (+ comp.): the
  _____-er . . . the _____-er
tantus . . . quantus: as great . . . as
tot . . . quot: as many . . . as
totiēns . . . quotiēns: as often . . . as

Verbs
emō, emere, ēmī, ēmptus: buy
reddō, reddere, reddidī, redditus: give back

Readings

Required

25.1. Perdit majōra quī spernit dōna minōra.—Werner
25.2. Nihil est majus, in rēbus hūmānīs, philosophiā.—Plato (trans.)
25.3. Tot hominēs, quot sententiae sunt.—Terence (adapted)
25.4. Nihil est vēritātis lūce dulcius.—Cicero

25.5. Bona opīniō hominum tūtior pecūniā est.—Publilius Syrus
25.6. Hominēs, quō plūra habent, eō ampliōra cupiunt.—Justinian
25.7. Quis amīcior quam frāter frātrī?—Sallust

Vocabulary

25.1. perdō, perdere, perdidī, perditus: lose
     spernō, spernere, sprēvī, sprētus: scorn, spurn
     dōnum, dōnī, n.: gift
25.2. philosophia, philosophiae, f.: philosophy
25.3. sententia, sententiae, f.: opinion, sentiment
25.5. opīniō, opīniōnis, f.: opinion, reputation
     tūtus, tūta, tūtum: safe
25.6. amplior, amplius: more

Optional

25.8. Dē minimīs nōn cūrat lēx.—Legal
25.9. Fidēliōrēs sunt oculī auribus.—Binder
25.10. Famēs est optimus coquus.—Anon.
25.11. Ācta exteriōra indicant interiōra sēcrēta.—Legal
25.12. Graviōra quaedam sunt remedia perīculīs.—Anon.
25.13. Quantō *altior est ascēnsus, tantō dūrior dēscēnsus.—St. Jerome
25.14. Numquam ego mē tam sēnsī amārī, quam nunc.—Plautus
25.15. Ubi concordia, ibi victōria est.—Publilius Syrus (adapted)
25.16. Quālis dominus, tālis servus.—Petronius
25.17. Homō totiēns moritur, quotiēns āmittit suōs.—Publilius Syrus

Word Study: English Derivatives

From Lesson	Latin	From Readings	Latin
1. ameliorate		1. donate	
2. imagine		2. majority	
3. intolerant		3. minority	
4. leonine		4. pecuniary	
5. optimal		5. plural	
6. render		6. quotient	
7. species		7. translucent	
8. specimen		8. tutor	

Summary Tasks

____ 1. Rewrite sentences 1–10 of exercise 5, changing the subject from the singular to the plural and making any other necessary change(s).

____ 2. Copy from Readings 25.1 through 25.7 the adjectives that are morphologically ambiguous. Identify all possibilities, choose one that seems correct, and give the possible evidence.

____ 3. Write the complete paradigms of *major leō* and *vīnum dulcius*.

____ 4. Translate into Latin showing comparison in two ways: Nothing is better than a friend.

Lesson 26

The Past Imperfective Tense
The Future Imperfective Tense

All finite verbs in the previous lessons were identified as *present imperfective* or *present perfective*. This lesson introduces *past* and *future imperfective* verbs. Lesson 27 will introduce *past* and *future perfective* verbs.

Basic Sentences

26.1. Nox erat, et caelō fulgēbat lūna serēnō inter minōra sīdera.—Horace
  It was night, and in the clear sky the moon shone among the lesser stars.

26.2. Sed quis custōdiet ipsōs custōdēs?—Juvenal
  But who will guard the guards themselves?

26.3. Vēritās vōs līberābit.—Motto
  The truth will make you free.

26.4. Aut inveniam viam aut faciam.—Motto
  Either I will find a way or I will make a way.

The Past Imperfective Tense

The past imperfective is an easy tense to recognize because it always has the morpheme {bā} on the imperfective stem and uses the regular person endings: *-m, -s, -t, -mus, -tis, -nt* (active voice) and *-r, -ris, -tur, -mur, -minī, -ntur* (passive voice).

	First Conjugation	
	Singular	Plural
Active		
First person	laudābam	laudābāmus
Second person	laudābās	laudābātis
Third person	laudābat	laudābant
Passive		
First person	laudābar	laudābāmur
Second person	laudābāris (-re)	laudābāminī
Third person	laudābātur	laudābantur

Here are other examples of verbs in this tense. The examples show only the singular; see Appendix pages 404–26 for a complete listing of regular and irregular verbs.

	First	Second	Third	Third -iō	Fourth
	Singular	Singular	Singular	Singular	Singular

Active

First person	amābam	vidēbam	regēbam	capiēbam	audiēbam
Second person	amābās	vidēbās	regēbās	capiēbās	audiēbās
Third person	amābat	vidēbat	regēbat	capiēbat	audiēbat

Passive

First person	amābar	vidēbar	regēbar	capiēbar	audiēbar
Second person	amābāris (-re)	vidēbāris (-re)	regēbāris (-re)	capiēbāris (-re)	audiēbāris (-re)
Third person	amābātur	vidēbātur	regēbātur	capiēbātur	audiēbātur

The irregular verbs follow the pattern of the verbs above.

	Singular	Singular	Singular	Singular	Singular
First person	ferēbam	volēbam	nōlēbam	fīēbam	ībam
Second person	ferēbās	volēbās	nōlēbās	fīēbās	ībās
Third person	ferēbat	volēbat	nōlēbat	fīēbat	ībat

Note that there is regular vowel shortening in {bā} before -nt- and before final *m, r,* and *t.* (See lesson 6, p. 54.)

The verb *esse* (and its compounds, e.g., *posse*) is unique.

	Singular	Plural	Singular	Plural
First person	eram	erāmus	poteram	poterāmus
Second person	erās	erātis	poterās	poterātis
Third person	erat	erant	poterat	poterant

The past imperfective tense indicates an action in past time that is not regarded as a completed action, either because it was:

Repeated: "I used to go." "I went every day."
Continuous: "I kept going again and again."
Begun: "I started to go there."
Attempted: "I tried to go there (but I couldn't make it and turned back)."

The most common translation, one that covers many of these meanings, is "was _____-ing."

Sometimes this tense is used to provide descriptions or circumstances surrounding the main event in the narrative tense and may be translated as "_____-ed."

■ Exercise 1
Underline all past imperfective verb forms.

1. currēbant

2. scrībō

3. erāmus

4. pōnēbāmur

5. bibit

6. ībam

7. petēbar

8. habēmus

■ Exercise 2

Each Latin verb is past imperfective. Underline all possible English equivalents.

1. regēbant: they used to rule, they had ruled, they have ruled

2. vidēbās: you see, you have seen, you were seeing

3. capiēbāmur: we were being caught, we have been caught, we are being caught

4. stābat: she stood, she has stood, she was standing

5. veniēbam: I used to come, I have come, I can come

6. erat: it was, it has been, it had been

The Future Imperfective Tense

There are two separate morphological signals for the future imperfective tense in Latin. The first and second conjugations have {b} plus a variable vowel; the third and fourth conjugations have {ē}, except for the first person singular, which has {a}. The person endings are -ō/m, -s, -t, -mus, -tis, -nt (active voice) and -r, -ris (-re), -tur, -mur, -minī, -ntur (passive voice). Here are sample paradigms of this tense in the active and passive voices.

	First		Second		Third	
	Singular	Plural	Singular	Plural	Singular	Plural
Active						
First person	amābō	amābimus	vidēbō	vidēbimus	regam	regēmus
Second person	amābis	amābitis	vidēbis	vidēbitis	regēs	regētis
Third person	amābit	amābunt	vidēbit	vidēbunt	reget*	regent*

	Third -iō		Fourth	
	Singular	Plural	Singular	Plural
Active				
First person	capiam	capiēmus	audiam	audiēmus
Second person	capiēs	capiētis	audiēs	audiētis
Third person	capiet*	capient*	audiet*	audient*

*Again, regular vowel shortening occurs.

	First		Second		Third	
	Singular	Plural	Singular	Plural	Singular	Plural
Passive						
First person	amābor	amābimur	vidēbor	vidēbimur	regar	regēmur
Second person	amāberis (-re)	amābiminī	vidēberis (-re)	vidēbiminī	regēris (-re)	regēminī
Third person	amābitur	amābuntur	vidēbitur	vidēbuntur	regētur	regentur*

	Third -iō		Fourth	
	Singular	Plural	Singular	Plural
Passive				
First person	capiar	capiēmur	audiar	audiēmur
Second person	capiēris (-re)	capiēminī	audiēris (-re)	audiēminī
Third person	capiētur	capientur*	audiētur	audientur*

*Again, regular vowel shortening occurs.

Here are the paradigms in the singular for irregular verbs. See Appendix pages 419–26 for a complete listing of these verbs.

	Singular	Singular	Singular	Singular	Singular
First person	feram	volam	nōlam	fīam	ībō
Second person	ferēs	volēs	nōlēs	fīēs	ībis
Third person	feret	volet	nōlet	fīet	ībit

The verb *esse* (and its compounds) is unique:

	Singular	Plural	Singular	Plural
First person	erō	erimus	poterō	poterimus
Second person	eris	eritis	poteris	poteritis
Third person	erit	erunt	poterit	poterunt

The future imperfective tense indicates future time and imperfective aspect. One common way of translating this tense in English is "going to _____"; thus *Rem quaeret amīcus* might in English be "A friend is *going to look* for assistance." The other common way of translating this tense is to use "will" with the verb as in "They will play here soon."

Summary

Latin verb system, imperfective tenses, first conjugation: *amō, amāre, amāvī, amātus*. (See appendix for complete verb system of other conjugations.)

	Past Imperfective		Present Imperfective		Future Imperfective	
	Singular	Plural	Singular	Plural	Singular	Plural
Active						
First person	amābam	amābāmus	amō	amāmus	amābō	amābimus
Second person	amābās	amābātis	amās	amātis	amābis	amābitis
Third person	amābat	amābant	amat	amant	amābit	amābunt
Passive						
First person	amābar	amābāmur	amor	amāmur	amābor	amābimur
Second person	amābāris (-re)	amābāminī	amāris (-re)	amāminī	amāberis (-re)	amābiminī
Third person	amābātur	amābantur	amātur	amantur	amābitur	amābuntur

■ Exercise 3

Based on the verb information provided in the dictionary entries given, underline all future imperfective verb forms.

    cūrō, cūrāre, cūrāvī, cūrātus
    moveō, movēre, mōvī, mōtus
    premō, premere, pressī, pressus
    vestiō, vestīre, vestīvī, vestītus

1. movēbant

2. premēs

3. cūrābis

4. movēs

5. vestiet

6. vestit

7. premēbāmus

8. movēbunt

■ Exercise 4

Identify the part of speech and form of each of these words.

1. inveniam

2. viam

3. habēs

4. dīcēs

5. amōrēs

6. audior

7. audiar

8. fortior

■ Exercise 5

Underline all possible English equivalents of each of these verbs.

1. quaerimus: we are seeking, we were seeking, we seek

2. erunt: they were, they will be, they are

3. audiēmus: we are going to listen, we listen, we will listen

4. vincēmur: we are being overcome, we will be overcome, we overcame

5. regēbat: he was ruling, he will rule, he used to rule

6. capiēbātur: he will be caught, he was catching, he was caught

7. laudābunt: they are praising, they will praise, they were praising

■ Exercise 6
Identify the tense of each verb and give at least one metaphrase of each sentence.

	Identification	*Metaphrase*
1. Oculī sunt in amōre ducēs.		
2. Oculī erant in amōre ducēs.		
3. Oculī erunt in amōre ducēs.		
4. Vēritās numquam perībit.		
5. Vēritās numquam perībat.		
6. Vēritās numquam perit.		
7. Effugere nōn poteris.		
8. Effugere nōn potes.		
9. Effugere nōn poterās.		
10. Gladiātor capit cōnsilium.		
11. Gladiātor capiet cōnsilium.		
12. Gladiātor capiēbat cōnsilium.		

Lesson Vocabulary

Nouns
caelum, caelī, n.: heaven, sky
custōs, custōdis, m. & f.: guard
lūna, lūnae, f.: moon
sīdus, sīderis, n.: star; constellation
via, viae, f.: road, way

Adjective
serēnus, serēna, serēnum: bright, fair, clear

Indeclinables
Coordinating Conjunctions
aut: or
aut . . . aut: either . . . or

Verbs

custōdiō, custōdīre, custōdīvī, custōdītus: guard
fulgeō, fulgēre, fulsī: shine, flash
inveniō, invenīre, invēnī, inventus: find, come upon
līberō, līberāre, līberāvī, līberātus: free, make free, liberate

Readings

Required

26.1. Hoc fuit, est, et erit: similis similem sibi quaerit.—Werner
26.2. Jamque quiēscēbant vōcēs hominumque canumque
        lūnaque nocturnōs alta regēbat equōs.—Ovid
26.3. Jam ego ūnō in saltū lepidē aprōs capiam duōs.—Plautus
26.4. Paucīs cārior fidēs quam pecūnia fuit.—Sallust
26.5. Sum quod eris.—Grave Inscription
26.6. Aut amat aut ōdit mulier; nīl est tertium.—Publilius Syrus

Vocabulary

26.2.   quiēscō, quiēscere, quiēvī: be quiet, be still
      nocturnus, nocturna, nocturnum: of night
      equus, equī, m.: horse
26.3.   saltus, saltūs, m.: jump, leap
      lepidē (adv.): gracefully, neatly
26.4.   *paucī, paucae, pauca: few
      fidēs, fideī, f.: faith, trust
26.6.   *mulier, mulieris, f.: woman

Optional

26.7. Plautus Selection to Be Read after Lesson 26 (p. 356)
26.8. In *lūmine tuō vidēbimus lūmen.—Motto of Columbia University
26.9. Orbem jam tōtum victor Rōmānus habēbat.—Petronius
26.10. Plūs apud mē vēra ratiō valēbit quam vulgī *opīniō.—Cicero
26.11. Bonīs nocet quisquis pepercit malīs.—Anon.
26.12. Ōdimus quem laesimus.—Anon.
26.13. Quam diū stābit Colysēus, stābit et Rōma;
    quandō cadet Colysēus, cadet et Rōma;
    quandō cadet Rōma, cadet et *mundus.
    (A pilgrim proverb of the early Middle Ages, used by Byron in *Childe Harold's
    Pilgrimage* 4.145. *Colysēus:* the Colosseum in Rome)
26.14. Forsan et haec *ōlim meminisse juvābit.—Vergil

Word Study: English Derivatives

From Lesson	**Latin**		**From Readings**	**Latin**
1. effulgent			1. charity	
2. invent			2. insult	
3. lunar			3. quiescent	
4. lunatic			4. require	
5. serenity			5. result	
6. sidereal (time)			6. simile	
7. via			7. vocation	

Summary Tasks

___ 1. Copy from the Plautus Selection for lesson 26, lines 5–8, all examples of "unequal" and "equal" comparisons.

___ 2. Write the Latin verb for each English equivalent in exercise 5.

___ 3. Name the tense of each verb in the Required Readings.

___ 4. Copy all kernels of Basic Sentences 26.1 and 26.2.

___ 5. Embed Basic Sentences 26.3 and 26.4 as indirect statements after *dīcō/dīxī* and give a final metaphrase.

Review Lesson 8

Lesson Vocabulary

Nouns
aedēs, aedium, f. pl.: house
Belgae, Belgārum, m. pl.: the Belgians
caelum, caelī, n.: heaven, sky
custōs, custōdis, m. & f.: guard
Gallus, Gallī, m.: a Gaul
leō, leōnis, m.: lion
lūna, lūnae, f.: moon
plūs, plūris, n.: more
sīdus, sīderis, n.: star; constellation
speculum, speculī, n.: mirror
via, viae, f.: road, way

Adjectives
dīves (dīvitis): rich
gracilis, gracile: graceful
humilis, humile: humble, lowly
intolerābilis, intolerābile: intolerable
mājor, mājus: greater, bigger
maximus, maxima, maximum: greatest,
    biggest
melior, melius: better
minimus, minima, minimum: least, smallest
minor, minus: less, smaller
mortuus, mortua, mortuum: dead
nōbilis, nōbile: noble
optimus, optima, optimum: best
pejor, pejus: worse
pessimus, pessima, pessimum: worst
plūrēs, plūra (pl.): more
plūrimus, plūrima, plūrimum: most
serēnus, serēna, serēnum: bright, fair, clear
tālis, tāle: such, of such a kind
vīvus, vīva, vīvum: alive, living

Indeclinables
Adverbs
ibi: there
ita: thus, so

tam: so
totiēns: so often

Adjective
tot: so many

Connectors
aut: or
aut . . . aut: either . . . or
quam: than; (as a correlative) as

Correlatives
eō . . . quō (+ comparatives):
    the ___-er . . . the ___-er
ibi . . . ubi: there . . . where
ita . . . ut: in the same way . . . as
tālis . . . quālis: such . . . as
tam . . . quam: as/so . . . as
tantō . . . quantō (+ comparatives):
    the ___-er . . . the ___-er
tantus . . . quantus: as great . . . as
tot . . . quot: as many . . . as
totiēns . . . quotiēns: as often . . . as

Verbs
custōdiō, custōdīre, custōdīvī, custōdītus:
    guard
emō, emere, ēmī, ēmptus: buy
fulgeō, fulgēre, fulsī: shine, flash
inveniō, invenīre, invēnī, inventus: find,
    come upon
līberō, līberāre, līberāvī, līberātus: free, make
    free, liberate
reddō, reddere, reddidī, redditus: give back

Readings Vocabulary

altus, alta, altum: high, deep
lūmen, lūminis, n.: light, lamp
mulier, mulieris, f.: woman
mundus, mundī, m.: world
ōlim (adv.): once upon a time, sometime
opīniō, opīniōnis, f.: opinion
paucī, paucae, pauca: few

Morphology Review

New Morphology: Lessons 25 and 26

adjective: comparative and superlative degrees, regular and irregular
adverb: comparative and superlative degrees
verb: past and future imperfective tenses, active and passive

Form Identification

    a. līberō, līberāre, līberāvī, līberātus: free, make free, liberate
    b. līber, lībera, līberum: free
    c. lībertās, lībertātis, f.: freedom
    d. līberālis, līberāle: befitting a free person, noble; generous, liberal

1. lībertātum _____
2. līberātum _____
3. līberius _____
4. līberābās _____
5. līberissimās _____
6. līberālium _____
7. līberior _____
8. līberō _____
9. līberābuntur _____
10. līberābimus _____

■ Exercise: English to Latin Sentences
Using the Latin sentences as models, translate the English sentences into Latin.

1. Melior est canis vīvus leōne mortuō. (S25.1)
2. Intolerābilius nihil est quam fēmina dīves. (S25.2)
3. Omnium Gallōrum fortissimī sunt Belgae. (S25.3)
4. Nox erat et caelō fulgēbat lūna serēnō inter minōra sīdera. (S26.1)
5. Aut inveniam viam aut faciam. (S26.4)

a. The house of the girlfriend is more elegant than the house of the woman. (1)

b. Nothing is worse for a parasite than a meal missed. (2)

c. Of all women you are dearest to me. (3)

d. With whom did the woman continue to talk? (4)

e. The parasite will approach and address the husband. (5)

Vocabulary

Nouns

girlfriend: amīca
house: domus
husband: vir
meal: prandium, prandiī, n.
nothing: nihil
parasite: parasītus, parasītī, m.
woman: fēmina

Pronouns

I, me, etc.: ego
who, etc.: quī

Adjectives

all: omnis
dear: cārus, cāra, cārum
elegant: pulcher
worse: pejor

Verbs

address: adloquor, adloquī, adlocūtus
approach: adeō, adīre, adiī
be: sum
miss: āmittō
talk: dīcō

Stem List

Enter the following words in the Stem List found in the back of this book. Also add the dictionary listing for each word entered.

1. inveniam
2. mortuō
3. redditur
4. speculum

Lesson 27

The Past Perfective Tense
The Future Perfective Tense

Lesson 9 introduced the present perfective tense, e.g., *audīvit* (active voice) and *audītus est* (passive voice). This lesson introduces the last two tenses of the indicative verb system, the *past perfective* and the *future perfective* tenses.

Basic Sentences

27.1. Nōn sum ego quod fueram.—Ovid
      I am not what I had been.
27.2. Āctiō rēcta nōn erit, nisi rēcta fuerit voluntās.—Seneca
      It will not be a proper act unless the motivation has been (will have been) proper.

The Past Perfective Tense

The past perfective tense in the active voice consists of the perfective active stem (the third principal part minus the *-ī*) plus the morpheme {erā} plus the active person endings: *-m, -s, -t, -mus, -tis, -nt.*
    The passive voice forms of the past perfective tense, like the present perfective, are periphrastic forms made up of the perfective passive participle and forms of *sum, esse.* Here are forms of the verb *audiō, audīre, audīvī, audītus.* See the appendix for models of other verbs.

	Singular	Plural
Active		
First person	audīveram	audīverāmus
Second person	audīverās	audīverātis
Third person	audīverat	audīverant
Passive		
First person	audītus, -a, -um eram	audītī, -ae, -a erāmus
Second person	audītus, -a, -um erās	audītī, -ae, -a erātis
Third person	audītus, -a, -um erat	audītī, -ae, -a erant

Because these forms have *perfective* aspect, they indicate *completed* action; because they are *past* in time, they stress that the action was already complete at some time in the past. Therefore *audīverat* means "＿＿＿ had heard," as in "He *had heard* the news before he arrived here." *Audītī erant* means "＿＿＿s had been heard," as in "Strange sounds *had been heard* before the roof collapsed."

The Future Perfective Tense

The future perfective tense in the active voice consists of the perfective active stem plus the morpheme {eri} (except for the first person singular that has only {er}) plus the active person endings: *-ō, -s, -t, -mus, -tis, -nt.*

The passive voice form of the future perfective tense is again a periphrastic form made up of the perfective passive participle and forms of *sum, esse.* For example:

	Singular	Plural
Active		
First person	audīverō	audīverimus
Second person	audīveris	audīveritis
Third person	audīverit	audīverint
Passive		
First person	audītus, -a, -um erō	audītī, -ae, -a erimus
Second person	audītus, -a, -um eris	audītī, -ae, -a eritis
Third person	audītus, -a, -um erit	audītī, -ae, -a erunt

Again, because these forms have perfective aspect, they indicate completed action, but because they are *future* in time they indicate an action completed at some time in the future. For example, *perfēcerit* means "_____ will have completed," as in "When he *will have completed* the work, I will pay him." It is interesting to observe that English usually does not use the future perfective in such sentences, but instead expresses this relationship as "When he has completed the work, I will pay him," or "When he completes the work, I will pay him." S27.2 provides an example of this difference between English and Latin inasmuch as *fuerit* is expressed in the literary translation as "_____ has been," but literally means "_____ will have been."

The future perfective tense occurs most frequently in subordinate clauses.

Note: Contractions are common in verbs in the perfective active system: e.g., *laudā'rō* for *laudāverō, laudā'runt* for *laudāvērunt.*

■ Exercise 1

Identify each verb by person, number, tense, and voice.

1. Fūrēs captī erant.

2. Fūrēs capientur.

3. Fūrēs capiuntur.

4. Fūrēs captī sunt.

5. Fūrēs capiēbantur.

6. Fūrēs captī erunt.

7. Sapientēs fortūnam ferunt.

8. Sapientēs fortūnam ferent.

9. Sapientēs fortūnam tulerant.

10. Sapientēs fortūnam tulēre.[1]

11. Sapientēs fortūnam tulerint.

12. Sapientēs fortūnam ferēbant.

13. Rēgem laudō.

14. Rēgem laudāvī.

15. Rēgem laudā'rō.

16. Rēgem laudābō.

17. Rēgem laudā'ram.

18. Rēgem laudābam.

Note

1. *-ēre* on the perfective active stem is the alternative form for *-ērunt*.

■ Exercise 2

Translate each verb form or sentence.

1. vincar

2. vīcerō

3. vincēbar

4. vīcī

5. victus sum

6. victus eram

7. loquiminī

8. locūtī estis

9. loquēbāris

10. loquēmur

11. locūtī sunt

12. locūta erās

13. Quis ā nōbīs custōdītus erat?

14. Quis ā nōbīs custōdiēbātur?

15. Quis ā nōbīs custōdiētur?

16. Quis ā nōbīs custōdītus erit?

17. Quis ā nōbīs custōdītur?

18. Quis ā nōbīs custōdītus est?

19. Quis custōdiet ipsōs custōdēs?

20. Quis custōdiēbat ipsōs custōdēs?

21. Quis custōdīverat ipsōs custōdēs?

22. Quis custōdit ipsōs custōdēs?

23. Quis custōdīverit ipsōs custōdēs?

24. Quis custōdīvit ipsōs custōdēs?

Lesson Vocabulary

Nouns
āctiō, āctiōnis, f.: action, act
voluntās, voluntātis, f.: wish, will

Adjective
rēctus, rēcta, rēctum: right, correct

Indeclinable
Subordinating Conjunction
nisi: if not, unless

Readings

Required

27.1. Glōriam quī sprēverit, vēram habēbit.—Livy

27.2. Cito rumpēs arcum, semper sī tēnsum habueris; at sī laxā'ris, cum volēs, erit ūtilis.—Phaedrus

27.3. Quae fuerant vitia, mōrēs sunt.—Seneca

27.4. Dōnec eris fēlīx, multōs numerābis amīcōs; tempora sī fuerint nūbila, sōlus eris.—Ovid

27.5. In quō . . . jūdiciō jūdicāveritis, jūdicābiminī.—St. Matthew

Vocabulary

27.1. glōria, glōriae, f.: glory

spernō, spernere, sprēvī, sprētus: despise

27.2. rumpō, rumpere, rūpī, ruptus: break

tendō, tendere, tetendī, tēnsus: stretch, stretch out

at (coord. conj.): but

laxō, laxāre, laxāvī, laxātus: loosen, release

ūtilis, ūtile: useful

27.4. dōnec (subord. conj.): as long as

numerō, numerāre, numerāvī, numerātus: count

nūbilus, nūbila, nūbilum: cloudy, unhappy

27.5. jūdicium, jūdiciī, n.: judgment

Optional

27.6. Vīxī, et quem dederat cursum fortūna perēgī,

et *nunc magna meī sub terrās ībit imāgō.

(Vergil *Aeneid* 4.653–54: Dido sums up the meaning of her life and her death.)

27.7. Dum loquimur, fūgerit invida aetās.—Horace

27.8. "The Wolf and the Lamb"

Ad rīvum eundem lupus et agnus vēnerant,

sitī compulsī. Superior stābat lupus,

longēque īnferior agnus. Tunc fauce improbā

latrō incitātus jūrgiī causam intulit.

"Cūr" *inquit "turbulentam fēcistī mihi

aquam bibentī?" Lāniger contrā timēns:

"Quī[1] possum, quaesō, facere quod quereris, lupe?

Ā tē dēcurrit ad meōs haustūs liquor."

Repulsus ille vēritātis vīribus:

"Ante hōs sex mēnsēs male," ait, "dīxistī mihi."

Respondit agnus: "Equidem nātus nōn eram."

"Pater herclē tuus" ille inquit "maledīxit mihi."

Atque ita correptum[2] lacerat injūstā nece.

Haec propter illōs scrīpta est hominēs fābula

quī fictīs causīs innocentēs opprimunt.—Phaedrus 1.1

Paraphrasis: Ad idem flūmen vēnerant et lupus et agnus quod aquam bibere cupīvērunt. Suprā stābat lupus, agnus īnfrā. Tum lupus, quod agnum edere volēbat, lītem cum īnfēlīcī generābat et ait, "Quā rē tū aquam meam cōnfūdistī?" Agnus timōre *commōtus respondit: "Quō modō facere possum id quod tū expostulās? Flūmen ā tē ad mē dēfluit; ergō ego aquam tibi turbulentam facere nōn possum." Vēritāte ipsā lupus *quidem victus aliam causam lītis invēnit: "Ante sex mēnsēs tū mihi maledīxistī." Timidus agnus: "Ego quidem" inquit "ante sex mēnsēs nōn nātus eram." Nōn dēstitit lupus: "Erat certē pater tuus quī mihi maledīxit." Hōc dictō, agnum īnfēlīcem injūstē necāvit. Haec fābula est scrīpta propter illōs quī falsīs causīs innocentēs *laedunt.

Notes
1. quī = quō modō
2. A typical Latin use of subordination. Where English would use two parallel verbs, "He seized the lamb and tore him to pieces," Latin says *correptum lacerat*.

Word Study: English Derivatives

From Lesson	Latin	From Readings	Latin
1. action		1. relaxation	
2. direct		2. repulsive	
3. egotist		3. tense	
4. rectitude		4. utility	
5. volunteer		5. vicious	

Summary Tasks

——— 1. Write a synopsis (all tenses in both voices) of *superō,* in the first person plural.
——— 2. Write all participles of *superō.*
——— 3. Write all infinitives of *superō.*
——— 4. Write a cumulative metaphrase of Readings 27.1 and 27.3.
——— 5. Copy from Optional Reading 27.8 all words that *look like* participles.

Lesson 28

The Imperative Mood
The Vocative Case
The Negative Command

Finite verbs have occurred so far in sentences that express direct questions or direct statements of fact. This lesson introduces verb forms that occur only in sentences expressing direct commands, e.g., in English, "Matt, *close* the door!" All previous finite verb forms were in the *indicative mood*. The new verb forms are in the *imperative mood*. There are three moods of Latin verbs. The third will be introduced in lesson 29.

Sentences with a verb in the imperative are often expanded by the name of the person addressed. This name occurs in the *vocative case*.

Basic Sentences

28.1. Dīc hominem lepidissimum esse mē.—Plautus
   Say that I am a very charming person.
28.2. Contrā verbōsōs nōlī contendere verbīs.—Dionysius Cato
   Do not struggle against the wordy with words.
28.3. Ūtere[1] quaesītīs opibus; fuge nōmen avārī.—Dionysius Cato
   Use the riches which have been acquired; flee the name of "miser."

Note
1. The verb *ūtor*, and a few others, takes a complement in the ablative case.

The Imperative Mood

The imperative occurs in both active and passive voice, and both singular and plural number. It is imperfective in aspect, present in time, and second in person. Here are examples from each of the conjugations.

			Active Voice		
	First	Second	Third	Third -iō	Fourth
Singular	laudā	vidē	vīve	cape	audī
Plural	laudāte	vidēte	vīvite	capite	audīte

Dīc, dūc, fac, and *fer* are imperative singulars without the *-e*. The plurals are *dīcite, dūcite, facite,* and *ferte*.

Here are examples of the imperative of deponent verbs from each conjugation.

	Deponents				
	First	Second	Third	Third -iō	Fourth
Singular	mīrāre	verēre	sequere	patere	mentīre
Plural	mīrāminī	verēminī	sequiminī	patiminī	mentīminī

Passive imperatives are rare; those that do occur look the same as the deponent imperatives. Note that deponent imperatives are analogous with second person indicative forms.

There are some other imperative forms restricted primarily to legal and poetic language; they need not be learned here.

The Vocative Case

Morphology

The form of a noun in the vocative is the same as that of the nominative in both singular and plural with these exceptions: nouns of the second declension ending in -us have the morpheme {e} in the singular, e.g., *amīce* (from *amīcus, amīcī*); nouns of the second declension ending in -ius have the morpheme {ī} in the singular, e.g., *fīlī* (from *fīlius, fīliī*).

Syntax

Sentences with a verb in the imperative mood express a *direct command*. There is no difference in kernel types or in syntax between statements, questions, and commands. Because the verb is automatically in the second person, the subject *tū* or *vōs* usually is not expressed except for special emphasis. However, a noun in the vocative, if present, identifies the referent of the *tū* or *vōs*.

The vocative is best understood as an expansion that can appear with statements and questions as well as commands.

The Negative Command

S28.2 is an example of a *negative command*. In contrast to the positive commands expressed by the imperative alone, this command consists of the imperative *nōlī/nōlīte* (from the irregular verb *nōlō, nōlle* [be unwilling]) plus the complementary infinitive in the active or passive voice.

Singular	Nōlī abīre! (Don't go away!)
Plural	Nōlīte capī! (Don't be caught!)

Kernel Information

Contrā verbōsōs nōlī contendere verbīs. (S28.2)

Clause Marker	Item: Function	Item: Function	Item: Function	Kernel Type	F/NF	M/D	Adj./Adv./ Noun	Name
—	nōlī contendere: verb	— Ø tū: subj.	—	IA	F	M	—	command

■ Exercise 1

Underline all possible imperatives and identify as singular or plural. All words are verb forms. The principal parts of these verbs are provided.

morior, morī, mortuus
vincō, vincere, vīcī, victus

1. morere

2. morī

3. moriminī

4. moriēminī

5. vincēs

6. vince

7. vincite

8. vincitis

■ Exercise 2

Fully identify each word according to the dictionary entry provided.

1. canis, canis, m.:	cane	_____
2. canō, canere:	cane	_____
3. regō, regere:	rege	_____
4. rēx, rēgis, m.:	rēge	_____
5. vestiō, vestīre:	vestī	_____
6. vestis, vestis, f.:	vestī	_____
7. laudō, laudāre:	laudā	_____
8. laus, laudis, f.:	laude	_____
9. audeō, audēre:	audē	_____
10. audiō, audīre:	audī	_____

■ Exercise 3

Write the positive and negative commands for these verbs in the plural number and active voice. Translate each form.

1. mittō, mittere

2. accipiō, accipere

3. laudō, laudāre

4. veniō, venīre

5. teneō, tenēre

Lesson Vocabulary

Noun

ops, opis, f.: power; (pl.) wealth, resources

Adjectives

avārus, avāra, avārum: greedy
lepidus, lepida, lepidum: charming, graceful
verbōsus, verbōsa, verbōsum: wordy, verbose

Verb

contendō, contendere, contendī, contentus: strive, stretch, struggle

Readings

Required

28.1. Tū quī lēgistī nōmina nostra, valē.—Grave Inscription
28.2. Invēnī portum. Spēs et Fortūna, valēte!
      Sat mē lūsistis; lūdite nunc aliōs.—Grave Inscription
28.3. Bene ferre magnam disce fortūnam.—Horace
28.4. Audī, vidē, tacē, sī vīs vīvere in pāce.—Medieval
28.5. Sī vīs pācem, parā bellum.—Vegetius
28.6. Servā mē, servābō tē.—Petronius

Vocabulary

28.1. *valeō, valēre, valuī: be well, fare well
28.2. portus, portūs, m.: harbor
     lūdō, lūdere, lūsī, lūsus: mock, play with, play
28.3. bene (adv.): well
28.4. taceō, tacēre, tacuī: be quiet
     pāx, pācis, f.: peace
28.5. *parō, parāre, parāvī, parātus: prepare
     pāx, pācis, f.: peace
     bellum, bellī, n.: war
28.6. servō, servāre, servāvī, servātus: save

Optional

28.7. Plautus Selection to Be Read after Lesson 28 (p. 358)
28.8. "An Unsatisfactory Lawyer"
     Nōn dē vī neque caede nec venēnō,
     sed līs est mihi dē tribus capellīs:
     vīcīnī queror hās abesse fūrtō.
     Hoc jūdex sibi postulat *probārī.
     Tū Cannās Mithridāticumque bellum
     et perjūria Pūnicī *furōris
     et Sullās Mariōsque Mūciōsque
     magnā vōce sonās manūque tōtā.
     Jam dīc, Postume, dē tribus capellīs.—Martial 6.19

28.9. Catilīna, perge, quō coepistī. Ēgredere aliquandō ex urbe. Patent *portae, proficīscere.—Cicero

Word Study: English Derivatives

From Lesson	Latin	From Readings	Latin
1. acquisition		1. allusion	
2. attend		2. bellicose	
3. avaricious		3. conservation	
4. extend		4. legible	
5. opulence		5. pacify	
6. refugee		6. preparatory	
7. utilize		7. taciturn	
8. verbose		8. valedictorian	

Summary Tasks

____ 1. Change all verb forms in exercise 1 from singular to plural or vice versa.

____ 2. Copy the kernels of all Basic Sentences in this lesson onto a kernel chart.

____ 3. Rewrite the following Basic Sentences, changing the subject from nominative to vocative, and the verb from indicative to imperative: S4.4, 5.5, 8.3, 16.4.

____ 4. Review and explain all relative clauses in the Basic Sentences and the Required Readings of lesson 13.

Lesson 29

The Subjunctive Mood in Independent Clauses

So far all finite verbs have been in either the indicative mood or the imperative mood. This lesson introduces the third mood, the *subjunctive*. Verbs in the subjunctive, like those in the indicative, occur in both independent and dependent clauses. A subjunctive verb in an *independent* clause *always* implies some meaning not implied by an indicative verb.

Most often an independent verb in the subjunctive suggests an action or state of being as *possible* or *willed* or *wished for*. This contrasts with the indicative, which indicates simply that an action has occurred, is occurring, or will occur. For example, *tempus fugit*, with verb in the indicative, can be translated "time flies," but *tempus fugiat*, with verb in the subjunctive, may have these, and other, translations: "time may fly," "time should fly," or "I hope time flies."

Note: A special meaning is *not always* implied when the subjunctive verb occurs in a *dependent* clause. Dependent clauses with verbs in the subjunctive will be introduced in lesson 30.

Basic Sentences

29.1. Rapiāmus, amīcī, occāsiōnem dē diē.—Horace
   My friends, let us seize the opportunity from the moment.
29.2. Longiōrem ōrātiōnem causa forsitan postulet, tua certē natūra breviōrem.[1]—Cicero
   The (legal) case may perhaps require a rather long speech, but your character certainly requires only a rather short one.
29.3. Utinam id sit quod spērō.—Plautus
   May it be that which I hope it is.

Note
1. Ø = postulat (indicative mood)

The Subjunctive Mood in Independent Clauses

There are four tenses of the subjunctive mood. This lesson introduces the present imperfective; lesson 30 will introduce the remaining three tenses. Most of the subjunctives in independent clauses are present imperfective.

The Present Imperfective Subjunctive

The signal for the present imperfective subjunctive is -*ā*- in the second, third, and fourth conjugations, and -*ē*- in the first conjugation. This tense is formed on the imperfective stem. Vowel shortening occurs in the usual places.

	First		Second		Third	
	Singular	Plural	Singular	Plural	Singular	Plural
Active						
First person	laudem	laudēmus	videam	videāmus	dīcam	dīcāmus
Second person	laudēs	laudētis	videās	videātis	dīcās	dīcātis
Third person	laudet	laudent	videat	videant	dīcat	dīcant
Passive						
First person	lauder	laudēmur	videar	videāmur	dīcar	dīcāmur
Second person	laudēris (-re)	laudēminī	videāris (-re)	videāminī	dīcāris (-re)	dīcāminī
Third person	laudētur	laudentur	videātur	videantur	dīcātur	dīcantur

	Third -iō		Fourth	
	Singular	Plural	Singular	Plural
Active				
First person	capiam	capiāmus	audiam	audiāmus
Second person	capiās	capiātis	audiās	audiātis
Third person	capiat	capiant	audiat	audiant
Passive				
First person	capiar	capiāmur	audiar	audiāmur
Second person	capiāris (-re)	capiāminī	audiāris (-re)	audiāminī
Third person	capiātur	capiantur	audiātur	audiantur

Note that the first person singular, active and passive, is ambiguous with the future imperfective indicative in the third and fourth conjugations.

The present imperfective subjunctive of seven irregular verbs follows.

	sum		possum		volō	
	Singular	Plural	Singular	Plural	Singular	Plural
First person	sim	sīmus	possim	possīmus	velim	velīmus
Second person	sīs	sītis	possīs	possītis	velīs	velītis
Third person	sit	sint	possit	possint	velit	velint

	nōlō		mālō		ferō	
	Singular	Plural	Singular	Plural	Singular	Plural
First person	nōlim	nōlīmus	mālim	mālīmus	feram	ferāmus
Second person	nōlīs	nōlītis	mālīs	mālītis	ferās	ferātis
Third person	nōlit	nōlint	mālit	mālint	ferat	ferant

	eō	
	Singular	Plural
First person	eam	eāmus
Second person	eās	eātis
Third person	eat	eant

■ Exercise 1

Notice that in order to interpret verb morphology, a reader must know the conjugation to which a verb belongs. Identify the conjugation, then identify the tense and mood.

1. tenet

2. dīcet

3. laudet

4. dūcat

5. corōnat

6. rapiat

7. arbitrātur

8. sequātur

9. vetat

10. veniat

■ Exercise 2

Name the mood of each verb form.

1. veniētis

2. veniātis

3. venī

4. vēnī

5. sequere

6. sequātur

7. sequitur

8. fuit

9. sumus

10. sīmus

■ Exercise 3

Name the mood of each verb form; then, if the word listed is indicative, write the subjunctive, and vice versa.

1. faciant

2. loquantur

3. arbitrantur

4. capiunt

5. sint

6. possunt

7. velint

8. ferunt

9. eant

10. nōlunt

Syntax and Semantics

An independent clause with a verb in the subjunctive mood must fulfill the same syntactic expectations as a clause with a verb in the indicative or the imperative mood.

Semantically a subjunctive verb in an independent clause has one of three interpretations. Thus, S29.1 is a sentence that might express:

1. the notion of *possibility*, e.g., "we might seize the opportunity,"
2. the notion of an *action willed*, e.g., "we should seize the opportunity,"
3. the notion of an *action wished for*, e.g., "if only we could seize the opportunity."

It does not mean "we are seizing the opportunity." This is the translation of an indicative verb.

Grammarians have traditionally assigned interpretive labels to subjunctives. These labels are provided in this textbook because they are "fixed in grammatical usage" even though they are "not precisely descriptive" (from Allen and Greenough's *New Latin Grammar*, ed. Greenough, Kittredge, Howard, and D'ooge [Boston: Ginn and Co., 1931], p. 282). The terms commonly used to name the three interpretations above are:

1. potential subjunctive (from *possum, posse:* is able)
2. hortatory subjunctive (from *hortor, hortārī:* exhort, urge strongly)
3. optative subjunctive (from *optō, optāre:* wish for)

The selection of a meaning leading to an appropriate English translation usually depends on the context. A hortatory interpretation has been selected for S29.1.

In a question the subjunctive almost always implies *doubt*. Doubt is implied in R29.7, *quid agam?* (What am I to do . . . ?). This is called the *deliberative* subjunctive.

Certain words, when they appear with a subjunctive verb, assign to the subjunctive verb a particular semantic meaning. The most common of these words are:

forsitan: signals possibility
utinam: signals wish

In S29.2, the word *forsitan* (perhaps) in the first clause signals possibility, i.e., "the case *may* perhaps require. . . ." The word *certē* in the second clause suggests that the verb would be in the indicative mood if it weren't gapped.

There are two possible negators associated with independent subjunctives: *nē* and *nōn*. *Nē* occurs when the semantic interpretation of the subjunctive is an action *willed* or *wished*. *Nōn* occurs when the interpretation is *possibility* or *doubt*.

Nē vincat vēritās. (May truth not conquer.)
Nōn vincat vēritās. ([It is possible that] truth may not conquer.)

■ Exercise 4

All of the Latin verbs in the following list are in the indicative mood. Underline English verb forms that are possible translations. (Note: The incorrect choices are translations of verbs in the imperative or subjunctive moods.)

1. bibit: may he drink, he is drinking, he may drink, he does drink

2. tacēmus: we are silent, we should be silent, let's be silent, we can be silent

3. laudāris: you could be praised, you must be praised, you are being praised, you are praised

4. venīs: come, you are coming, you come, you may come

5. capiuntur: they may be caught, let them be caught, they are being caught, they should be caught

■ Exercise 5
All of the Latin verbs in the following list are in the subjunctive mood. Underline the choices that are possible translations.

1. gaudeāmus: let's rejoice, we do rejoice, we might rejoice, we are rejoicing

2. vincant: they are conquering, they should conquer, may they conquer, they might conquer

3. vīvat: may he live, he may live, would that he live, he does live

4. imprimātur: it is being printed, may it be printed, it may be printed, let it be printed

5. patiāminī: you may suffer, you are suffering, you should be suffering, may you suffer

■ Exercise 6
Give the metaphrase(s) of each sentence. Some have several possibilities.

1. Faciāmus dē necessitāte virtūtem.

2. Nē cēdāmus timōrī.

3. Vincat vēritās.

4. Utinam vincat vēritās.

5. Nōn impediat īra animum.

Lesson Vocabulary

Noun
ōrātiō, ōrātiōnis, f.: speech, oration

Indeclinables
Adverbs
certē: assuredly, certainly
forsitan: perhaps (signals potential subjunctive)
nē: signals negative hortatory or optative subjunctive
utinam: would that (signals optative subjunctive)

Verbs

postulō, postulāre, postulāvī, postulātus: demand, require

rapiō, rapere, rapuī, raptus: seize, grab

spērō, spērāre, spērāvī, spērātus: hope, hope for

Readings

Required

29.1. Sī quid agis, prūdenter agās et respice fīnem. — Aesop (trans.)

29.2. Quī dedit beneficium, taceat; nārret quī accēpit. — Seneca

29.3. Ergō ego germānam frātremque patremque deōsque

et nātāle solum ventīs ablāta relinquam? — Ovid *Metamorphoses*

(spoken by Medea, wrestling with her overpowering love for Jason, who is the enemy
of her family)

29.4. Dum vīvimus, vīvāmus. — Anon.

29.5. Quod sentīmus, loquāmur; quod loquimur, sentiāmus: concordet sermō cum

vītā. — Seneca

29.6. Nec mē miserior est neque ūlla videātur magis. — Plautus

(spoken by an unhappy woman)

29.7. Quid agam, jūdicēs? Quō mē vertam? — Cicero

Vocabulary

29.1. prūdenter (adv.): wisely, prudently

respiciō, respicere, respexī, respectus: look back at, consider

29.2. taceō, tacēre, tacuī: be quiet

29.3. *ergō (sentence connector): therefore

germāna, germānae, f.: twin

nātālis, nātāle: native

solum, solī, n.: earth, soil

ventus, ventī, m.: wind

auferō, auferre, abstulī, ablātus: carry away

29.5. concordō, concordāre, concordāvī, concordātus: be in harmony with

sermō, sermōnis, f.: talk

29.6. *miser, misera, miserum: unhappy, wretched

*neque (coord. conj.): nor

magis (adv., comp. of multum): more

29.7. jūdex, jūdicis, m.: judge

vertō, vertere, vertī, versus: turn

Optional

29.8. Plautus Selection No. 1 to Be Read after Lesson 29 (p. 359)

29.9. Plautus Selection No. 2 to Be Read after Lesson 29 (p. 362)

29.10. Ferās, nōn culpēs, quod mūtārī nōn potest. — Publilius Syrus

29.11. Fīat jūstitia, *ruat caelum. — Legal

29.12. *Edāmus, vīvāmus, gaudeāmus; post mortem nūlla voluptās. — Anon.

29.13. Omnia vincit Amor; et nōs cēdāmus Amōrī.—Vergil

29.14. Populus vult dēcipī; dēcipiātur.—Anon.

29.15. Utinam quae dīcis dictīs facta suppetant.—Plautus

29.16. Quis genus Aeneadum, quis Trōjae nesciat urbem,
virtūtēsque virōsque aut tantī incendia bellī.—Vergil *Aeneid*

29.17. *Bella gerant aliī; tū, fēlīx Austria, nūbe!
*Nam quae Mars aliīs, dat tibi *rēgna Venus.—Anon.
(The first three words come from a line of Ovid (*Her.* 13.84). The significance of the couplet lies in the fact that Austria grew to power through a series of advantageous marriages.)

29.18. Quisquis amat, valeat; pereat quī nescit amāre.
Bis tantō pereat quisquis amāre vetat.—Inscription

29.19. *Gaudeāmus Igitur:* A famous student song written in the seventeenth century

> Gaudeāmus igitur,
> juvenēs dum sumus:
> post jūcundam juventūtem,
> post molestam senectūtem,
> > nōs habēbit humus.
>
> Ubi sunt quī ante nōs
> in mundō fuēre?
> Vādite ad superōs,
> trānsīte ad īnferōs,
> > ubi jam fuēre.
>
> Vīta nostra brevis est,
> brevī fīniētur;
> venit mors vēlōciter,
> rapit nōs atrōciter:
> > nēminī parcētur.
>
> Vīvat acadēmia;
> vīvant professōrēs;
> vīvat membrum quodlibet;
> vīvant membra quaelibet:
> > semper sint in flōre.
>
> Vīvat et rēs pūblica
> et quī illam regit;
> vīvat nostra cīvitās,
> vīvat haec sodālitās
> > quae nōs hūc collēgit.
>
> Alma Mater flōreat,
> quae nōs ēducāvit,
> cārōs et commīlitōnēs
> dissitās in regiōnēs
> > sparsōs congregāvit.

Word Study: English Derivatives

From Lesson	Latin	From Readings	Latin
1. because		1. ablative	
2. cause		2. acceptance	
3. certificate		3. concordance	
4. certify		4. consent	
5. despair		5. convert	
6. desperate		6. divert	
7. oracle		7. sermon	
8. rapture		8. soil	

Summary Tasks

____ 1. Write the Latin equivalent for each English item in exercise 4.

____ 2. Change the verb in each of these Basic Sentences from indicative to subjunctive, and give one possible translation of the sentence: 1.1, 1.6, 4.2, 4.4, 5.3.

____ 3. What syntactic and/or semantic expectations are raised by the first words in Readings 29.1, 29.2, 29.4, 29.5, and 29.7?

____ 4. Review and explain all participle clauses in the Basic Sentences and Required Readings of lessons 14 and 15.

Lesson 30

The Indirect Question: A Finite Noun Clause

In the early lessons of this textbook all clauses were direct statements or direct questions; direct commands first appeared in lesson 28. Each of these can also be found embedded in the form of a dependent clause. In this form they are called indirect statements, indirect questions, and indirect commands. Lessons 23 and 24 described the indirect statement as a non-finite clause. This lesson describes the *indirect question* and the next lesson will describe the indirect command. Both of these are finite noun clauses with the verb in the subjunctive.

Basic Sentences

30.1. Sciō quid sit amor.—Ovid
      I know what love is.
30.2. Interrogāvī ipsōs an essent Christiānī.—Pliny (in a letter to Trajan)
      I asked them themselves whether they were Christians.
30.3. Forsitan et Priamī fuerint quae Fāta requīrās.—Vergil
      Perhaps you may also ask what the fate of Priam was.
      (a reference to the fall of Troy, whose king was Priam)

The Indirect Question: A Finite Noun Clause

Lesson 29 introduced the present imperfective subjunctive. Below is the morphology of the *present perfective subjunctive* and of the *past imperfective* and *past perfective subjunctives*. (There are no future subjunctives.)

Present Perfective Subjunctive

The morpheme for the present perfective subjunctive in the active voice is {erī} with regular shortening of the *i;* this tense is built on the perfective active stem. The passive is a periphrastic form consisting of the perfective participle and the present imperfective subjunctive of *sum, esse.*

	Singular	Plural
Active		
First person	amāverim	amāverīmus
Second person	amāverīs	amāverītis
Third person	amāverit	amāverint
Passive		
First person	amātus sim	amātī sīmus
Second person	amātus sīs	amātī sītis
Third person	amātus sit	amātī sint

See the Appendix for complete listings of verbs of other conjugations.

Past Imperfective Subjunctive

In practical terms, both the past subjunctives, imperfective and perfective, are easy to recognize because they look like infinitives with person endings.

The past imperfective subjunctive of regular verbs has the morpheme {rē} with regular shortening of the *ē; this tense is built on the imperfective stem.

	First		Second		Third	
	Singular	Plural	Singular	Plural	Singular	Plural
Active						
First person	amārem	amārēmus	vidērem	vidērēmus	regerem	regerēmus
Second person	amārēs	amārētis	vidērēs	vidērētis	regerēs	regerētis
Third person	amāret	amārent	vidēret	vidērent	regeret	regerent
Passive						
First person	amārer	amārēmur	vidērer	vidērēmur	regerer	regerēmur
Second person	amārēris (-re)	amārēminī	vidērēris (-re)	vidērēminī	regerēris (-re)	regerēminī
Third person	amārētur	amārentur	vidērētur	vidērentur	regerētur	regerentur

	Third -iō		Fourth		sum	
	Singular	Plural	Singular	Plural	Singular	Plural
Active						
First person	caperem	caperēmus	audīrem	audīrēmus	essem*	essēmus
Second person	caperēs	caperētis	audīrēs	audīrētis	essēs	essētis
Third person	caperet	caperent	audīret	audīrent	esset	essent
Passive						
First person	caperer	caperēmur	audīrer	audīrēmur	—	—
Second person	caperēris (-re)	caperēminī	audīrēris (-re)	audīrēminī	—	—
Third person	caperētur	caperentur	audīrētur	audīrentur	—	—

*For *essem, essēs,* etc., the forms *forem, forēs,* etc., are sometimes used.

Past Perfective Subjunctive

The past perfective subjunctive in the active voice has the morpheme {issē} with regular shortening of the *ē.* This tense is built on the perfective active stem. The passive is a periphrastic form consisting of the perfective passive participle and the past imperfective subjunctive of *sum.*

	Singular	Plural
Active		
First person	amāvissem	amāvissēmus
Second person	amāvissēs	amāvissētis
Third person	amāvisset	amāvissent
Passive		
First person	amātus essem	amātī essēmus
Second person	amātus essēs	amātī essētis
Third person	amātus esset	amātī essent

See the Appendix for complete listings of verbs of other conjugations.

■ Exercise 1

Identify the person, number, tense, mood, and voice of each verb. Do not translate the verbs since most subjunctive verbs can be translated correctly only in context. All forms come from the dictionary entries given.

tractō, tractāre, tractāvī, tractātus
mittō, mittere, mīsī, missus

1. tractāverās _____

2. tractāvisset _____

3. tractēmus _____

4. mittam _____

5. mittam _____

6. mīserim _____

7. mitterēris _____

8. tractantur _____

9. missus sit _____

10. tractāvistis _____

Syntax and Semantics

Just as the indirect statement is a noun clause functioning as subject or direct object of a kernel, so too the indirect question is a noun clause functioning as subject or direct object of a kernel. Both of these clauses are finite in English but only the indirect question is finite in Latin.

A Latin indirect question can be recognized by three features:

1. a question word as clause marker
2. a verb in the subjunctive—the subjunctive is obligatory in indirect questions
3. a governing verb having the general semantic notions "ask," "say," "tell," "know," like *rogō, quaerō, dīcō, sciō.*

Quid est amor? (What is love?) is a direct question. In S30.1, *quid sit amor* is an indirect question. The reader reacts to it as such because *sciō* raises the syntactic expectation of a direct object, which must be a noun or a noun clause. Semantically the verb *sciō* raises the expectation of an embedded statement or question. Here the question word *quid* as clause marker and the subjunctive mood of the verb in the clause confirmed the construction as an indirect question.

A sentence with an indirect question has at least two kernels. The question word, like the relative pronoun in a relative clause, is always a clause marker, whether it is part of the kernel or not.

If the governing verb has the semantic notion of "asking," the person to whom the question is directed is expressed by a noun or pronoun in the *accusative*, e.g., *ipsōs* in S30.2, or by a prepositional phrase, e.g., *(quaerō) ex ipsīs*. For practical purposes it is convenient to treat both the accusative of the person asked and the question itself as objects of the governing verb. The traditional term for this is *double accusative*.

The expectation of an indirect question is raised by expressions with the semantic notions "ask," "say," "know." Verbs of "asking" include:

> rogō (ask)
> quaerō (ask)
> interrogō (ask, inquire)
> requīrō (ask for, look for)

See also the list of verbs that introduce indirect statements in lesson 23.

Frequently Occurring Question Words

> ā quō? (by whom?)
> an? (or; whether, if [ind. quest.])
> cūr? (why?)
> num? (whether [ind. quest.])
> quā condiciōne? (under what condition?)
> quālis, quāle? (what kind of?)
> quam? with adj., adv. (how?)
> quam diū? (how long?)
> quandō? quō tempore? (when?)
> quantum? (how greatly?)
> quantus, quanta, quantum? (how great a _____ ?)
> quī, quae, quod? (which? what?)
> quis, quid? (who? what?)
> quō auxiliō? (by what means?)
> quō cōnsiliō? (for what purpose?)
> quō modō? (in what manner?)
> quō? quem ad locum? (where to?)
> quōcum? (with whom?)
> quot? (how many?)
> quotiēns? (how often?)
> ubi? quō in locō? (where?)
> unde? quō ā/dē/ē locō? (where from?)
> ut? with clause (how?)
> uter, utra, utrum? (which of two _____ ?)
> utrum . . . an? (whether . . . or?)

Note: Indefinite relative clauses, which have *qu-* clause markers, need not be confused with indirect questions: (1) their governing verbs usually have different semantic notions from those governing indirect questions; (2) the *qu-* words are relative and not interrogative pronouns; and (3) the embedded verb is usually indicative. In contrast, the two are easily confused in English because they look alike. For example,

Indefinite relative clause: I don't like *what has happened.*
Indirect question: I don't know *what has happened.*

Kernel Information

Interrogāvī ipsōs an essent Christiānī.

Clause Marker	Item: Function	Item: Function	Item: Function	Kernel Type	F/NF	M/D	Adj./Adv./ Noun	Name
—	interrogāvī: verb	ipsōs: dir. obj. an essent Christiānī: dir. obj.	$\emptyset$ = ego: subj.	TA	F	M	—	statement
an	essent: verb	Christiānī: subj. compl.	$\emptyset$ = ipsī: subj.	Lkg.	F	D	noun	ind. quest.

■ Exercise 2

Copy the kernels for S30.1 (*Sciō quid sit amor*).

Clause Marker	Item: Function	Item: Function	Item: Function	Kernel Type	F/NF	M/D	Adj./Adv./ Noun	Name
1.								
2.								

■ Exercise 3

Each of the English sentences contains an embedded clause, either an indirect question or an indirect statement. Rewrite the indirect statement or question as a direct statement or question.

1. I know that she is the teacher.

2. I know who the teacher is.

3. I know what science she teaches.

4. I know that she teaches science.

5. He is asking who teaches science.

6. Does this schedule indicate that he is the teacher?

7. This schedule does not indicate who the teacher is.

8. The teacher assumes that the class will meet.

9. Does the teacher know that the book is not available?

10. Why doesn't the teacher know why the books have not come?

■ Exercise 4

Copy the verbs governing the indirect statements in exercise 3. Then copy the verbs governing the indirect questions. Underline the verbs that appear on both lists.

Verbs Governing Indirect Statements   *Verbs Governing Indirect Questions*

Relative Time

Just as an imperfective infinitive in an indirect statement expresses *time simultaneous* with that of the governing verb (see lesson 23), so also does an imperfective subjunctive in an indirect question. *Sit* in S30.1 and *essent* in S30.2 are both imperfective subjunctives.

Likewise, both the perfective infinitive in an indirect statement (see lesson 24) and the perfective subjunctive in an indirect question express *time before* that of the governing verb. *Fuerint* in S30.3 is a perfective subjunctive.

■ Exercise 5

On the basis of the subjunctive being imperfective or perfective, indicate by a check mark whether the event described by the indirect question happened/happens *before* the time of the governing verb or *not before*. (It is irrelevant for this exercise whether the subjunctive is a past or present form.)

	Before	*Not Before*
1. Scīmus quis fūrem cognōscat.	————	————
2. Scīmus quem fūr cognōverit.	————	————
3. Nesciō quid gladiātor in harēnā vīderit.	————	————
4. Nescīvī quid gladiātor in harēnā vīdisset.	————	————
5. Rogāvērunt quō modō prūdēns vīveret.	————	————
6. Nesciunt cūr fēlīx sīs.	————	————

Metaphrasing

The question word always comes at the beginning of the dependent clause in English, no matter whether it is the subject, direct object, adjectival modifier, or adverbial modifier within the embedded clause.

The dependent subjunctives in this lesson are translated as if they were indicatives. This is so because the subjunctive mood is an obligatory feature in an indirect question and therefore does not usually demand a special semantic interpretation.

Back-shift, introduced in lessons 23 and 24, applies to both English and Latin indirect questions because they both have finite verbs. It means that a finite verb in a present tense in a dependent clause shifts to the past when the time of the governing verb is past.[1] For example,

---

1. There are other terms used in discussing this general topic, e.g., "sequence of tense" and "tense agreement." While there is some overlap with back-shift, the rules for sequence of tense are more detailed than metaphrasing requires. They are also phrased for writing rather than for reading Latin.

Fēmina *quaerit* quis *veniat*. (The woman *wants to know* who *is arriving*.)
Fēmina *quaesīvit* quis *venīret*. (The woman *wanted to know* who *was arriving*.)

The time change from *quaerit* to *quaesīvit* necessitates the shift from *veniat* to *venīret*, without any change in meaning. Both *veniat* (is arriving) and *venīret* (was arriving) show the same time relative to the governing verb, namely *same time*.

Back-shift, of course, occurs also with perfective tenses. For example, *vēnerit* would shift to *vēnisset* after a verb with past time meaning.

Sciō quis *vēnerit*. (I *know* who *has arrived*.)
Scīvī quis *vēnisset*. (I *knew* who *had arrived*.)

"Has arrived" and "had arrived" both show the same time relative to the governing verb, namely, *time before*.

Back-shift should be observed in metaphrasing, although it is fair to say that many speakers of English do not consistently observe it. It was sometimes disregarded in Latin also.

■ Exercise 6
Rewrite sentences 3, 5, 7, and 10 in exercise 3, putting the governing verb into the past time and applying back-shift to the dependent verb.

3.

5.

7.

10.

■ Exercise 7
Write a metaphrase of each of the sentences in exercise 5 (not exercise 6).

1.

2.

3.

4.

5.

6.

■ Exercise 8

Identify each italicized *qu-* clause or sentence as:

    a. direct question

    b. indirect question

    c. adjectival relative clause

    d. noun relative clause

1. Nīl agit exemplum, *lītem quod līte resolvit.*

2. Sciō *quid sit amor.*

3. *Quid gladiātor in harēnā videt?*

4. Quī *quod vult* dīcit, *quod nōn vult* saepius audit.

5. *Quī quod vult dīcit,* quod nōn vult saepius audit.

Lesson Vocabulary

Noun

fātum, fātī, n.: fate, destiny

Adjective

Christiānus, Christiāna, Christiānum: Christian

Indeclinables

Question Words

an?: or; whether, if (ind. quest.)

nōnne: introduces direct questions that expect the answer "yes"

num?: introduces direct questions that expect the answer "no"; whether (ind. quest.)

utrum . . . an?: whether . . . or?

Verbs

interrogō, interrogāre, interrogāvī, interrogātus: ask, inquire

requīrō, requīrere, requīsīvī, requīsītus: ask for, look for

rogō, rogāre, rogāvī, rogātus: ask

Readings

Required

30.1. Scīre cupiō quid agās, quid exspectēs.—Cicero

30.2. An dīves sit, omnēs quaerunt; nēmō an bonus.—Anon.

30.3. "Servus est." Sed fortasse līber animō. "Servus est." Hoc illī nocēbit? Ostende quis nōn sit. Alius libīdinī servit, alius avāritiae, alius ambitiōnī, omnēs timōrī.—Seneca

30.4. Quis sim, sciēs ex eō quem ad tē mīsī.—Cicero

30.5. Amīcum an nōmen habeās aperit calamitās.—Publilius Syrus

    (Note: The first question word *utrum* has been omitted.)

Vocabulary

30.1. *exspectō, exspectāre, exspectāvī, exspectātus: look for, wait for

30.3. *servus, servī, m.: slave

    fortasse (adv.): perhaps

    ostendō, ostendere, ostendī, ostentus: show

    libīdō, libīdinis, f.: pleasure, desire

    ambitiō, ambitiōnis, f.: ambition

30.5. aperiō, aperīre, aperuī, apertus: reveal

    calamitās, calamitātis, f.: disaster

Optional

30.6. Plautus Selection to Be Read after Lesson 30 (p. 363)

30.7. Quid Deus intendat, nōlī perquīrere sorte; quid statuat dē tē, sine tē dēlīberat
    ille.—Cato

30.8. Tum genus omne tuum et quae dentur moenia, discēs.—Vergil

30.9. Rāna Rupta et Bōs

    Inops, potentem dum vult imitārī, perit.
    In prātō quondam rāna cōnspexit bovem,
    et *tacta invidiā tantae magnitūdinis
    rūgōsam īnflāvit pellem. Tum *nātōs suōs
    interrogāvit an bove esset lātior.
    Illī negā'runt. Rursus intendit cutem
    majōre nīsū, et similī quaesīvit modō
    quis major esset. Illī dīxērunt bovem.
    Novissimē indīgnāta, dum vult *validius
    īnflāre sēsē, ruptō *jacuit corpore.—Phaedrus 1.24

Paraphrasis: *Pauper, sī vult dīvitem imitārī, semper obit. Ōlim in agrō rāna bovem
pāscentem *aspexit, et magnitūdinī ejus invidēns suum corpus parvulum īnflāvit. Hōc
factō, ē fīliīs suīs quaesīvit, "Nōnne ego grandior bove sum?" Illī "Nōn tam grandis
es" respondērunt. Iterum conātū majōre corpus īnflāvit et iterum quaesīvit, "Quis
major est, utrum bōs an māter vestra?" Nātī ejus "Bōs major est" respondēre.
Tandem īrāta fortius sē īnflāre volēbat et hōc modō sē rūpit.

30.10. Caesar finds it difficult to gather information about Britain:

    Neque enim temere praeter mercātōrēs illō adit quisquam, neque eīs ipsīs
    quicquam praeter ōram maritimam atque regiōnēs eās quae sunt contrā Galliās
    nōtum est. Itaque vocātīs ad sē undique mercātōribus, neque quanta esset īnsulae
    magnitūdō, neque quae aut quantae nātiōnēs incolerent, neque quem ūsum bellī
    habērent aut quibus īnstitūtīs ūterentur, neque quī essent ad majōrum *nāvium
    multitūdinem idōneī portūs reperīre poterat.—Caesar *B.G.* 4.20

Word Study: English Derivatives

From Lesson	Latin		From Readings	Latin
1. fatal			1. admission	
2. interrogate			2. expectation	
3. question			3. liberator	
4. request			4. ostentatious	
5. scientific			5. query	

Summary Tasks

____ 1. Write a synopsis of *rogō* in the second person singular, indicative and subjunctive, active and passive.

____ 2. Embed Basic Sentences 3.2 and 3.3 as indirect questions with *rogō* and then with *rogāvī*.

____ 3. Which of the question words on page 298 are answered by an adverbial modifier?

____ 4. Name the semantic notions that raise the expectation of an indirect question.

Review Lesson 9

Lesson Vocabulary

Nouns
āctiō, āctiōnis, f.: action, act
fātum, fātī, n.: fate, destiny
ops, opis, f.: power; (pl.) wealth, resources
ōrātiō, ōrātiōnis, f.: speech, oration
voluntās, voluntātis, f.: wish, will

Adjectives
avārus, avāra, avārum: greedy
Christiānus, Christiāna, Christiānum: Christian
lepidus, lepida, lepidum: charming
rēctus, rēcta, rēctum: right, correct
verbōsus, verbōsa, verbōsum: wordy, verbose

Indeclinables
Adverbs
certē: assuredly, certainly
forsitan: perhaps
nē: signals negative hortatory or optative subjunctive
utinam: would that

Subordinating Conjunction
nisi: if not, unless

Question Words
an?: or; whether, if
nōnne: introduces direct questions that expect the answer "yes"
num?: introduces direct questions that expect the answer "no"; whether
utrum . . . an?: whether . . . or?

Verbs
contendō, contendere, contendī, contentus: strive, stretch, struggle
interrogō, interrogāre, interrogāvī, interrogātus: ask, inquire
postulō, postulāre, postulāvī, postulātus: demand, require
rapiō, rapere, rapuī, raptus: seize, grab
requīrō, requīrere, requīsīvī, requīsītus: ask for, look for
rogō, rogāre, rogāvī, rogātus: ask
spērō, spērāre, spērāvī, spērātus: hope, hope for

Readings Vocabulary

aspiciō, aspicere, aspexī, aspectus: look at, see
bellum, bellī, n.: war
commoveō, commovēre, commōvī, commōtus: move deeply, alarm
edō, edere, ēdī, ēsus: eat
ergō (sentence connector): therefore
exspectō, exspectāre, exspectāvī, exspectātus: look for, wait for
furor, furōris, m.: madness, fury
inquit: "_____ says"
jaceō, jacēre, jacuī: lie
laedō, laedere, laesī, laesus: harm, injure
miser, misera, miserum: unhappy, miserable
nam (sentence connector): for
nātus, nātī, m.: son
nāvis, nāvis, f.: ship
neque (coord. conj.): nor, and not
nunc (adv.): now
parō, parāre, parāvī, parātus: prepare, get ready
pauper (pauperis): poor
porta, portae, f.: gate
probō, probāre, probāvī, probātus: prove, approve
quidem (intensifier): indeed, in fact, certainly
rēgnum, rēgnī, n.: kingdom
ruō, ruere, ruī: fall
servus, servī, m.: slave
tangō, tangere, tetigī, tactus: touch, affect
valeō, valēre, valuī: be strong, be effective, prevail
validus, valida, validum: strong

Morphology Review

New Morphology: Lessons 27 through 30

noun: vocative case
verb: past and future perfective tenses, active and passive
      imperative mood, singular and plural, active and passive
      subjunctive mood, present imperfective and perfective, past imperfective and
      perfective, active and passive

Form Identification

    a. spērō, spērāre, spērāvī, spērātus: hope
    b. spēs, speī, f.: hope, expectation
    c. spērābilis, spērābile: possible (able to be hoped for)

1. spērāta erit _____
2. spērem _____
3. spērāveram _____
4. spērāte _____
5. spērābilis _____
6. spērātī erant _____
7. nōlī spērāre _____
8. spērāveris _____
9. spem _____
10. spērāvissem _____

■ Exercise: English to Latin Sentences
Using the Latin sentences as models, translate the English sentences into Latin.

1. Nōn sum quod fueram. (S27.1)
2. Dīc hominem lepidissimum esse mē. (S28.1)
3. Contrā verbōsōs nōlī contendere verbīs. (S28.2)
4. Rapiāmus, amīcī, occāsiōnem dē diē. (S29.1)
5. Interrogāvī ipsōs an essent Christiānī. (S30.2)

   a. The brother continued to say whatever the girlfriend had said. (1)

   b. Say that you love me! (2)

   c. Don't approach this house! (3)

   d. May the gods destroy him! (4)

   e. The husband asked the woman why she was angry. (5)

Vocabulary
Nouns
brother: frāter
girlfriend: amīca
god: deus
house: domicilium, domiciliī, n.
husband: vir
woman: fēmina

Pronouns
him: is
me: ego
what: qui, quae, quod
you: tū

Adjectives
angry: īrātus, īrāta, īrātum
this: hic, haec, hoc

Question Word
why?: cūr?

Verbs
approach: adeō, adīre, adiī
ask: rogō
destroy: perdō, perdere, perdidī, perditus
love: amō
say: dīcō
was: sum

Stem List

Enter the following words in the Stem List found in the back of this book. Also add the dictionary listings for each word entered.

1. āctiō
2. certē
3. contendere
4. fāta
5. opibus

6. ōrātiōnem
7. quaerō
8. rēcta
9. requīrās
10. voluntās

Lesson 31

The Indirect Command: A Finite Noun Clause

Indirect statements are statements depending on expressions with the semantic notions "say," "think," "feel," etc. Indirect questions are questions depending on many of the same expressions and, in addition, those with the semantic notions "inquire," "ask," etc. *Indirect commands* are commands depending on expressions with the semantic notions "order," "ask," "want," "urge." This lesson introduces indirect commands that are finite noun clauses. Lesson 23 introduced non-finite clauses that express commands (see objective infinitive).

Basic Sentences

31.1. Mediō ut līmite currās moneō.—Ovid

I advise that you fly on the middle course. (Daedalus addresses his son Icarus, for whose escape from Crete he has constructed wings of wax and feathers. The middle course is between the risks of sun and water.)

31.2. Orgetorīx Helvētiīs persuāsit ut dē fīnibus suīs exīrent.—Caesar

Orgetorix persuaded the Helvetians to leave their territory.

The Indirect Command: A Finite Noun Clause

Syntax and Semantics

The indirect command, like the indirect statement and the indirect question, is a noun clause and functions as either subject or object of the kernel.

A Latin indirect command can be recognized by these features:

1. the clause markers *ut/utī* (for positive command), *nē* (for negative command) (note: *ut* is not always present in positive commands)
2. a verb in the subjunctive
3. a governing expression with the semantic notions "order," "ask," "want," or "urge," etc.

In S31.1, the clause *mediō ut līmite currās* is the indirect command which functions here as direct object of the verb *moneō*. In S31.2, the clause *ut dē fīnibus suīs exīrent* is the indirect command. An indirect command may of course also be subject of the kernel, e.g., *ut exīrent imperātum est* (It was ordered that they leave).

Kernel Information

Mediō ut līmite currās moneō. (S31.1)

Clause Marker	Item: Function	Item: Function	Item: Function	Kernel Type	F/NF	M/D	Adj./Adv./ Noun	Name
—	moneō: verb	mediō ut līmite currās: dir. obj.	∅ = ego: subj.	TA	F	M	—	statement
ut	currās: verb	∅ = tū: subj.		IA	F	D	noun	indirect command

The subjunctives are imperfective since the relative time of the indirect command is never "time before" that of the governing verb: that which is commanded *cannot* precede the act of commanding. *Exīrent* is past imperfective, rather than present imperfective, because of back-shift after *persuāsit,* a verb expressing past time.

A personal noun or pronoun in the accusative,[1] in the dative, e.g., *Helvētiīs* in S31.2, or within a prepositional phrase may be present to indicate the person(s) to whom the command is given.

Listed below are some of the most common of the expressions that raise the expectation of an indirect command. Also included are some of the many English equivalents.

One group of expressions that raises the expectation of an indirect command includes verbs with the semantic notion "order/urge."

hortor (urge, encourage) + accusative
imperō (order, command, impose) + dative
moneō (warn, advise) + accusative
ōrō (beg, entreat) + accusative
persuādeō (persuade, convince) + dative
petō (ask, request) + *ab* + ablative
postulō (demand, desire) + *ab* + ablative
precor (pray, entreat) + accusative
quaerō (desire, ask) + *ex/ab* + ablative
rogō (ask, beg, request) + accusative
suādeō (persuade, convince) + dative

A second group includes those verbs with the semantic notion "wish."

volō (wish)
nōlō (not wish)
mālō (prefer)
cupiō (wish, desire)

A third group includes verbs with the semantic notion "resolve."

---

1. See double accusatives in lesson 30.

cēnseō (propose)
cōnstituō (decide)
statuō (decide, determine)

A fourth group of such expressions includes verbs with the semantic notion "allow."

permittō (allow, permit) + dative
sinō (allow) + accusative
patior (allow) + accusative

Some of the above verbs that pattern with a finite clause may pattern also with an objective infinitive construction, especially in poetry. In contrast, there are a few verbs with the semantic notion "command," e.g., *jubeō*, that pattern almost always with an infinitive clause. See lesson 23 for the objective infinitive construction.

Metaphrasing

In English too there are two ways of expressing most indirect commands. For example, S31.2.

Orgetorīx Helvētiīs persuāsit *ut dē fīnibus suīs exīrent.*
a. Orgetorix persuaded the Helvetians *that they should go out of their country.*
b. Orgetorix persuaded the Helvetians *to go out of their country.*

The beginning student will be safe in metaphrasing the finite indirect command of Latin as a finite clause in English, as in *a* above. (Speakers of English differ as to whether to include "should" in the finite clause.) However, the non-finite clause in *b* is more common after certain English verbs.

■ Exercise 1
Below are five sentences containing indirect commands. Replace forms of *imperō* by the equivalent forms of *jubeō, jubēre, jussī, jussus* and replace the finite clauses by accusative with infinitive clauses. Look at the example.

Imperō tibi ut veniās: Jubeō tē venīre.

1. Imperāvī tibi ut venīrēs:

2. Imperāvī eī ut venīret:

3. Imperāveram vōbīs ut venīrētis:

4. Imperābis illīs ut effugiant:

5. Imperāvistī puerīs ut effugerent:

■ Exercise 2

The sentences below contain indirect statements and both types of indirect commands. Copy all kernels onto a kernel chart and give a final metaphrase of each sentence.

1. Dux Helvētiōs exīre dīxit.

2. Dux Helvētiōs exīre jussit.

3. Dux Helvētiīs ut exīrent persuāsit.

4. Dux Helvētiōs exīre voluit.

5. Petō ut effugiat.

6. Dīxī eum effugere.

7. Jussī eum effugere.

Semantic Note

It is interesting, as well as pertinent, to consider that some verbs may introduce more than one of the three indirect utterances: indirect statements, indirect questions, indirect commands. For example, *dīcō* (say) introduces all three; the same holds true for English.

> Indirect statement: They say that Caesar is coming.
> Indirect question: They say who is coming.
> Indirect command: They say that Caesar should come.

Sciō (know) introduces two indirect utterances.

> Indirect statement: They know that Caesar is coming.
> Indirect question: They know who is coming.

Rogō (ask) introduces a different set of two indirect utterances.

> Indirect question: They ask who is coming.
> Indirect command: They ask that Caesar (should) come.

The Semantic Notion of Indefiniteness

The semantic notion of indefiniteness is expressed by different words according to the environment. So far *quis* (who) and *quid* (what) have occurred as interrogative pronouns, and *quī, quae, quod* (what/which _____) as interrogative adjectives. However, in a dependent clause introduced by *nē*, or by *sī, nisi, num*, the pronoun *quis, quid*, and forms of *quī* express indefiniteness corresponding to English "anyone, anything." For example,

> Monuit *nē quid* inexpertum relinquerent. (He warned that they should *not* leave *anything* unexplored.)

Other words that express indefiniteness are unambiguous because they are morphologically much like English "who*ever*," "*some*one," "*any*one," etc. These include:

*ali*quis, *ali*quid (someone, something)
qu**ī***cumque*, quae*cumque*, quod*cumque* (whoever, whatever)
quis*quam*, quae*quam*, quic*quam* (or quid*quam*) (anyone, anything)

Caution: *quisque, quaeque, quodque* (each, every person/thing) and *quīdam, quaedam, quoddam* (a certain person/thing) are *not* indefinites.

■ Exercise 3
Label each *quis* as *interrogative* or *indefinite*. Write a metaphrase of each sentence.

1. Scīs quis veniat.

2. Imperō nē quis veniat.

3. Sī quis venit, grātus est.

4. Quis veniat rogāmus.

Lesson Vocabulary

Nouns
Helvētiī, Helvētiōrum, m. pl.: the Helvetians (a people living in what is now Switzerland)
līmes, līmitis, m.: track, course
Orgetorīx, Orgetorīgis, m.: Orgetorix (chief of the Helvetians)

Pronouns
aliquis, aliquid: someone, something
quisquam, quaequam, quicquam (or quidquam): anyone, anything

Adjective
medius, media, medium: middle, middle of

Indeclinable
Subordinating Conjunction
nē as clause marker: that . . . not; indicates negative dependent clause

Verbs
cēnseō, cēnsēre, cēnsuī, cēnsus: propose
cōnstituō, cōnstituere, cōnstituī, cōnstitūtus: decide; set up
exeō, exīre, exiī (exīvī), exitūrus: leave, go out
hortor, hortārī, hortātus: encourage, urge
imperō, imperāre, imperāvī, imperātus: order, command
permittō, permittere, permīsī, permissus: allow, permit
persuādeō, persuādēre, persuāsī, persuāsūrus: persuade, convince
precor, precārī, precātus: pray, entreat
sinō, sinere, sīvī, situs: allow
statuō, statuere, statuī, statūtus: decide, determine; set up
suādeō, suādēre, suāsī, suāsūrus: persuade, convince

Readings

Required

31.1. Dēcrēvit quondam senātus ut cōnsul vidēret, nē quid rēs pūblica dētrīmentī caperet.—Cicero

31.2. Tē rogō atque ōrō ut eum juvēs.—Cicero

31.3. Exigis ut nostrōs dōnem tibi, Tucca, libellōs.

  Nōn faciam. Nam vīs vendere, nōn legere.—Martial

Vocabulary

31.1. dēcernō, dēcernere, dēcrēvī, dēcrētus: decree

  quondam (adv.): once, at one time

  cōnsul, cōnsulis, m.: consul (chief magistrate in Rome)

  rēs pūblica, reī pūblicae, f.: the state, republic

  dētrīmentum, dētrīmentī, n.: harm, detriment

31.3. exigō, exigere, exēgī, exāctus: demand, require

  dōnō, dōnāre, dōnāvī, dōnātus: give

  libellus, libellī, m.: small book, booklet

  vendō, vendere, vendidī, venditus: sell

Optional

31.4. Plautus Selection to Be Read after Lesson 31 (p. 365)

31.5. Here is an invitation to dinner with a humorous twist.

  Cēnābis *bene, mī Fabulle, *apud mē

  paucīs, sī tibi dī favent, diēbus,

  sī tēcum attuleris bonam atque magnam

  cēnam, nōn sine candidā puellā

  et vīnō et sale et omnibus cachinnīs.

  Haec sī, inquam, attuleris, venuste noster,

  cēnābis bene: nam tuī Catullī

  plēnus sacculus est arāneārum.

  Sed contrā accipiēs merōs amōrēs

  seu quid suāvius ēlegantiusve est:

  nam unguentum dabō, quod meae puellae

  dōnā'runt Venerēs Cupīdinēsque,

  quod tū cum olfaciēs, deōs rogābis,

  tōtum ut tē faciant, Fabulle, nāsum.—Catullus

31.6. Martial didn't mind accepting gifts but he did object to being reminded of it:

  Quae mihi praestiterīs *meminī semperque tenēbō.

    Cūr igitur *taceō? Postume, tū loqueris.

  Incipiō quotiēns alicui tua dōna *referre,

    prōtinus exclāmat: "Dīxerat ipse mihi."

  Nōn bellē quaedam faciunt duo: sufficit ūnus

    huic operī. Sī vīs ut loquar, ipse tacē.

  Crēde mihi, quamvīs ingentia, Postume, dōna

    auctōris pereunt garrulitāte suī.—Martial

31.7. Martial knew how to handle a free-loader:

> Exigis ut dōnem nostrōs tibi, Quīnte, libellōs.
> Nōn habeō, sed habet bybliopōla Tryphōn.
> "Aes dabō prō nūgīs et emam tua *carmina sānus?
> Nōn" inquis "faciam tam fatuē." Nec ego.—Martial

31.8. A good and honorable life:

> Hōrae quidem cēdunt et diēs et *mēnsēs et annī, nec praeteritum tempus umquam revertitur nec quid sequātur scīrī potest. Quod cuique temporis ad vīvendum datur, eō dēbet esse contentus. Breve enim tempus aetātis satis longum ad bene honestēque vīvendum.—Cicero

Word Study: English Derivatives

From Lesson	Latin	From Readings	Latin
1. current		1. detrimental	
2. exhortation		2. donate	
3. exit		3. exact	
4. imprecation		4. libel	
5. limited		5. oration	
6. median		6. pardon	
7. monitor		7. senior	
8. persuasion		8. vendor	

Summary Tasks

____ 1. Embed the three Basic Sentences of lesson 28 as indirect commands with *imperō* and then with *imperāvī*.

____ 2. Name the semantic notions which raise the expectation of an indirect command.

____ 3. Describe and contrast the characteristics of indirect statements, indirect questions, and indirect commands.

____ 4. Write the Latin for: They say that the boy is running; They say/tell why the boy is running; They say that the boy should run.

Lesson 32

Noun Result Clause: A Finite Noun Clause
Clause of Fearing: A Finite Noun Clause

This lesson introduces two more dependent noun clauses that, like the indirect command, have *ut* as clause marker and a verb in the subjunctive. These are the *noun result clause* and the *clause of fearing*. For the reader, semantic information about the governing verb is necessary in order to determine whether a particular noun clause with the marker *ut* expresses a command, a fear, or a result.

Caution: Any discussion of *ut* refers to both positive *ut* and "negative" *ut*, i.e., *nē* or *ut . . . nōn*.

Basic Sentences

32.1. Hīs rēbus fīēbat ut minus facile fīnitimīs bellum īnferre possent.—Caesar
    Because of this it happened that they could less easily make war on their neighbors.
32.2. Nē tē uxor sequātur, timēs.—Plautus
    You are afraid that your wife is following you.

Noun Result Clause: A Finite Noun Clause

A noun result clause can be recognized by the following features.

1. the clause marker *ut/utī*. *Nē* does *not* occur as a clause marker in noun result clauses. Instead there is a negator, such as *nōn*, within the *ut* clause.
2. a verb in the subjunctive
3. a governing verb or expression with the semantic notion "bring about," "happen," for example:

    efficiō (bring about) + noun clause as direct object
    fit (come about) + noun clause as subject
    accidit (happen) + noun clause as subject

The *ut* clause in S32.1 is a noun result clause patterning with *fīēbat*; it is the subject of the verb *fīēbat*. Here is a kernel chart for S32.1.

316

Clause Marker	Item: Function	Item: Function	Item: Function	Kernel Type	F/NF	M/D	Adj./Adv./ Noun	Name
	fīēbat: verb	ut . . . bellum īnferre possent: subj.	—	IA	F	M	—	statement
ut	bellum: dir. obj.	īnferre possent: verb	∅ = eī: subj.	TA	F	D	noun	noun result

Clause of Fearing: A Finite Noun Clause

A clause of fearing can be recognized by these features.

1. the clause marker *nē*, metaphrased "that," for something one fears *will* happen, and the clause marker *ut* or *nē nōn*, metaphrased "that . . . not" for something one fears *will not* happen
2. a verb in the subjunctive
3. a governing verb or expression with the general semantic notion "fear,"[1] for example:

   timeō (fear)
   metuō (fear)
   vereor (fear)
   metus est (there is fear)

The *nē* clause in S31.2 (*Nē tē uxor sequātur, timēs*) is a noun clause, object of the governing verb *timēs*. S32.2 is kernelized as follows.

Clause Marker	Item: Function	Item: Function	Item: Function	Kernel Type	F/NF	M/D	Adj./Adv./ Noun	Name
nē	tē: dir. obj.	uxor: subj.	sequātur: verb	TA	F	D	noun	cl. fear.
—	nē tē uxor sequātur: dir. obj.	timēs: verb	∅ = tū: subj.	TA	F	M	—	statement

S32.2, if rewritten with *ut* or *nē nōn* instead of *nē* as clause marker, would be translated "You are afraid that your wife is *not* following you."

---

1. There are various explanations as to why the clause markers *ut* and *nē* seem to be semantically reversed in clauses of fearing. D. Taylor proposes that verbs of fearing may be thought to have the semantic feature *negative*. In Latin, as in some other languages, two negatives cancel each other. Therefore, in practical terms, the negator *nē* cancels out the feature *negative* in the verb to produce a positive expression of what is feared. (From a paper read at the 1973 Kentucky Foreign Language Conference; published as "Verbs of 'Fearing' in Latin," *Classical Outlook* 61, no. 3 [March-April 1984]: 83–84.)

■ Exercise 1

Copy all kernels onto a kernel chart. Each sentence has an embedded noun clause, i.e., an indirect command, a noun result clause, or a clause of fearing.

1. Dux monuit ut hostēs ex urbe exīrent.
2. Dux timuit nē hostēs ex urbe exīrent.
3. Dux effēcit ut hostēs ex urbe exīrent.

Clause Marker	Item: Function	Item: Function	Item: Function	Kernel Type	F/NF	M/D	Adj./Adv./ Noun	Name
1.								
1.								
2.								
2.								
3.								
3.								

■ Exercise 2

Metaphrase the following in the structural context of a complete sentence. Look at the example.

Dux efficit ut: the leader brings it about that ____ ____s ± ____

1. Dux effēcit ut

2. Dux rogābat nē

3. Dux postulat ut

4. Dux monēbit ut

5. Dux timuerat nē

6. Accidit ut dux

7. Dux metuit ut

■ Exercise 3

Do not translate these sentences. Copy all kernels onto a kernel chart. Each sentence has an embedded clause.

1. Quid metuis? Metuō nē mihi damnum in Epidamnō faciās.—Plautus *Menaechmi* 267
2. Hunc[1] metuēbam nē meae uxōrī renūntiāret dē pallā et prandiō.—Ibid. 420[2]

Clause Marker	Item: Function	Item: Function	Item: Function	Kernel Type	F/NF	M/D	Adj./Adv./ Noun	Name
1.								
1.								
1.								
2.								
2.								

Lesson Vocabulary

Nouns

bellum, bellī, n.: war
fīnitimī, fīnitimōrum, m. pl.: neighbors
metus, metūs, m.: fear
uxor, uxōris, f.: wife

Verbs

accidō, accidere, accidī: happen
efficiō, efficere, effēcī, effectus: bring about
īnferō, īnferre, intulī, illātus: bring in, bring upon; *bellum īnferre:* make war on (+ dat.)
metuō, metuere, metuī: fear

Readings

Required

32.1. Eādem nocte accidit ut esset lūna plēna.—Caesar
32.2. Accidit ut ūnā nocte omnēs Hermae dējicerentur.—Nepos
(Hermae = statues of the god Hermes)
32.3. Rēgem ut in suā potestāte habēret, Caesar effēcit.—Caesar
32.4. Timeō nē malefacta mea sint inventa omnia.—Plautus
32.5. Metuō nē nōn sit surda.—Plautus

---

1. A verb of fearing, etc., can have a personal object in addition to the noun clause. Write both in one kernel column. See double accusatives in lesson 30.
2. *Ibid.* is an abbreviation for the Latin word *ibidem* (in the same place), and is used when the source is the same as that just cited.

Vocabulary

32.1. plēnus, plēna, plēnum: full
32.2. dējiciō, dējicere, dējēcī, dējectus: throw down
32.3. potestās, potestātis, f.: power, authority
32.4. malefactum, malefactī, n.: wrongdoing, misdeed
32.5. surdus, surda, surdum: deaf; unheeding

Optional

32.6. Plautus Selection to Be Read after Lesson 32 (p. 367)
32.7. Hīs erat rēbus effectum ut (mīlitēs) equitum impetum *sustinēre audērent neque magnopere eōrum multitūdine terrerentur.—Caesar
32.8. Metuō, illa mihi rēs nē malō magnō sit.—Plautus
32.9. Metuō nē morbus aggravēscat.—Terence
32.10. In Plautus' play *Amphitryon* the slave Sosia is afraid he might be the fifth man to be knocked out by the god Mercury, who boasts of his having "put to sleep" four men. *Quintus*, the Latin word for "fifth," is a common name in Rome.

Formīdō male

nē ego hīc nōmen meum commūtem et Quīntus fīam ē Sōsiā.
quattuor virōs somnō sē dedisse hic dīcit:
metuō nē numerum augeam illum.

Word Study: English Derivatives

From Lesson	Latin	From Readings	Latin
1. accident		1. absurd	
2. bellicose		2. dejected	
3. effect		3. incident	
4. facility		4. inventor	
5. inference		5. lunacy	
6. minister		6. malefactor	
7. sequence		7. replenish	

Summary Tasks

___ 1. Underline all clause markers and bracket the dependent clauses in the Eutropius Section, "Battle of Cannae" in the back of the book (p. 374).
___ 2. Write a synopsis, indicative and subjunctive, active and passive of *agō*, in the third person singular.
___ 3. Review and be able to explain all infinitive constructions in lessons 21 through 24.
___ 4. Name all the kinds of noun clauses, finite and non-finite, that have occurred in this course.

Review Lesson 10

Lesson Vocabulary

Nouns
bellum, bellī, n.: war
fīnitimī, fīnitimōrum, m. pl.: neighbors
Helvētiī, Helvētiōrum, m. pl.: Helvetians
līmes, līmitis, m.: track, course
metus, metūs, m.: fear
Orgetorīx, Orgetorīgis, m.: Orgetorix
uxor, uxōris, f.: wife

Pronouns
aliquis, aliquid: someone, something
quisquam, quaequam, quicquam (or quidquam): anyone, anything

Adjective
medius, media, medium: middle, middle of

Indeclinable
Subordinating Conjunction
nē (as clause marker): indicates negative dependent clause

Verbs
accidō, accidere, accidī: happen
cēnseō, cēnsēre, cēnsuī, cēnsus: propose
cōnstituō, cōnstituere, cōnstituī, cōnstitūtus: decide; set up
efficiō, efficere, effēcī, effectus: bring about
exeō, exīre, exiī (exīvī), exitūrus: leave, go out
hortor, hortārī, hortātus: encourage, urge
imperō, imperāre, imperāvī, imperātus: order, command, impose
īnferō, īnferre, intulī, illātus: bring in, bring upon; *bellum īnferre:* make war on (+ dat.)
metuō, metuere, metuī: fear
permittō, permittere, permīsī, permissus: allow, permit
persuādeō, persuādēre, persuāsī, persuāsūrus: persuade, convince
precor, precārī, precātus: pray, entreat
sinō, sinere, sīvī, situs: allow
statuō, statuere, statuī, statūtus: decide, determine; set up
suādeō, suādēre, suāsī, suāsūrus: persuade, convince

Readings Vocabulary

apud (prep. + acc.): in the presence of, among
bene (adv.): well
carmen, carminis, n.: song, poem
meminī, meminisse: remember
mēnsis, mēnsis, m.: month
referō, referre, rettulī, relātus: carry back, bring back
sustineō, sustinēre, sustinuī, sustentus: hold up, endure
taceō, tacēre, tacuī, tacitus: be silent

Morphology Review

New Morphology: Lessons 31 and 32

no new forms

Form Identification

    a. fīnis, fīnis, m.: end, goal; boundary
    b. fīnitimī, fīnitimōrum, m. pl.: neighbors
    c. fīniō, fīnīre, fīnīvī, fīnītus: put an end to, finish

1. fīniam _____
2. fīnēs _____
3. fīnitimīs _____
4. fīnīrēs _____
5. fīnīverīs _____
6. fīnītī _____
7. fīnītum esse _____
8. fīnitimī _____
9. fīnīrēminī _____
10. fīnium _____

■ Exercise: English to Latin Sentences
Using the Latin sentences as models, translate the following English sentences into Latin.

1. Mediō ut līmite currās moneō. (S31.1)
2. Orgetorīx Helvētiīs persuāsit ut dē fīnibus suīs exīrent. (S31.2)
3. Hīs rēbus fīēbat ut minus facile fīnitimīs bellum īnferre possent. (S32.1)
4. Nē tē uxor sequātur, timēs. (S32.2)

a. The father warned the woman not to observe what her husband was doing. (1)

b. The woman and her father order the brother to flee. (2)

c. It happened that the slave brought help to the husband. (3)

d. The brother is afraid that he is being caught by the slaves. (4)

Vocabulary

Nouns

brother: frāter
father: pater
help: auxilium
husband: vir
slave: servus
woman: fēmina

Verbs

be afraid: metuō
bring: īnferō
catch: capiō
do: agō
flee: fugiō
happen: accidō; fīō
observe: observō, observāre
order: imperō
warn: moneō

Indeclinables

by: ā/ab (prep. + abl.)
not: nōn (adv.)

Question Word

what: quis, quid

Stem List

Enter the following words into the Stem List found in the back of this book. Also list dictionary entries for the words entered.

1. accidit
2. cēnseō
3. cōnstituit
4. effēcit
5. exīrent
6. īnferre
7. metuō
8. metus
9. permittō
10. possent
11. statuō

Lesson 33

Adverbial Clauses
Clause of Result: An Adverbial Clause
Clause of Purpose: An Adverbial Clause
Relative Clause with Verb in the Subjunctive

By now it is no doubt apparent that proficiency in recognizing dependent clauses either as noun clauses or as modifiers is necessary for reading Latin. The three previous lessons have dealt with noun clauses. This lesson and the next will reexamine dependent clauses that are adjectival and adverbial modifiers. Such clauses have occurred with a verb in the indicative since lessons 11 and 12, but they also occur with a verb in the subjunctive. It will turn out that the mood of the dependent verb must be taken into account for the semantic interpretation of these clauses.

This lesson examines two adverbial clauses with the clause marker *ut: clauses of result* and *clauses of purpose*. It also examines relative clauses with a verb in the subjunctive mood.

Basic Sentences

33.1. Tanta vīs[1] probitātis est, ut eam in hoste etiam dīligāmus.—Cicero
   So great is the power of honesty that we esteem it even in an enemy.
33.2. Nōn ut edam vīvō, sed ut vīvam edō.—Quintilian
   I do not live to eat, but I eat to live.

Note
1. *Vīs* is an irregular noun that has no form surviving for the genitive or dative singular. The accusative singular is *vim;* the ablative singular is *vī.* It has a regular plural: *vīrēs, vīrēs, vīribus, vīribus, vīrium.*

Adverbial Clauses

If an *ut* clause is not part of the governing clause, i.e., if the governing kernel is complete without it, it is not a noun clause but an adverbial clause. Lesson 11 introduced two semantic categories for adverbial *ut* clauses, *comparison* and *temporal*. The dependent verb in these two clauses is usually indicative. Accordingly, in exercise 3 of lesson 11 *ut fortūna* was metaphrased "as fortune ＿＿＿s" and "when fortune ＿＿＿s."

Two other categories expressed by adverbial *ut* clauses are *result* and *purpose*. The verb of the clause is in the subjunctive.

Clause of Result: An Adverbial Clause

The *ut* clause in S33.1 (*ut eam in hoste etiam dīligāmus*) expresses result. The reader may expect a clause of this category if the governing clause contains a signal word that has the semantic notion "so" or "such." These signal words include:

adeō (to such a degree)
ita (thus, so)
tālis, tāle (such)
tam (so)
tantus, tanta, tantum (so great)
tot (so many)
totiēns (so often)

The signal word in the main clause of S33.1 (*Tanta vīs probitātis est*) is *tanta*. This word raises the expectation of a clause that will answer the question *quanta*? "*how great* is the power of honesty?"

Nē does not occur as a clause marker in clauses of result. Instead there is a negator such as *nōn* or *numquam* within the *ut* clause.

Metaphrasing

Ut as clause marker of a result clause is always metaphrased "that." The subjunctive verb is most often metaphrased as if it were indicative.

■ Exercise 1
Write a final metaphrase of each of the following. Assume that the *ut* clause is a clause of result. Look at the example.

Tot hominēs adsunt ut: There are so many people that _____ _____s ± _____ .

1. Puella tam celeriter currit ut

2. Totiēns urbem adjūvistī ut

3. Tanta est urbs ut

4. Tālem sapientiam tenētis ut

5. Pater adeō contendit ut

Clause of Purpose: An Adverbial Clause

The *ut* clauses in S33.2 (*ut edam* and *ut vīvam*) both express purpose. They answer the question *quō cōnsiliō*? (for what purpose [does somebody do something]?) There is no special signal outside the *ut* clause to raise the expectation that an expression of purpose will occur. This is so although, or perhaps because, any activity has a purpose—but this purpose may or may not be expressed.

Nē is the clause marker for a negative purpose clause.

Metaphrasing

Ut as clause marker of a purpose clause is metaphrased "in order that," followed by a finite verb (e.g., S33.2 "I eat *in order that I may live.*"). Back-shift applies in Latin and English after a verb expressing past time. English commonly expresses purpose also by an infinitive, e.g., "we eat *to live,*" or "we eat *in order to live.*"

The negative clause marker *nē* can be metaphrased "in order that <u>(subject)</u> not _____ ± _____ ."

■ Exercise 2

Copy all the kernels from the following sentences onto a kernel chart.

1. Ut discessī ā tē, vīdī amīcōs.
2. Numquam imperātor ita pācī crēdit ut nōn sē paret bellō.
3. Eāmus ut edāmus.

Clause Marker	Item: Function	Item: Function	Item: Function	Kernel Type	F/NF	M/D	Adj./Adv./ Noun	Name
1.								
1.								
2.								
2.								
3.								
3.								

■ Exercise 3

These sentences contain adverbial *ut* clauses with four different semantic categories. Name them and translate each sentence.

1. Omne parātum est ut jussistī atque ut voluistī.

2. Eāmus ut edāmus.

3. Numquam imperātor ita pācī crēdit ut nōn sē paret bellō. (See R33.5.)

4. Haec rēs est ut nārrō tibi.

5. Ut discessī ā tē, vīdī amīcōs.

Relative Clause with Verb in the Subjunctive

Most relative clauses with a verb in the subjunctive differ in meaning from the same clause with a verb in the indicative. A relative clause in the subjunctive may have the same semantic categories as other clauses in the subjunctive (e.g., purpose, characteristic, cause, possibility, etc.). Study these examples and read the discussion regarding two of them: *relative clauses of purpose* and *relative clauses of characteristic*.

> Rōmulus lēgātōs circā vīcīnās gentēs mīsit quī societātem cōnūbiumque novō populō peterent.—Livy
>> Romulus sent envoys around the neighboring tribes who should/were to ask for an alliance and the right of intermarriage for the new people.
> At sunt quī dīcant. . . .—Cicero
>> But there are some who might say that. . . .

In the first sentence the subjunctive *peterent* in the relative clause presents the purpose of Romulus in sending envoys. The same clause with a verb in the indicative would express a simple fact: "Romulus sent envoys who asked. . . ." In the second sentence the subjunctive verb in the relative clause indicates that the clause is describing a characteristic rather than stating an actual fact. This clause is an indefinite relative clause since there is no antecedent.

As the Latin language became "classical," the subjunctive in certain relative clauses became the rule, with the result that it no longer contrasted with the indicative. Nevertheless in most circumstances there is a contrast, and the subjunctive must be carefully considered.[1]

■ Exercise 4
Write a translation of each of the following contrasting sentences.

1. Mittit lēgātōs quī auxilium offerunt.

2. Mittit lēgātōs quī auxilium offerant.

3. Mīsit lēgātōs quī auxilium offerēbant.

4. Mīsit lēgātōs quī auxilium offerrent.

Lesson Vocabulary

Nouns
probitās, probitātis, f.: honesty
vīs (gen. and dat. sing. not in use), pl. vīrēs, vīrium, f.: force, violence; power

Indeclinable
Adverb
adeō: to such a degree

Verbs
dīligō, dīligere, dīlēxī, dīlēctus: choose; esteem, value, honor
edō, edere, ēdī, ēsus: eat

---

1. In indirect speech (ōrātiō oblīqua) all finite verbs are automatically in the subjunctive. Therefore it is sometimes not possible to determine the exact significance of the subjunctive.

Readings

Required

33.1. Ūnī nāvī nē committās omnia.—Anon.

33.2. Lēgum servī sumus ut līberī esse possīmus.—Cicero

33.3. Edās, bibās ut bene vīvās; nē vīvās ut tantum edās et bibās.—Medieval

33.4. Dīcere . . . solēbat nūllum esse librum tam malum ut nōn aliquā parte prōdesset.—Pliny the Younger

33.5. Numquam imperātor ita pācī crēdit ut nōn sē praeparet bellō.—Seneca

33.6. Est quidem haec nātūra mortālium ut nihil magis placeat quam quod āmissum est.—Seneca

33.7. Quis homō est quī dīcat mē dīxisse istud?—Plautus

33.8. Nūllum est iam dictum quod nōn sit dictum prius.—Terence

33.9. Ego is sum, quī nihil umquam meā magis quam meōrum cīvium causā fēcerim.—Cicero

33.10. Nōn tū is es quī quid sīs nesciās.—Cicero

Vocabulary

33.1.   committō, committere, commīsī, commissus: entrust, commit

33.3.   *bibō, bibere, bibī: drink

33.4.   liber, librī, m.: book
pars, partis, f.: part
prōsum, prōdesse, prōfuī: be useful, be helpful

33.5.   imperātor, imperātōris, m.: commander, general
pāx, pācis, f.: peace
praeparō, praeparāre, praeparāvī, praeparātus: prepare, get ready

33.6.   *mortālis, mortāle: mortal

33.8.   prius (adv.): before, earlier

33.9.   cīvis, cīvis, m. & f.: citizen, fellow citizen

33.10. nesciō, nescīre, nescīvī: not know

Optional

33.11. Plautus Selection to Be Read after Lesson 33 (p. 368)

33.12. Inventa sunt specula ut homō ipse sē *nō'sset.—Seneca

33.13. The verb *agō* is used with many different objects. Martial exploits this for humorous effect.

> Semper agis causās, et rēs agis, Attale, semper;
> > est, nōn est quod agās, Attale, semper agis.
> Sī rēs et causae dēsunt, agis, Attale, mūlās.
> > Attale, nē quod agās dēsit, agās animam.—Martial 1.79

33.14. Then, as now, poets exchanged their work:

> Cūr nōn mittō meōs tibi, Pontiliāne, libellōs?
> > Nē mihi tū mittās, Pontiliāne, tuōs.—Martial 7.3

33.15. This poem has the same point as the one addressed to Pontilianus that precedes.

> Nōn *dōnem tibi cūr meōs *libellōs
> ōrantī totiēns et exigentī
> mīrāris, Theodōre? Magna causa est:
> dōnēs tū mihi nē tuōs libellōs.—Martial 5.73

33.16. The Path to a Happy Life

The Roman author Juvenal wrote satires in which he attacked the vices of his time. The lines below are from a famous satire, often imitated, especially by Dr. Samuel Johnson in his "Vanity of Human Wishes."

> Ōrandum est[1] ut sit mēns sāna in corpore sānō.
> Fortem posce animum, mortis terrōre carentem,
> quī spatium[2] vītae extrēmum[2] inter mūnera pōnat
> nātūrae, quī ferre queat quōscumque[3] labōrēs,
> nesciat[4] īrāscī, cupiat[4] nihil et potiōrēs
> Herculis aerumnās crēdat[4] *saevōsque labōrēs
> et Venere[5] et cēnīs et plūmā[6] Sardanapallī.[7]
> Mōnstro quod ipse tibi possīs dare. Sēmita certē
> tranquillae per virtūtem patet ūnica vītae.—Juvenal *Satire X*

Notes

1. Ōrandum est: "one should pray"
2. spatium . . . extrēmum: "the end of life"
3. quōscumque labōrēs: "any labors whatsoever"
4. There are five *quī* clauses, but the *quī* is not repeated.
5. Venere: the goddess Venus; here "love"
6. plūma: feather, translate "soft (downy) couch"
7. Sardanapallus: a king of Assyria, noted for his love of luxury

Word Study: English Derivatives

From Lesson	Latin	From Readings	Latin
1. diligence		1. credit	
2. edible		2. emperor	
3. probable		3. imbibe	
4. prove		4. imperative	
5. tantamount		5. navigate	
6. violence		6. placid	

Summary Tasks

—— 1. Copy from the Required Readings all nouns that are ambiguous in form.

—— 2. Copy each noun-adjective pair from Optional Reading 33.16 in the order in which the items occur.

—— 3. Write a cumulative metaphrase of Reading 33.2.

—— 4. Label the relative clauses in the Required Readings as adjectival or noun clauses.

Lesson 34

More Adverbial Clauses

Adverbial modifiers, whether adverbs, prepositional phrases, adverbial noun phrases, or adverbial clauses, express a variety of semantic relationships with other units within the sentence. The following semantic categories for adverbial clauses were first introduced in lessons 11 and 33:

time, cause, comparison, condition, place, purpose, and result.

Three additional semantic categories of clauses occur in this lesson. They are:

circumstance, concession, and *proviso.*

As stated in the introduction of lesson 33, the mood of the verb in these dependent clauses must be taken into account for the semantic interpretation of the clauses.

There will now be new clause markers as well as additional meanings for old clause markers. The following sections examine clauses with the markers *cum, dum,* and *sī.* A chart will provide information about other clause markers.

Basic Sentences

34.1. Caesarī cum id nūntiātum esset, mātūrāvit ab urbe proficīscī.—Caesar
    Since/because/when this had been announced to Caesar, he hastened to set out from the city.

34.2. Cum prīmī ōrdinēs hostium concidissent, tamen ācerrimē reliquī resistēbant.—Caesar
    Although the first ranks of the enemy had fallen, the rest nevertheless continued to resist most vigorously.

34.3. Multa quoque et bellō passus (est), dum conderet urbem.—Vergil
    And he (Aeneas) also suffered much in war, until he could found the city (of Rome).

34.4. Ōderint,[1] dum metuant.—Accius (a favorite motto of the emperor Caligula)
    Let them hate me, provided that they fear me.

34.5. Magis valērem, sī hīc manērēs.—Plautus
    I would be better off, if you were staying here.

34.6. Sī vēnissēs ad exercitum, ā tribūnīs mīlitāribus vīsus essēs; nōn es autem ab hīs vīsus; nōn igitur profectus es ad exercitum.—Cicero
    If you had come to the army, you would have been seen by the military tribunes; yet you were not seen by them; therefore you did not come to the army.

Note

1. *Ōderint* comes from the defective verb *ōdī*, which has only perfective forms. *Ōderint* is thus equivalent to the present imperfective subjunctive. Verbs which have only the perfective forms are few in number, but occur frequently, e.g., *coepī, coepisse* (begin), *meminī, meminisse* (remember), *novī, novisse* (know).

More Adverbial Clauses

Cum Clauses

The clause marker *cum* indicates either a clause of *time* (when), *circumstance* (when), *cause* (since, because), or *concession* (although). A clause of time is signaled by a verb in the indicative (see lesson 11); the others are signaled by a verb in the subjunctive. It is not always possible, and sometimes not even necessary, to select one meaning over another as, e.g., in S34.1. However, the presence of the word *tamen* (nevertheless) in the main clause, as in S34.2, indicates that a *cum* clause is one of concession.

Dum Clauses

The clause marker *dum* indicates either a clause of *time* (while); a clause of *time* with the added idea of *anticipation* (until), e.g., S34.3; or a clause of *proviso* (provided that, if only), e.g., S34.4. As with *cum*, a clause expressing only time is signaled by a verb in the indicative and the others by a verb in the subjunctive. A proviso clause is indicated also by the clause marker *dummodo*.

■ Exercise 1
Metaphrase the following in the context of a complete sentence. Follow the example.

Dum loquimur: While we are speaking, _____ _____ s ± _____ .

1. Cum timeāmus, tamen
2. Cum timeāmus,
3. Cum timeāmus,
4. Cum timēmus,
5. Dum metuunt,
6. Dum metuant,
7. Dum metuant,
8. Dummodo metuant,

Conditions or *Sī* Clauses

The clause markers *sī* (if), *sī nōn* (if not), *nisi* (unless), and *etsī* (even if) indicate a conditional clause. Such a clause usually forms a rather tight unit with the main clause and together they are spoken of as a *conditional sentence*. The main clause may be a statement, question, or command, and is usually called a *conditional statement/question/command* in contrast to the *conditional clause*, i.e., the *sī* clause. The verbs in conditional sentences are indicative or subjunctive. The subjunctive adds information about the "degree of probability" of the conditional sentence. Often the verb of the main clause and of the *sī* clause are in the same mood and tense.

A *sī* clause with the verb in the indicative, in any tense, presents a condition as open, and implies nothing about its probability. It is often called a *simple condition*. For example,

> Sī amīcus hoc legit, multa discit. (If my friend is reading this, he is learning many things.)

In contrast, a *sī* clause with the verb in the subjunctive is a hypothetical condition. The Latin language expresses two types. One is the *potential condition,* which implies *possibility* for the condition. The verb in the subjunctive is present imperfective (or, less often, present perfective). This is often called the *should-would* condition. For example,

> Sī amīcus id legat, multa discat. (If my friend should [and he may] read this, he would learn many things.)

The other is the *contrary-to-fact condition,* which implies the *impossibility* of the condition. The verb in the subjunctive is past imperfective (S34.5) or past perfective (S35.6). A past *imperfective* subjunctive indicates a condition that is in effect *now*, i.e., *at the time of speaking*. For example,

> Sī amīcus hoc legeret, multa disceret. (If my friend were reading this [but he isn't], he would be learning many things.)

A past *perfective* subjunctive indicates a condition that was in effect *before the time of speaking*. For example,

> Sī amīcus hoc lēgisset, multa didicisset. (If my friend had read this [but he has not], he would have learned many things.)

It is not easy to offer suggestions for "safe" metaphrasing of conditional sentences because present-day American English does not always use verb morphology to signal different kinds of conditions.

■ Exercise 2
From the English sentences provided, copy a translation for each Latin sentence.

1. Sī veniātis, gaudeam.

2. Sī venītis, gaudeō.

3. Sī venīrētis, gaudērem.

4. Sī vēnissētis, gāvīsus essem.

  a. If you are coming, I rejoice.
  b. If you were coming (but you aren't), I would be rejoicing.
  c. If you had come, I would have rejoiced.
  d. If you should come, I would rejoice.

■ Exercise 3

Rewrite the simple conditional sentences as potential and as contrary-to-fact sentences. Give a final metaphrase of each.

1. Simple condition: Sī vulpēs mūneribus capitur, stulta est.

                                    If the fox is caught by gifts, she is stupid.

   Potential condition:

   Contrary-to-fact condition
   (indicating current time):

2. Simple condition: Respondēbō,[1] sī scrībēs.

                                      If you will write, I will answer.

   Potential condition:

   Contrary-to-fact condition
   (indicating earlier time):

Note

1. respondeō, respondēre, respondī

Summary of Adverbial Clause Markers

The following chart presents summary information about adverbial clause markers.

Subordinating Conjunction	Dependent Clause		English Equivalent of Clause Marker
	Mood of Verb	Semantic Category	
antequam/priusquam	indicative	time	before (i.e., before they did _____)
antequam/priusquam	subjunctive	time + anticipation*	before (i.e., before they could _____)
cum	indicative	time	when/whenever
cum	subjunctive	circumstance	when
cum	subjunctive	cause	since, because
cum	subjunctive	concessive	although
dum/dōnec	indicative	time	while/as long as
dum/dummodo	subjunctive	proviso	if only
dum/quoad	subjunctive	time + anticipation*	until/as long as
postquam	indicative	time	after
quamquam/etsī	indicative	concession	although
quamvīs	subjunctive	concession	although
quasi	indicative	comparison	as if
quasi	subjunctive	comparison + anticipation*	as if

*These subjunctives add the extra notion of probability and/or anticipation.

Dependent Clause			English Equivalent
Subordinating Conjunction	Mood of Verb	Semantic Category	of Clause Marker
quia/quod/quoniam	indicative	cause	because
quotiēns	indicative	comparison	as often as
quotiēns	subjunctive	comparison + anticipation*	as often as
sī (nisi, nī, sīn, sīve . . . sīve)	indicative	condition	if (if not, unless, but if, whether . . . or)
	subjunctive	condition + probability*	if (if not, unless, but if, whether . . . or)
simul ac, atque	indicative	time	as soon as
ubi	indicative	time	when, as soon as
ubi	indicative	place	where
ut	indicative	time	when, as
ut	indicative	comparison	as
ut/nē	subjunctive	purpose	in order that (. . . not)
ut/ut nōn	subjunctive	result	that (. . . not)

*These subjunctives add the extra notion of probability and/or anticipation.

Lesson Vocabulary

Nouns
ōrdō, ōrdinis, m.: order, rank, class
tribūnus, tribūnī, m.: tribune

Adjectives
ācer, ācris, ācre: sharp
mīlitāris, mīlitāre: military
prīmus, prīma, prīmum: first
reliquus, reliqua, reliquum: remaining,
   the other

Indeclinables
Adverbs
hīc: here, in this place
quoque: also
tamen: nevertheless

Subordinating Conjunctions
antequam: before
dōnec: while, as long as
dummodo: provided that
etsī: even if, although
nī: if not
priusquam: before

quamquam: although
quamvīs: although
quasi: as if
quoad: until, as long as
quoniam: since
simul ac: as soon as
sīn: but if
sīve: or if
sīve . . . sīve: whether . . . or

Sentence Connectors
autem: however; moreover
igitur: therefore

Verbs
concidō, concidere, concidī: fall, collapse
mātūrō, mātūrāre, mātūrāvī: hurry, hasten
nūntiō, nūntiāre, nūntiāvī, nūntiātus:
   announce
ōdī, ōdisse: hate, dislike
proficīscor, proficīscī, profectus: set out,
   start
valeō, valēre, valuī, valitūrus: be strong,
   be effective, prevail

Readings

Required

34.1. Sī tacuissēs, philosophus mānsissēs.—Boethius

34.2. Rūsticus exspectat dum dēfluat amnis.—Horace

34.3. Ut spatium intercēdere posset dum mīlitēs . . . convenīrent, lēgātīs respondit diem sē ad dēlīberandum sumptūrum.—Caesar

34.4. Sī foret (= esset) in terrīs, rīdēret Dēmocritus.—Horace

34.5. Dummodo sit dīves, barbarus ipse placet.—Ovid

34.6. Haec cum animadvertisset, convocātō cōnciliō, vehementer eōs incūsāvit.—Caesar

Vocabulary

34.1. philosophus, philosophī, m.: philosopher

34.2. rūsticus, rūstica, rūsticum: unsophisticated, rustic
 amnis, amnis, m.: river

34.3. spatium, spatiī, n.: space (of time)
 intercēdō, intercēdere, intercessī: intervene
 conveniō, convenīre, convēnī: come together, convene
 lēgātus, lēgātī, m.: legate, envoy
 *respondeō, respondēre, respondī, respōnsus: answer
 dēlīberō, dēlīberāre, dēlīberāvī, dēlīberātus: deliberate
 sūmō, sūmere, sūmpsī, sūmptus: take

34.4. *terra, terrae, f.: land, earth

34.5. barbarus, barbara, barbarum: barbarian (person)

34.6. animadvertō, animadvertere, animadvertī, animadversus: notice
 convocō, convocāre, convocāvī, convocātus: call together
 concilium, conciliī, n.: council, meeting, assembly
 vehementer (adv.): violently, vehemently
 incūsō, incūsāre, incūsāvī, incūsātus: reproach

Optional

34.7. Plautus Selection No. 1 to Be Read after Lesson 34 (p. 369)

34.8. Plautus Selection No. 2 to Be Read after Lesson 34 (p. 370)

Word Study: English Derivatives

From Lesson	Latin	From Readings	Latin
1. convention		1. assume	
2. enunciate		2. council	
3. extraordinary		3. fluid	
4. odious		4. intercede	
5. passive		5. responsible	
6. permanent		6. spacious	
7. prevail		7. terrace	

Summary Tasks

____ 1. Name all dependent clauses that can be introduced by *ut* and describe their characteristics.

____ 2. Name the semantic categories of each dependent clause in the Readings.

____ 3. Write the Latin for: If I were strong (*valeō*), I would be brave; If I had been strong, I would have been brave.

____ 4. Write a complete synopsis of *īnferō* in the third person plural.

Review Lesson 11

Lesson Vocabulary

Nouns
ōrdō, ōrdinis, m.: order, rank, class
probitās, probitātis, f.: honesty
tribūnus, tribūnī, m.: tribune
vīs (gen. and dat. sing. not in use), pl. vīrēs,
    vīrium, f.: force, violence; power

Adjectives
ācer, ācris, ācre: sharp
mīlitāris, mīlitāre: military
prīmus, prīma, prīmum: first
reliquus, reliqua, reliquum: the rest,
    the other(s)

Indeclinables
Adverbs
adeō: to such a degree
hīc: here, in this place
quoque: also
tamen: nevertheless

Subordinating Conjunctions
antequam: before
dōnec: while, as long as
dummodo: provided that
etsī: even if, although
nī: if not
priusquam: before

quamquam: although
quamvīs: although
quasi: as if
quoad: until, as long as
quoniam: since
simul ac: as soon as
sīn: but if
sīve: or if
sīve . . . sīve: whether . . . or

Sentence Connectors
autem: however; moreover
igitur: therefore
tamen: nevertheless

Verbs
concidō, concidere, concidī: fall, collapse
dīligō, dīligere, dīlēxī, dīlēctus:
    choose; esteem, value, honor
edō, edere, ēdī, ēsus: eat
mātūrō, mātūrāre, mātūrāvī: hurry, hasten
nūntiō, nūntiāre, nūntiāvī, nūntiātus:
    announce
ōdī, ōdisse: hate, dislike
proficīscor, proficīscī, profectus: set out,
    start
valeō, valēre, valuī, valitūrus: be strong,
    be effective, prevail

Readings Vocabulary

bibō, bibere, bibī: drink
dōnō, dōnāre, dōnāvī, dōnātus: give
libellus, libellī, m.: small book, booklet
mortālis, mortāle: mortal, human
nōvī, nōvisse, nōtus: know

respondeō, respondēre, respondī,
    respōnsus: answer
saevus, saeva, saevum: fierce
terra, terrae, f.: land, earth

Morphology Review

New Morphology: Lessons 33 and 34

no new forms

Form Identification

  a. probitās, probitātis, f.: honesty
  b. probō, probāre, probāvī, probātus: approve, commend
  c. probus, proba, probum: good, honest
  d. probātiō, probātiōnis, f.: approval

1. probābam _____

2. probātī essent _____

3. probitāte _____

4. probāvissem _____

5. probitātem _____

6. probōrum _____

7. probātiōnum _____

8. probārī _____

9. probātīs _____

10. probāvērunt _____

■ Exercise: English to Latin Sentences
Using the Latin sentences as models, translate the English sentences that follow into Latin.

1. Nōn ut edam vīvō, sed ut vīvam edō. (S33.2)
2. Multa quoque et bellō passus Ø=est dum conderet urbem. (S34.3)
3. Sī vēnissēs ad exercitum, ā tribūnīs mīlitāribus vīsus essēs; nōn es autem ab hīs vīsus; nōn igitur profectus es ad exercitum. (S34.6)

  a. We observe ourselves in order to understand others; we observe others in order to understand ourselves. (1)

  b. The slave suffered much until he could recognize the husband. (2)

  c. If the husband had not been living, the brother would not have found him; but the brother did find him; therefore the husband was living. (3)

Vocabulary

Nouns
brother: frāter
husband: vir
slave: servus

Pronouns
him: is
ourselves: nōs

Adjectives
much, many: multus
others: cēterī

Indeclinables
but: at (sentence connector)
however: autem (sentence connector)
therefore: ergō (sentence connector)

Subordinating Conjunctions
if: sī
until: dum

Verbs
find: inveniō
live: vīvō
observe: observō, observāre
recognize: cognōscō
suffer: patior
understand: intellegō, intellegere

Stem List

Enter the following words in the Stem List found in the back of this book. Also give dictionary listings for each word entered.

1. acerrimē
2. concidissent
3. dīligāmus
4. manērēs
5. passus

6. reliquī
7. valērem
8. vēnissēs
9. vī
10. vīsus

Lesson 35

The Gerundive and Future Passive Periphrastic
The Impersonal Passive Kernel

The topics named in the title of this lesson have been tirelessly researched and discussed by famous ancient and modern grammarians. No definitive theory explaining their development and nature has yet been put forward. Therefore, the information presented in this lesson has been selected and organized only for the practical needs of readers.

The Gerundive and Future Passive Periphrastic

Basic Sentences

35.1. In voluptāte spernendā et repudiandā virtūs vel maximē cernitur.—Cicero
   Virtue is certainly most clearly distinguished in casting aside or denying pleasure.

35.2. Sapientia ars vīvendī putanda est.—Caesar
   Wisdom should be considered the art of living.

35.3. Caesarī omnia ūnō tempore erant agenda.—Caesar
   All things had to be done by Caesar at the same time.

Morphology: The Future Passive Participle

In addition to the three participles—imperfective active, future active, perfective passive—Latin verbs have a form with the characteristic morpheme {nd} added to the imperfective stem and with the -us, -a, -um set of endings. This is commonly called the future passive participle.

	Masculine	Feminine	Neuter
Singular			
Nominative	agendus	agenda	agendum
Accusative	agendum	agendam	agendum
Ablative	agendō	agendā	agendō
Dative	agendō	agendae	agendō
Genitive	agendī	agendae	agendī
Plural			
Nominative	agendī	agendae	agenda
Accusative	agendōs	agendās	agenda
Ablative	agendīs	agendīs	agendīs
Dative	agendīs	agendīs	agendīs
Genitive	agendōrum	agendārum	agendōrum

The future passive participle occurs in both constructions introduced in this lesson.

340

■ Exercise 1

Underline those items that could be *gerunds* (see lesson 22). Then circle the words that could be *future passive participles*. (Some of these are also gerunds.)

1. agendus

2. agenda

3. agendī

4. agentī

5. agendae

6. agendō

7. agentēs

8. agendā

9. agendam

10. agentem

The Gerundive

One of the constructions in which the *-nd-* participle occurs is the *gerundive* construction. Like all participial constructions, this consists of a noun-head and the participle. Readers will meet this construction most often in the ablative or genitive case, or in the accusative with the preposition *ad*.

The literal English equivalent for a gerundive construction sounds rather awkward. For example, in S35.1, *in voluptāte spernendā* would be "in pleasure to be spurned." Therefore, it is practical to translate the gerundive as if it were a gerund and to treat its noun-head as the direct object of the "_____-ing" word, e.g., *in voluptāte spernendā* "in spurning pleasure."

The preposition *ad* plus the accusative of a gerundive phrase or *causā* after the genitive express purpose, just as the gerund phrase does, e.g., *ad pācem petendam* or *pācis petendae causā* "for (the purpose of) seeking peace."

■ Exercise 2

Draw an arrow from each gerundive to its noun-head. Caution: some of these *-nd-* items are gerunds. (Some of the vocabulary is unfamiliar.)

1. inter rēs agendās

2. tempora frūctibus percipiendīs accommodāta

3. ob absolvendum accipere pecūniam

4. dē contemnendā morte liber

5. prō līberandā amīcā

6. loquendī ēlegantia augētur legendīs ōrātōribus et poētīs

7. cupiditās bellī gerendī

8. cupidōs videndī urbem

9. cupidōs videndae urbis

10. ad urbem condendam

■ Exercise 3

First give the literal English equivalent of each gerundive construction. Then write a translation that is practical. Follow the example.

ad pācem petendam
a. for (the purpose of) peace to be sought
b. for seeking peace

1. studium reī pūblicae līberandae

   a.

   b.

2. timor bellī gerendī

   a.

   b.

3. ad urbem videndam

   a.

   b.

4. pecūniae accipiendae causā

   a.

   b.

The Future Passive Periphrastic

Just as there are periphrastic verb forms consisting of the perfective passive participle combined with forms of *esse* (e.g., *ācta sunt* and *ācta esse*), so also are there combinations of the *-nd-* participle and forms of *esse*, e.g., *agenda sunt* and *agenda esse*. (Forms of *sum, esse* are often omitted.) This particular combination is traditionally called the *future passive periphrastic*. In classical Latin the future passive periphrastic is the usual way of expressing *obligation*. In S35.2, *putanda est* is translated "should be considered." There are several alternative ways of expressing this idea in English. Thus *putanda est* might also be translated "has to be considered" or "is to be considered."

In S35.3, the verb *erant agenda* is in the past imperfective tense. The options for translating *erant agenda* are "had to be done" or "were to be done." There is no past form of "must" in English.

A dative of a personal noun signals the agent of a passive periphrastic verb. This is in contrast to the ablative of agent that patterns with other passive verbs. In S35.3, *Caesarī* is a dative signaling the agent of *erant agenda*, and is translated "by Caesar."

Clauses with the passive periphrastic are often transformed into the active voice in final translations. For example, S35.3 could be translated "Caesar had to do everything. . . ."

■ Exercise 4

Identify each *-nd-* form as a passive periphrastic or as a gerundive. Write a metaphrase of each sentence or phrase.

1. mīlitēs revocandī sunt

2. pācis petendae causā

3. pācem petendam esse dīcit

4. dē pāce petendā

5. manūs lavandae sunt

■ Exercise 5

Rewrite the verb in each sentence as passive periphrastic, and change the ablative of agent to the dative. Next, metaphrase each sentence as passive. Then translate each sentence, using the active voice.

Mare ā nōbīs trānsītur.
a. Mare nōbīs transeundum est.
b. The sea has to be/must be crossed by us.
c. We must cross the sea.

1. Mīlitēs ā Caesare revocantur.

    a.

    b.

    c.

2. Ā Gallīs pāx petitur.

    a.

    b.

    c.

The Impersonal Passive Kernel

Basic Sentences

35.4. Ītur in antīquam silvam.—Vergil

> One enters into the ancient forest.

35.5. Quid agitur, Calidōre? Amātur atque egētur ācriter.—Plautus

> What's up, Calidorus? Loving and being very poor.

35.6. Prīvātum. Precāriō adītur.—Inscription

> Private property. Entrance by request only.

35.7. Nunc est bibendum, nunc pede līberō tellūs pulsanda.—Horace

> Now there must be drinking, now the ground must be tapped with light foot.

Morphology

Certain verb forms that look like third person singular passive verb forms in the present imperfective are probably not what they seem, but rather fossilized remnants of the language from which Latin developed, where a final verb morpheme {r} indicated action without indicating the agent. Probably by analogy other tenses were formed. Among the few more common verbs occurring as impersonal passives are:

> venītur, ventum est
>
> pūgnātur, pūgnābātur, pūgnābitur, pūgnātum est
>
> bibitur, bibendum est

Syntax and Metaphrasing

As one would expect, the so-called impersonal passive *never* has a subject. A seemingly passive form of an intransitive verb must therefore be the *impersonal passive* because intransitive verbs have *no* personal passive. Such is the case for *ītur* in S35.4 and *adītur* in S35.6. On the other hand, *agitur* in S35.5 has the subject *quid*. *Amātur* in the same sentence could be personal or impersonal, but in combination with *egētur*, it is probably impersonal. And indeed this is confirmed by the context, which does not speak of a particular person being loved, but of the misery of being poor and in love. In S35.6, *est bibendum*, a passive periphrastic verb, is an impersonal passive; the other verb, ∅ = *est pulsanda*, also a passive periphrastic, has the subject *tellūs*.

A literal English equivalent of the impersonal passive is impossible because English has no kernels without a subject expressed or understood. There are several options for translating such a verb in English:

> use "one" as a subject, e.g., *pūgnātur* (one fights)
>
> use a gerund or an abstract noun, e.g., *pūgnātur* (fighting/a fight takes place)
>
> use the dummy-word "there" and a gerund or abstract noun, e.g., *pūgnātur* (there is fighting/a fight)

Lesson Vocabulary

Nouns

pēs, pedis, m.: foot
silva, silvae, f.: forest
tellūs, tellūris, f.: soil, earth
voluptās, voluptātis, f.: pleasure

Adjectives

antīquus, antīqua, antīquum: old, ancient
prīvātus, prīvāta, prīvātum: private

Verbs

adeō, adīre, adiī, aditūrus: go to, approach
bibō, bibere, bibī: drink
cernō, cernere, crēvī, crētus: perceive, distinguish
egeō, egēre, eguī (with abl. or gen.): be needy, be in want
pūgnō, pūgnāre, pūgnāvī, pūgnātūrus: fight
pulsō, pulsāre, pulsāvī, pulsātus: tap, beat, shake
repudiō, repudiāre, repudiāvī, repudiātus: reject, repudiate
spernō, spernere, sprēvī, sprētus: scorn, reject

Indeclinables
Adverbs
ācriter: sharply; keenly
nunc: now
precāriō: upon request
vel: even, actually

Readings

Required

35.1. Nihil . . . sine ratiōne faciendum est.—Seneca
35.2. Praetereā cēnseō Carthāginem esse dēlendam.—Marcus Cato
35.3. Dēlīberandum est saepe, statuendum est semel.—Publilius Syrus

Vocabulary
35.2. *praetereā (adv.): moreover, in addition
     Carthāgō, Carthāginis, f.: Carthage
     dēleō, dēlēre, dēlēvī, dēlētus: destroy, demolish
35.3. *dēlīberō, dēlīberāre, dēlīberāvī, dēlīberātus: deliberate
     semel (adv.): once, one time

Optional

35.4. Vitium uxōris aut tollendum aut ferendum est.—Varro
35.5. Est tempus quandō nihil, est tempus quandō aliquid, nūllum tamen est tempus in quō
     dīcenda sunt omnia.—Anon.
35.6. Ratiō docet quid faciendum fugiendumve sit.—Cicero (adapted)
35.7. Maximae cuique fortūnae minimē crēdendum est.—Livy

35.8. Aeneas takes leave of Helenus and Andromache, Trojan refugees who have already found a new home:

> Vīvite fēlīcēs, quibus est fortūna perācta
> jam sua; nōs alia ex aliīs in fāta vocāmur.
> Vōbīs *parta quiēs; nūllum maris aequor arandum,
> arva neque Ausoniae semper cēdentia retrō quaerenda.—Vergil *Aeneid*

35.9. Caesar had to do everything:

> Caesarī omnia ūnō tempore erant agenda; vexillum prōpōnendum, quod erat īnsigne cum ad arma concurrere oportēret; signum tubā dandum; ab opere revocandī mīlitēs; quī paulō longius aggeris petendī causā *prōcesserant arcessendī; aciēs īnstruenda; mīlitēs cohortandī; signum dandum.—Caesar

35.10. The value of praise:

> Trahimur omnēs studiō laudis, et optimus quisque maximē gloriā dūcitur. Ipsī illī *philosophī etiam in eīs libellīs, quōs dē contemnendā gloriā scrībunt, nōmen suum īnscrībunt; in eō ipsō in quō praedicātiōnem nōbilitātemque dēspiciunt, praedicārī dē sē ac *nōminārī volunt.—Cicero

Word Study: English Derivatives

From Lesson	Latin	From Readings	Latin
1. agenda		1. constitution	
2. artist		2. delete	
3. contemporary		3. deliberation	
4. discern		4. indelible	
5. insipid		5. institution	
6. repudiate		6. irrational	
7. reputation		7. rationalize	

Summary Tasks

____ 1. Enjoy: *Fīnis corōnat opus*.

Readings

T. Maccī Plautī: *Menaechmī*

T. Maccius Plautus wrote this comedy of lost brothers, mistaken identity, shrewish spouses, grasping mistresses, and hungry flatterers; of concerned fathers, quack doctors, and faithful slaves during or after the second war between Carthage and Rome. He aimed to please a nation fighting for its life. He succeeded so well that he has been imitated many times since, just as he had imitated the Greeks. The musical comedy, *A Funny Thing Happened on the Way to the Forum*, is the latest but not the last of these imitations.

Personae (Cast of Characters)

Peniculus: a hungry hanger-on

Menaechmus I: a well-settled, but hen-pecked citizen

Menaechmus II: his unknown happy-go-lucky twin

Erotium: an elegant lady-about-town

Cylindrus: her chef

Messenio: the faithful slave of Menaechmus II

Matrona: the shrewish wife of Menaechmus I

Senex: her rich father

Medicus: a fashionable doctor

Scene

A street in Epidamnus, 200 B.C. Stage left, the house of Menaechmus I. Stage right, the house of Erotium.

The following passages can be read after the indicated lessons, beginning with lesson 22. Except when noted, the selections follow the order of the play. While many lines have been left out, the text has been adapted only slightly. The lines have been numbered consecutively in each selection.

Many of the words Plautus uses occur elsewhere in this textbook and are listed in the Review Lessons or in the General Vocabulary. New vocabulary as well as notes, indicated by line number, and words to be entered onto the Stem List appear after each selection.

Plautus wrote in various rhythms, called meters, and his lines should and can be read aloud, regardless of your knowledge of meters.

Selection to Be Read after Lesson 22

These lines are selected from the prologue to *Menaechmī* (*The Menaechmus Twins*). Either Plautus himself wrote it, or one of his producers. The purpose of the prologue is to acquaint the audience with the events leading up to the opening scene of the play.

1 Mercātor quīdam fuit Syrācūsīs senex.
    eī sunt nātī fīliī geminī duo.
    postquam jam puerī septuennēs sunt, pater
    onerāvit nāvem magnam multīs mercibus;
5 impōnit geminum alterum in nāvem pater,
    Tarentum āvexit sēcum ad mercātum simul.
    geminum relīquit alterum apud mātrem domī.
    puer aberrāvit inter hominēs ā patre.
    Epidamniēnsis quīdam ibi mercātor fuit,
10 is puerum tollit āvehitque Epidamnum.
    pater ejus autem postquam puerum perdidit,
    animum dēspondit, eāque is aegritūdine
    paucīs diēbus post Tarentī mortuus est.

    Postquam Syrācūsās dē eā rē rediit nūntius
15 immūtat nōmen avus huic geminō alterī:
    idem est ambōbus nōmen geminīs frātribus.
    Epidamniēnsis ille mercātor, . . .
    geminum illum puerum quī surrupuit alterum,
    adoptat sibi fīlium eīque uxōrem dōtātam dedit,
20 eumque hērēdem fēcit cum ipse obiit diem.

    Nunc ille geminus quī Syrācūsīs habet
    hodiē in Epidamnum veniet cum servō suō
    hunc quaeritātum geminum germānum suum.

The next three lines are taken from the *argumentum*, a short overview written much later by a *grammaticus*, a professor of literature. *Argumenta* tell what the problem or plot is going to be, and how it is going to be solved.

    Menaechmum omnēs cīvem crēdunt advenam
25 eumque appellant meretrix, uxor et socer.
    Eī sē cognōscunt frātrēs postrēmō in vicem.

Line Notes

  5. *geminum alterum:* Menaechmus I
  6. *ad mercātum = ad mercandum*
  7. *geminum alterum:* the other twin, to be renamed Menaechmus II
  7. *domī:* "at home." The morpheme {ī} may mean "place where," if the stem has the feature *place*. This form is called the *locative*. See line 13, *Tarentī* (at Tarentum).
  8. *puer:* Menaechmus II
 15. *huic geminō alterī:* Menaechmus II
 18. *geminum illum puerum:* Menaechmus I
 19. *uxōrem:* Matrona
 21. *habet = habitat*
 22. *veniet:* "will come," future tense of *venit,* see lesson 26
 22. *cum servō suō:* Messenio
 23. *quaeritātum = ad quaerendum*
 24. This line has a factitive kernel: "all believe Menaechmus, the newcomer, to be Menaechmus, the citizen."
 25. This line too has a factitive kernel: "the courtesan, the wife, and the father-in-law call him Menaechmus."

25. *meretrix:* Erotium
25. *uxor:* Matrona
25. *socer:* Matrona's father

Supplementary Plautus Vocabulary, Lesson 22[1]

adoptō (1): adopt
advena, -ae, m. or f.: newcomer, stranger
aegritūdō, -inis, f.: sorrow
ambō, -ae, -ō (adj.): both, two; dat. pl., *ambōbus*
animum dēspondēre: lose heart
apud (prep. + acc.): at the house of
āvehō, -ere: carry away
avus, -ī, m.: grandfather
dōtō (1): provide with a dowry
Epidamniēnsis, -e: of the city of Epidamnus (a city on the Illyrian coast opposite Brundisium)
geminus, -ī, m.: twin
germānus, -a, -um: having same parents; *germānus, -ī,* m.: brother
hērēs, -ēdis, m.: heir
immūtō (1): change, substitute
in vicem: mutually
mercātor, -ōris, m.: merchant
mercor, -ārī, -ātus: trade (in merchandise)
meretrīx, -īcis, f.: courtesan

merx, -cis, f.: merchandise
nāvis, -is, f.: ship
obeō, -īre + *diem:* meet one's death, die
onerō (1): load
paucī, -ae, -a: few
perdō, -dere, -didī, -ditus: lose
postrēmō (adv.): finally
quīdam senex: a certain older man (the father of the twins)
redeō, -īre, -iī: go back, return
septuennis, -e: seven years old
simul (adv.): together
socer, -erī, m.: father-in-law
surripiō, -ere, -rupuī, -reptus: snatch secretly, steal
Syrācūsae, -ārum, f. pl.: Syracuse (chief city in Sicily); *Syrācūsīs:* at Syracuse
Tarentum, -ī, n.: Tarentum (a city in Italy)
tollō, tollere, sustulī, sublātus: lift up, take away
uxor, -ōris, f.: wife

Words to Be Entered into the Stem List (identified by line number)

6. āvexit
10. tollit
10. āvehit
13. mortuus est
14. rediit
18. surrupuit
20. obiit
21. habet
23. quaeritātum
24. advenam
25. cognōscunt

Here is a rundown on the characters in this play.

Menaechmus I is tired of Matrona, his wife, and his daily routine. He seeks relief in the company of Erotium.

Menaechmus II has been searching for five years for his twin brother, Menaechmus I, and loves adventure.

---

1. In the vocabulary, (1) following a verb indicates that it is a regular first conjugation verb.

Matrona is a wealthy, spoiled, heiress wife and demands assistance from her father.
Messenio, Menaechmus II's slave, has sense and loyalty and is longing for freedom.
Erotium, Menaechmus I's girlfriend, is an accomplished and successful girl in the
    oldest profession in the world.
Senex, Matrona's father, regrets his daughter's obnoxious behavior.

In addition there are three supporting persons.

Peniculus, a man with no visible means of support, has food on his mind.
Cylindrus, Erotium's cook, without whom she could not carry on.
Medicus, a fashionable quack doctor.

In the next selections you will meet these same persons in different situations, all
of them comic rather than tragic. You should remember these persons easily and recognize
them wherever you meet them, like cartoon or television series characters. The comic irony
is that they do not recognize each other!

Selection to Be Read after Lesson 23

In the comedy *Menaechmi,* Plautus achieves a high degree of dramatic unity. One of his
means is the repeated appearance or reference to the same dramatic property. In the
selections below, mention is made of a *palla,* a cloak or stole, that keeps appearing and
disappearing. Of similar importance is a *prandium* or *cēna* (lunch or dinner) that is eaten
or not.

Peniculus is a "parasite." This Greek word means a professional dinner guest, a person
who has no means of support and eats well only when he is invited out. In order to eat he
has to make himself agreeable or to be in the possession of a dark secret for blackmailing
someone. Some of Shakespeare's fools play similar roles. At the beginning of the play
Peniculus is looking forward eagerly to dinner at the house of the well-to-do Menaechmus I,
for a valid reason.

1   nam ille homō hominēs nōn alit, sed ēducat
      recreatque; nūllus melius medicīnam facit.

But Menaechmus and his wife Matrona are quarreling. Menaechmus cancels the dinner, and
announces that he will eat out with his girlfriend. Peniculus fears he won't get to eat at all.

    ille homō sē uxōrī simulat male loquī, loquitur mihi.
    nam, sī forīs cēnat, mē, nōn uxōrem, ulcīscitur.

Menaechmus is, however, delighted to see Peniculus.

5   nōn potuistī magis per tempus mihi advenīre quam advenīs.

He shows Peniculus the *palla* that he has stolen from his wife and will give to his girlfriend
Erotium. For this feat he wishes to be admired. He will order dinner for the three of them
at Erotium's place.

Men I Dīc hominem lepidissimum esse mē! *Pen* Dīcō: homō es lepidissimus.
Men I Ab uxōre hanc pallam surrupuī meā; nunc ad amīcam dēferētur.
Mihi, tibi atque illī jubēbō jam adparārī prandium.

When Erotium enters, Men I arranges for the dinner.

    Men I Scīsne quid volō ego tē adcūrāre? *Erot* Sciō: cūrābō quae volēs.
10   *Men I* Jubē igitur tribus nōbīs apud tē prandium adcūrārī.

Line Notes

2. *melius:* an adverb in the comparative degree, translate "better"; see lesson 25
5. *per tempus:* "at the right moment"
6. *dīc:* an imperative, the command form of the verb, translate "say!" See lesson 28 for imperatives.
6. *lepidissimum:* an adjective in the superlative degree, "very/most charming"; see lesson 25
7. *dēferētur:* future imperfective, "will be carried away"; see lesson 26
8. *jubēbō:* also future imperfective, "I will order"; so is *cūrābō* (I will attend to), in line 9
10. *jubē:* also an imperative; see note on *dīc*, line 6

Supplementary Plautus Vocabulary, Lesson 23

adcūrō (1): take care of
adparō (1): prepare
adveniō, -īre, -vēnī: arrive
apud (prep. + acc.): at the house of
cēnō (1): dine
dēferō, -ferre, -tulī, -lātus: carry away
ēducō (1): rear, bring up, educate, train
forīs (adv.): outside of the house
igitur (adv.): therefore
magis . . . quam: more . . . than (see lesson 25)
medicīna, -ae, f.: medicine, cure
melior, melius (comp. of *bonus, -a, -um*): better

nam (sentence connector): for (introduces an explanation of the preceding comment)
palla, -ae, f.: robe, stole
prandium, -ī, n.: dinner, luncheon
recreō (1): revive
simulō (1): imagine, pretend
surripiō, -ere, -rupuī, -reptus: take away secretly, steal
ulcīscor, ulcīscī, ultus: punish
uxor, -ōris, f.: wife

Words to Be Entered into the Stem List (identified by line number)

1. alit
1. ēducat
2. recreat
3. simulat
5. advenīre
7. dēferētur
8. adparārī
9. adcūrāre

Selection to Be Read after Lesson 24

Like most comic authors, Plautus relies heavily on puns as a means to make the audience feel "in the know" and involved. In the selections below, Menaechmus II and his faithful slave Messenio have arrived in the city of Epidamnus in their long search for Menaechmus I. Plautus puns on the name Epidamnus, because the Latin word *damnum, damnī* (n.) means "damage" or "financial loss." Plautus also puns on the Latin word *geminus, geminī* (m.) meaning "twin," because it begins with the same sound sequence as the verb *gemō, gemere, gemuī* for "sigh, regret" (when one does not win!). Epidamnus is described as a sort of Las Vegas, with playboys, alcoholics, sharpers, and shady ladies such as Erotium, the elegant courtesan in this play. Two verbs, *caveō, cavēre, cāvī, cautus* and *metuō, metuere, metuī,* occur frequently, because under such circumstances one needs *caution* and there is reason to *be afraid.*

Messenio, carrying a *marsuppium,* which looks rather empty:

1   hic sextus annus est postquam ē Siciliā excessimus.

We have been all around the Mediterranean Sea:

Histrōs, Hispānōs, Massiliēnsēs, Illyriōs,
mare superum omne Graeciamque exōticam
ōrāsque Ītalicās omnēs, quā adgreditur mare,
5   adiimus.

But we have found nothing because

hominem inter vīvōs quaerītāmus mortuum.

Men II Ego quaerō quī mihi dīcat (= dīcere potest) sē scīre geminum esse mortuum. Vērum aliter vīvus numquam dēsistam exsequī. Cārissimus mihi est.

10   *Mess* Quīn domum redīmus? Audīsne, Menaechme? Cum īnspiciō marsuppium, minimum est. Nisī domum redīmus, gemēs, geminum dum quaerēs. In urbe hāc habitant voluptāriī et potātōrēs maximī, tum sycophantae et meretrīcēs mulierēs. Huic urbī nōmen Epidamnō datum est, quia nēmō hūc sine damnō venit.

15   *Men II* Ego id cavēbō. Cedo mihi marsuppium.
Mess Quid vīs? *Men II* Metuō dē verbīs tuīs.
Mess Quid metuis? *Men II* Damnum in Epidamnō metuō.
Tū magnus amātor mulierum es, Messeniō, ego autem homō īrācundus.
Id sī habēbō, neque tū dēlinquēs neque ego īrātus tibi erō.

Erotium's cook Cylindrus is returning from shopping. He, of course, mistakes Menaechmus II for Menaechmus I and accordingly welcomes him with open arms. Messenio reminds his master that the town is full of sharpers:

20   Dīxīne tibi esse hīc sycophantās plūrimōs?

Menaechmus II agrees and tells the cook to seek medical help (for his mind):

> Jubē tē piārī dē meā pecūniā;
> nam ego īnsānum esse tē certē sciō.

But the cook answers that he will tell Erotium that Menaechmus stands outside:

> Ībō intrō et dīcam tē hīc adstāre Erōtiō:

Messenio keeps warning him:

> Nam istīc meretrīcem crēdō habitāre mulierem
> 25 ut quidem ille īnsānus dīxit quī hinc abiit modo

and Men II is inclined to accept the warning:

> Monēs quidem hercle rēctē

Messenio still admonishes him to be cautious:

> Tum quidem sciam rēctē monuisse, sī tū rēctē cāveris.

Line Notes

The following are all future imperfective verb forms (see lesson 28): *dēsistam* (8), *gemēs* (11), *quaerēs* (12), *cavēbō* (15), *habēbō* (19), *dēlinquēs* (19), *erō* (19), *ībō* (23), *dīcam* (23), *sciam* (27). Translate as "will _____ ."

3. *mare superum:* the Adriatic Sea
10. *quīn:* "why . . . not?"
10. *Menaechme:* vocative (see lesson 28)
15. *cedo* (archaic imperative): "hand over"
21. *jubē tē piārī: jubē* is a verb form in the imperative mood; translate as "order yourself to be purified!" In modern terms: "go see a shrink!" See lesson 26.
21. *dē meā pecūniā:* literally "from my money," that is, "at my expense"
27. There is a subject gapped with *monuisse: sciam ∅ = mē rēctē monuisse* "I will know that I have warned you well if you will have been cautious well!"
27. *cāveris:* a verb form in the future perfective, "you will have been cautious"

Supplementary Plautus Vocabulary, Lesson 24

abeō, -īre, -iī: go away
adeō, -īre, -iī: go to, visit
adgredior, -gredī, -gressus: approach, come up to
adstō (1): stand nearby
aliter (adv.): otherwise
amātor, -ōris, m.: lover
annus, -ī, m.: year
caveō, -ēre, cāvī: guard against, beware of

cedo (old imperative form): "bring here"
certē (adv.): certainly
damnum, -ī, n.: damage
dēlinquō, -ere: do wrong
dēsistō, -ere: cease, stop
excēdō, -ere, -cessī: depart
exōticus, -a, -um: foreign
exsequor, -sequī: follow to the end
gemō, -ere: sigh

Graecia, -ae: Greece
habitō (1): dwell
hercle (interjection): by Hercules
hīc (adv.): here
hinc (adv.): from here
Hispānī, -ōrum, m. pl.: the Spaniards
Histrī, -ōrum, m. pl.: people of the Lower
    Danube region
hūc (adv.): (to) here
Illyriī, -ōrum, m. pl.: a people on the
    Adriatic coast of northern Greece
īnspiciō, -ere: look into, examine
intrō (adv.): inside
īrācundus, -a, -um: easily angered
istīc (adv.): there, here
mare, -is, n.: sea
marsuppium, -ī, n.: pouch, purse
Massiliēnsēs, -ium, m. pl.: people of
    Massilia, on the Mediterranean coast
    of Gaul

meretrix, -īcis, f.: courtesan
metuō, -ere: be afraid
modo (adv.): just now
mulier, -ieris, f.: woman
nam (sentence connector): for
ōra, -ae, f.: coast; region
plūrimus, -a, -um: very many
potātor, -ōris, m.: a drinker, alcoholic
quā (adv.): where
quaeritō (1): seek
quidem (adv.): indeed, certainly
quīn: why . . . not?
rēctē (adv.): correctly, properly
redeō, -īre, -iī: return
sextus, -a, -um: sixth
Sicilia, -ae: Sicily
superus, -a, -um: upper
sycophanta, -ae, m.: blackmailer, informer
vērum (adv.): but yet, however
voluptārius, -ī, m.: playboy

Words to Be Entered into the Stem List (identified by line number)

4. adgreditur
9. exsequī
10. redīmus

10. īnspiciō
23. adstāre
25. abiit

Selection to Be Read after Lesson 26

Greek and Roman students had to write many exercises and compositions to learn the use
of comparisons in clear speaking and writing. Not surprisingly, comparisons often occur
in comedies, another means for strengthening dramatic unity. Watch for them in this
selection. You remember that Menaechmus II loves adventure and that Messenio keeps
warning him against the sharpers and courtesans of "Damage City." Here she comes—
Erotium herself makes a grand entrance from her elegant establishment. She thinks that it is
Menaechmus I who has come for the dinner he had ordered earlier. We know better!

1 *Erot* Ubi ille est quem coquus ante aedīs esse dīcit? atque eum videō!
    Nunc eum adībō atque ultrō adloquar!
    "Animule mī, mihi mīrum vidētur
    tē hīc stāre forīs,
5 magis quam domus tua domus cum haec tua est;
    omne parātum est ut jussistī
    atque ut voluistī . . .
    prandium, ut jussistī, hīc cūrātum est.

Menaechmus II is a bit taken aback:

> Quōcum haec mulier loquitur? *Erot* Equidem tēcum. *Men II* Quid mēcum tibi
> 10 fuit umquam aut nunc est negōtī?

Erotium wants to know why he has ordered her to have dinner prepared:

> Cūr igitur mē tibi jussistī parāre prandium?

Menaechmus II doesn't understand:

> Egone tē jussī parāre? *Erot* Certō, tibi et parasītō tuō.
> *Men II* Cui parasītō? Certō, haec mulier nōn sāna satis.
> *Erot* Pēniculō. *Men II* Quis iste est Pēniculus?
> 15 *Erot* Ille, quī tēcum vēnit, cum pallam mihi
> dētulistī, quam ab uxōre tuā surrupuistī. *Men II* Quid est?
> Tibi pallam dedī, quam uxōrī surrupuī? Sānane es?

But he cannot resist the invitation to adventure and accepts the opportunity as offered by the gods. Meanwhile Peniculus comes back from the Forum, where he has "immersed" himself into an assembly. He is late, he thinks, for the dinner, and is very angry with himself and Menaechmus I:

> Plūs quam trīgintā annōs vīxī. . . .
> numquam facinus fēcī pejus neque scelestius
> 20 quam hodiē, cum in contiōnem mediam mē immersī miser.
> Sed quid ego videō? Menaechmus cum corōnā exit forās!
> Sublātum est convivium, observābō hominem. Post adībō atque adloquar.

Menaechmus II comes out of Erotium's house, a garland on his head, and over his arm the *palla* that Erotium wants restyled at the embroiderer's shop. He is ecstatic!

> Prō dī immortālēs, cui hominī umquam ūnō diē
> bonī dedistis plūs, quī minus spērāverit?
> 25 Prandī, pōtāvī, amāvī; abstulī hanc pallam.
> Dīcit hanc dedisse mē sibi atque eam meae
> uxōrī surrupuisse!

Line Notes

3. *animule mī:* vocative case, or address form, translate "oh my darling"; see lesson 28
5. Note the postponed clause marker: "Since this house is yours more than your house ∅ = is yours"
9. *quōcum, tēcum, mēcum: cum quō, cum tē, cum mē*
9. *quid negōtī: negōtī* (variant of *negōtiī*) is an example of a partitive genitive, translate "what of business," or in good English "what business"; see lesson 17
24. *bonī . . . plūs:* see note on line 9
26. *dīcit:* the ∅ subject is *Erōtium*
27. *uxōrī:* dative of separation (with personal nouns only), "from my wife"

Supplementary Plautus Vocabulary, Lesson 26

adeō, -īre, -iī: go to, approach
adloquor, -loquī, -locūtus: speak to, address
aedēs, -is, f.: house, building
animule mī: [see Line Notes]
auferō, auferre, abstulī, ablātus: take away
certō (adv.): certainly, for sure
contiō, -ōnis, f.: people's assembly
convivium, -ī, n.: banquet
coquus, -ī, m.: cook
corōna, -ae, f.: crown, wreath, garland
dēferō, -ferre, -tulī, -lātus: bring, deliver
equidem (intensifier): to be sure
facinus, -oris, n.: crime
forās (adv.): outside (place to which)
forīs (adv.): outside, out-of-doors (place where)
hīc (adv.): here
hodiē (adv.): today
igitur (sentence connector): therefore
immergō, -ere, -mersī, -mersus: get involved in, immerse
immortālis, -e: immortal

medius, -a, -um: middle of
mīrus, -a, -um: astonishing, wonderful
miser, -era, -erum: wretched, unhappy
negōtium, -ī, n.: business [see Line Notes]
nunc (adv.): now
observō (1): watch, observe
palla, -ae, f.: robe, stole
parasītus, -ī, m.: freeloader, parasite
parō (1): prepare
pōtō (1): drink heavily
prandeō, -ēre, prandī: eat
prandium, -ī, n.: dinner, luncheon
prō (interjection): oh
sānus, -a, -um: sane
scelestus, -a, -um: wicked
spērō (1): hope
surripiō, -ere, -rupuī, -reptus: take away secretly, steal
tollō, tollere, sustulī, sublātus: take away
trīgintā (indecl. numeral adj.): thirty
ultrō (adv.): on one's own accord
uxor, -ōris, f.: wife

Words to Be Entered into the Stem List (identified by line number)

1. aedīs
2. adībō
2. adloquar
4. stāre
6. parātum est
11. parāre

16. dētulistī
17. dedī
19. facinus
19. fēcī
22. adībō

Selection to Be Read after Lesson 28

For the ancients dramatic unity demands that the play take place in one location, here the street in front of the house of Erotium and Menaechmus I. It also demands that the action not last longer than one day. Hence the word *hodiē* in line 12 reminds the audience that the stealing of the stole and its presentation to Erotium have happened on the same day.

Menaechmus II claims he has capitalized on the courtesan's error in mistaking him for somebody who he is not:

1   Quōniam sentiō
errāre, coepī adsentārī mulierī; quidquid dīxerat,
idem ego dīcēbam.
Minōre nusquam bene fuī dispendiō.

Peniculus steps up and threatens to reveal to Matrona the secret of the *palla,* which obviously means nothing to Menaechmus II.

5   Adībō ad hominem. Quid dīcis, homō

      levior quam plūma, pessime et nequissime?

      Men II Adulēscēns, quaesō, quid tibi mēcum est reī?

      Nōn edepol ego tē umquam ante hunc diem

      vīdī neque nōvī.

10   *Pen* Menaechme, vigilā, nōn mē nōvistī? Tuum parasītum nōn nōvistī?

      Surrupuistīne uxōrī tuae

      pallam istam hodiē et dedistī Erōtiō?

      Men II Neque hercle ego uxōrem habeō, neque ego Erōtiō

      dedī nec pallam surrupuī.

15   *Pen* Uxōrī rem omnem jam ēloquar.

      Omnēs in tē istae recident contumēliae.

      Nōn impūnē prandium comēderis.

Supplementary Plautus Vocabulary, Lesson 28

adeō, -īre, -iī: go to, approach

adsentor, -ārī: (+ dat.) assent constantly, agree with

adulēscēns, -entis, m.: young man

bene (adv. of *bonus, -a, -um*): well

coepī, coepisse: (+ complementary inf.) begin

comedō, -ere, comēdī: eat up

contumēlia, -ae, f.: insult

dispendium, -ī, n.: cost

edepol (interjection): by Pollux

ēloquor, ēloquī, ēlocūtus: speak out, report

hercle (interjection): by Hercules

hodiē (adv., from *hōc diē*): on this day, today

impūnē (adv.): unpunished, unpaid for

neque (coord. conj.): nor, and not

nequissimus, -a, -um: most worthless

nōvī, nōvisse: know

nusquam (adv.): never

parasītus, -ī, m.: blackmailer, parasite

plūma, -ae, f.: feather

quaesō, -ere: beg, ask (usually parenthetical)

quisquis, quaeque, quidquid: whoever, whatever

quoniam (subord. conj.): since

recidō, -ere, recidī: fall back

surripiō, -ere, -rupuī, -reptus: take away secretly, steal

uxor, -ōris, f.: wife

vigilō (1): keep awake

Words to Be Entered into the Stem List (identified by line number)

1. sentiō
2. adsentārī
9. nōvī
15. ēloquar
16. recident

Selection No. 1 to Be Read after Lesson 29

The scene of Plautus' plays is supposed to be Greece, and the persons are never supposed to be Romans, probably because the Romans considered the subject matter of comedy to be below a Roman's dignity. But Plautus introduces quite a few details that are typically

Roman. In this selection, the audience, being Roman, knows why Menaechmus I is late for the dinner he has ordered. A well-established Roman citizen had a larger or smaller number of clients, i.e., persons who because of their socially inferior status could not plead their own cases in court and had to rely on the help of a *patrōnus*, a patron. The clients had to support their patron's political career. Menaechmus and others like him knew law from their study in the rhetorical schools, and from listening to the famous orators in the courts. The courts were in the public buildings comprising the Roman Forum; some of them can be seen even today.

Menaechmus I, already late for his dinner with the courtesan Erotium because a client kept him in the Forum, runs into his wife and the parasite Peniculus, who has told her all about Menaechmus' stealing of her stole.

1   *Men I* Dī illum omnēs perdant! ita mihi hunc hodiē corrūpit diem;
       mēque adeō, quī hodiē forum umquam oculīs īnspexī meīs.
       Diem corrūpī optimum. Jussī adparārī prandium,
       amīca exspectat mē, sciō. Ubi prīmum est licitum, īlicō
5   properāvī abīre dē forō. Īrāta est, crēdō, nunc mihi; placābit palla quam dedī,
       quam hodiē uxōrī abstulī atque dētulī huic Erōtiō.
       Pen (to Matrona, the wife) Quid āis? *Matr* Virō mē malō male nuptam.
       Pen Satisne audīs quae ille loquitur? *Matr* Satis. *Men I* Sī sapiam, hinc
       intrō abeam, ubi mī bene est. *Pen (to Men I)* Manē: male erit potius.
10   *Matr* Clanculum tē ista flagitia facere cēnsēbās posse?
       Men I Quid illud est, uxor, negōtī? *Matr* Mē rogās? *Men I* Vīsne mē rogāre illum?
       Matr Aufer hinc palpātiōnēs! *Pen* Perge tū. *Men I* Quid tū mihi trīstis es?
       Matr Tē scīre oportet. *Pen* Scit, sed dissimulat malus.
       Men I Quid negōtī est? *Matr* Pallam. *Men I* Pallam? *Matr* Quīdam pallam . . .
15   *Pen* Quid pavēs? *Men I* Nihil equidem paveō. *Pen* Nisī ūnum: palla pallōrem incutit.
       Illūc redī. *Men I* Quō ego redeam? *Pen* Equidem ad phrygiōnem, cēnseō.
       Ī, pallam refer. *Men I* Quae ista palla est? *Matr* Nai, ego ēcastor mulier misera!
       Men I Cūr tū misera es? Mihi expedī. Num quis servōrum dēlīquit? Num ancillae
       aut servī tibi respōnsant? Ēloquere, impūne nōn erit. *Matr* Nūgās agis.
20   *Men I* Certē familiārium alicuī īrāta es. *Matr* Nūgās agis.
       Men I Num mihi es īrāta saltem? *Matr* Nunc tū nōn nūgās agis.

Line Notes

1. *illum:* referring to the client for whom Menaechmus had been pleading in court
4. *īlicō = ad eum locum*
8. *sī sapiam, hinc intrō abeam:* "If I had wisdom, I would go from here inside" (i.e., into Erotium's house where it is fine for me). This conditional sentence is in the present imperfective subjunctive, to indicate "possibility"; see lesson 34.
11. *quid . . . negōtī:* see note on Selection to Be Read after Lesson 26, line 9
12. *palpātiōnēs:* the word begins with the same sound sequence as *palla* in line 14, *pavēs* in line 15, and *pallōrem* in line 15. The Romans enjoyed such sound sequences. In this case the English word "pale" has similar sound associations.
17. *nai:* a Greek word meaning "truly." Most educated Romans knew Greek quite well, which explains why so much of Roman literature is new creation inspired by Greek models.
18. *num:* indicates a question to which the expected answer is "no"

18. *quis:* after *num* the word *quis* means "anybody," not "who?"

20. *familiārium alicuī: familiārium* is another partitive genitive, "someone of the persons in the household," perhaps a slave. The word *familia* does not refer to the nuclear family, but to anybody connected with and living in the household or the estate. Caesar tells us that one of the Gallic chiefs had a *familia* of ten thousand people.

Supplementary Plautus Vocabulary, Selection No. 1, Lesson 29

abeō, -īre, -iī: go away

adeō (adv.): to such a degree

adparō (1): prepare

āis (second person sing. of *āit*): you say

aliquis, aliquid: someone, something

ancilla, -ae, f.: maid, female servant

auferō, auferre, abstulī, ablātus: carry away

cēnseō, -ēre, cēnsuī: be of an opinion, think

clanculum (adv.): secretly, privately

corrumpō, -ere, -rūpī, -ruptus: break up, destroy

dēferō, -ferre, -tulī, -lātus: carry down, deliver

dēlinquō, -ere, -līquī, -lictus: do wrong

dissimulō (1): pretend (that something is *not* so)

ēcastor (interjection): by Castor (twin brother of Pollux: cf. *edepol*)

ēloquor, -loquī, -locūtus: speak out

equidem (intensifier): indeed, to be sure

est licitum: it was possible

expediō, -īre, -pediī, -pedītus: set free, explain

exspectō (1): wait for

familiāris, -is, m.: familiar person, servant, friend

flagitium, -ī, n.: disgrace

forum, -ī, n.: forum (place of public business)

hinc (adv.): from here, from this place

illūc (adv.): to that place

impūne (adv.): unpunished

incutiō, -ere, -cussī, -cussus: strike into

īnspiciō, -ere, -spexī, -spectus: see, lay eyes on

intrō (adv.): inside

miser, -era, -erum: miserable

nai (Greek, "truly"): [see Line Notes]

negōtium, -ī, n.: business, concern, affair

nūbō, -ere, nupsī, nuptus: (+ dat.) marry (a man), be married to

nūgae, -ārum, f.: nonsense

num (question word): introduces a direct question, expecting a negative answer

pallor, -ōris, m.: paleness, fear

palpātiō, -ōnis, f.: caress

paveō, -ēre: be scared of

perdō, -dere, -didī, -ditus: destroy

pergō, -gere, -rēxī: go straight on, continue, proceed

phrygiō, -ōnis, m.: embroiderer

potius (adv.): rather, more

properō (1): hurry

quīdam, quaedam, quiddam (adj.): a certain

quō (adv.): where, to what place?

referō, -ferre, rettulī, -lātus: carry back

respōnsō (1): answer, talk back

rogō (1): ask

saltem (adv.): at least, in any event

servus, -ī, m.: servant, slave

tristis, -e: sad, gloomy

ubi prīmum (subord. conj.): as soon as

Words to Be Entered into the Stem List (identified by line number)

1. corrūpit
3. jussī
5. placābit
6. abstulī
17. refer

Selection No. 2 to Be Read after Lesson 29

Plautus often uses comparisons and imagery from houses and from building. In another play, *The Haunted House,* a young man compares himself to a building well planned and constructed by his parents, but neglected by himself. Although the inside of houses is never shown in a Roman play, the audience is quite aware of its existence, and of the contrast between inside and outside. The idea that one's home is one's castle goes back to ancient beliefs and feelings. Every house had the hearth as a holy place for worship of the household gods. The Latin word for the hearth is *focus.* Plautus' housing vocabulary includes the words *domus* and *aedēs* for house, *jānua* and *ōstium* for door. All forms of the stem *for-* mean "outside." A *for*eigner is an *out*sider.

Menaechmus I has been excluded from his house. So far he does not mind, because he expects to be welcome at the house of Erotium. But she also excludes him. This is an almost tragi-comic moment.

1   *Men I* Male mihi uxor sēsē fēcisse cēnset, cum exclūsit forās,
    quasi nōn habeam quō intrōmittar, alium meliōrem locum.
    Sī tibi displiceō, patiundum; at placuerō huic Erōtiō,
    quae mē nōn exclūdet ab sē, sed apud sē occlūdet domī.

5   Aperīte atque Erōtium aliquis ēvocāte ante ōstium.
    Erot Quis hīc mē quaerit? *Men I* Sibi inimīcus magis quam aetātī tuae.
    Erot Mī Menaechme, cūr ante aedīs astās? Sequere intrō! *Men I* Manē!
    Scīsne cūr ego ad tē veniō? *Erot* Sciō, venīs ad amandum.
    Men I Immō edepol pallam illam, amābō tē, quam tibi dūdum dedī,

10 mihi eam redde: uxor rescīvit rem omnem, ut factum est.
    Erot Tibi dedī equidem illam . . . paulō prius.
    Men I Mihi dedistī pallam? Numquam fēcistī. Nam ego quidem, postquam
    illam dūdum tibi dedī atque abiī ad forum, nunc redeō, nunc tē videō.
    Erot Videō cōnsilium tuum. Vīs mē dēfraudāre, quia commīsī tibi pallam.

15 *Men I* Nōn ego tē dēfraudāre volō. Tibi dīcō uxōrem rem omnem rescīvisse.
    Erot Tū ultrō ad mē dētulistī, dedistī eam dōnō mihi:
    eandem nunc reposcis; patiar. Tibi habē, aufer, ūtere,
    vel tū, vel tua uxor, vel etiam in loculōs compingite.
    Tū post hunc diem pedem intrō nōn ferēs,

20 nisi ferēs argentum; frūstrā mē ductāre nōn potes. *(exit)*
    Men I Heus tū, tibi dīcō, manē! Redī! Abiit intrō, occlūsit aedīs.
    Nunc ego sum exclūsissimus.
    Neque domī neque apud amīcam mihi jam quicquam crēditur.

Line Notes

2. *quasi . . . locum:* "as if I wouldn't have another better place to which I would be admitted"; see note to line 8 in the previous selection

3. *tibi = uxōrī*

3. *patiundum = patiundum est:* "it must be suffered," i.e., "I must bear it"; see lesson 35

9. *amābō tē:* "please"; literally "I will love you"

23. *quicquam = quidquam:* "anything"

Supplementary Plautus Vocabulary, Selection No. 2, Lesson 29

abeō, -īre, -iī: go away

aedēs, aedium, f. pl.: house

aliquis, aliquid (indef. pronoun): someone, something

aperiō, -īre: open

apud (prep. + acc.): in the house of

argentum, -ī, n.: silver; money

astō (1) (for adstō): stand, stand near

auferō, auferre, abstulī, ablātus: take away

cēnseō, -ēre, cēnsuī, cēnsūrus: be of an opinion, think

committō, -ere, -mīsī, -missus: entrust

compingō, -ere, -pēgī, -pāctus: confine, cram down

dēferō, -ferre, -tulī, -lātus: bring

dēfraudō (1): cheat, trick

displiceō, -plicēre, -plicuī: (+ dat.) displease

domī (adv.): at home

donum, -ī, n.: gift, present

ductō (1): lead on

dūdum (adv.): a little while ago, just now

edepol (interjection): by Pollux

equidem (intensifier): indeed, in fact

ēvocō (1): call out, summon

exclūdō, -ere, -clūsī, -clūsus: shut out

forās (adv.): out, outside (place to which)

forum, -ī, n.: forum (place of public business)

frūstrā (adv.): for free

hīc (adv.): here, in this place

immō (adv., in contradiction or correction of preceding words): no, rather, on the contrary

intrō (adv.): inside

intrōmittō, -ere: let in

loculus, -ī, m.: money-box

neque . . . neque: neither . . . nor

occlūdō, -ere, -clūsī, -clūsus: shut in

ōstium, -ī, n.: door, entrance

paulō prius (adv.): a little earlier, a little while ago

quasi (subord. conj.): as if

quidem (intensifier): indeed, in fact

redeō, -īre, -iī, -itūrus: come back, return

reposcō, -ere: demand back

rescīscō, -ere, rescīvī: find out

ultrō (adv.): of one's own accord, without being asked

uxor, -ōris, f.: wife

vel . . . vel . . . vel etiam (coord. conj.): either . . . or . . . or even

Words to Be Entered into the Stem List (identified by line number)

1. exclūsit
3. displiceō
3. patiundum
4. occlūdet
5. ēvocāte
7. astās

10. rescīvit
13. redeō
17. aufer
20. ductāre
22. exclūsissimus

Selection to Be Read after Lesson 30

The selections given here do not follow the previous selections but deal with general topics. In the very beginning of the play, Menaechmus I berates his wife for her interference and her spying on him. The interfering wife is a favorite topic of Roman satire.

1 Nam quotiēns forās īre volō, mē retinēs, revocās, rogitās,
   quō ego eam, quam rem agam, quid negōtī geram,
   quid petam, quid feram, quid forīs ēgerim.
   Portitōrem domum dūxī: ita omnem mihi rem necesse ēloquī est,
5 quidquid ēgī atque agō.

How does the cook know Menaechmus II's name? The slave Messenio explains the ways of courtesans.

   Men II Sed mīror, quī (= ut) ille nōverit nōmen meum.
   Mess Minimē hercle mīrum. Mōrem hunc meretrīcēs habent:
   ad portum mittunt servulōs, ancillulās.
   sī quae peregrīna nāvis in portum advenit,
10 rogitant, unde sit, quid eī nōmen sit.
   Men II Monēs quidem hercle rēctē. *Mess* Tum sciam rēctē monuisse,
   sī tū rēctē cāveris. *Men II* Tacē dum parumper: nam concrepuit ōstium.
   Videāmus, quī hinc ēgreditur.

Menaechmus II still wonders how the courtesan Erotium knows his name. Messenio suggests that the money pouch "smells good" to her.

   Men II Haec quidem edepol rēctē appellat meō mē nōmine mulier.
15 Nimis mīror, quid hoc sit negōtī. *Mess* Oboluit marsuppium
   huic istud, quod habēs. *Men II* Atque edepol tū mē monuistī probē.
   Accipe dum hoc: jam scībō, utrum haec mē magis amet an marsuppium.
   Erot Eāmus intrō.

Line Notes

7. Notice the alliteration of initial *m* and the assonance *mīrum—mōrem*. Roman ears relished these sound patterns.
11. *monuisse = mē monuisse*
17. *scībō* = a variant of the future imperfective of *sciō*

Supplementary Plautus Vocabulary, Lesson 30

adveniō, -īre, -vēnī: come to, arrive
ancillula, -ae, f. (dim. of *ancilla, ancillae*): little maid
caveō, cavēre, cāvī, cautus: beware, be on one's guard
concrepō, -ere, concrepuī: rattle, creak, make noise
dum (adv.): now
edepol (interjection): by Pollux
ēgredior, -ī, ēgressus: step out
ēloquor, -ī, ēlocūtus: speak out, explain
forās (adv.): out, outside (place to which)
hinc (adv.): here, to this place

intrō (adv.): inside
marsuppium, -ī, n.: purse, pocketbook, wallet
meretrīx, -īcis, f.: courtesan
mīrus, -a, -um: wonderful, surprising
mulier, -ieris, f.: woman
nāvis, -is, f.: ship
necesse est: it is necessary
negōtium, -ī, n.: business
nimis (adv.): very much, a lot
nōvī, nōvisse: know
oboleō, -ēre, oboluī: smell, give off a scent
ōstium, -ī, n.: door

parumper (adv.): for a little while, for a moment

peregrīnus, -a, -um: foreign

portitor, -ōris, m.: doorguard, concierge

portus, -ūs, m.: port, harbor

probē (adv.): correctly, wisely

quae (here indef. = *aliquae*): any, some

quisquis, quaeque, quidquid: whoever, whatever

retineō, -ēre, -tinuī, -tentus: hold back, restrain

revocō (1): call back

rogitō (1): keep on asking, question continuously

servulus, -ī, m. (dim. of *servus, -ī*): little slave, servant

taceō, -ēre, tacuī: keep quiet

tum (adv.): then, at that time

utrum . . . an (question word): whether . . . or

Words to Be Entered into the Stem List (identified by line number)

1. retinēs
1. revocās
2. eam
2. agam
2. geram

6. nōverit
7. mōrem
12. tacē
13. ēgreditur

Selection to Be Read after Lesson 31

Matrona's father, Senex, is an almost pathetic figure, quite unlike the almighty *pater familiās* of whom Roman stories tell. Perhaps this is so because in comedy things are topsy-turvy, not at all like they are in reality. This is the thesis of a book *Roman Laughter* by Erich Segal, the well-known author of *Love Story*.

Matrona wants to see her husband bring back the *palla,* and Menaechmus II wants to see Messenio take it to the ship. Notice the cross-fit of their purposes, when they come face to face.

1   *Matr* Prōvīsam quam mox vir meus redeat domum.
     Sed eum videō! Salva sum, pallam refert!
     Men II Dēmīror, ubi nunc ambulet Messēniō.
     Matr Nōn tē pudet prōdīre in cōnspectum meum
5   cum istōc ornātū?
     Men II Quid est? Quae tē rēs agitat, mulier?

Matrona's father knows her behavior only too well and reminds her of it.

     Sen Quotiēns mōnstrāvī tibi, virō ut mōrem gerās,
     quid ille faciat, nē id observēs, quō eat, quid rērum gerat!
     Matr Mē dēspoliat, mea ōrnamenta clam ad amīcam dēgerit.
10 *Sen* Male facit, sī istud facit; sī nōn facit, tū male facis.
     Dīc mihi istūc, Menaechme, quod vōs dissertātis.
     Men II Quisquis es, quidquid tibi nōmen est, senex, summum Jovem
     deōsque dō testīs
     mē neque istī male fēcisse mulierī neque eam nōvisse.

15 Sī ego intrā aedīs hujus umquam, ubi habitat, penetrāvī pedem,
    omnium hominum exoptō ut fīam miserōrum miserrimus.

Matrona and Senex conclude that he is mad, so Senex goes for a doctor and Menaechmus II
sees a chance to get away. Menaechmus II speaks to the audience:

    Jamne istī abiērunt ex cōnspectū meō,
    quī mē vī cōgunt, ut valēns īnsāniam?
    Quid cessō abīre ad nāvem?
20 Vōs omnīs quaesō, sī senex revēnerit,
    nē mē indicētis, quā plateā hinc aufūgerim.

Line Notes

4. *nōn tē pudet prōdīre:* "is it not shameful for you to go forward . . . ?" See lesson 21 on
   the infinitive as subject of a verb.
7. *quotiēns mōnstrāvī tibi, virō ut mōrem gerās:* "how often have I pointed out to you that
   you should humor your husband?" *Mōnstrāvī* here has the semantic feature *command*.
11. *Dic . . . istūc:* "Speak to that point."
12. *quisquis, quidquid:* a clause marker, equivalent to *quīcumque* (whoever)

Supplementary Plautus Vocabulary, Lesson 31

abeō, -īre, -iī: go away
aedēs, aedium, f. pl.: house
agitō (1): stir up, bother
aufugiō, -fugere, -fūgī: flee, make off
cessō (1): let up, slack off
clam (adv.): secretly, stealthily
cōnspectus, -ūs, m.: sight, view
dēgerō, -gerere, -gessī: carry off
dēmīror (1): wonder (about something)
dēspoliō (1): strip, rob
dissertō (1): discuss
exoptō (1): hope, pray
hinc (adv.): from here, from this place
indicō (1): reveal, disclose; betray
īnsāniō, -īre, īnsāniī: be crazy, mad, insane
intrā (prep. + acc.): inside, within
Juppiter, Jovis, m.: Jupiter, Jove
miser, -era, -erum: wretched, unhappy
mōnstrō (1): point out
nāvis, -is, f.: ship

neque . . . neque (coord. conj.):
   neither . . . nor
nōvī, nōvisse: know
observō (1): watch
ornāmentum, -ī, n.: trinket, jewel
ornātus, -ūs, m.: apparel, outfit, attire
penetrō (1): enter, penetrate
platea, -ae, f.: street
prōdeō, -īre, -iī: go forth, come forward
prōvīsō, -ere: go to see
pudet: it makes somebody ashamed, it is
   shameful for somebody
quaesō, -ere: beg, ask
quam mox? (adv.): how soon?
referō, -ferre, rettulī, -lātus: bring back
reveniō, -īre, revēnī: come back
salvus, -a, -um: safe
senex, senis, m.: old man
testis, -is, m.: witness

Selection to Be Read after Lesson 32

This selection contains a scene of physical violence such as occurs in many Greek and Roman comedies. Of course, there was always dancing and music, and most of Plautus' plays contain what we would call arias. None of the music has survived, but the whole play is composed in rhythms. For example, line 13 has the same rhythm as Basic Sentence 11.3 (*Postquam Crassus carbō factus, Carbō crassus factus est*). Here are the lines with stress marks:

1 Póstquam Crássus cárbō fáctus, Cárbō crássus fáctus ést
  Vós sceléstī, vós rapácēs, vós praedónēs. Périimús

This rhythm is called trochaic octonarius and was very popular. One of the great rewards for learning to read Plautus in its original unadapted form is the feeling for the differences in meaning produced by the different rhythms.

Senex sits, watches, and waits for the doctor. In the plays of Plautus, doctors and cooks were favorite butts of caricature.

1 Lumbī sedendō, oculī spectandō dolent
  manendō medicum.
  Med Quid illī esse morbī dīxerās? Nārrā, senex!
  Sen Quīn eā tē causā dūcō, ut id dīcās mihi
5 atque illum ut sānum faciās.

Enters Menaechmus I, unaware of the situation and very dejected.

  Sen Obsecrō hercle, medice, quidquid factūrus es, fac;
  nōn vidēs hominem īnsānīre? *Med* Ad mē fac ut dēferātur. Ibi poterō cūrāre hominem.
  Ī, vocā hominēs quī illum ad mē dēferant. *Sen* Quot sunt satis?
  Med Quattuor, nihilō minus. *Sen* Jam hīc erunt. *Med* Ībō domum. Hunc ad mē ferant.

Four strong men with ropes and chains now go after Menaechmus I.

10 *Men I* Quid vultis? Quid quaeritātis? Quid mē circumsistitis?
  Quō rapitis mē? Quō fertis mē? Periī. Subvenīte, cīvēs!

And he is rescued by Messenio, who mistakes him for Menaechmus II.

  Mes Numquam tē patiar perīre, mē perīre aequius est.
  Vōs scelestī, vōs rapācēs, vōs praedōnēs. *The Four* Periimus.
  Mess Agite, abīte, fugite hinc in malam crucem.

Line Notes

3. *Quid . . . dīxerās?:* "What disease did you say he had?"
4. *ut:* so that, see lesson 33. See also line 5.

Supplementary Plautus Vocabulary, Lesson 32

aequus, -a, -um: fair, just
circumsistō, -ere, -stetī: surround
cīvis, -is, m.: citizen
crux, crucis, f.: cross, gallows
dēferō, -ferre, -tulī, -lātus: carry, deliver
hercle (interjection): by Hercules
hīc (adv.): here
hinc (adv.): from here, from this place
īnsāniō, -īre: be mad
lumbus, -ī, m.: loin
nihilō minus (adv.): no less, no fewer

obsecrō (1): beg, pray, entreat
praedō, -ōnis, m.: robber, pirate
quaeritō (1): seek, go after
quīn (adv.): (raises an objection to a
    previous remark) but
rapax (rapācis): greedy, grasping, grabby
sānus, -a, -um: sane, healthy
scelestus, -a, -um: wicked, criminal
senex, senis, m.: old man
subveniō, -īre, -vēnī: come up to aid, help

Words to Be Entered into the Stem List (identified by line number)

1. spectandō
10. circumsistitis
11. rapitis
11. subvenīte

12. perīre
12. aequius
13. rapācēs
14. fugite

Selection to Be Read after Lesson 33

Menaechmus I has been "excluded" by wife and mistress and saved by Messenio, whom he does not know. He marvels at it all.

1 Aliī mē negant eum esse quī sum atque exclūdunt forās,
    etiam hic (= Messēniō) servum sē meum esse aībat quem ego ēmīsī manū.
    Is (= Messēniō) ait sē mihi allātūrum cum argentō marsuppium.
    Id sī attulerit, dīcam ut ā mē abeat līber quō volet,
5 nē tum, quandō sānus factus sit, ā mē argentum petat.
    Socer et medicus mē īnsānīre aiēbant. Quid sit mīra sunt.
    Nunc ībō ad hanc meretrīcem, quamquam suscēnset mihi,
    sī possum exōrāre ut pallam reddat, quam referam domum.

Line Notes

3. *allātūrum = allātūrum esse*
5. *quandō sānus factus sit:* "when he should have become well." For the subjunctive use, see lesson 34.

Supplementary Plautus Vocabulary, Lesson 33

abeō, -īre, -iī: go away, depart
afferō, afferre, attulī, allātus: bring
    (something) to
aībat: third person sing., past imperfective
    of *ait:* cf. *aiēbant* in line 6

argentum, -ī, n.: silver; money
ēmittō, -ere, ēmīsī, ēmissus: let go (from
    one's hand), emancipate
exclūdō, -ere, -clūsī, -clūsus: shut out
exōrō (1): entreat, prevail

forās (adv.): out, outside
īnsāniō, -īre, īnsāniī: be mad
meretrīx, -īcis, f.: courtesan
mīrus, -a, -um: strange
palla, -ae, f.: robe, stole

quamquam (subord. conj.): although
sānus, -a, -um: sane, healthy
socer, soceri, m.: father-in-law
suscēnseō, -ēre, suscēnsuī: (+ dat.) be
    enraged at

Words to Be Entered into the Stem List (identified by line number)

1. exclūdunt
3. allātūrum
8. referam

Selection No. 1 to Be Read after Lesson 34

These selections do not continue the story but are interesting passages from early in the play.

The first words of Menaechmus II and of the homesick Messenio:

1   *Men II* Voluptās nūlla est nautīs, Messēniō,
     major meō animō quam cum ex altō procul
     terram cōnspiciunt. *Mess* Major, nōn dīcam dolō
     sī adveniēns terram videās quae fuerit tua.

Messenio has had enough of searching:

5   Sī acum, crēdō, quaererēs,
     acum invēnissēs, sī adesset, jam diū.
     Hominem inter vīvōs quaeritāmus mortuum,
     nam invēnissēmus jam diū, sī vīveret.

Supplementary Plautus Vocabulary, Selection No. 1, Lesson 34

acus, acūs, f.: needle, pin
adveniō, -īre, -vēnī: arrive
dolus, -ī, m.: deceit
jam diū (adv.): a long time ago
nauta, -ae, m.: sailor
procul (adv.): at a distance, far away
quaeritō (1): keep on seeking
terra, -ae, f.: land
voluptās, -ātis, f.: pleasure

Words to Be Entered into the Stem List (identified by line number)

3. cōnspiciunt
8. invēnissēmus

Selection No. 2 to Be Read after Lesson 34

The two Menaechmi recognize each other. They decide to return to Syracuse after selling everything at auction. Messenio asks to be the auctioneer.

1   *Men II* Mī germāne gemine frāter, salvē! Ego sum geminus.
   Men I Ō salvē, īnspērāte, multīs post annīs quem cōnspicor.
   Men II Frāter, et tū, quem ego multīs miseriīs, labōribus
   ūsque adhūc quaesīvī quemque ego esse inventum gaudeō.
5   *Mess* Hoc erat, quod haec tē meretrīx hujus vocābat nōmine:
   hunc cēnsēbat tē esse, crēdō, cum vocat tē ad prandium.
   Men I Namque edepol jussī hīc mihi hodiē prandium apparārier (= apparārī)
   clam meam uxōrem, cui pallam surrupuī dūdum domō:
   eam dedī huic. Quō modō haec ad tē pervēnit?
10 *Men II* Meretrīx hūc ad prandium mē abdūxit, mē sibi dedisse aiēbat. . . .
   In patriam redeāmus ambō. *Men I* Frāter, faciam ut tū volēs,
   auctiōnem hīc faciam et vendam quidquid est. *Men II* Fīat.
   Mess Scītisne quid ego vōs rogō? Praecōnium ut mihi dētis. *Men I* Dabitur.
   Mess Auctiō fiet Menaechmī māne sānē septimī.
15 Vēnībunt servī, supellex, fundī, aedēs, omnia.
   Vēnībit uxor quoque etiam, sī quis ēmptor vēnerit.
   Nunc spectātōrēs, valēte et nōbīs clārē plaudite!

FĪNIS

Line Notes

2. *multīs post annīs: post* here equals *posteā,* meaning "afterward" or "later." *Multīs annīs* is an ablative and expresses the "degree of difference": "later by many years/many years later."

13. *scītisne quid . . . rogō:* Plautus often uses the indicative mood in an indirect question where classical Latin uses the subjunctive.

14. *māne sānē septimī:* You should read lines 14–17 aloud to enjoy the sound pattern and the rhythm.

Supplementary Plautus Vocabulary, Selection No. 2, Lesson 34

abdūcō, -ere, -dūxī, -ductus: lead away
aedēs, aedium, f. pl.: house
aiēbat: third person sing., past imperfective of *ait*
ambō, -ae, -ō: both
apparō (1): get ready, prepare
auctiō, -ōnis, f.: sale, auction
cēnseō, -ēre, cēnsuī: think
clam (prep.): without the knowledge of
clārus, -a, -um: loud, clear
cōnspicor, -ārī, -ātus: see, lay eyes on
dūdum (adv.): a little while ago, just now

ēmptor, -ōris, m.: buyer
fundus, -ī, m.: land, acreage
geminus, -a, -um: twin
germānus, -a, -um: having the same parents, full brother
hīc (adv.): here, in this place
hodiē (adv., from *hōc diē*): today, on this day
hūc (adv.): here, to this place
īnspērātus, -a, -um: unhoped for
māne: in the morning
meretrīx, -īcis, f.: courtesan

miseria, -ae, f.: trouble

palla, -ae, f.: robe, stole

plaudō, -ere, plausī, plausus: applaud

praecōnium, -ī, n.: the job of auctioneer

prandium, -ī, n.: dinner, luncheon

salvē: be well, hello, greetings

sānē (adv.): definitely

septimus, -a, -um: seventh (day)

spectātor, -ōris, m.: member of the audience

supellex, supellectilis, f.: furniture

surripiō, -ere, -rupuī, -reptus: take away secretly, steal

usque adhūc (adv.): even up to this point

valeō, -ēre, valuī: fare well; *valēte:* goodbye

vendō, -ere, vendī, venditus: sell

vēneō, -īre: go for sale, be sold

Words to Be Entered into the Stem List (identified by line number)

2. cōnspicor
4. inventum
5. vocābat

7. apparārier
9. pervēnit
10. abdūxit

Eutropius

Roman war elephant
carrying a tower (Pompeii)

Little is known about the life of Eutropius. He was
proconsul in Asia in A.D. 371 and is said to have been the
secretary of the Emperor Constantine. The *Breviarium* is
a summary of the history of Rome from 753 B.C. to A.D. 364.
He followed standard sources, such as Livy and Suetonius,
and was an impartial historian. He made some mistakes, but
most of these were in connection with dates. His style is
simple and direct.

The Second Punic War was one of the great crises that the Romans had to face.
After the First Punic War (264–41 B.C.) the Carthaginians prepared for a renewal of the
struggle with Rome for control of the Western Mediterranean Sea. Hannibal, a sworn enemy
of Rome and one of the great military geniuses of all time, was put in command of the
Carthaginian forces. He crossed the Alps and for some fifteen years ravaged Italy, but he did
not succeed in bringing about the surrender of Rome. Finally, Hannibal was forced to return
to Africa, where Scipio defeated him at the battle of Zama in 202 B.C. In 149 B.C. the
Romans forced the Carthaginians into the third and final Punic War. The Carthaginians were
crushed, and their city destroyed in 146 B.C.

See the map accompanying these selections for Hannibal's route and for the places
mentioned in the text.

From the End of the First to the End of the Second Punic War, 241–201 B.C.

Fīnītō igitur Pūnicō bellō, quod per XXIII annōs tractum est, Rōmānī jam clārissimā glōriā
nōtī lēgātōs ad Ptolemaeum, Aegyptī rēgem, mīsērunt auxilia prōmittentēs, quia rēx Syriae
Antiochus bellum eī intulerat. Ille grātiās Rōmānīs ēgit, auxilia nōn accēpit. Jam enim fuerat
pūgna trānsācta. Eōdem tempore potentissimus rēx Siciliae Hierō Rōmam vēnit ad lūdōs
spectandōs.

L. Cornēliō Lentulō, Fulviō Flaccō cōnsulibus, quibus Hierō Rōmam vēnerat, etiam
contrā Ligurēs intrā Ītaliam bellum gestum est et dē hīs triumphātum. Karthāginiēnsēs tamen
bellum reparāre temptābant, Sardiniēnsēs, quī ex condiciōne pācis Rōmānīs pārēre dēbēbant,
ad rebellandum impellentēs. Vēnit tamen Rōmam lēgātiō Karthāginiēnsium et pācem
impetrāvit.

T. Manliō Torquātō, C. Atiliō Bulcō cōnsulibus, dē Sardīs triumphātum est, et pāce
omnibus locīs factā Rōmānī nūllum bellum habuērunt, quod hīs post Rōmam conditam semel
tantum, Numā Pompiliō rēgnante, contigerat.

Reprinted from Waldo E. Sweet, ed., *Latin Workshop Experimental Materials*, bk. 2, rev. ed. (Ann Arbor:
University of Michigan Press, 1956), pp. 1–10.

L. Postumius Albīnus, Cn. Fulvius Centumalus cōnsulēs bellum contrā Īllyriōs gessērunt et multīs cīvitātibus captīs etiam rēgēs in dēditiōnem accēpērunt. Ac tum prīmum ex Īllyriīs triumphātum est.

L. Aemiliō cōnsule, ingentēs Gallōrum cōpiae Alpēs trānsiērunt. Sed prō Rōmānīs tōta Ītalia cōnsēnsit, trāditumque est ā Fabiō historicō, quī eī bellō interfuit, DCCC mīlia hominum parāta ad id bellum fuisse. Sed rēs per cōnsulem tantum prosperē gesta est. XL mīlia hostium interfecta sunt et triumphus Aemiliō dēcrētus.

Aliquot deinde annīs post contrā Gallōs intrā Ītaliam pūgnātum est, fīnītumque bellum M. Claudiō Marcellō et Cn. Cornēliō Scīpiōne cōnsulibus. Tum Marcellus cum parvā manū equitum dīmicāvit et rēgem Gallōrum, Viridomarum nōmine, manū suā occīdit. Posteā cum conlēgā ingentēs cōpiās Gallōrum perēmit, Mediolānum expūgnāvit, grandem praedam Rōmam pertulit. Ac triumphāns Marcellus spolia Gallī stīpitī imposita umerīs suīs vexit.

Beginning of the Second Punic War, 218 B.C.

M. Minuciō Rūfō, P. Cornēliō cōnsulibus, Histrīs bellum inlātum est, quia latrōcinātī nāvibus Rōmānōrum fuerant, quae frūmenta exhibēbant, perdomitīque sunt omnēs. Eōdem annō bellum Pūnicum secundum Rōmānīs inlātum est per Hannibalem, Karthāginiēnsium ducem, quī Saguntum, Hispāniae cīvitātem Rōmānīs amīcam, oppūgnāre aggressus est, annum agēns vīcēsimum aetātis, cōpiīs congregātīs CL mīlium. Huic Rōmānī per lēgātōs dēnūntiāvērunt ut bellō abstinēret. Is lēgātōs admittere nōluit. Rōmānī etiam Karthāginem mīsērunt, ut mandārētur Hannibalī nē bellum contrā sociōs populī Rōmānī gereret. Dūra respōnsa ā Karthāginiēnsibus data sunt. Saguntīnī intereā famē victī sunt, captīque ab Hannibale ultimīs poenīs adficiuntur. Bellum Karthāginiēnsibus indictum est.

The Western Mediterranean in the Time of Hannibal

Hannibal Crosses the Alps

Tum P. Cornēlius Scīpiō cum exercitū in Hispāniam profectus est, Ti. Semprōnius in
Siciliam. Hannibal, relictō in Hispāniā frātre Hasdrubale, Pȳrēnaeum trānsiit. Alpēs, adhūc
eā parte inviās, sibi patefēcit. Trāditur ad Ītaliam LXXX mīlia peditum, X mīlia equitum,
septem et XXX elephantōs addūxisse. Intereā multī Ligurēs et Gallī Hannibalī sē
conjūnxērunt. Semprōnius Gracchus, cognitō ad Ītaliam Hannibalis adventū, ex Siciliā
exercitum Arīminum trājēcit.

Battle of Lake Trasimene

P. Cornēlius Scīpiō Hannibalī prīmus occurrit. Commissō proeliō, fugātīs suīs ipse vulnerātus
in castra rediit. Semprōnius Gracchus et ipse cōnflīgit apud Trebiam amnem. Is quoque
vincitur. Hannibalī multī sē in Ītaliā dēdidērunt. Inde ad Tusciam veniēns Hannibal Flāminiō
cōnsulī occurrit. Ipsum Flāminium interēmit; Rōmānōrum XXV mīlia caesa sunt, cēterī
diffūgērunt. Missus adversus Hannibalem posteā ā Rōmānīs Q. Fabius Maximus. Is eum
differendō pūgnam ab impetū frēgit, mox inventā occāsiōne vīcit.

Battle of Cannae, 216 B.C.

Quīngentēsimō et quadrāgēsimō annō ā conditā urbe L. Aemilius Paulus, P. Terentius Varrō
contrā Hannibalem mittuntur Fabiōque succēdunt, quī abiēns ambō cōnsulēs monuit ut
Hannibalem, callidum et impatientem ducem, nōn aliter vincerent quam proelium differendō.
Vērum cum impatientiā Varrōnis cōnsulis contrādīcente alterō cōnsule apud vīcum, quī
Cannae appellātur, in Āpūliā pūgnātum esset, ambō cōnsulēs ab Hannibale vincuntur. In eā
pūgnā tria mīlia Afrōrum pereunt; magna pars dē exercitū Hannibalis sauciātur. Nūllō tamen
proeliō Pūnicō bellō Rōmānī gravius acceptī sunt. Periit enim in eō cōnsul Aemilius Paulus,
cōnsulārēs aut praetōriī XX, senātōrēs, captī aut occīsī XXX, nōbilēs virī CCC, mīlitum XL
mīlia, equitum III mīlia et quīngentī. In quibus malīs nēmō tamen Rōmānōrum pācis
mentiōnem habēre dīgnātus est. Servī, quod numquam ante, manūmissī et mīlitēs factī sunt.

Post eam pūgnam multae Ītaliae cīvitātēs, quae Rōmānīs pāruerant, sē ad Hannibalem
trānstulērunt. Hannibal Rōmānīs obtulit ut captīvōs redimerent respōnsumque est ā senātū
eōs cīvēs nōn esse necessāriōs quī, cum armātī essent, capī potuissent. Ille omnēs posteā
variīs suppliciīs interfēcit et trēs modiōs ānulōrum aureōrum Karthāginem mīsit, quōs ex
manibus equitum Rōmānōrum, senātōrum et mīlitum dētrāxerat. Intereā in Hispāniā, ubi
frāter Hannibalis Hasdrubal remānserat cum magnō exercitū, ut eam tōtam Āfrīs subigeret,
ā duōbus Scīpiōnibus, Rōmānīs ducibus, vincitur. Perdit in pūgnā XXXV mīlia hominum; ex
hīs capiuntur X mīlia, occīduntur XXV mīlia. Mittuntur eī ā Karthāginiēnsibus ad reparandās
vīrēs XII mīlia peditum, IV mīlia equitum, XX elephantī.

Annō quārtō postquam ad Ītaliam Hannibal vēnit, M. Claudius Marcellus cōnsul apud
Nōlam, cīvitātem Campāniae, contrā Hannibalem bene pūgnāvit. Hannibal multās cīvitātēs
Rōmānōrum per Āpūliam, Calabriam, Bruttiōs occupāvit. Quō tempore etiam rēx
Macedoniae Philippus ad eum lēgātōs mīsit, prōmittēns auxilia contrā Rōmānōs sub hāc
condiciōne, ut dēlētīs Rōmānīs ipse quoque contrā Graecōs ab Hannibale auxilia acciperet.
Captīs igitur lēgātīs Philippī et rē cognitā, Rōmānī in Macedoniam M. Valerium Laevīnum īre
jussērunt, in Sardiniam T. Manlium Torquātum prōcōnsulem. Nam etiam ea sollicitāta ab
Hannibale Rōmānōs dēseruerat.

Ita ūnō tempore quattuor locīs pūgnābātur: in Ītaliā contrā Hannibalem, in Hispāniīs contrā frātrem ejus Hasdrubalem, in Macedoniā contrā Philippum, in Sardiniā contrā Sardōs et alterum Hasdrubalem Karthāginiēnsem. Is ā T. Mānliō prōcōnsule, quī ad Sardiniam missus fuerat, vīvus est captus, occīsa duodecim mīlia, captī cum eō mīlle quīngentī, et ā Rōmānīs Sardinia subācta. Manlius victor captīvōs et Hasdrubalem Rōmam reportāvit. Intereā etiam Philippus ā Laevīnō in Macedoniā vincitur et in Hispāniā ab Scīpiōnibus Hasdrubal et Māgō, tertius frāter Hannibalis.

Campaign in Sicily

Decimō annō postquam Hannibal in Ītaliam vēnerat, P. Sulpiciō, Cn. Fulviō cōnsulibus, Hannibal usque ad quārtum mīliārium urbis accessit, equitēs ejus usque ad portam. Mox cōnsulum cum exercitū venientium metū Hannibal ad Campāniam sē recēpit. In Hispāniā ā frātre ejus Hasdrubale ambō Scīpiōnēs, quī per multōs annōs victōrēs fuerant, interficiuntur, exercitus tamen integer mānsit; cāsū enim magis erant quam virtūte dēceptī. Quō tempore etiam ā cōnsule Marcellō Siciliae magna pars capta est, quam tenēre Āfrī coeperant, et nōbilissima urbs Syrācūsāna; praeda ingēns Rōmam perlāta est. Laevīnus in Macedoniā cum Philippō et multīs Graeciae populīs et rēge Asiae Attalō amīcitiam fēcit, et ad Siciliam profectus Hannōnem quendam, Āfrōrum ducem, apud Agrigentum cīvitātem cum ipsō oppidō cēpit eumque Rōmam cum captīvīs nōbilissimīs mīsit. XL cīvitātēs in dēditiōnem accēpit, XXVI expūgnāvit. Ita omnis Sicilia recepta est; ingentī glōriā Rōmam regressus est. Hannibal in Ītaliā Cn. Fulvium cōnsulem subitō aggressus cum octō mīlibus hominum interfēcit.

War in Spain

Intereā ad Hispāniās, ubi occīsīs duōbus Scīpiōnibus nūllus Rōmānus dux erat, P. Cornēlius Scīpiō mittitur, fīlius P. Scīpiōnis, quī ibīdem bellum gesserat, annōs nātus quattuor et vīgintī, vir Rōmānōrum omnium et suā aetāte et posteriōre tempore ferē prīmus. Is Karthāginem Hispāniae capit, in quā omne aurum, argentum et bellī apparātum Āfrī habēbant, nōbilissimōs quoque obsidēs, quōs ab Hispānīs accēperant. Māgōnem etiam, frātrem Hannibalis, ibīdem capit, quem Rōmam cum aliīs mittit. Rōmae ingēns laetitia post hunc nūntium fuit. Scīpiō Hispānōrum obsidēs parentibus reddidit; quā rē omnēs ferē Hispānī ūnō animō ad eum trānsiērunt. Post quae Hasdrubalem, Hannibalis frātrem, victum fugat et praedam maximam capit.

Intereā in Ītaliā cōnsul Q. Fabius Maximus Tarentum recēpit, in quā ingentēs cōpiae Hannibalis erant. Ibi etiam ducem Hannibalis Carthalōnem occīdit, XXV mīlia hominum cāptīvōrum vēndidit, praedam mīlitibus dispertīvit, pecūniam hominum vēnditōrum ad fiscum rettulit. Tum multae cīvitātēs Rōmānōrum, quae ad Hannibalem trānsierant prius, rūrsus sē Fabiō Maximō dēdidērunt. Īnsequentī annō Scīpiō in Hispāniā ēgregiās rēs ēgit et per sē et per frātrem suum L. Scīpiōnem; LXX cīvitātēs recēpērunt. In Italiā tamen male pūgnātum est. Nam Claudius Marcellus cōnsul ab Hannibale occīsus est.

Tertiō annō postquam Scīpiō ad Hispāniās profectus fuerat, rūrsus rēs inclutās gerit. Rēgem Hispāniārum magnō proeliō victum in amīcitiam accēpit et prīmus omnium ā victō obsidēs nōn poposcit.

Dēspērāns Hannibal Hispāniās contrā Scīpiōnem diūtius posse retinērī, frātrem suum Hasdrubalem ad Ītaliam cum omnibus cōpiīs ēvocāvit. Is, veniēns eōdem itinere quō etiam

Hannibal vēnerat, ā cōnsulibus Ap. Claudiō Nerōne et M. Liviō Salīnātōre apud Sēnam, Pīcēnī cīvitātem, in īnsidiās compositās incidit. Strēnuē tamen pūgnāns occīsus est; ingentēs ejus cōpiae captae aut interfectae sunt, magnum pondus aurī atque argentī Rōmam relātum est. Post haec Hannibal diffīdere jam dē bellī coepit ēventū. Rōmānīs ingēns animus accessit; itaque et ipsī ēvocāvērunt ex Hispāniā P. Cornēlium Scīpiōnem. Is Rōmam cum ingentī glōriā vēnit.

Q. Caeciliō, L. Valeriō cōnsulibus, omnēs cīvitātēs, quae in Bruttiīs ab Hannibale tenēbantur, Rōmānīs sē trādidērunt.

Scipio Invades Africa, 204 B.C.

Annō quārtō decimō posteāquam in Ītaliam Hannibal vēnerat, Scīpiō, quī multa bene in Hispāniā ēgerat, cōnsul est factus et in Āfricam missus. Cui virō dīvīnum quiddam inesse exīstimābātur, adeō ut putārētur etiam cum nūminibus habēre sermōnem. Is in Āfricā contrā Hannōnem, ducem Āfrōrum pūgnat; exercitum ejus interficit. Secundō proeliō castra capit cum quattuor mīlibus et quīngentīs mīlitibus, XI mīlibus occīsīs. Syphācem, Numidiae rēgem, quī sē Āfrīs conjūnxerat, capit et castra ejus invādit. Syphāx cum nōbilissimīs Numidīs et īnfīnītīs spoliīs Rōmam ā Scīpiōne mittitur. Quā rē audītā omnis ferē Ītalia Hannibalem dēserit. Ipse ā Karthāginiēnsibus redīre in Āfricam jubētur, quam Scīpiō vāstābat.

Ita annō septimō decimō ab Hannibale Ītalia līberāta est. Lēgātī Karthāginiēnsium pācem ā Scīpiōne petīvērunt; ab eō ad senātum Rōmam missī sunt. Quadrāgintā et quīnque diēbus hīs indūtiae datae sunt, quousque īre Rōmam et regredī possent; et trīgintā mīlia pondō argentī ab hīs accepta sunt. Senātus ex arbitriō Scīpiōnis pācem jussit cum Karthāginiēnsibus fierī. Scīpiō hīs condiciōnibus dedit: nē amplius quam trīgintā nāvēs habērent, ut quīngenta mīlia pondō argentī darent, captīvōs et perfugās redderent.

Interim Hannibale veniente ad Āfricam pāx turbāta est, multa hostīlia ab Āfrīs facta sunt. Lēgātī tamen eōrum ex urbe venientēs ā Rōmānīs captī sunt, sed jubente Scīpiōne dīmissī. Hannibal quoque frequentibus proeliīs victus ā Scīpiōne petit etiam ipse pācem. Cum ventum esset ad conloquium, īsdem condiciōnibus data est quibus prius, additīs quīngentīs mīlibus pondō argentī centum mīlibus lībrārum propter novam perfidiam. Karthāginiēnsibus condiciōnēs displicuērunt jussēruntque Hannibalem pūgnāre. Īnfertur ā Scīpiōne et Masinissā, aliō rēge Numidārum, quī amīcitiam cum Scīpiōne fēcerat, Karthāginī bellum. Hannibal trēs explōrātōrēs ad Scīpiōnis castra mīsit, quōs captōs Scīpiō circumdūcī per castra jussit ostendīque hīs tōtum exercitum, mox etiam prandium darī dīmittīque, ut renūntiārent Hannibalī quae apud Rōmānōs vīdissent.

Battle of Zama, 202 B.C.

Intereā proelium ab utrōque duce īnstrūctum est, quāle vix ūllā memoriā fuit, cum perītissimī virī cōpiās suās ad bellum ēdūcerent. Scīpiō victor recēdit paene ipsō Hannibale captō, quī prīmum cum multīs equitibus, deinde cum vīgintī, postrēmō cum quattuor ēvāsit. Inventa in castrīs Hannibalis argentī pondō vīgintī mīlia, aurī octōgintā, cētera supellectilis cōpiōsa. Post id certāmen pāx cum Karthāginiēnsibus facta est. Scīpiō Rōmam rediit, ingentī glōriā triumphāvit atque Āfricānus ex eō appellārī coeptus est. Fīnem accēpit secundum Pūnicum bellum post annum nōnum decimum quam coeperat.

Vocabulary for the Selections from Eutropius

Vocabulary that appears in the General Vocabulary at the end of the book is not included here.

abeō, -īre, -iī, -itūrus: go away, depart

abstineō, -ēre, -tinuī, -tentus: (+ abl.) keep away from, abstain from

ac (coord. conj.): and

accēdō, -ere, -cessī: come to

addō, -ere, -didī, -ditus: add, increase

addūcō, -ere, -dūxī, -ductus: lead to

adficiō, -ficere, -fēcī, -fectus: afflict

adhūc (adv.): thus far, still

admittō, -ere, -mīsī, -missus: let in, admit

adventus, -ūs, m.: arrival

adversus (prep. + acc.): facing, against

Aegyptus, -ī, f.: Egypt

Āfrī, -ōrum, m. pl.: Africans

Āfricānus, -ī, m.: Africanus (the honorary name of Scipio, given for his success in Africa)

aggredior, -gredī, -gressus: attack; begin

Agrigentum, -ī, n.: Agrigentum (a city on the south coast of Sicily)

aliquot (indecl. adj.): some, several, a few

aliter (adv.): otherwise, in another way

Alpēs, -ium, m. pl.: Alps (mountain range to the north of Italy)

ambō, -ae, -ō: both

amnis, -is, m.: river

amplior, amplius: more; (with numerals) more than

Antiochus, -ī, m.: Antiochus (a king of Egypt)

ānulus, -ī, m.: ring

apparātus, -ūs, m.: equipment

Āpūlia, -ae, f.: Apulia (a region in southwest Italy)

arbitrium, -ī, n.: judgment, decision

argentum, -ī, n.: silver

Arīminum, -ī, n.: Arimini (a town in south Italy)

armō (1): furnish with arms, arm

Asia, -ae, f.: Asia

Attalus, -ī, m.: Attalus (an Asian king)

aurum, -ī, n.: gold

Bruttiī, -ōrum, m. pl.: the Bruttians (inhabitants of a region in extreme southwest Italy)

caedō, -ere, cecīdī, caesus: kill, cut down, slaughter

Calabria, -ae, f.: Calabria (a region in extreme southeast Italy)

callidus, -a, -um: skillful, experienced, crafty

Campānia, -ae, f.: Campania (a region of Italy, around modern Naples)

Cannae, -ārum, f. pl.: Cannae (with singular verb; a village in Apulia in south Italy)

captīvus, -ī, m.: captive, prisoner

Carthalō, -ōnis, m.: Carthalo (an African general)

cāsus, -ūs, m.: chance; misfortune, accident

certāmen, -inis, n.: struggle, confrontation

circumdūcō, -ere, -dūxī, -ductus: lead around

cīvis, -is, m. & f.: citizen

clārus, -a, -um: famous, renowned

coepī, coepisse (defective verb): begin

committō, -ere, -mīsī, -missus: start, commence

compositus, -a, -um: prepared, well-arranged

cōnflīgō, -ere, -flīxī, -flīctus: come into conflict, fight

congregō (1): herd together; assemble

conjungō, -ere, -jūnxī, -jūnctus: join together with

conlēga, -ae, f.: colleague, comrade

conloquium, -ī, n.: conversation, conference

cōnsentiō, -īre, -sēnsī: agree, unite

cōnsul, cōnsulis, m.: consul (chief magistrate of Rome)

cōnsulāris, -e: consular, having the rank of consul

contingō, -ere, -tigī, -tāctus: (+ dat.) happen to

contrādīcō, -ere, -dīxī, -dictus: speak against, object

cōpiōsus, -a, -um: abundant, copious

dēcernō, -ere, -crēvī, -crētus: decree

decimus, -a, -um: tenth

dēcipiō, -ere, -cēpī, -ceptus: deceive

dēditiō, -ōnis, f.: surrender

dēdō, -ere, -didī, -ditus: give up, surrender

dēleō, -ēre, -ēvī, -ētus: destroy, annihilate

dēnūntiō (1): announce officially; give official warning to

dēspērō (1): despair, give up hope

dētrahō, -ere, -trāxī, -tractus: pull off, pull from

differō, -ferre, distulī, dīlātus: defer, delay

diffīdō, -ere, -fīsus: distrust, despair of

diffugiō, -ere, -fūgī: flee, run away

dignō (1): think worthy

dīmicō (1): fight

dīmittō, -ere, -mīsī, -missus: send away

dispertiō, -īre, -īvī, -ītus: distribute, divide

displiceō, -ēre, -plicuī: (+ dat.) displease

diūtius: longer, still longer, for any more time

dūrus, -a, -um: hard, harsh

ēdūcō, -ere, -dūxī, -ductus: lead out, march out (an army)

ēgregius, -a, -um: outstanding, excellent

elephantus, -ī, m.: elephant

enim (sentence connector): for (introduces an explanation)

eques, equitis, m.: knight, (in pl.) cavalry

ēvādō, ēvādere, ēvāsī: escape, evade

ēventus, -ūs, m.: outcome

ēvocō (1): call, summon (from somewhere)

exīstimō (1): believe

explōrātor, -ōris, m.: scout, spy

expūgnō (1): assault, storm

Fabius, -ī, m.: Fabius (one of the earliest Roman historians, his full name was Fabius Pictor)

famēs, -is, f.: hunger

ferē (adv.): almost, nearly

fīniō, -īre, -iī, -ītus: finish

fiscus, -ī, m.: treasury

Flāminius, -ī, m.: Flaminius (a Roman general)

frequēns (-entis): frequent, numerous

frūmentum, -ī, n.: grain

fugō (1): put to flight

Gallī, -ōrum, m. pl.: Gauls (people of modern France)

glōria, -ae, f.: glory, fame

Graecī, -ōrum, m. pl.: Greeks

Graecia, -ae, f.: Greece

grandis, -e: large, great

grātiās agere: give thanks

gravis, -e: heavy; severe, serious

Hannibal, -balis, m.: Hannibal (the famous Carthaginian general)

Hannō, -ōnis, m.: Hanno (an African general)

Hasdrubal, -balis, m.: Hasdrubal (brother of Hannibal)

Hierō, -ōnis, m.: Hiero (king of Sicily)

Hispānī, -ōrum, m. pl.: Spaniards, inhabitants of Spain

Hispānia, -ae, f.: Spain

historicus, -ī, m.: historian, writer of history

Histrī, -ōrum, m. pl.: the Histrī (a people in modern Yugoslavia)

hostīlis, -e: hostile, appropriate to an enemy

ibīdem (adv.): in the same place

Illyriī, -ōrum, m. pl.: Illyrians (people living on the east coast of the Adriatic Sea)

impatientia, -ae, f.: impatience

impellō, -ere, -pulsī, -pulsus: drive, urge, impel

impetrō (1): obtain, procure (by asking)

incidō, -ere, -cidī: fall into, fall in with

inclutus, -a, -um: famous

inde (adv.): thence, from that place

indīcō, -ere, -dīxī, -dictus: declare; *bellum indīcere:* (+ dat.) declare war against

indūtiae, -ārum, f. pl.: armistice, truce

īnfīnītus, -a, -um: countless, infinite

īnsequēns (-entis): next, following, succeeding

īnsidiae, -ārum, f. pl.: ambush, trap

īnsum, -esse, -fuī: (+ dat.) be contained in, be in, belong to

integer, -gra, -grum: whole, unbroken, undivided

intereā (adv.): in the meantime, meanwhile

interficiō, -ere, -fēcī, -fectus: destroy, kill

interim (adv.): in the meantime, meanwhile

interimō, -imere, -ēmī, -emptus: kill

intersum, -esse, -fuī: (+ dat.) be involved in, participate in

invius, -a, -um: without a road, trackless

Ītalia, -ae, f.: Italy

Karthāginiēnsēs, -ium, m. pl.:
Carthaginians

Karthāgō, -inis, f.: Carthage (rival city of
Rome in North Africa, opposite Sicily)

laetitia, -ae, f.: happiness, rejoicing

Laevīnus, -ī, m.: Laevinus (last name of
M. Valerius Laevinus)

latrōcinor, -ārī, -ātus: be a pirate

lēgātiō, -ōnis, f.: embassy, legation

lēgātus, -ī, m.: legate, envoy

lībra, -ae, f.: a pound (of twelve ounces)

Ligurēs, Ligurum, m. pl.: Ligurians (people
of Northwest Alpine Italy)

lūdus, -ī, m.: game, sport

Macedonia, -ae, f.: Macedonia (northern
Greece)

magis (adv.): more; *magis . . . quam:*
more . . . than

Māgō, -ōnis, m.: Mago (brother of
Hannibal)

mandō (1): (+ dat.) command, order

manumittō, -ere, -mīsī, -missus: set free,
emancipate

manus, -ūs, f.: hand; band, company

Marcellus, -ī, m.: Marcellus (a Roman
general)

Masinissa, -ae, m.: Masinissa (a Numidian
king)

Mediolānum, -ī, n.: Milan (a town in
northern Italy)

memoria, -ae, f.: memory, remembrance

mentiō, -ōnis, f.: mention; *mentiōnem
habēre:* make mention

mīliārium, -ī, n.: milestone

modius, -ī, m.: peck (a unit of measure)

necessārius, -a, -um: necessary, needed

Nōla, -ae, f.: Nola (a town in Campania)

nōnus decimus, -a, -um: nineteenth

Numa Pompilius, Numae Pompiliī, m.:
Numa Pompilius (the second legendary
king of Rome)

nūmen, -inis, n.: supernatural being

Numidia, -ae, f.: Numidia (a region of
Africa)

Numidiae, -ārum, f. pl.: Numidians,
inhabitants of Numidia

nūntius, -ī, m.: message, announcement,
news

occupō (1): besiege, occupy

occurrō, -ere, -currī: (+ dat.) rush against,
meet with

oppidum, -ī, n.: town

oppūgnō (1): besiege

ostendō, -ere, -tendī, -tentus: show, display

parēns, -entis, m. & f.: parent

pareō, -ēre, -uī: (+ dat.) be obedient to,
obey

pars, partis, f.: part, portion

pateficiō, -ere, -fēcī, -factus: open up, make
open

pāx, pācis, f.: peace

pedes, peditis, m.: foot soldier, (in pl.)
infantry

perdō, -ere, -didī, -ditus: lose

perdomō, -āre, -uī, -itus: subdue

perferō, -ferre, -tulī, -lātus: bring to

perfidia, -ae, f.: deceit, perfidy

perfuga, -ae, m.: military deserter

perimō, -ere, -ēmī, -emptus: destroy, kill

perītus, -a, -um: experienced, expert

Philippus, -ī, m.: Philip (king of Macedonia)

Pīcēnī, -ōrum, m. pl.: the Piceni (a tribe of
northern Italy)

poena, -ae, f.: punishment

pondō (indecl.): pound, pounds; *trigintā
mīlia pondō argentī:* thirty thousand
pounds of silver

pondus, -eris, n.: weight

poscō, -ere, poposcī: (with acc. of thing
asked, *ab* + abl. for person from whom)
demand, require

posteā (adv.): afterward, later

posteāquam (conj.): after

posterior, -ius: later

postrēmō (adv.): finally, at last

potēns (-entis): powerful

praeda, -ae, f.: booty, loot, plunder

praetōrius, -ī, m.: praetorian, having the
rank of praetor

prandium, -ī, n.: dinner, luncheon

prius (adv.): earlier

prōcōnsul, -is, m.: proconsul (a Roman
magistrate, former consul)

proelium, -ī, n.: battle

prōmittō, -ere, -mīsī, -missus: promise

prosperē (adv.): successfully

Ptolemaeus, -ī, m.: Ptolemy (a king of
Egypt)

pūgna, -ae, f.: battle

Pūnicus, -a, -um: Punic, Carthaginian

quadrāgēsimus, -a, -um: fortieth

quā rē (adv.): wherefore, on which account

quārtus, -a, -um: fourth

quārtus decimus, -a, -um: fourteenth

quīdam, quaedam, quiddam: a certain

quīngentēsimus, -a, -um: five hundredth

quousque (adv.): until the time when

rebellō (1): renew war

recēdō, -ere, -cessī: give ground, fall back, retreat

recipiō, -ere, -cēpī, -ceptus: take back; *sē recipere:* to take oneself back, withdraw

redimō, -ere, -ēmī, -emptus: buy back, redeem

rēgnō (1): rule, reign

regredior, -gredī, -gressus: return, come back

remaneō, -ēre, -mānsī: stay behind, remain

renūntiō (1): carry back news, report

reparō (1): get ready again, renew

reportō (1): carry back

respōnsum, -ī, n.: answer

retineō, -ēre, -tinuī, -tentus: keep, keep back, retain

rūrsus (adv.): again

Saguntīnī, -ōrum, m. pl.: Saguntians (people of Saguntum)

Saguntum, -ī, n.: Saguntum (a town in Spain)

Sardī, -ōrum, m. pl.: Sardinians (inhabitants of Sardinia)

Sardinia, -ae, f.: Sardinia (a large island off the west coast of Italy)

Sardiniēnsēs, -ium, m. pl.: Sardinians

sauciō (1): wound

Scīpiō, -ōnis, m.: Scipio (the name of a Roman family)

secundus, -a, -um: second

semel (adv.): once, one time

Sēna, -ae, f.: Sienna (a town in northern Italy)

senātor, -ōris, m.: senator, member of the senate

septimus decimus, -a, -um: seventeenth

sermō, -ōnis, m.: conversation, talk

Sicilia, -ae, f.: Sicily

socius, -ī, m.: ally

sollicitō (1): stir up, incite to revolt

spolium, -ī, n.: loot, booty, spoils

stīpes, stīpitis, m.: stick, pole

strēnuē (adv.): vigorously, strenuously

subigō, -ere, -ēgī, -āctus: subdue, conquer

succēdō, -ere, -cessī: come after, succeed

supellex, -ectilis, f.: furniture, household goods

supplicium, -ī, n.: penalty, torture

Syphāx, -ācis, m.: Syphax (king of Numidia)

Syrācūsānus, -a, -um: Syracusan, having to do with the city of Syracuse

Syria, -ae, f.: Syria

tantum (adv.): only, just

temptō (1): try, attempt

tertius, -a, -um: third

trādō, -ere, -didī, -ditus: hand down, hand over, relate

trānseō, -īre, -iī: go across, cross

trānsferō, -ferre, -tulī, -lātus: carry across, transfer

trānsigō, -igere, -ēgī, -āctus: finish

Trebia, -ae, f.: the Trebia (a river in Italy)

triumphō (1): celebrate a triumph

triumphus, -ī, m.: triumph

turbō (1): disturb, break

Tuscia, -ae, f.: Etruria

ultimus, -a, -um: final, ultimate

umerus, -ī, m.: shoulder

usque (adv.): (with *ad* + acc.) all the way to

varius, -a, -um: different, varied

Varrō, Varrōnis, m.: Varro (a Roman consul and general)

vastō (1): lay waste, devastate

vehō, -ere, vexī, vectus: carry

vendō, -ere, -didī, -itus: put up for sale

vīcēsimus, -a, -um: twentieth; *annum agere vīcēsimum:* to be nineteen years old

vīcus, -ī, m.: village, town

Viridomarus, -ī, m.: Viridomarus (king of Gauls)

vix (adv.): scarcely, hardly

vulnerō (1): wound

Cardinal Numbers

XI (undecim): 11
XII (duodecim): 12
XX (vīgintī): 20
XXIII (trēs et vīgintī): 23
XXV (vīgintī et quīnque): 25
XXVI (vīgintī et sex): 26
XXX (trīgintā): 30
XXXV (trīgintā et quīnque): 35

XL (quadrāgintā): 40
XLV (quadrāgintā et quīnque): 45
LXX (septuāgintā): 70
LXXX (octōgintā): 80
CL (centum et quīnquāgintā): 150
CCC (trecentī, -ae, -a): 300
D (quīngentī, -ae, -a): 500
DCCC (octingentī, -ae, -a): 800

Stem List

While the number of words in the Latin dictionary is large, the number of frequently occurring stems is not. Familiarity with them is one of the best means to enlarge a beginner's vocabulary, especially when used together with a study of prefixes and suffixes. Stems and prefixes undergo, however, certain sound changes according to their environment. The sounds, and therefore the spellings, of many Latin words and their English derivatives are determined by *vowel weakening* and by *assimilation*. By reference to meaning and sound changes you will learn to recognize the stems of many Latin words.

Vowel Weakening

Vowel weakening is a universal feature. For example, the vowel *a* in the English word *land* is weakened in the compound *England*. In the compound word *Newfoundland* the vowels in both *found* and *land* are weakened so that the word is pronounced something like *Newf'ndl'nd*. In Latin there are four main patterns of vowel weakening. These can be observed in some of the compound words to be entered in the stem list.

1. short *a* becomes *i*, e.g., ca*d*ō → inc*i*dō
2. short *a* becomes *e*, e.g., ca*p*iō, ca*p*tus → reci*p*iō, rece*p*tus
3. short *e* becomes *i*, e.g., le*g*ō → coll*i*gō
4. *ae* becomes *ī*, e.g., ca*e*dō → inc*ī*dō

Assimilation

Assimilation is most obvious in compound words where prefixes assimilate (i.e., become similar) to the initial consonant of a stem with which they are compounded. The very word *assimilation* is a compound of the prefix *ad-* and the stem *simil*. This explains variations like *addūcō, accurrō, afferō, assistō, attendō,* all of which have the prefix *ad-*. A combination of vowel weakening and assimilation explains words like *acceptus* where *adcaptus* would be expected.

This list is just a beginning of your study of Latin stems. You may want to expand the number of stems as you begin to read the works of various Latin authors. This is not meant to be a scholarly list of stems; rather it is meant to be a practical aid for beginners.

A Selective List of Productive Latin Stems

āc-: sharp

aud-/audīt-: hear

aed-: build

aud-/aus-: dare

aequ-: level

aug-/auct-: increase

ag-/āct-: do

cad-/cās-: fall

al-: nourish

caed-/caes-: fell, cut

al-/ali-: other

cap-/capt-: take

am-/amāt-: love

cēd-/cess-: yield, go

anim-: breath

cēns-: assess, rate

cern-/cert-/crēt-: perceive

cing-/cīnct-: surround

claud-/claus-: close

col-/cult-: care for

cord-: heart

cre-/creāt-: bring forth, create

cup-/cupit-: wish

cūr-/cūrāt-: care

da-/dat-: give

dīc-/dict-: say, tell

doc-/doct-: teach

dūc-/duct-: lead

e-/ī-/it: go

es-: be, live

fā-/fāt-: speak

fac-/fact-: make, do

fall-/fals-: deceive

fer-/tul-/lāt-: carry, bear

fid-/fīd-: trust

fing-/fict-: mold, form

frang-/frag-/frāct-: break

fug-/fugit-: flee

fund-/fūs-: pour

gen-: birth

ger-/gest-: carry, do

gnō-/nō-: learn

grad-/gress-: walk, step

hab-/habit-: have

ī-/it-: go (see e-/ī-/it-)

jac-: lie

jac-/jact-: lay, throw

jub-/juss-: command, order

jung-/jūnct-: join, bind

jūr-/jūs-: swear, just, right

juv-/jūt-: help

laed-/laes-: hurt

leg-/lēct-: pick, read

linqu-/līqu-/lict-: leave

loqu-/locūt-: speak

man-/māns-: stay

metu-: fear

mīr-/mīrāt-: wonder

mitt-/miss-: send, let go

mon-/monit-: warn, advise

mōr-: custom

mor-/morāt-: delay

mori-/mort-/morit-: die

mov-/mōt-: move

op-: means, power

oper-: work

or-/ort-: rise, grow

ōr-/ōs-: mouth, speak

pand-/pass-/pat-: open up

parā-/parāt-: prepare

parc-/pars-: spare

pari-/part-: produce

pāsc-/pāst-: feed

pati-/pass-: suffer, endure

pell-/puls-: push

pet-/petit-: seek

plac-: please

plē-: -fill

plec-/plex-: fold, weave

pōn-/posit-: put, place

pot-: power

prehend-/prehēns-: catch

prem-/press-: press

quaer-/quaesīt-: ask, seek

rap-/rapt-: snatch

reg-/rēct-: stretch, guide

rump-/rupt-: break

scī-: know

scrīb-/scrīpt-: write

sent-/sēns-: discern by senses

sequ-/secūt-: follow

simul-/simulāt-: pretend

solv-/solūt-: solve, loosen

spec-/spect-: see, spy

stā-/stat-: stand, set

sūm-/sūmpt-: take

tac-/tacit-: be quiet

tang-/tāct-: touch

ten-/tent-: hold

tend-/tēns-/tent-: stretch

toll-: lift

tra-/tract-: drag

ūt-/ūs-: use

val-: strong

veh-/vect-: carry, ride

ven-/vent-: come

vert-/vers-: turn

vi-: force

vid-/vīs-: see

vinc-/vict-: conquer

voc-/vocāt-: call

vol-: wish

Basic Sentences

1.1. Manus manum lavat.

1.2. Impedit īra animum.

1.3. Spem successus alit.

1.4. Fugit hōra.

1.5. Occāsiō facit fūrem.

1.6. Vincit vēritās.

2.1. Fūrem fūr cognōscit et lupum lupus.

2.2. Diem nox premit, diēs noctem.

2.3. Pecūnia nōn satiat avāritiam sed irrītat.

2.4. Vītam regit fortūna, nōn sapientia.

2.5. Senātus populusque Rōmānus.

3.1. Fūrem fūr cognōscere potest.

3.2. Quis fūrem cognōscere potest?

3.3. Quem occāsiō facit?

4.1. Fortiter, fidēliter, fēlīciter.

4.2. Vēritās numquam perit.

4.3. Prūdēns cum cūrā vīvit, stultus sine cūrā.

4.4. Gladiātor in harēnā capit cōnsilium.

5.1. Ā fonte pūrō pūra dēfluit aqua.

5.2. Fīnis corōnat opus.

5.3. In omnī rē vincit imitātiōnem vēritās.

5.4. Vānēscit absēns et intrat novus amor.

5.5. Fortem Fortūna adjuvat.

6.1. Occāsiō aegrē offertur, facile āmittitur.

6.2. Ā cane nōn magnō saepe tenētur aper.

6.3. Multitūdō nōn ratiōne dūcitur sed impetū.

7.1. Magna dī cūrant, parva neglegunt.

7.2. Ācta deōs numquam hūmāna fallunt.

7.3. Crūdēlis lacrimīs pāscitur, nōn frangitur.

8.1. Parva levēs capiunt animōs.

8.2. Astra regunt hominēs, sed regit astra Deus.

8.3. Vulpēs nōn capitur mūneribus.

9.1. Dīvīna nātūra dedit agrōs; ars hūmāna aedificāvit urbēs.

9.2. Ālea jacta est.

9.3. Caesar prō castrīs cōpiās prōdūxit et aciem īnstrūxit.

10.1. Oculī sunt in amōre ducēs.

10.2. Ars longa, vīta brevis.

10.3. Necessitūdō etiam timidōs fortēs facit.

11.1. Hominēs, dum docent, discunt.

11.2. Ut fragilis glaciēs, interit īra morā.

11.3. Postquam Crassus carbō factus, Carbō crassus factus est.

12.1. Cōgitur ad lacrimās oculus, dum cor dolet intus.

12.2. Noctēs atque diēs patet jānua.

12.3. Multum lacrimās verba inter singula fundit.

13.1. Condidit urbem Rōmulus quam ex nōmine suō Rōmam vocāvit.

13.2. Nīl agit exemplum, lītem quod līte resolvit.

13.3. Citō fit quod dī volunt.

13.4. Semper inops quīcumque cupit.

14.1. Invādunt urbem somnō vīnōque sepultam.

14.2. Stēlla facem dūcēns multā cum lūce cucurrit.

14.3. Vōx audīta perit, littera scrīpta manet.

15.1. Fortūnā fortēs adjuvante, perīculum vincitur.

15.2. Caesar, obsidibus acceptīs, exercitum in Bellovacōs dūcit.

16.1. Sōlitūdō placet Mūsīs, urbs est inimīca poētīs.

16.2. Hōc tempore nūlla cīvitās Athēniēnsibus auxiliō fuit praeter Plataeēnsēs.

16.3. Inopī beneficium bis dat quī dat celeriter.

16.4. Impōnit fīnem sapiēns et rēbus honestīs.

17.1. Imāgō animī vultus; indicēs oculī.

17.2. Jūstitia omnium est domina et rēgīna virtūtum.

18.1. Caecī . . . ducem quaerunt; nōs sine duce errāmus.

18.2. Ex ōre tuō tē jūdicō.

18.3. Vēnī, vīdī, vīcī.

18.4. Effugere nōn potes necessitātēs; potes vincere.

19.1. Trahimur omnēs studiō laudis.

19.2. Quī sēsē accūsat ipse, ab aliō nōn potest.

20.1. Nōn omnēs eadem mīrantur amantque.

20.2. Ubi lībertās cecidit, audet līberē nēmō loquī.

21.1. Et monēre et monērī proprium est vērae amīcitiae.

21.2. Difficile est longum subitō dēpōnere amōrem.

21.3. Labōrāre est ōrāre.

21.4.   Juvat īre et Dōrica castra
dēsertōsque vidēre locōs lītusque relictum.

22.1. Hominis mēns discendō alitur et cōgitandō.

22.2. Timendī causa est nescīre.

23.1. Caesar mīlitēs pontem facere jubet/jussit.

23.2. Caesar dīcit mīlitēs pontem facere.

23.3. Caesar dīxit mīlitēs pontem facere.

24.1. Caesar mīlitēs pontem fēcisse dīcit.

24.2. Caesar mīlitēs pontem factūrōs (esse) dīcit.

24.3. Victōrem ā victō superātum esse saepe vidēmus.

25.1. Melior est canis vīvus leōne mortuō.

25.2. Intolerābilius nihil est quam fēmina dīves.

25.3. Omnium Gallōrum fortissimī sunt Belgae.

25.4. Nihil tam cito redditur quam ā speculō imāgō.

26.1. Nox erat, et caelō fulgēbat lūna serēnō inter minōra sīdera.

26.2. Sed quis custōdiet ipsōs custōdēs?

26.3. Vēritās vōs līberābit.

26.4. Aut inveniam viam aut faciam.

27.1. Nōn sum ego quod fueram.

27.2. Āctiō rēcta nōn erit, nisi rēcta fuerit voluntās.

28.1. Dīc hominem lepidissimum esse mē.

28.2. Contrā verbōsōs nolī contendere verbīs.

28.3. Ūtere quaesītīs opibus; fuge nōmen avārī.

29.1. Rapiāmus, amīcī, occāsiōnem dē diē.

29.2. Longiōrem ōrātiōnem causa forsitan postulet, tua certē natūra breviōrem.

29.3. Utinam id sit quod spērō.

30.1. Sciō quid sit amor.

30.2. Interrogāvī ipsōs an essent Christiānī.

30.3. Forsitan et Priamī fuerint quae Fāta requīrās.

31.1. Mediō ut līmite currās moneō.

31.2. Orgetorīx Helvētiīs persuāsit ut dē fīnibus suīs exīrent.

32.1. Hīs rēbus fīēbat ut minus facile fīnitimīs bellum īnferre possent.

32.2. Nē tē uxor sequātur, timēs.

33.1. Tanta vīs probitātis est, ut eam in hoste etiam dīligāmus.

33.2. Nōn ut edam vīvō, sed ut vīvam edō.

34.1. Caesarī cum id nūntiātum esset, mātūrāvit ab urbe proficīscī.

34.2. Cum prīmī ōrdinēs hostium concīdissent, tamen ācerrimē reliquī resistēbant.

34.3. Multa quoque et bellō passus (est), dum conderet urbem.

34.4. Ōderint, dum metuant.

34.5. Magis valērem, sī hīc manērēs.

34.6. Sī vēnissēs ad exercitum, ā tribūnīs mīlitāribus vīsus essēs; nōn es autem ab hīs vīsus; nōn igitur profectus es ad exercitum.

35.1. In voluptāte spernendā et repudiandā virtūs vel maximē cernitur.

35.2. Sapientia ars vīvendī putanda est.

35.3. Caesarī omnia ūnō tempore erant agenda.

35.4. Ītur in antīquam silvam.

35.5. Quid agitur, Calidōre? Amātur atque egētur ācriter.

35.6. Prīvātum. Precāriō adītur.

35.7. Nunc est bibendum, nunc pede līberō tellūs pulsanda.

Appendix: Summary of Morphology

Nouns

First Declension

Singular			
Nominative	hōra	īra	fēmina
Accusative	hōram	īram	fēminam
Ablative	hōrā	īrā	fēminā
Dative	hōrae	īrae	fēminae
Genitive	hōrae	īrae	fēminae
Plural			
Nominative	hōrae	īrae	fēminae
Accusative	hōrās	īrās	fēminās
Ablative	hōrīs	īrīs	fēminīs
Dative	hōrīs	īrīs	fēminīs
Genitive	hōrārum	īrārum	fēminārum

Second Declension

Singular				
Nominative	animus	populus	vir	aper
Accusative	animum	populum	virum	aprum
Ablative	animō	populō	virō	aprō
Dative	animō	populō	virō	aprō
Genitive	animī	populī	virī	aprī
Plural				
Nominative	animī	populī	virī	aprī
Accusative	animōs	populōs	virōs	aprōs
Ablative	animīs	populīs	virīs	aprīs
Dative	animīs	populīs	virīs	aprīs
Genitive	animōrum	populōrum	virōrum	aprōrum

Second Declension—Neuter Gender

Singular		
Nominative	cōnsilium	vīnum
Accusative	cōnsilium	vīnum
Ablative	cōnsiliō	vīnō
Dative	cōnsiliō	vīnō
Genitive	cōnsiliī	vīnī
Plural		
Nominative	cōnsilia	vīna
Accusative	cōnsilia	vīna
Ablative	cōnsiliīs	vīnīs
Dative	cōnsiliīs	vīnīs
Genitive	cōnsiliōrum	vīnōrum

Third Declension

Singular						
Nominative	fūr	occāsiō	vēritās	nox	mēns	piscis
Accusative	fūrem	occāsiōnem	vēritātem	noctem	mentem	piscem
Ablative	fūre	occāsiōne	vēritāte	nocte	mente	pisce
Dative	fūrī	occāsiōnī	vēritātī	noctī	mentī	piscī
Genitive	fūris	occāsiōnis	vēritātis	noctis	mentis	piscis
Plural						
Nominative	fūrēs	occāsiōnēs	vēritātēs	noctēs	mentēs	piscēs
Accusative	fūrēs	occāsiōnēs	vēritātēs	noctēs (-īs)	mentēs (-īs)	piscēs (-īs)
Ablative	fūribus	occāsiōnibus	vēritātibus	noctibus	mentibus	piscibus
Dative	fūribus	occāsiōnibus	vēritātibus	noctibus	mentibus	piscibus
Genitive	fūrum	occāsiōnum	vēritātum	noctium	mentium	piscium

Third Declension—Neuter Gender

Singular			
Nominative	opus	culmen	animal (*i*-stem)
Accusative	opus	culmen	animal
Ablative	opere	culmine	animālī
Dative	operī	culminī	animālī
Genitive	operis	culminis	animālis
Plural			
Nominative	opera	culmina	animālia
Accusative	opera	culmina	animālia
Ablative	operibus	culminibus	animālibus
Dative	operibus	culminibus	animālibus
Genitive	operum	culminum	animālium

Fourth Declension

Singular			
Nominative	manus	successus	senātus
Accusative	manum	successum	senātum
Ablative	manū	successū	senātū
Dative	manuī	successuī	senātuī
Genitive	manūs	successūs	senātūs
Plural			
Nominative	manūs	successūs	senātūs
Accusative	manūs	successūs	senātūs
Ablative	manibus	successibus	senātibus
Dative	manibus	successibus	senātibus
Genitive	manuum	successuum	senātuum

Fifth Declension

Singular		
Nominative	rēs*	diēs*
Accusative	rem	diem
Ablative	rē	diē
Dative	reī	diēī
Genitive	reī	diēī
Plural		
Nominative	rēs	diēs
Accusative	rēs	diēs
Ablative	rēbus	diēbus
Dative	rēbus	diēbus
Genitive	rērum	diērum

*The only fifth declension nouns with common plural forms are *diēs* and *rēs*.

Adjectives

First-Second Declension

	Masc.	Fem.	Neut.
Singular			
Nominative	novus	nova	novum
Accusative	novum	novam	novum
Ablative	novō	novā	novō
Dative	novō	novae	novō
Genitive	novī	novae	novī
Plural			
Nominative	novī	novae	nova
Accusative	novōs	novās	nova
Ablative	novīs	novīs	novīs
Dative	novīs	novīs	novīs
Genitive	novōrum	novārum	novōrum

Third Declension

	Masc. & Fem.	Neut.	Masc.	Fem.	Neut.
Singular					
Nominative	omnis	omne	acer	acris	acre
Accusative	omnem	omne	acrem	acrem	acre
Ablative	omnī	omnī	acrī	acrī	acrī
Dative	omnī	omnī	acrī	acrī	acrī
Genitive	omnis	omnis	acris	acris	acris
Plural					
Nominative	omnēs	omnia	acrēs	acrēs	acria
Accusative	omnēs (-īs)	omnia	acrēs (-īs)	acrēs (-īs)	acria
Ablative	omnibus	omnibus	acribus	acribus	acribus
Dative	omnibus	omnibus	acribus	acribus	acribus
Genitive	omnium	omnium	acrium	acrium	acrium

One-ending Third Declension Adjectives (including imperfective participles)

	Masc. & Fem.	Neut.
Singular		
Nominative	tacēns	tacēns
Accusative	tacentem	tacēns
Ablative	tacentī (-e)*	tacentī (-e)*
Dative	tacentī	tacentī
Genitive	tacentis	tacentis
Plural		
Nominative	tacentēs	tacentia
Accusative	tacentēs (-īs)	tacentia
Ablative	tacentibus	tacentibus
Dative	tacentibus	tacentibus
Genitive	tacentium	tacentium

*The imperfective participle, when used as a non-finite verb, ends in -*e* in the ablative.

Comparison of Adjectives

Regular

Positive	Comparative	Superlative
fortis, -is, -e	fortior, -ior, -ius	fortissimus, -a, -um
pūrus, -a, -um	pūrior, -ior, -ius	pūrissimus, -a, -um
celer, celeris, celere	celerior, -ior, -ius	celerrimus, -a, -um
pulcher, pulchra, pulchrum	pulchrior, -ior, -ius	pulcherrimus, -a, -um

Six adjectives in -lis (facilis, difficilis, similis, dissimilis, gracilis, humilis) are compared *facilis, facilior, facillimus*. All the other adjectives in -lis, e.g., *crūdēlis, nōbilis,* etc., have the -issimus superlative.

Irregular

Positive	Comparative	Superlative
bonus, -a, -um	melior, melior, melius	optimus, -a, -um
magnus, -a, -um	major, major, majus	maximus, -a, -um
malus, -a, -um	pejor, pejor, pejus	pessimus, -a, -um
multus, -a, -um	plūs*; plūrēs, plūrēs, plūra	plurimus, -a, -um
parvus, -a, -um	minor, minor, minus	minimus, -a, -um
— (prae, prō: prep.)	prior, prior, prius	prīmus, -a, -um
— (prope: prep.)	propior, propior, propius	proximus, -a, -um
— (ultrā: prep.)	ulterior, ulterior, ulterius	ultimus, -a, -um

Plūs is a neuter singular noun, not an adjective.

Paradigm of the Comparative Adjective

	Masc. & Fem.	Neut.
Singular		
Nominative	fortior	fortius
Accusative	fortiōrem	fortius
Ablative	fortiōre	fortiōre
Dative	fortiōrī	fortiōrī
Genitive	fortiōris	fortiōris
Plural		
Nominative	fortiōrēs	fortiōra
Accusative	fortiōrēs	fortiōra
Ablative	fortiōribus	fortiōribus
Dative	fortiōribus	fortiōribus
Genitive	fortiōrum	fortiōrum

Formation of Adverbs from Adjectives

Adverbs are regularly formed from adjectives by the morphemes {ē} or {ter}.

-*ē* is used if the adjective is first and second declension: *honestē*.
-*ter* is used if the adjective is third declension: *fortiter*.

The comparative adverb is the accusative singular neuter of the comparative adjective: *honestius*.

Pronouns and Special Adjectives

Pronouns

Personal and Reflexive Pronouns

	First Person	Second Person	Third Person
Singular			
Nominative	ego	tū	—
Accusative	mē	tē	sē, sēsē
Ablative	mē	tē	sē, sēsē
Dative	mihi, mī	tibi	sibi
Genitive	meī	tuī	suī
Plural			
Nominative	nōs	vōs	—
Accusative	nōs	vōs	sē, sēsē
Ablative	nōbīs	vōbīs	sē, sēsē
Dative	nōbīs	vōbīs	sibi
Genitive	nostrum, nostrī	vestrum, vestrī	suī

Note: *is, hic, ille, ipse,* and *īdem,* when used without a noun, function as personal pronouns, third person.

Relative Pronoun

	Masc.	Fem.	Neut.
Singular			
Nominative	quī	quae	quod
Accusative	quem	quam	quod
Ablative	quō	quā	quō
Dative	cui	cui	cui
Genitive	cujus	cujus	cujus
Plural			
Nominative	quī	quae	quae
Accusative	quōs	quās	quae
Ablative	quibus	quibus	quibus
Dative	quibus	quibus	quibus
Genitive	quōrum	quārum	quōrum

Interrogative Pronoun

	Animate	Nonanimate
Singular		
Nominative	quis	quid
Accusative	quem	quid
Ablative	quō	quō
Dative	cui	cui
Genitive	cujus	cujus

The plural is like that of the relative pronoun.

Demonstrative Pronouns

	Masc.	Fem.	Neut.	Masc.	Fem.	Neut.
Singular						
Nominative	hic	haec	hoc	ille	illa	illud
Accusative	hunc	hanc	hoc	illum	illam	illud
Ablative	hōc	hāc	hōc	illō	illā	illō
Dative	huic	huic	huic	illī	illī	illī
Genitive	hujus	hujus	hujus	illīus	illīus	illīus
Plural						
Nominative	hī	hae	haec	The plural has the regular		
Accusative	hōs	hās	haec	endings of first-second		
Ablative	hīs	hīs	hīs	declension adjectives.		
Dative	hīs	hīs	hīs			
Genitive	hōrum	hārum	hōrum			

	Masc.	Fem.	Neut.	Masc.	Fem.	Neut.
Singular						
Nominative	iste	ista	istud	ipse	ipsa	ipsum
Accusative	istum	istam	istud	ipsum	ipsam	ipsum
Ablative	istō	istā	istō	ipsō	ipsā	ipsō
Dative	istī	istī	istī	ipsī	ipsī	ipsī
Genitive	istīus	istīus	istīus	ipsīus	ipsīus	ipsīus
Plural						
Nominative	The plural is regular.			The plural is regular.		
Accusative						
Ablative						
Dative						
Genitive						

	Masc.	Fem.	Neut.	Masc.	Fem.	Neut.
Singular						
Nominative	is	ea	id	īdem	eadem	idem
Accusative	eum	eam	id	eundem	eandem	idem
Ablative	eō	eā	eō	eōdem	eādem	eōdem
Dative	eī	eī	eī	eīdem	eīdem	eīdem
Genitive	ejus	ejus	ejus	ejusdem	ejusdem	ejusdem
Plural						
Nominative	eī, ī	eae	ea	eīdem*	eaedem	eadem
Accusative	eōs	eās	ea	eōsdem	eāsdem	eadem
Ablative	eīs, īs	eīs, īs	eīs, īs	eīsdem*	eīsdem*	eīsdem*
Dative	eīs, īs	eīs, īs	eīs, īs	eīsdem*	eīsdem*	eīsdem*
Genitive	eōrum	eārum	eōrum	eōrundem	eārundem	eōrundem

*Same variant as *is*.

Interrogative Adjective

	Masc.	Fem.	Neut.
Singular			
Nominative	quī	quae	quod
Accusative	quem	quam	quod
Ablative	quō	quā	quō
Dative	cui	cui	cui
Genitive	cujus	cujus	cujus
Plural			
Nominative	quī	quae	quae
Accusative	quōs	quās	quae
Ablative	quibus	quibus	quibus
Dative	quibus	quibus	quibus
Genitive	quōrum	quārum	quōrum

Note: The interrogative adjective has the same forms as the relative pronoun.

Special Adjectives

ūnus, tōtus, sōlus, ūllus ⎫ Dative singular in -*ī*
uter, alter, neuter, nūllus ⎬ Genitive singular in -*īus*
uterque, alius (n. aliud) ⎭ Otherwise like *novus, -a, -um*

Paradigms of ūnus, duo, trēs, and mīlia

	Masc.	Fem.	Neut.	Masc.	Fem.	Neut.	Masc. & Fem.	Neut.	Neut.
Singular									
Nominative	ūnus	ūna	ūnum						
Accusative	ūnum	ūnam	ūnum						
Ablative	ūnō	ūnā	ūnō						
Dative	ūnī	ūnī	ūnī						
Genitive	ūnīus	ūnīus	ūnīus						
Plural									
Nominative				duo	duae	duo	trēs	tria	mīlia
Accusative				duōs	duās	duo	trēs	tria	mīlia
Ablative				duōbus	duābus	duōbus	tribus	tribus	mīlibus
Dative				duōbus	duābus	duōbus	tribus	tribus	mīlibus
Genitive				duōrum	duārum	duōrum	trium	trium	mīlium

Numerals

Latin numerals belong to one of these sets:

1. Cardinals answer the question *quot?* How many?
2. Ordinals answer the question *quotus, -a, -um?* Which in order?
3. Distributives (often used in place of cardinals) answer the question *quotēnī, -ae, -a?* How many apiece? How many at a time?
4. Numeral adverbs answer the question *quotiēns?* How often?

In the following list of numerals the indeclinables are indented:

	Cardinal	*Ordinal*	*Distributive*
I	ūnus, -a, -um	prīmus, -a, -um	singulī, -ae, -a
II	duo, duae, duo	secundus, -a, -um	bīnī, -ae, -a
III	trēs, tria	tertius, -a, -um	ternī, -ae, -a
IV	quattuor	quārtus, -a, -um	quaternī, -ae, -a
V	quīnque	quīntus, -a, -um	quīnī, -ae, -a
VI	sex	sextus, -a, -um	sēnī, -ae, -a
VII	septem	septimus, -a, -um	septēnī, -ae, -a
VIII	octō	octāvus, -a, -um	octōnī, -ae, -a
IX	novem	nōnus, -a, -um	novēnī, -ae, -a
X	decem	decimus, -a, -um	dēnī, -ae, -a
XI	ūndecim	ūndecimus, -a, -um	etc.
XII	duodecim	duodecimus, -a, -um	
XIII	tredecim	tertius, -a, -um decimus, -a, -um	
XIV	quattuordecim	quārtus, -a, -um decimus, -a, -um	
XV	quīndecim	quīntus, -a, -um decimus, -a, -um	
XVI	sēdecim	sextus, -a, -um decimus, -a, -um	
XVII	septendecim	septimus, -a, -um decimus, -a, -um	
XVIII	duodēvīgintī	duodēvīcēsimus, -a, -um	
XIX	ūndēvīgintī	ūndēvīcēsimus, -a, -um	
XX	vīgintī	vīcēsimus, -a, -um	
XXI	vīgintī ūnus	etc.	
XXX	trīgintā		
XL	quadrāgintā		
L	quīnquāgintā		
LX	sexāgintā		
LXX	septuāgintā		
LXXX	octōgintā		
XC	nōnāgintā		
C	centum		
CC	ducentī, -ae, -a		
CCC	trecentī, -ae, -a		
CCCC	quadringentī, -ae, -a		
D	quīngentī, -ae, -a		
M	mīlle		
MM	duo mīlia (neuter noun)		

Numeral Adverbs

semel	once
bis	twice
ter	three times
quater	four times
quīnquiēns	five times
centiēns	one hundred times
mīliēns	one thousand times

Verbs

Person Endings

Present Perfective Active

	Sing.	Pl.
First person	-ī	-imus
Second person	-istī	-istis
Third person	-it	-ērunt (-ēre)

All Others Active

	Sing.	Pl.
First person	-ō, -m	-mus
Second person	-s	-tis
Third person	-t	-nt

Passive

	Sing.	Pl.
First person	-r, -or	-mur
Second person	-ris (-re)	-minī
Third person	-tur	-ntur

Latin Verb System

First Conjugation: amō, amāre, amāvī, amātus

Indicative

	Past Imperfective		Present Imperfective		Future Imperfective	
	Sing.	Pl.	Sing.	Pl.	Sing.	Pl.
Active						
First person	amābam	amābāmus	amō	amāmus	amābō	amābimus
Second person	amābās	amābātis	amās	amātis	amābis	amābitis
Third person	amābat	amābant	amat	amant	amābit	amābunt
Passive						
First person	amābar	amābāmur	amor	amāmur	amābor	amābimur
Second person	amābāris (-re)	amābāminī	amāris (-re)	amāminī	amāberis (-re)	amābiminī
Third person	amābātur	amābantur	amātur	amantur	amābitur	amābuntur

	Past Perfective		Present Perfective		Future Perfective	
	Sing.	Pl.	Sing.	Pl.	Sing.	Pl.
Active						
First person	amāveram	amāverāmus	amāvī	amāvimus	amāverō	amāverimus
Second person	amāverās	amāverātis	amāvistī	amāvistis	amāveris	amāveritis
Third person	amāverat	amāverant	amāvit	amāvērunt (-ēre)	amāverit	amāverint
Passive						
First person	amātus eram	amātī erāmus	amātus sum	amātī sumus	amātus erō	amātī erimus
Second person	amātus erās	amātī erātis	amātus es	amātī estis	amātus eris	amātī eritis
Third person	amātus erat	amātī erant	amātus est	amātī sunt	amātus erit	amātī erunt

Subjunctive

	Past Imperfective		Present Imperfective	
	Sing.	Pl.	Sing.	Pl.
Active				
First person	amārem	amārēmus	amem	amēmus
Second person	amārēs	amārētis	amēs	amētis
Third person	amāret	amārent	amet	ament
Passive				
First person	amārer	amārēmur	amer	amēmur
Second person	amārēris (-re)	amārēminī	amēris (-re)	amēminī
Third person	amārētur	amārentur	amētur	amentur

	Past Perfective		Present Perfective	
	Sing.	Pl.	Sing.	Pl.
Active				
First person	amāvissem	amāvissēmus	amāverim	amāverīmus
Second person	amāvissēs	amāvissētis	amāverīs	amāverītis
Third person	amāvisset	amāvissent	amāverit	amāverint
Passive				
First person	amātus essem	amātī essēmus	amātus sim	amātī sīmus
Second person	amātus essēs	amātī essētis	amātus sīs	amātī sītis
Third person	amātus esset	amātī essent	amātus sit	amātī sint

Imperatives

	Sing.	Pl.
Active	amā	amāte
Passive	amāre	amāminī

Infinitives

	Active	Passive
Imperf.	amāre	amārī
Perf.	amāvisse	amātus, -a, -um esse
Fut.	amātūrus, -a, -um esse	

Participles

	Active	Passive
Imperf.	amāns	—
Perf.	—	amātus, -a, -um
Fut.	amātūrus, -a, -um	amandus, -a, -um

Supines[1]

amātum
amātū

---

1. A supine is a verbal noun of the fourth declension. It occurs only infrequently in Latin texts. The form in *-um* is used after verbs of motion to express purpose and the form in *-ū* is used as an ablative of specification or respect.

Second Conjugation: vídeō, vidēre, vīdī, vīsus

Indicative

	Past Imperfective		Present Imperfective		Future Imperfective	
	Sing.	Pl.	Sing.	Pl.	Sing.	Pl.
Active						
First person	vidēbam	vidēbāmus	videō	vidēmus	vidēbō	vidēbimus
Second person	vidēbās	vidēbātis	vidēs	vidētis	vidēbis	vidēbitis
Third person	vidēbat	vidēbant	videt	vident	vidēbit	vidēbunt
Passive						
First person	vidēbar	vidēbāmur	videor	vidēmur	vidēbor	vidēbimur
Second person	vidēbāris (-re)	vidēbāminī	vidēris (-re)	vidēminī	vidēberis (-re)	vidēbiminī
Third person	vidēbātur	vidēbantur	vidētur	videntur	vidēbitur	vidēbuntur

	Past Perfective		Present Perfective		Future Perfective	
	Sing.	Pl.	Sing.	Pl.	Sing.	Pl.
Active						
First person	vīderam	vīderāmus	vīdī	vīdimus	vīderō	vīderimus
Second person	vīderās	vīderātis	vīdistī	vīdistis	vīderis	vīderitis
Third person	vīderat	vīderant	vīdit	vīdērunt (-ēre)	vīderit	vīderint
Passive						
First person	vīsus eram	vīsī erāmus	vīsus sum	vīsī sumus	vīsus erō	vīsī erimus
Second person	vīsus erās	vīsī erātis	vīsus es	vīsī estis	vīsus eris	vīsī eritis
Third person	vīsus erat	vīsī erant	vīsus est	vīsī sunt	vīsus erit	vīsī erunt

Subjunctive

	Past Imperfective		Present Imperfective	
	Sing.	Pl.	Sing.	Pl.
Active				
First person	vidērem	vidērēmus	videam	videāmus
Second person	vidērēs	vidērētis	videās	videātis
Third person	vidēret	vidērent	videat	videant
Passive				
First person	vidērer	vidērēmur	videar	videāmur
Second person	vidērēris (-re)	vidērēminī	videāris (-re)	videāminī
Third person	vidērētur	vidērentur	videātur	videantur

	Past Perfective		Present Perfective	
	Sing.	Pl.	Sing.	Pl.
Active				
First person	vīdissem	vīdissēmus	vīderim	vīderīmus
Second person	vīdissēs	vīdissētis	vīderīs	vīderītis
Third person	vīdisset	vīdissent	vīderit	vīderint
Passive				
First person	vīsus essem	vīsī essēmus	vīsus sim	vīsī sīmus
Second person	vīsus essēs	vīsī essētis	vīsus sīs	vīsī sītis
Third person	vīsus esset	vīsī essent	vīsus sit	vīsī sint

Imperatives

	Sing.	Pl.
Active	vidē	vidēte
Passive	vidēre	vidēminī

Infinitives

	Active	Passive
Imperf.	vidēre	vidērī
Perf.	vīdisse	vīsus, -a, -um esse
Fut.	vīsūrus, -a, -um esse	

Participles

	Active	Passive
Imperf.	vidēns	—
Perf.	—	vīsus, -a, -um
Fut.	vīsūrus, -a, -um	videndus, -a, -um

Supines

vīsum
vīsū

Third Conjugation: regō, regere, rēxī, rēctus

Indicative

	Past Imperfective		Present Imperfective		Future Imperfective	
	Sing.	Pl.	Sing.	Pl.	Sing.	Pl.
Active						
First person	regēbam	regēbāmus	regō	regimus	regam	regēmus
Second person	regēbās	regēbātis	regis	regitis	regēs	regētis
Third person	regēbat	regēbant	regit	regunt	reget	regent
Passive						
First person	regēbar	regēbāmur	regor	regimur	regar	regēmur
Second person	regēbāris (-re)	regēbāminī	regeris (-re)	regiminī	regēris (-re)	regēminī
Third person	regēbātur	regēbantur	regitur	reguntur	regētur	regentur

	Past Perfective		Present Perfective		Future Perfective	
	Sing.	Pl.	Sing.	Pl.	Sing.	Pl.
Active						
First person	rēxeram	rēxerāmus	rēxī	rēximus	rēxerō	rēxerimus
Second person	rēxerās	rēxerātis	rēxistī	rēxistis	rēxeris	rēxeritis
Third person	rēxerat	rēxerant	rēxit	rēxērunt (-ēre)	rēxerit	rēxerint
Passive						
First person	rēctus eram	rēctī erāmus	rēctus sum	rēctī sumus	rēctus erō	rēctī erimus
Second person	rēctus erās	rēctī erātis	rēctus es	rēctī estis	rēctus eris	rēctī eritis
Third person	rēctus erat	rēctī erant	rēctus est	rēctī sunt	rēctus erit	rēctī erunt

Subjunctive

	Past Imperfective		Present Imperfective	
	Sing.	Pl.	Sing.	Pl.
Active				
First person	regerem	regerēmus	regam	regāmus
Second person	regerēs	regerētis	regās	regātis
Third person	regeret	regerent	regat	regant
Passive				
First person	regerer	regerēmur	regar	regāmur
Second person	regerēris (-re)	regerēminī	regāris (-re)	regāminī
Third person	regerētur	regerentur	regātur	regantur

	Past Perfective		Present Perfective	
	Sing.	Pl.	Sing.	Pl.
Active				
First person	rēxissem	rēxissēmus	rēxerim	rēxerīmus
Second person	rēxissēs	rēxissētis	rēxerīs	rēxerītis
Third person	rēxisset	rēxissent	rēxerit	rēxerint
Passive				
First person	rēctus essem	rēctī essēmus	rēctus sim	rēctī sīmus
Second person	rēctus essēs	rēctī essētis	rēctus sīs	rēctī sītis
Third person	rēctus esset	rēctī essent	rēctus sit	rēctī sint

Imperatives

	Sing.	Pl.
Active	rege	regite
Passive	regere	regiminī

Infinitives

	Active	Passive
Imperf.	regere	regī
Perf.	rēxisse	rēctus, -a, -um esse
Fut.	rēctūrus, -a, -um esse	

Participles

	Active	Passive
Imperf.	regēns	—
Perf.	—	rēctus, -a, -um
Fut.	rēctūrus, -a, -um	regendus, -a, -um

Supines

rēctum
rēctū

Third -iō Conjugation: capiō, capere, cēpī, captus

Indicative

	Past Imperfective		Present Imperfective		Future Imperfective	
	Sing.	Pl.	Sing.	Pl.	Sing.	Pl.
Active						
First person	capiēbam	capiēbāmus	capiō	capimus	capiam	capiēmus
Second person	capiēbās	capiēbātis	capis	capitis	capiēs	capiētis
Third person	capiēbat	capiēbant	capit	capiunt	capiet	capient
Passive						
First person	capiēbar	capiēbāmur	capior	capimur	capiar	capiēmur
Second person	capiēbāris (-re)	capiēbāminī	caperis (-re)	capiminī	capiēris (-re)	capiēminī
Third person	capiēbātur	capiēbantur	capitur	capiuntur	capiētur	capientur

	Past Perfective		Present Perfective		Future Perfective	
	Sing.	Pl.	Sing.	Pl.	Sing.	Pl.
Active						
First person	cēperam	cēperāmus	cēpī	cēpimus	cēperō	cēperimus
Second person	cēperās	cēperātis	cēpistī	cēpistis	cēperis	cēperitis
Third person	cēperat	cēperant	cēpit	cēpērunt (-ēre)	cēperit	cēperint
Passive						
First person	captus eram	captī erāmus	captus sum	captī sumus	captus erō	captī erimus
Second person	captus erās	captī erātis	captus es	captī estis	captus eris	captī eritis
Third person	captus erat	captī erant	captus est	captī sunt	captus erit	captī erunt

Subjunctive

	Past Imperfective		Present Imperfective	
	Sing.	Pl.	Sing.	Pl.
Active				
First person	caperem	caperēmus	capiam	capiāmus
Second person	caperēs	caperētis	capiās	capiātis
Third person	caperet	caperent	capiat	capiant
Passive				
First person	caperer	caperēmur	capiar	capiāmur
Second person	caperēris (-re)	caperēminī	capiāris (-re)	capiāminī
Third person	caperētur	caperentur	capiātur	capiantur

	Past Perfective		Present Perfective	
	Sing.	Pl.	Sing.	Pl.
Active				
First person	cēpissem	cēpissēmus	cēperim	cēperīmus
Second person	cēpissēs	cēpissētis	cēperīs	cēperītis
Third person	cēpisset	cēpissent	cēperit	cēperint
Passive				
First person	captus essem	captī essēmus	captus sim	captī sīmus
Second person	captus essēs	captī essētis	captus sīs	captī sītis
Third person	captus esset	captī essent	captus sit	captī sint

Imperatives

	Sing.	Pl.
Active	cape	capite
Passive	capere	capiminī

Infinitives

	Active	Passive
Imperf.	capere	capī
Perf.	cēpisse	captus, -a, -um esse
Fut.	captūrus, -a, -um esse	

Participles

	Active	Passive
Imperf.	capiēns	—
Perf.	—	captus, -a, -um
Fut.	captūrus, -a, -um	capiendus, -a, -um

Supines

captum
captū

Fourth Conjugation: audiō, audīre, audīvī, audītus

Indicative

	Past Imperfective		Present Imperfective		Future Imperfective	
	Sing.	Pl.	Sing.	Pl.	Sing.	Pl.
Active						
First person	audiēbam	audiēbāmus	audiō	audīmus	audiam	audiēmus
Second person	audiēbās	audiēbātis	audīs	audītis	audiēs	audiētis
Third person	audiēbat	audiēbant	audit	audiunt	audiet	audient
Passive						
First person	audiēbar	audiēbāmur	audior	audīmur	audiar	audiēmur
Second person	audiēbāris (-re)	audiēbāminī	audīris (-re)	audīminī	audiēris (-re)	audiēminī
Third person	audiēbātur	audiēbantur	audītur	audiuntur	audiētur	audientur

	Past Perfective		Present Perfective		Future Perfective	
	Sing.	Pl.	Sing.	Pl.	Sing.	Pl.
Active						
First person	audīveram	audīverāmus	audīvī	audīvimus	audīverō	audīverimus
Second person	audīverās	audīverātis	audīvistī	audīvistis	audīveris	audīveritis
Third person	audīverat	audīverant	audīvit	audīvērunt (-ēre)	audīverit	audīverint
Passive						
First person	audītus eram	audītī erāmus	audītus sum	audītī sumus	audītus erō	audītī erimus
Second person	audītus erās	audītī erātis	audītus es	audītī estis	audītus eris	audītī eritis
Third person	audītus erat	audītī erant	audītus est	audītī sunt	audītus erit	audītī erunt

Subjunctive

	Past Imperfective		Present Imperfective	
	Sing.	Pl.	Sing.	Pl.
Active				
First person	audīrem	audīrēmus	audiam	audiāmus
Second person	audīrēs	audīrētis	audiās	audiātis
Third person	audīret	audīrent	audiat	audiant
Passive				
First person	audīrer	audīrēmur	audiar	audiāmur
Second person	audīrēris (-re)	audīrēminī	audiāris (-re)	audiāminī
Third person	audīrētur	audīrentur	audiātur	audiantur

	Past Perfective		Present Perfective	
	Sing.	Pl.	Sing.	Pl.
Active				
First person	audīvissem	audīvissēmus	audīverim	audīverīmus
Second person	audīvissēs	audīvissētis	audīverīs	audīverītis
Third person	audīvisset	audīvissent	audīverit	audīverint
Passive				
First person	audītus essem	audītī essēmus	audītus sim	audītī sīmus
Second person	audītus essēs	audītī essētis	audītus sīs	audītī sītis
Third person	audītus esset	audītī essent	audītus sit	audītī sint

Imperatives

	Sing.	Pl.
Active	audī	audīte
Passive	audīre	audīminī

Infinitives

	Active	Passive
Imperf.	audīre	audīrī
Perf.	audīvisse	audītus, -a, -um esse
Fut.	audītūrus, -a, -um esse	

Participles

	Active	Passive
Imperf.	audiēns	—
Perf.	—	audītus, -a, -um
Fut.	audītūrus, -a, -um	audiendus, -a, -um

Supines

audītum
audītū

Deponent Verbs

First Conjugation: mīror, mīrārī, mīrātus

Indicative

	Past Imperfective		Present Imperfective		Future Imperfective	
	Sing.	Pl.	Sing.	Pl.	Sing.	Pl.
First person	mīrābar	mīrābāmur	mīror	mīrāmur	mīrābor	mīrābimur
Second person	mīrābāris (-re)	mīrābāminī	mīrāris (-re)	mīrāminī	mīrāberis (-re)	mīrābiminī
Third person	mīrābātur	mīrābantur	mīrātur	mīrantur	mīrābitur	mīrābuntur

	Past Perfective		Present Perfective		Future Perfective	
	Sing.	Pl.	Sing.	Pl.	Sing.	Pl.
First person	mīrātus eram	mīrātī erāmus	mīrātus sum	mīrātī sumus	mīrātus erō	mīrātī erimus
Second person	mīrātus erās	mīrātī erātis	mīrātus es	mīrātī estis	mīrātus eris	mīrātī eritis
Third person	mīrātus erat	mīrātī erant	mīrātus est	mīrātī sunt	mīrātus erit	mīrātī erunt

Subjunctive

	Past Imperfective		Present Imperfective	
	Sing.	Pl.	Sing.	Pl.
First person	mīrārer	mīrārēmur	mīrer	mīrēmur
Second person	mīrārēris (-re)	mīrārēminī	mīrēris (-re)	mīrēminī
Third person	mīrārētur	mīrārentur	mīrētur	mīrentur

	Past Perfective		Present Perfective	
	Sing.	Pl.	Sing.	Pl.
First person	mīrātus essem	mīrātī essēmus	mīrātus sim	mīrātī sīmus
Second person	mīrātus essēs	mīrātī essētis	mīrātus sīs	mīrātī sītis
Third person	mīrātus esset	mīrātī essent	mīrātus sit	mīrātī sint

Imperative

Sing.	Pl.
mīrāre	mīrāminī

Infinitives

Imperf.	mīrārī
Perf.	mīrātus, -a, -um esse
Fut.	mīrātūrus, -a, -um esse

Participles

Imperf.	mīrāns
Perf.	mīrātus, -a, -um
Fut.	mīrātūrus, -a, -um
Fut. pass.	mīrandus, -a, -um

Supines

mīrātum
mīrātū

Second Conjugation: vereor, vererī, veritus

Indicative

	Past Imperfective		Present Imperfective		Future Imperfective	
	Sing.	Pl.	Sing.	Pl.	Sing.	Pl.
First person	verēbar	verēbāmur	vereor	verēmur	verēbor	verēbimur
Second person	verēbāris (-re)	verēbāminī	verēris (-re)	verēminī	verēberis (-re)	verēbiminī
Third person	verēbātur	verēbantur	verētur	verentur	verēbitur	verēbuntur

	Past Perfective		Present Perfective		Future Perfective	
	Sing.	Pl.	Sing.	Pl.	Sing.	Pl.
First person	veritus eram	veritī erāmus	veritus sum	veritī sumus	veritus erō	veritī erimus
Second person	veritus erās	veritī erātis	veritus es	veritī estis	veritus eris	veritī eritis
Third person	veritus erat	veritī erant	veritus est	veritī sunt	veritus erit	veritī erunt

Subjunctive

	Past Imperfective		Present Imperfective	
	Sing.	Pl.	Sing.	Pl.
First person	verērer	verērēmur	verear	vereāmur
Second person	verērēris (-re)	verērēminī	vereāris (-re)	vereāminī
Third person	verērētur	verērentur	vereātur	vereantur

	Past Perfective		Present Perfective	
	Sing.	Pl.	Sing.	Pl.
First person	veritus essem	veritī essēmus	veritus sim	veritī sīmus
Second person	veritus essēs	veritī essētis	veritus sīs	veritī sītis
Third person	veritus esset	veritī essent	veritus sit	veritī sint

Imperative

Sing.	Pl.
verēre	verēminī

Infinitives

Imperf.	vererī
Perf.	veritus, -a, -um esse
Fut.	veritūrus, -a, -um esse

Participles

Imperf.	verēns
Perf.	veritus, -a, -um
Fut.	veritūrus, -a, -um
Fut. pass.	verendus, -a, -um

Supines

veritum
veritū

Third Conjugation: sequor, sequī, secūtus

Indicative

	Past Imperfective		Present Imperfective		Future Imperfective	
	Sing.	Pl.	Sing.	Pl.	Sing.	Pl.
First person	sequēbar	sequēbāmur	sequor	sequimur	sequar	sequēmur
Second person	sequēbāris (-re)	sequēbāminī	sequeris (-re)	sequiminī	sequēris (-re)	sequēminī
Third person	sequēbatur	sequēbantur	sequitur	sequuntur	sequētur	sequentur

	Past Perfective		Present Perfective		Future Perfective	
	Sing.	Pl.	Sing.	Pl.	Sing.	Pl.
First person	secūtus eram	secūtī erāmus	secūtus sum	secūtī sumus	secūtus erō	secūtī erimus
Second person	secūtus erās	secūtī erātis	secūtus es	secūtī estis	secūtus eris	secūtī eritis
Third person	secūtus erat	secūtī erant	secūtus est	secūtī sunt	secūtus erit	secūtī erunt

Subjunctive

	Past Imperfective		Present Imperfective	
	Sing.	Pl.	Sing.	Pl.
First person	sequerer	sequerēmur	sequar	sequāmur
Second person	sequerēris (-re)	sequerēminī	sequāris (-re)	sequāminī
Third person	sequerētur	sequerentur	sequātur	sequantur

	Past Perfective		Present Perfective	
	Sing.	Pl.	Sing.	Pl.
First person	secūtus essem	secūtī essēmus	secūtus sim	secūtī sīmus
Second person	secūtus essēs	secūtī essētis	secūtus sīs	secūtī sītis
Third person	secūtus esset	secūtī essent	secūtus sit	secūtī sint

Imperative

Sing.	Pl.
sequere	sequiminī

Infinitives

Imperf.	sequī
Perf.	secūtus, -a, -um esse
Fut.	secūtūrus, -a, -um esse

Participles

Imperf.	sequēns
Perf.	secūtus, -a, -um
Fut.	secūtūrus, -a, -um
Fut. pass.	sequendus, -a, -um

Supines

secūtum
secūtū

Third -iō Conjugation: patior, patī, passus

Indicative

	Past Imperfective		Present Imperfective		Future Imperfective	
	Sing.	Pl.	Sing.	Pl.	Sing.	Pl.
First person	patiēbar	patiēbāmur	patior	patimur	patiar	patiēmur
Second person	patiēbāris (-re)	patiēbāminī	pateris (-re)	patiminī	patiēris (-re)	patiēminī
Third person	patiēbātur	patiēbantur	patitur	patiuntur	patiētur	patientur

	Past Perfective		Present Perfective		Future Perfective	
	Sing.	Pl.	Sing.	Pl.	Sing.	Pl.
First person	passus eram	passī erāmus	passus sum	passī sumus	passus erō	passī erimus
Second person	passus erās	passī erātis	passus es	passī estis	passus eris	passī eritis
Third person	passus erat	passī erant	passus est	passī sunt	passus erit	passī erunt

Subjunctive

	Past Imperfective		Present Imperfective	
	Sing.	Pl.	Sing.	Pl.
First person	paterer	paterēmur	patiar	patiāmur
Second person	paterēris (-re)	paterēminī	patiāris	patiāminī
Third person	paterētur	paterentur	patiātur	patiantur

	Past Perfective		Present Perfective	
	Sing.	Pl.	Sing.	Pl.
First person	passus essem	passī essēmus	passus sim	passī sīmus
Second person	passus essēs	passī essētis	passus sīs	passī sītis
Third person	passus esset	passī essent	passus sit	passī sint

Imperative

Sing.	Pl.
patere	patiminī

Infinitives

Imperf.	patī
Perf.	passus, -a, -um esse
Fut.	passūrus, -a, -um esse

Participles

Imperf.	patiēns
Perf.	passus, -a, -um
Fut.	passūrus, -a, -um
Fut. pass.	patiendus, -a, -um

Supines

passum
passū

Fourth Conjugation: mentior, mentīrī, mentītus

Indicative

	Past Imperfective		Present Imperfective		Future Imperfective	
	Sing.	Pl.	Sing.	Pl.	Sing.	Pl.
First person	mentiēbar	mentiēbāmur	mentior	mentīmur	mentiar	mentiēmur
Second person	mentiēbāris (-re)	mentiēbāminī	mentīris (-re)	mentīminī	mentiēris (-re)	mentiēminī
Third person	mentiēbātur	mentiēbantur	mentītur	mentiuntur	mentiētur	mentientur

	Past Perfective		Present Perfective		Future Perfective	
	Sing.	Pl.	Sing.	Pl.	Sing.	Pl.
First person	mentītus eram	mentītī erāmus	mentītus sum	mentītī sumus	mentītus erō	mentītī erimus
Second person	mentītus erās	mentītī erātis	mentītus es	mentītī estis	mentītus eris	mentītī eritis
Third person	mentītus erat	mentītī erant	mentītus est	mentītī sunt	mentītus erit	mentītī erunt

Subjunctive

	Past Imperfective		Present Imperfective	
	Sing.	Pl.	Sing.	Pl.
First person	mentīrer	mentīrēmur	mentiar	mentiāmur
Second person	mentīrēris (-re)	mentīrēminī	mentiāris (-re)	mentiāminī
Third person	mentīrētur	mentīrentur	mentiātur	mentiantur

	Past Perfective		Present Perfective	
	Sing.	Pl.	Sing.	Pl.
First person	mentītus essem	mentītī essēmus	mentītus sim	mentītī sīmus
Second person	mentītus essēs	mentītī essētis	mentītus sīs	mentītī sītis
Third person	mentītus esset	mentītī essent	mentītus sit	mentītī sint

Imperative

Sing.	Pl.
mentīre	mentīminī

Infinitives

Imperf.	mentīrī
Perf.	mentītus, -a, -um esse
Fut.	mentītūrus, -a, -um esse

Participles

Imperf.	mentiēns
Perf.	mentītus, -a, -um
Fut.	mentītūrus, -a, -um
Fut. pass.	mentiendus, -a, -um

Supines

mentītum
mentītū

Irregular Verbs

sum, esse, fuī, futūrus

Indicative

	Past Imperfective		Present Imperfective		Future Imperfective	
	Sing.	Pl.	Sing.	Pl.	Sing.	Pl.
First person	eram	erāmus	sum	sumus	erō	erimus
Second person	erās	erātis	es	estis	eris	eritis
Third person	erat	erant	est	sunt	erit	erunt

	Past Perfective		Present Perfective		Future Perfective	
	Sing.	Pl.	Sing.	Pl.	Sing.	Pl.
First person	fueram	fuerāmus	fuī	fuimus	fuerō	fuerimus
Second person	fuerās	fuerātis	fuistī	fuistis	fueris	fueritis
Third person	fuerat	fuerant	fuit	fuērunt (-ēre)	fuerit	fuerint

Subjunctive

	Past Imperfective		Present Imperfective	
	Sing.	Pl.	Sing.	Pl.
First person	essem	essēmus	sim	sīmus
Second person	essēs	essētis	sīs	sītis
Third person	esset	essent	sit	sint

	Past Perfective		Present Perfective	
	Sing.	Pl.	Sing.	Pl.
First person	fuissem	fuissēmus	fuerim	fuerīmus
Second person	fuissēs	fuissētis	fuerīs	fuerītis
Third person	fuisset	fuissent	fuerit	fuerint

Infinitives

Imperf.	esse
Perf.	fuisse
Fut.	futūrus, -a, -um esse (fore)

Participles

Imperf.	—
Perf.	—
Fut.	futūrus, -a, -um

possum, posse, potuī

Indicative

	Past Imperfective		Present Imperfective		Future Imperfective	
	Sing.	Pl.	Sing.	Pl.	Sing.	Pl.
First person	poteram	poterāmus	possum	possumus	poterō	poterimus
Second person	poterās	poterātis	potes	potestis	poteris	poteritis
Third person	poterat	poterant	potest	possunt	poterit	poterunt

	Past Perfective		Present Perfective		Future Perfective	
	Sing.	Pl.	Sing.	Pl.	Sing.	Pl.
First person	potueram	potuerāmus	potuī	potuimus	potuerō	potuerimus
Second person	potuerās	potuerātis	potuistī	potuistis	potueris	potueritis
Third person	potuerat	potuerant	potuit	potuērunt (-ēre)	potuerit	potuerint

Subjunctive

	Past Imperfective		Present Imperfective	
	Sing.	Pl.	Sing.	Pl.
First person	possem	possēmus	possim	possīmus
Second person	possēs	possētis	possīs	possītis
Third person	posset	possent	possit	possint

	Past Perfective		Present Perfective	
	Sing.	Pl.	Sing.	Pl.
First person	potuissem	potuissēmus	potuerim	potuerīmus
Second person	potuissēs	potuissētis	potuerīs	potuerītis
Third person	potuisset	potuissent	potuerit	potuerint

Infinitives

Imperf.	posse
Perf.	potuisse
Fut.	—

volō, velle, voluī

Indicative

	Past Imperfective		Present Imperfective		Future Imperfective	
	Sing.	Pl.	Sing.	Pl.	Sing.	Pl.
First person	volēbam	volēbāmus	volō	volumus	volam	volēmus
Second person	volēbās	volēbātis	vīs	vultis	volēs	volētis
Third person	volēbat	volēbant	vult	volunt	volet	volent

	Past Perfective		Present Perfective		Future Perfective	
	Sing.	Pl.	Sing.	Pl.	Sing.	Pl.
First person	volueram	voluerāmus	voluī	voluimus	voluerō	voluerimus
Second person	voluerās	voluerātis	voluistī	voluistis	volueris	volueritis
Third person	voluerat	voluerant	voluit	voluērunt (-ēre)	voluerit	voluerint

Subjunctive

	Past Imperfective		Present Imperfective	
	Sing.	Pl.	Sing.	Pl.
First person	vellem	vellēmus	velim	velīmus
Second person	vellēs	vellētis	velīs	velītis
Third person	vellet	vellent	velit	velint

	Past Perfective		Present Perfective	
	Sing.	Pl.	Sing.	Pl.
First person	voluissem	voluissēmus	voluerim	voluerīmus
Second person	voluissēs	voluissētis	voluerīs	voluerītis
Third person	voluisset	voluissent	voluerit	voluerint

Infinitives

Imperf.	velle
Perf.	voluisse
Fut.	—

Participles

Imperf.	volēns
Perf.	—
Fut.	—

nōlō, nōlle, nōluī

Indicative

	Past Imperfective		Present Imperfective		Future Imperfective	
	Sing.	Pl.	Sing.	Pl.	Sing.	Pl.
First person	nōlēbam	nōlēbāmus	nōlō	nōlumus	nōlam	nōlēmus
Second person	nōlēbās	nōlēbātis	nōn vīs	nōn vultis	nōlēs	nōlētis
Third person	nōlēbat	nōlēbant	nōn vult	nōlunt	nōlet	nōlent

	Past Perfective		Present Perfective		Future Perfective	
	Sing.	Pl.	Sing.	Pl.	Sing.	Pl.
First person	nōlueram	nōluerāmus	nōluī	nōluimus	nōluerō	nōluerimus
Second person	nōluerās	nōluerātis	nōluistī	nōluistis	nōlueris	nōlueritis
Third person	nōluerat	nōluerant	nōluit	nōluērunt (-ēre)	nōluerit	nōluerint

Subjunctive

	Past Imperfective		Present Imperfective	
	Sing.	Pl.	Sing.	Pl.
First person	nōllem	nōllēmus	nōlim	nōlīmus
Second person	nōllēs	nōllētis	nōlīs	nōlītis
Third person	nōllet	nōllent	nōlit	nōlint

	Past Perfective		Present Perfective	
	Sing.	Pl.	Sing.	Pl.
First person	nōluissem	nōluissēmus	nōluerim	nōluerīmus
Second person	nōluissēs	nōluissētis	nōluerīs	nōluerītis
Third person	nōluisset	nōluissent	nōluerit	nōluerint

Imperative

Sing.	Pl.
nōlī	nōlīte

Infinitives

Imperf.	nōlle
Perf.	nōluisse
Fut.	—

Participles

Imperf.	nōlēns
Perf.	—
Fut.	—

eō, īre, īvī (iī), itūrus

Indicative

	Past Imperfective		Present Imperfective		Future Imperfective	
	Sing.	Pl.	Sing.	Pl.	Sing.	Pl.
First person	ībam	ībāmus	eō	īmus	ībō	ībimus
Second person	ībās	ībātis	īs	ītis	ībis	ībitis
Third person	ībat	ībant	it	eunt	ībit	ībunt

	Past Perfective		Present Perfective		Future Perfective	
	Sing.	Pl.	Sing.	Pl.	Sing.	Pl.
First person	īveram	īverāmus	īvī	īvimus	īverō	īverimus
Second person	īverās	īverātis	īvistī	īvistis	īveris	īveritis
Third person	īverat	īverant	īvit	īvērunt (-ēre)	īverit	īverint

Subjunctive

	Past Imperfective		Present Imperfective	
	Sing.	Pl.	Sing.	Pl.
First person	īrem	īrēmus	eam	eāmus
Second person	īrēs	īrētis	eās	eātis
Third person	īret	īrent	eat	eant

	Past Perfective		Present Perfective	
	Sing.	Pl.	Sing.	Pl.
First person	īvissem	īvissēmus	īverim	īverīmus
Second person	īvissēs	īvissētis	īverīs	īverītis
Third person	īvisset	īvissent	īverit	īverint

Imperative

Sing.	Pl.
ī	īte

Infinitives

Imperf.	īre
Perf.	īvisse
Fut.	itūrus, -a, -um esse

Participles

Imperf.	iēns (euntis)
Perf.	—
Fut.	itūrus, -a, -um

fīō, fierī, factus

Indicative

	Past Imperfective		Present Imperfective		Future Imperfective	
	Sing.	Pl.	Sing.	Pl.	Sing.	Pl.
First person	fīēbam	fīēbāmus	fīō	—	fīam	fīēmus
Second person	fīēbās	fīēbātis	fīs	—	fīēs	fīētis
Third person	fīēbat	fīēbant	fit	fīunt	fīet	fīent

	Past Perfective		Present Perfective		Future Perfective	
	Sing.	Pl.	Sing.	Pl.	Sing.	Pl.
First person	factus eram	factī erāmus	factus sum	factī sumus	factus erō	factī erimus
Second person	factus erās	factī erātis	factus es	factī estis	factus eris	factī eritis
Third person	factus erat	factī erant	factus est	factī sunt	factus erit	factī erint

Subjunctive

	Past Imperfective		Present Imperfective	
	Sing.	Pl.	Sing.	Pl.
First person	fierem	fierēmus	fīam	fīāmus
Second person	fierēs	fierētis	fīās	fīātis
Third person	fieret	fierent	fīat	fīant

	Past Perfective		Present Perfective	
	Sing.	Pl.	Sing.	Pl.
First person	factus essem	factī essēmus	factus sim	factī sīmus
Second person	factus essēs	factī essētis	factus sīs	factī sītis
Third person	factus esset	factī essent	factus sit	factī sint

Infinitives

Imperf.	fierī
Perf.	factus, -a, -um esse
Fut.	—

Participles

Imperf.	—
Perf.	factus, -a, -um
Fut.	faciendus, -a, -um

ferō, ferre, tulī, lātus*

Indicative

	Past Imperfective		Present Imperfective		Future Imperfective	
	Sing.	Pl.	Sing.	Pl.	Sing.	Pl.
Active						
First person	ferēbam	ferēbāmus	ferō	ferimus	feram	ferēmus
Second person	ferēbās	ferēbātis	fers	fertis	ferēs	ferētis
Third person	ferēbat	ferēbant	fert	ferunt	feret	ferent
Passive						
First person	ferēbar	ferēbāmur	feror	ferimur	ferar	ferēmur
Second person	ferēbāris (-re)	ferēbāminī	ferris (-re)	feriminī	ferēris (-re)	ferēminī
Third person	ferēbātur	ferēbantur	fertur	feruntur	ferētur	ferentur

	Past Perfective		Present Perfective		Future Perfective	
	Sing.	Pl.	Sing.	Pl.	Sing.	Pl.
Active						
First person	tuleram	tulerāmus	tulī	tulimus	tulerō	tulerimus
Second person	tulerās	tulerātis	tulistī	tulistis	tuleris	tuleritis
Third person	tulerat	tulerant	tulit	tulērunt (-ēre)	tulerit	tulerint
Passive						
First person	lātus eram	lātī erāmus	lātus sum	lātī sumus	lātus erō	lātī erimus
Second person	lātus erās	lātī erātis	lātus es	lātī estis	lātus eris	lātī eritis
Third person	lātus erat	lātī erant	lātus est	lātī sunt	lātus erit	lātī erunt

Subjunctive

	Past Imperfective		Present Imperfective	
	Sing.	Pl.	Sing.	Pl.
Active				
First person	ferrem	ferrēmus	feram	ferāmus
Second person	ferrēs	ferrētis	ferās	ferātis
Third person	ferret	ferrent	ferat	ferant
Passive				
First person	ferrer	ferrēmur	ferar	ferāmur
Second person	ferrēris (-re)	ferrēminī	ferāris (-re)	ferāminī
Third person	ferrētur	ferrentur	ferātur	ferantur

	Past Perfective		Present Perfective	
	Sing.	Pl.	Sing.	Pl.
Active				
First person	tulissem	tulissēmus	tulerim	tulerīmus
Second person	tulissēs	tulissētis	tulerīs	tulerītis
Third person	tulisset	tulissent	tulerit	tulerint
Passive				
First person	lātus essem	lātī essēmus	lātus sim	lātī sīmus
Second person	lātus essēs	lātī essētis	lātus sīs	lātī sītis
Third person	lātus esset	lātī essent	lātus sit	lātī sint

*This verb also has passive voice morphology.

Imperatives

	Sing.	Pl.
Active	fer	ferte
Passive	ferre	feriminī

Infinitives

	Active	Passive
Imperf.	ferre	ferrī
Perf.	tulisse	lātus, -a, -um esse
Fut.	lātūrus, -a, -um esse	—

Participles

	Active	Passive
Imperf.	ferēns	—
Perf.	—	lātus, -a, -um
Fut.	lātūrus, -a, -um	ferendus, -a, -um

Supines

lātum
lātū

General Vocabulary

The number after an entry not marked by an asterisk (*) indicates the lesson number where the word first occurs in Lesson Vocabulary.

An asterisk before an entry indicates an item that occurs three or more times in Readings but not in Lesson Vocabulary. The lesson number indicates the third occurrence.

An asterisk before a lesson number indicates the third occurrence in Readings of a word that occurs also in the Lesson Vocabulary of a subsequent lesson.

ā/ab (prep. + abl.): from, away from; by (4)

ā quō: by whom? (with passive verb); from whom? (with verb of motion) (6)

absēns (absentis): absent (5)

accidō, accidere, accidī: happen (32)

accipiō, accipere, accēpī, acceptus: accept, receive (15)

accūsō, accūsāre, accūsāvī, accūsātus: accuse (19)

ācer, ācris, ācre: sharp (34)

aciēs, aciēī, f.: battle line (9)

ācriter (adv.): sharply, keenly (35)

āctiō, āctiōnis, f.: action, act (27)

āctum, āctī, n.: deed, act (7)

ad (prep. + acc.): to, toward (12)

adeō (adv.): to such a degree (33)

adeō, adīre, adiī, aditūrus: go to, approach (35)

adjuvō, adjuvāre, adjūvī, adjūtus: aid, help (5)

adsum, adesse, adfuī: be present, be at hand (16)

aedēs, aedium, f. pl.: house (25)

aedificō, aedificāre, aedificāvī, aedificātus: build (9)

aegrē (adv.): with difficulty (6)

*aetās, aetātis, f.: youth, age, period of life (22)

*afficiō, afficere, affēcī, affectus: affect (12)

ager, agrī, m.: field (9)

*agnus, agnī, m.: lamb (11)

agō, agere, ēgī, āctus: do, act, drive, lead (3)

*ait: _____ says (8)

ālea, āleae, f.: game of dice, a die (9)

aliquis, aliquid: someone, something (31)

alius, alia, aliud: another, other (19)

alō, alere, aluī, altus: feed, nourish (1)

alter, altera, alterum: one (of two), the other (20)

*altus, alta, altum: high, deep (25)

ambulō, ambulāre, ambulāvī: walk (4)

amīcitia, amīcitiae, f.: friendship (21)

amīcus, amīca, amīcum: friendly (5)

amīcus, amīcī, m.: friend (4)

āmittō, āmittere, āmīsī, āmissus: let go; lose (6)

amō, amāre, amāvī, amātus: love, like (3)

amor, amōris, m.: love (5)

an: or; whether? if? (30)

animal, animālis, n.: animal (8)

animus, animī, m.: mind (1)

annus, annī, m.: year (12)

ante (prep. + acc.): in front of; before; (also adv.) before, previously (12)

antequam (subord. conj.): before (34)

antīquus, antīqua, antīquum: old, ancient (*8, 35)

aper, aprī, m.: boar (6)

appellō, appellāre, appellāvī, appellātus: call; name (10)

*appropinquō, appropinquāre, appropinquāvī, appropinquātus: approach, draw near (RL3)

aptus, apta, aptum: fitting, suitable (16)

*apud (prep. + acc.): in the presence of, among (31)

aqua, aquae, f.: water (5)

arbitror, arbitrārī, arbitrātus: think (23)

*arcus, arcūs, m.: bow (RL4)

*ardeō, ardēre, arsī: burn (23)

*arma, armōrum, n. pl.: weapons (17)

ars, artis, f.: skill, an art (9)

*ascendō, ascendere, ascendī, ascēnsus: ascend; climb, mount (RL4)

*aspiciō, aspicere, aspexī, aspectus: look at, see (30)

astrum, astrī, n.: star, constellation (8)

*at (coord. conj.): but (27)

Athēniēnsēs, Athēniēnsium, m. pl.: (people of) Athens (16)

atque (coord. conj.): and (12)

audeō, audēre, ausus: dare (3, 20)

audiō, audīre, audīvī, audītus: hear, listen to (3)

*aureus, aurea, aureum: golden, of gold (16)

aut (coord. conj.): or; *aut . . . aut:* either . . . or (26)

autem (sentence connector): however; moreover (*8, 34)

auxilium, auxiliī, n.: help, aid (6)

avāritia, avāritiae, f.: greed, avarice (2)

avārus, avāra, avārum: greedy (28)

Belgae, Belgārum, m. pl.: the Belgians (25)

Bellovacī, Bellovacōrum, m. pl.: the Bellovaci (15)

bellum, bellī, n.: war (*29, 32)

*bene (adv.): well (31)

beneficium, beneficiī, n.: kindness, favor, service (16)

*bēstia, bēstiae, f.: beast (RL3)

bibō, bibere, bibī: drink (*33, 35)

bis (adv.): twice (16)

bonus, bona, bonum: good (5)

*bōs, bovis, m. & f.: ox, bull (RL5)

brevis, breve: short (10)

cadō, cadere, cecidī, cāsūrus: fall (20)

caecus, caeca, caecum: blind (18)

caelum, caelī, n.: heaven, sky (*18, 26)

Caesar, Caesaris, m.: Caesar (9)

canis, canis, m. & f.: dog (6)

capiō, capere, cēpī, captus: take, seize, get (4)

*caput, capitis, n.: head (17)

Carbō, Carbōnis, m.: Carbo (11)

carbō, carbōnis, m.: charcoal (11)

*carmen, carminis, n.: song, poem (31)

cārus, cāra, cārum: dear (16)

castra, castrōrum, n. (pl. only): camp (9)

causa, causae, f.: reason, cause (6); *causā* (+ preceding gen.) for the sake of, on account of (16, 22)

*cēdō, cēdere, cessī, cessūrus: grant; go, proceed (22)

celeriter (adv.): quickly (16)

cēnseō, cēnsēre, cēnsuī, cēnsus: propose (31)

centum (indecl. numeral adj.): hundred (8)

cernō, cernere, crēvī, crētus: perceive, distinguish (35)

certē (adv.): assuredly, certainly (29)

*certus, certa, certum: sure, certain (16)

*cēterī, cēterae, cētera (pl. only): the others, the rest (RL4)

Christiānus, Christiāna, Christiānum: Christian (30)

cito (adv.): quickly (13)

cīvitās, cīvitātis, f.: state, citizenship (16)

cōgitō, cōgitāre, cōgitāvī, cōgitātus: think, consider (22)

cognōscō, cognōscere, cognōvī, cognitus: recognize, learn; get to know (2)

cōgō, cōgere, cōēgī, cōāctus: force, compel (12)

*collum, collī, n.: neck (14)

*commoveō, commovēre, commōvī, commōtus: move deeply, alarm (27)

concēdō, concēdere, concessī, concessus: allow; give up, yield (21)

concidō, concidere, concidī: fall, collapse (34)

condiciō, condiciōnis, f.: condition (11)

condō, condere, condidī, conditus: found, establish (13)

*cōnficiō, cōnficere, cōnfēcī, cōnfectus: finish, complete (17)

cōnsilium, cōnsiliī, n.: plan, advice (4)

*cōnspiciō, cōnspicere, cōnspexī, cōnspectus: see, look at (RL4)

cōnstituō, cōnstituere, cōnstituī, cōnstitūtus: decide, set up (31)

contendō, contendere, contendī, contentus: strive, stretch, struggle (28)

contrā (prep. + acc.): against; (also adv.) on the contrary (12)

cōpia, cōpiae, f.: abundance; (pl.) troops, supplies (9)

cor, cordis, n.: heart (12)

corōnō, corōnāre, corōnāvī, corōnātus: crown (5)

corpus, corporis, n.: body (5)

crassus, crassa, crassum: fat (11)

Crassus, Crassī, m.: Crassus (11)

crēdō, crēdere, crēdidī, crēditus: (+ dat.) trust, rely on (16)

crēscō, crēscere, crēvī, crētus: grow, increase (15)

crūdēlis, crūdēle: cruel (7)

culmen, culminis, n.: peak, summit (5)

cum (prep. + abl.): with (4)

cum (subord. conj.): when, since, although (11)

cupiō, cupere, cupīvī, cupītus: desire, wish (3)

cūr (question word): why? (11)

cūra, cūrae, f.: concern, care (4)

cūrō, cūrāre, cūrāvī, cūrātus: care for (7)

currō, currere, cucurrī, cursūrus: run, hasten (14)

*cursus, cursūs, m.: running, course (19)

custōdiō, custōdīre, custōdīvī, custōdītus: guard (*16, 26)

custōs, custōdis, m. & f.: guard (26)

dē (prep. + abl.): from, down from; concerning (4)

dēbeō, dēbēre, dēbuī, dēbitus: owe; ought (with inf.) (3)

decem (indecl. numeral adj.): ten (8)

decet, decēre, decuit (impers.): is fitting, suitable (21)

dēfluō, dēfluere, dēflūxī: flow down (5)

*deinde (adv.): then, next (RL2)

*dēlīberō, dēlīberāre, dēlīberāvī, dēlīberātus: decide, deliberate (35)

dēpōnō, dēpōnere, dēposuī, dēpositus: lay aside (21)

dēserō, dēserere, dēseruī, dēsertus: leave, desert (21)

dēsum, dēesse, dēfuī: be lacking, fail (16)

deus, deī, m.: god (7)

dīcō, dīcere, dīxī, dictus: say, tell, speak; call, name (16, 20)

diēs, diēī, m. & f.: day; time (2)

difficilis, difficile: difficult (*17, 21)

dīligō, dīligere, dīlēxī, dīlēctus: choose; esteem, value, honor (33)

*discēdō, discēdere, discessī, discessūrus: go away, depart (RL3)

discō, discere, didicī: learn (11)

dissimilis, dissimile: not like, unlike (16)

diū (adv.): for a long time (12)

dīves (dīvitis): rich (25)

dīvīnus, dīvīna, dīvīnum: divine (9)

dō, dare, dedī, datus: give (9)

doceō, docēre, docuī, doctus: teach (9)

doleō, dolēre, doluī: grieve (12)

*dolor, dolōris, m.: grief (12)

domina, dominae, f.: mistress (17)

domus, domūs, f.: home (12)

dōnec (subord. conj.): while, as long as (34)

*dōnō, dōnāre, dōnāvī, dōnātus: give (33)

Dōricus, Dōrica, Dōricum: Doric (21)

*dormiō, dormīre, dormīvī: sleep; rest, be inactive (9)

dūcō, dūcere, dūxī, ductus: lead (6)

*dulcis, dulce: sweet (21)

dum (subord. conj.): while, until, provided that (11)

dummodo (subord. conj.): provided that (34)

duo, duae, duo (numeral adj.): two (8)

dux, ducis, m.: leader (10)

ē/ex (prep. + abl.): from, out of (4)

edō, edere, ēdī, ēsus: eat (*29, 33)

efficiō, efficere, effēcī, effectus: bring about (32)

effugiō, effugere, effūgī: escape (18)

egeō, egēre, eguī: (+ abl. or gen.) be needy, be in want (35)

ego, meī (personal pronoun): I, me (18)

emō, emere, ēmī, ēmptus: buy (25)

eō, īre, iī (īvī), itūrus: go (18)

eō . . . quō (+ comp.): the _____-er . . . the _____-er (25)

*equus, equī, m.: horse (22)

*ergō (sentence connector): therefore (29)

errō, errāre, errāvī: wander; err (18)

et (coord. conj.): and (2); et . . . et: both . . . and (21); (intensifier) even

etiam (intensifier): even, also; shortened form et (10)

etsī (subord. conj.): even if, although (34)

*excitō, excitāre, excitāvī, excitātus: arouse (11)

exemplum, exemplī, n.: example (13)

exeō, exīre, exiī (exīvī), exitūrus: leave, go out (31)

exercitus, exercitūs, m.: army (15)

*exspectō, exspectāre, exspectāvī, exspectātus: look for, wait for (30)

extrā (prep. + acc.): outside of (12)

*faciēs, faciēī, f.: face (23)

facile (adv.): easily (6)

facilis, facile: easy (5)

faciō, facere, fēcī, factus: make, do (1)

fallō, fallere, fefellī, falsus: deceive (7)

fātum, fātī, n.: fate, destiny (30)

faveō, favēre, fāvī: (+ dat.) favor, offer favor to (16)

fax, facis, f.: torch, light, flame (14)

fēlīcitās, fēlīcitātis, f.: success, happiness, prosperity (7)

fēlīciter (adv.): luckily, successfully (4)

fēlīx (fēlīcis): fortunate, happy, prosperous (7)

fēmina, fēminae, f.: woman (2)

ferō, ferre, tulī, lātus: bring, carry, endure (18)

fidēliter (adv.): faithfully (4)

*fīlia, fīliae, f.: daughter (RL4)

*fīlius, fīliī, m.: son (20)

fīnis, fīnis, m.: end, goal; boundary (5)

fīnitimī, fīnitimōrum, m. pl.: neighbors (32)

fīō, fierī, factus: be made, become, happen (10, 20)

flūmen, flūminis, n.: river (15)

fluō, fluere, flūxī: flow (15)

fōns, fontis, m.: spring, fountain (5)

forsitan (adv.): perhaps (signals possibility) (29)

fortis, forte: brave (5)

fortiter (adv.): bravely (4)

fortūna, fortūnae, f.: chance, luck (2)

fragilis, fragile: fragile, easily broken (11)

frangō, frangere, frēgī, frāctus: break (7)

*frāter, frātris, m.: brother (11)

fugiō, fugere, fūgī, fugitūrus: flee (1)

fulgeō, fulgēre, fulsī: shine, flash (26)

fundō, fundere, fūdī, fūsus: pour (12)

fūr, fūris, m.: thief (1)

*furor, furōris, m.: madness, fury (28)

Gallus, Gallī, m. & f.: a Gaul (25)

gaudeō, gaudēre, gāvīsus: rejoice (20)

*gerō, gerere, gessī, gestus: carry, bear; wear; do, carry on (24)

glaciēs, glaciēī, f.: ice (11)

gladiātor, gladiātōris, m.: gladiator (4)

gracilis, gracile: graceful (25)

grātus, grāta, grātum: pleasing, agreeable (16)

habeō, habēre, habuī, habitus: have (5)

*habitō, habitāre, habitāvī: live, dwell (RL2)

harēna, harēnae, f.: sand, arena (4)

Helvētiī, Helvētiōrum, m. pl.: Helvetians (31)

hic, haec, hoc (demonstrative pronoun): this; he, she, it, they; the latter (10)

hīc (adv.): here, in this place (34)

homō, hominis, m. & f.: human being, man (2)

honestus, honesta, honestum: honorable, respectable (16)

honor, honōris, m.: honor, distinction (16)

hōra, hōrae, f.: hour (1)

hortor, hortārī, hortātus: encourage, urge (31)

hostis, hostis, m. & f.: enemy (22)

hūmānus, hūmāna, hūmānum: human (7)

humilis, humile: humble, lowly (25)

ibi (adv.): there; *ibi . . . ubi:* there . . . where (25)

īdem, eadem, idem (pronoun): the same (20)

igitur (sentence connector): therefore (34)

*ignis, ignis, m.: fire (14)

ille, illa, illud (demonstrative pronoun): that; he, she, it, they; the former (10)

imāgō, imāginis, f.: image, likeness (17)

imitātiō, imitātiōnis, f.: imitation (5)

imitor, imitārī, imitātus: imitate (20)

impedīmentum, impedīmentī, n.: hindrance (16)

impediō, impedīre, impedīvī, impedītus: hinder (1)

imperō, imperāre, imperāvī, imperātus: order, command (31)

impetus, impetūs, m.: attack, impulse (6)

impōnō, impōnere, imposuī, impositus: place upon, impose (16)

in (prep. + abl.): in, on; (+ acc.) into, onto; against (4, 12)

*incipiō, incipere, incēpī, inceptus: begin (15)

index, indicis, m. & f.: indicator, sign; informer (17)

īnferō, īnferre, intulī, illātus: bring in, bring upon; *bellum īnferre:* make war on (+ dat.) (32)

*ingēns (ingentis): huge (20)

iniciō, inicere, injēcī, injectus: throw on or into (16)

inimīcus, inimīca, inimīcum: hostile, unfriendly (16)

inops (inopis): poor, helpless (13)

*inquit: _____ says (27)

īnstruō, īnstruere, īnstrūxī, īnstrūctus: draw up (9)

*intendō, intendere, intendī, intentus: stretch, bend; intend (RL4)

inter (prep. + acc.): between, among (12)

intereō, interīre, interiī, interitūrus: perish, die (11)

*interficiō, interficere, interfēcī, interfectus: kill, do away with (11)

interrogō, interrogāre, interrogāvī, interrogātus: ask, inquire (30)

intolerābilis, intolerābile: intolerable (25)

intrā (prep. + acc.): within (12)

intrō, intrāre, intrāvī, intrātus: enter (5)

intus (adv.): within, inside (12)

invādō, invādere, invāsī, invāsus: enter, attack (14)

inveniō, invenīre, invēnī, inventus: find, come upon (26)

ipse, ipsa, ipsum (intensive pronoun): _____self, e.g., myself, yourself, himself (19)

īra, īrae, f.: anger (1)

īrāscor, īrāscī, īrātus: be angry (20)

irrītō, irrītāre, irrītāvī, irrītātus: stir up, incite (2)

is, ea, id (demonstrative pronoun): he, she, it, they (pl.) (7)

iste, ista, istud (demonstrative pronoun): that (near you), that of yours (20)

ita (adv.): thus, so; *ita . . . ut:* just . . . as (25)

*itaque (sentence connector): and so (RL2)

*iter, itineris, n.: journey (17)

*jaceō, jacēre, jacuī: lie (30)

jaciō, jacere, jēcī, jactus: throw, cast, hurl (9)

*jam (adv.): now, already; *nōn jam:* no longer (7)

jānua, jānuae, f.: door (12)

jubeō, jubēre, jussī, jussus: order (*RL4, 23)

jūdicō, jūdicāre, jūdicāvī, jūdicātus: judge (18)

jūstitia, jūstitiae, f.: justice (17)

*jūstus, jūsta, jūstum: just (22)

juvō, juvāre, jūvī, jūtus: help; please; (impers.) it delights (21)

*labor, labōris, m.: toil, hardship (12)

labōrō, labōrāre, labōrāvī, labōrātus: work (21)

lacrima, lacrimae, f.: tear (7)

*laedō, laedere, laesī, laesus: harm, injure (27)

*laetus, laeta, laetum: happy (RL3)

laudō, laudāre, laudāvī, laudātus: praise (18)

laus, laudis, f.: praise, glory; fame (19)

lavō, lavāre, lāvī, lautus: wash (1)

*legō, legere, lēgī, lēctus: read, choose (22)

leō, leōnis, m.: lion (*RL4, 25)

lepidus, lepida, lepidum: charming, graceful, neat (28)

levis, leve: light, unstable (8)

*lēx, lēgis, f.: law (8)

*libellus, libellī, m.: small book, booklet (33)

līber, lībera, līberum: free (20)

līberō, līberāre, līberāvī, līberātus: free, make free, liberate (26)

lībertās, lībertātis, f.: freedom (20)

licet, licēre, licuit (impers.): is allowed/possible (21)

līmes, līmitis, m.: track, course (31)

līs, lītis, f.: quarrel; lawsuit (13)

littera, litterae, f.: letter (of the alphabet); (pl.) a letter, dispatch; literature (14)

lītus, lītoris, n.: shore, beach (21)

locus, locī, m.: place, position (4)

longus, longa, longum: long (10)

loquor, loquī, locūtus: say, speak, tell (20)

*lūmen, lūminis, n.: light, lamp (26)

lūna, lūnae, f.: moon (26)

lupus, lupī, m.: wolf (2)

lūx, lūcis, f.: light (14)

magnus, magna, magnum: great, large (5)

major, majus (comp. of *magnus*): greater, bigger (25)

mālō, mālle, māluī: prefer (18)

malus, mala, malum: bad, evil (5)

maneō, manēre, mānsī, mānsūrus: remain, stay (14)

manus, manūs, f.: hand (1)

mare, maris, n.: sea (8)

māter, mātris, f.: mother (13)

mātūrō, mātūrāre, mātūrāvī: hurry, hasten (34)

*maximē (adv.): very much (RL3)

maximus, maxima, maximum (superl. of *magnus*): greatest, biggest (25)

*medicus, medicī, m.: physician (10)

medius, media, medium: middle, middle of (31)

melior, melius (comp. of *bonus*): better (25)

*meminī, meminisse: remember (31)

mēns, mentis, f.: mind, judgment (5)

*mēnsis, mēnsis, m.: month (31)

mentior, mentīrī, mentītus: lie, tell a lie (20)

metuō, metuere, metuī: fear (32)

metus, metūs, m.: fear (32)

meus, mea, meum (possessive adj.): my, mine (18)

mīles, mīlitis, m.: soldier (23)

mīlitāris, mīlitāre: military (34)

mīlle (indecl. numeral adj. in sing.; pl. decl. *mīlia*): thousand (8)

minimus, minima, minimum (superl. of *parvus*): least, smallest (25)

minor, minus (comp. of *parvus*): less, smaller (25)

mīror, mīrārī, mīrātus: admire, love (20)

*miser, mīsera, mīserum: unhappy (29)

mittō, mittere, mīsī, missus: send (6)

modus, modī, m.: manner, way (4)

moneō, monēre, monuī, monitus: advise, warn (21)

*mōns, montis, m.: mountain (19)

mōnstrō, mōnstrāre, mōnstrāvī, mōnstrātus: show (16)

*mōnstrum, mōnstrī, n.: monster (RL5)

mora, morae, f.: delay (11)

*morbus, morbī, m.: disease (10)

morior, morī, mortuus: die (20)

*mors, mortis, f.: death (21)

*mortālis, mortāle: mortal, human (33)

mortuus, mortua, mortuum: dead (*17, 25)

mōs, mōris, m.: habit, custom; (pl.) morals, character (8)

*mox (adv.): soon (13)

*mulier, mulieris, f.: woman (26)

multitūdō, multitūdinis, f.: crowd, multitude (6)

multum (adv.): much, greatly (12)

multus, multa, multum: much, many (pl.) (7)

*mundus, mundī, m.: world (26)

mūnus, mūneris, n.: gift (8)

*mūrus, mūrī, m.: wall (19)

Mūsa, Mūsae, f.: a Muse (16)

*mūtō, mūtāre, mūtāvī, mūtātus: change (19)

*nam (sentence connector): for (29)

nārrō, nārrāre, nārrāvī, nārrātus: tell, relate, narrate (16, 23)

nāscor, nāscī, nātus: be born (20)

nātūra, nātūrae, f.: nature (9)

*nātus, nātī, m.: son (30)

*nāvis, nāvis, f.: ship (30)

-ne: signals a yes/no question (3)

nē: signals negative hortatory or optative subjunctive; (subord. conj.): indicates negative dependent clause (29)

*nec (coord. conj.): nor, and not (24)

necessitās, necessitātis, f.: necessity (*17, 18)

necessitūdō, necessitūdinis, f.: necessity (10)

neglegō, neglegere, neglēxī, neglēctus: neglect (7)

negō, negāre, negāvī, negātus: deny, say . . . not (23)

nēmō, nēminis, m. & f.: no one (20)

*neque (coord. conj.): nor, and not (29)

nesciō, nescīre, nescīvī: not know, be ignorant of (22)

neuter, neutra, neutrum: neither (20)

nī (subord. conj.): if not (34)

nihil (indecl. noun), n.: nothing (12); (adverb) not at all

nīl (indecl. noun), n.: nothing (13)

nisi (subord. conj.): if not, unless (27)

nōbilis, nōbile: noble (25)

noceō, nocēre, nocuī: (+ dat.) harm, do harm to (16)

nōlō, nōlle, nōluī: not wish, be unwilling (18)

nōmen, nōminis, n.: name (13)

*nōminō, nōmināre, nōmināvī, nōminātus:
    name, call (35)

nōn (adv.): not (2)

nōnne: interrogative adv. introducing direct
    questions expecting the answer "yes" (30)

nōs, nostrum: we, us (18)

noster, nostra, nostrum (possessive adj.): our
    (18)

novem (indecl. numeral adj.): nine (8)

*nōvī, nōvisse, nōtus: know (33)

novus, nova, novum: new, strange (5)

nox, noctis, f.: night (2)

nūllus, nūlla, nūllum: no (16)

num: interrogative adv. introducing direct
    questions expecting the answer "no"; clause
    marker introducing indirect questions asking
    whether (30)

numquam (adv.): never (4)

nunc (adv.): now (*27, 35)

nūntiō, nūntiāre, nūntiāvī, nūntiātus: announce
    (34)

ob (prep. + acc.): against; because of (12)

obses, obsidis, m.: hostage (15)

occāsiō, occāsiōnis, f.: opportunity (1)

*occīdō, occīdere, occīdī, occīsus: kill (RL3)

octō (indecl. numeral adj.): eight (8)

oculus, oculī, m.: eye (10)

ōdī, ōdisse: hate, dislike, be disgusted at (34)

offerō, offerre, obtulī, oblātus: offer (6)

*ōlim (adv.): once upon a time, sometime (26)

omnis, omne: every; (pl.) all (5)

*opīniō, opīniōnis, f.: opinion (26)

oportet, oportēre, oportuit (impers.): is
    necessary (21)

ops, opis, f.: power; (pl.) wealth, resources (28)

optimus, optima, optimum (superl. of *bonus*):
    best (25)

opus, operis, n.: a work, accomplishment (5)

ōrātiō, ōrātiōnis, f.: speech, oration (29)

ōrdō, ōrdinis, m.: order, class, rank (34)

Orgetorīx, Orgetorīgis, m.: Orgetorix (31)

ōrō, ōrāre, ōrāvī, ōrātus: pray, beg, beseech
    (21)

ōs, ōris, n.: mouth, face (18)

*pallidus, pallida, pallidum: pale (23)

parcō, parcere, pepercī: (+ dat.) spare, be
    lenient to (16)

pāreō, pārēre, pāruī: (+ dat.) obey (16)

*pariō, parere, peperī, partus: bring forth (35)

*parō, parāre, parāvī, parātus: prepare, get
    ready (28)

parvus, parva, parvum: small (5)

pāscō, pāscere, pāvī, pāstus: feed (7)

pateō, patēre, patuī: stand open (12)

pater, patris, m.: father (13)

patior, patī, passus: suffer, endure, allow (20)

*patria, patriae, f.: country, fatherland (17)

*paucī, paucae, pauca: few (26)

*pauper (pauperis): poor (30)

pecūnia, pecūniae, f.: money (2)

pejor, pejus (comp. of *malus*): worse (25)

*pellis, pellis, f.: skin, animal hide (RL4)

per (prep. + acc.): through (12)

pereō, perīre, periī: perish, die, pass away (4)

*perficiō, perficere, perfēcī, perfectus: complete,
    finish, bring to an end (17)

perīculum, perīculī, n.: danger (5)

permittō, permittere, permīsī, permissus: allow,
    permit (31)

persuādeō, persuādēre, persuāsī, persuāsūrus:
    (+ dat.) persuade, convince (31)

*perveniō, pervenīre, pervēnī: arrive (17)

pēs, pedis, m.: foot (*RL3, 35)

pessimus, pessima, pessimum (superl. of
    malus): worst (25)

*petō, petere, petīvī, petītus: seek, look for
    (RL4)

*philosophus, philosophī, m.: philosopher (35)

piscis, piscis, m.: fish (8)

placeō, placēre, placuī: (+ dat.) please, be
    pleasing to (16)

Plataeēnsēs, Plataeēnsium, m. pl.: Plataeans;
    people of Plataea (16)

plūrēs, plūra (pl.) (comp. of *multus*): more (25)

plūrimum (adv.): very much, greatly (12)

plūrimus, plūrima, plūrimum (superl. of
    multus): most (25)

plūs, plūris, n.: more (12, 25)

poēta, poētae, m.: poet (16)

*pōmum, pōmī, n.: fruit, apple (17)

pōns, pontis, m.: bridge (23)

populus, populī, m.: the people, a nation;
    populus Rōmānus: Roman people (2)

*porta, portae, f.: gate (28)

*portō, portāre, portāvī, portātus: carry (14)

possum, posse, potuī: be able, can (3)

post (prep. + acc.): behind, after; (adv.)
    afterward (12)

postquam (subord. conj.): after (11)

postulō, postulāre, postulāvī, postulātus:
    demand, require (23, 29)

praeter (prep. + acc.): in addition to, except
    (12)

*praetereā (adv.): moreover, in addition (35)

precāriō (adv.): upon request (35)

precor, precārī, precātus: pray, entreat (31)

premō, premere, pressī, pressus: press, pursue
    (2)

*prīmum (adv.): at first (14)

prīmus, prīma, prīmum: first (34)

priusquam (subord. conj.): before (34)

prīvātus, prīvāta, prīvātum: private (35)

prō (prep. + abl.): before, in front of; for, on behalf of (9)

probitās, probitātis, f.: honesty (33)

*probō, probāre, probāvī, probātus: prove, approve (28)

*prōcēdō, prōcēdere, prōcessī, prōcessūrus: proceed, go forward (35)

prōdūcō, prōdūcere, prōdūxī, prōductus: bring forth (9)

proficīscor, proficīscī, profectus: set out, start (34)

prohibeō, prohibēre, prohibuī, prohibitus: prevent, hinder, keep from (23)

prope (prep. + acc.): near (12)

*properō, properāre, properāvī, properātus: hasten (16)

proprius, propria, proprium: appropriate, proper (21)

propter (prep. + acc.): because of (12)

proximus, proxima, proximum: nearest, next (16)

*prōvocō, prōvocāre, prōvocāvī, prōvocātus: call forth, challenge (16)

prūdēns, prūdentis, m.: sensible person (4)

puella, puellae, f.: girl (19)

puer, puerī, m.: boy (7)

pūgnō, pūgnāre, pūgnāvī, pūgnātūrus: fight (*16, 35)

pulcher, pulchra, pulchrum: beautiful (5)

pulsō, pulsāre, pulsāvī, pulsātus: beat, tap, shake (35)

pūrus, pūra, pūrum: pure (5)

putō, putāre, putāvī, putātus: think, consider (23)

quā condiciōne (question word): under what condition? (11)

quā dē causā (question word): why? for what reason? (6)

quaerō, quaerere, quaesīvī, quaesītus: look for, search for, ask (18, 30)

quālis, quāle: what kind of? (5)

quam (connector): than; (as correlative) as (25)

quam diū (question word): how long? (12)

quamquam (subord. conj.): although (34)

quamvīs (subord. conj.): although (34)

quandō (adv.): when? (6)

quantum (interrogative adv.): how greatly? (12)

quantus, quanta, quantum: how great a? what size? quantum: to what extent? (5, 12)

quasi (subord. conj.): as if (34)

quattuor (indecl. numeral adj.): four (8)

-que (coord. conj.): and (2)

quem ad locum (question word): where? to what place? (12)

quī, quae, quod (interrogative adj.): what, which? (13)

quī, quae, quod (relative pronoun): who, which, that (13)

quia (subord. conj.): because (11)

quīcumque, quaecumque, quodcumque (indef. pronoun): whoever, whatever, whichever (13)

quīdam, quaedam, quoddam (pronoun): a certain person/thing (31)

*quidem (intensifier): indeed, in fact, certainly (27)

quīnque (indecl. numeral adj.): five (8)

quis, quid (interrogative pronoun): who, what? (3)

quisquam, quaequam, quicquam (or quidquam) (indef. pronoun): anyone, anything, any (31)

*quisque, quaeque, quodque (pronoun): each, every person/thing (20)

quisquis, quaeque, quidquid: whosoever, whatsoever (31)

quō (question word): where to? to what place? (12)

quō ā/dē/ē locō (question word): where from? (4)

quō auxiliō (question word): by what means? (6)

quō factō (question word): with what (having been) done? (15)

quō (in) locō (question word): in what place? (4)

quō modō (question word): in what manner? how? (4)

quō tempore (question word): when? (6)

quoad (subord. conj.): until, as long as (34)

quōcum (question word): with whom? (4)

quod (subord. conj.): because (11)

quoniam (subord. conj.): since (34)

*quoque (adv.): also (RL3, 34)

quot (question word): how many? (8)

quotiēns (question word): how often? (4)

rapiō, rapere, rapuī, raptus: seize, grab (*11, 29)

ratiō, ratiōnis, f.: reason (6)

rēctē (adv.): correctly, rightly (4)

rēctus, rēcta, rēctum: right, correct (27)

reddō, reddere, reddidī, redditus: give back (25)

*redeō, redīre, rediī, reditūrus: go back, return (17)

*redūcō, redūcere, redūxī, reductus: bring back, lead back (17)

*referō, referre, rettulī, relātus: carry back, bring back (31)

rēgīna, rēgīnae, f.: queen (17)

*rēgnum, rēgnī, n.: kingdom (29)

regō, regere, rēxī, rēctus: rule, direct (2)

relinquō, relinquere, relīquī, relictus: leave behind, abandon (*17, 21)

reliquus, reliqua, reliquum: the rest, the
     other(s) (34)
repudiō, repudiāre, repudiāvī, repudiātus:
     reject, repudiate (35)
requīrō, requīrere, requīsīvī, requīsītus: ask for,
     look for (30)
rēs, reī, f.: thing, affair, circumstance (1)
resistō, resistere, restitī: (+ dat.) resist, offer
     resistance to (16)
resolvō, resolvere, resolvī, resolūtus: resolve
     (13)
*respondeō, respondēre, respondī, respōnsus:
     answer (34)
*rēx, rēgis, m.: king (15)
*rīdeō, rīdēre, rīsī, rīsus: laugh (RL2)
rogō, rogāre, rogāvī, rogātus: ask (30)
Rōma, Rōmae, f.: (city of) Rome (12)
*Rōmānus, Rōmāna, Rōmānum: Roman (18)
Rōmulus, Rōmulī, m.: Romulus (13)
*ruō, ruere, ruī: fall (29)

saepe (adv.): often (6)
*saevus, saeva, saevum: fierce (33)
*sagitta, sagittae, f.: arrow (15)
salūs, salūtis, f.: health, safety (16)
*sanguis, sanguinis, m.: blood (21)
sapiēns (sapientis): wise (10)
sapientia, sapientiae, f.: wisdom (2)
*sapiō, sapere, sapīvī: be wise (17)
satiō, satiāre, satiāvī, satiātus: satisfy, fill (2)
*satis (indecl. adj., also noun and adv.): enough
     (22)
sciō, scīre, scīvī, scītus: know (23)
scrībō, scrībere, scrīpsī, scrīptus: write (14)
sē, sē, sibī, suī (reflexive pronoun): himself,
     herself, itself, themselves (19)
sed (coord. conj.): but (2)
*sedeō, sedēre, sēdī: sit (22)
semper (adv.): always (4)
senātus, senātūs, m.: senate (2)
*senectūs, senectūtis, f.: old age (16)
*senex, senis, m.: old man (17)
sēnsus, sēnsūs, m.: sensation, feeling (22)
sentiō, sentīre, sēnsī, sēnsus: feel, perceive (23)
sepeliō, sepelīre, sepelīvī, sepultus: bury (14)
septem (indecl. numeral adj.): seven (8)
sequor, sequī, secūtus: follow (20)
serēnus, serēna, serēnum: bright, fair, clear
     (26)
*serpēns, serpentis, m. & f.: snake, serpent (11)
serviō, servīre, servīvī: (+ dat.) serve, help,
     offer service to (16)
*servus, servī, m.: slave (30)
sex (indecl. numeral adj.): six (8)
sī (subord. conj.): if (11)
*sīc (adv.): thus, so (22)
sīdus, sīderis, n.: star, constellation (26)

silva, silvae, f.: forest (35)
similis, simile: similar, like (16)
simul ac (subord. conj.): as soon as (34)
sīn (subord. conj.): but if (34)
sine (prep. + abl.): without (4)
singulī, singulae, singula: single (12)
sinō, sinere, sīvī, situs: allow (31)
sīve (subord. conj.): or if; sīve . . . sīve:
     whether . . . or (34)
*sōl, sōlis, m.: sun (RL5)
soleō, solēre, solitus: be accustomed (3, 20)
sōlitūdō, sōlitūdinis, f.: loneliness, solitude (16)
sōlus, sōla, sōlum: alone, the only (*RL3, 20)
*solvō, solvere, solvī, solūtus: loosen, destroy
     (24)
somnus, somnī, m.: sleep (14)
speculum, speculī, n.: mirror (25)
*spēlunca, spēluncae, f.: cave (19)
spernō, spernere, sprēvī, sprētus: scorn, reject
     (35)
spērō, spērāre, spērāvī, spērātus: hope, hope
     for (29)
spēs, speī, f.: hope, expectation (1)
*statim (adv.): immediately (14)
statuō, statuere, statuī, statūtus: decide,
     determine; set up (31)
stēlla, stēllae, f.: star (14)
*stō, stāre, stetī, statūrus: stand (RL3)
studium, studiī, n.: eagerness, zeal; study (19)
stultus, stulta, stultum: foolish, stupid (5)
stultus, stultī, m.: a fool (4)
suādeō, suādēre, suāsī, suāsūrus: persuade,
     convince (31)
sub (prep. + acc., abl.): under (12)
subitō (adv.): suddenly, abruptly (*RL3, 21)
successus, successūs, m.: success (1)
sum, esse, fuī, futūrus: be, exist (4)
*summus, summa, summum: greatest, best,
     highest (17)
super (prep. + acc.): over, above; (also adv.)
     above; moreover, besides (12)
*superbus, superba, superbum: proud (RL5)
superō, superāre, superāvī, superātus:
     overcome, surpass (24)
suprā (prep. + acc.): above, over; (also adv.)
     above, over (12)
*sustineō, sustinēre, sustinuī, sustentus: hold up,
     endure (32)
suus, sua, suum (reflexive adj.): his/her/its own,
     their own (13)

*taceō, tacēre, tacuī, tacitus: be silent (31)
tālis, tāle: such, of such a kind; tālis . . .
     quālis: such . . . as (25)
tam (adv.): so; tam . . . quam: as . . . as (25)
tamen (adv.): nevertheless (34)
*tandem (adv.): finally, at last (8)

*tangō, tangere, tetigī, tāctus: touch, affect (30)

tantum (adv.): so much, only (12)

tantus, tanta, tantum: so great a, of such a size (12); *tantus . . . quantus:* as great . . . as; *tantō . . . quantō* (+ comp.): the _____-er . . . the _____-er (25)

tellūs, tellūris, f.: soil, earth (35)

tempus, temporis, n.: time (6)

teneō, tenēre, tenuī, tentus: hold; keep (6)

*terra, terrae, f.: land, earth (34)

*terreō, terrēre, terruī, territus: frighten (17)

timeō, timēre, timuī: fear (*16, 20)

timidus, timida, timidum: timid (10)

timor, timōris, m.: fear, dread (*19, 22)

tot (adj.): so many; *tot . . . quot:* as many . . . as (25)

totiēns (adv.): so often; *totiēns . . . quotiēns:* as often . . . as (25)

tōtus, tōta, tōtum: whole, entire (20)

trahō, trahere, trāxī, tractus: drag, draw, pull (19)

*trājiciō, trājicere, trājēcī, trājectus: throw across, pierce (16)

trāns (prep. + acc.): across (12)

trēs, tria (numeral adj., pl. only): three (8)

tribūnus, tribūnī, m.: tribune (34)

tū, tuī (personal pronoun): you (18)

*tum (adv.): then (14)

tuus, tua, tuum (possessive adj.): your (sing.) (18)

ubi (question word, subord. conj.): where; when (4, 11)

ūllus, ūlla, ūllum: any (20)

*umbra, umbrae, f.: shadow, shade (18)

*umquam (adv.): ever (23)

unde (question word): where from? (4)

ūnus, ūna, ūnum (numeral adj.): one (8)

urbs, urbis, f.: city (12)

ūsus, ūsūs, m.: advantage, use, practice (16)

ut (subord. conj.): when, as; that; (in questions) how? (11)

uter, utra, utrum: which (of two)? (20)

uterque, utraque, utrumque: (usually sing.) each (of two) (20)

utinam (adv.): would that (signals wish) (29)

ūtor, ūtī, ūsus: (+ abl.) use (20)

utrum . . . an: whether . . . or (30)

uxor, uxōris, f.: wife (32)

valeō, valēre, valuī, valitūrus: be strong, be effective, prevail (*28, 34)

*validus, valida, validum: strong (30)

vānēscō, vānēscere, vānuī: vanish (5)

*vastus, vasta, vastum: huge, vast (20)

vel (coord. conj. or adv.): even, actually (35)

venēnum, venēnī, n.: poison (5)

veniō, venīre, vēnī, ventūrus: come (4)

verbōsus, verbōsa, verbōsum: wordy, verbose (28)

verbum, verbī, n.: word (12)

vereor, verērī, veritus: fear, respect (20)

vēritās, vēritātis, f.: truth (1)

vērus, vēra, vērum: true, real (21)

vester, vestra, vestrum (possessive adj.): your (pl.) (18)

vetō, vetāre, vetuī: forbid, prohibit (23)

via, viae, f.: road, way (*16, 26)

*viātor, viātōris, m.: wayfarer, traveler (16)

victor, victōris, m.: victor, conqueror (24)

*victōria, victōriae, f.: victory (19)

videō, vidēre, vīdī, vīsus: see (3)

vincō, vincere, vīcī, victus: conquer, prevail (1)

vīnum, vīnī, n.: wine (5)

vir, virī, m.: man (2)

virtūs, virtūtis, f.: excellence, courage, goodness, virtue (17)

*vīs (gen., dat. sing. not in use), pl. vīrēs, vīrium, f.: force, violence; power (*13, 33)

vīta, vītae, f.: life (2)

vitium, vitiī, n.: fault, vice (5)

vīvō, vīvere, vīxī, vīctūrus: live, be alive (4)

vīvus, vīva, vīvum: living, alive (25)

vocō, vocāre, vocāvī, vocātus: call, invite (10)

volō, velle, voluī: want, wish, be willing (3)

voluntās, voluntātis, f.: wish, will (27)

voluptās, voluptātis, f.: pleasure (35)

vōs, vestrum: you (pl.) (18)

vōx, vōcis, f.: voice, utterance, cry (14)

vulpēs, vulpis, f.: fox (8)

vultus, vultūs, m.: appearance, face (17)

Abbreviations

abl.	ablative	ind. st.	indirect statement
abl. abs.	ablative absolute	inf.	infinitive
acc.	accusative	intr.	intransitive
act.	active	irreg.	irregular
adj.	adjective	lkg.	linking
adv.	adverb	M	main
cl.	clause	m./masc.	masculine
comp.	comparative	mod.	modifier
compl.	complement	n./neut.	neuter
conj.	conjunction	nom.	nominative
conn.	connector	NF	non-finite
coord.	coordinating	obj.	object
D	dependent	P/pass.	passive
dat.	dative	perf.	perfective
decl.	declension	pl.	plural
dim.	diminutive	prep.	preposition
dir. obj.	direct object	pres.	present
f./fem.	feminine	qu-	words beginning with letters qu
F	finite	R	Readings
fut.	future	rel.	relative
gen.	genitive	S	Basic Sentence
IA	intransitive active	sing.	singular
imperf.	imperfective	spec. intr.	special intransitive
impers.	impersonal	spec. lkg.	special linking
indecl.	indeclinable	subj.	subject
indef.	indefinite	subord.	subordinate, subordinating
indep.	independent	superl.	superlative
ind. quest.	indirect question	TA/trans. act.	transitive active

Glossary

Adjectival Clause: Syntactic equivalent of an adjective: relative clause with a finite verb, participle with a non-finite verb.

Adverbial Clause: Syntactic equivalent of an adverb. They are both finite and non-finite.

Ambiguous Items: Ambiguous items have the same form, but different meanings according to the environment.

Aspect: Refers to the contrast between verb forms that describe an action as ongoing or incomplete (imperfective aspect) and those that describe it as completed (perfective aspect).

Clauses: Parts of the sentence that have their own kernel. A clause is either independent or dependent and finite or non-finite.

Command: The name of one of three major sentence types. The other two are statements and questions.

Conjugations, First through Fourth and Irregulars: Name of the sets of verb forms.

Declensions, First through Fifth: Name of the five sets or paradigms for the case forms of nouns, the three sets for the case forms of adjectives.

Dependent Clauses: Also called subordinate or embedded in contrast with independent clauses, also called main clauses.

Dictionary Entry: The way in which a word is listed in the dictionary.

Expectations: The universal ability to approach speech with morphological, syntactic, and semantic notions of completeness.

Form Identification: The first level of recognition. On the morphological level it means description in terms of the properties of parts of speech.

Governing: The term applies to the relation of head of construction to modifier. The head governs the modifier. It also applies to the relation between clauses.

Head of Construction: The item modified, in contrast to the modifier.

Kernel: The minimum framework of a complete clause.

Main Clause: Another term for independent clause. Every sentence must have a main clause.

Metaphrase: A technique for translating.

Modification: The process of modifying the head of a construction.

Modifier, Adjectival: Every modifier that modifies a noun-head is an adjectival modifier: adjective, relative clause, participle, genitive.

Modifier, Adverbial: Every modifier that modifies a verb or an adjective or an adverb is an adverbial modifier.

Morpheme: Name for the minimum unit of meaning in a word. There are two main groups: stem morphemes and inflectional morphemes.

Morphology: The description of morphemes in a systematic way.

Noun Clause: Syntactic equivalent of a noun. They are both finite and non-finite.

Parts of Speech: Classes of words arranged according to their meaning and function.

Question: The name of one of three major sentence types. The other two are statements and commands.

Semantics: The area of language study concerned with meaning.

Sentence Connector: Indeclinable particles (adverbs and conjunctions) that carry forward the meaning of a passage by showing the semantic relationship of a sentence to one or more preceding sentences.

Statement: The name of one of three major sentence types. The other two are commands and questions.

Subordinate Clause: Another name for dependent clause, in contrast to governing clause or main clause.

Syntactic Equivalent: Parts of the sentence that can replace each other are syntactic equivalents.

Index